30 years of Rock

30 years of Rock

John Tobler

Exeter Books

NEW YORK

First published in the USA 1985
by Exeter Books
Distributed by Bookthrift
Exeter is a trademark of Simon & Schuster, Inc
Bookthrift is a registered trademark of Simon & Schuster, Inc
New York, New York

Prepared by
Deans International Publishing
52–54 Southwark Street, London SE1 1UA
A division of The Hamlyn Publishing Group Limited
London · New York · Sydney · Toronto

ISBN 0–671–07671–X

Printed in Italy

Contents

1955

SIDE ONE
45 RPM
STEREO

Rock Around The Clock

JOHNNY ACE

CHUCK BERRY

PAT BOONE

THE CADILLACS

RAY CHARLES

THE CHORDS

THE CROWS

BO DIDDLEY

FATS DOMINO

ALAN FREED

Blame Bill Haley! Until he came along, everything was firmly under control. Popular music in Britain was comfortable and cosy, characterized by songs reflecting idealistic romance, traditional values and good clean fun. Ballads and novelty items were the order of the day and the Tin Pan Alley establishment felt no sense of alarm about a brash, noisy record called *Shake Rattle And Roll*, which stood at number four on the hit parade as the year opened. It was, they thought, just a temporary aberration ... no threat to the likes of Dickie Valentine, David Whitfield and Jimmy Young.

They thought wrong!

In America rock'n'roll had been brewing for several years, in the form of rhythm and blues (R&B), but its popularity was localized and generally restricted to black urban communities. However, a handful of records did make an impact nationally: *Crying In The Chapel* by Sonny Til and the Orioles; *Money Honey* by the Drifters; *Gee* by the Crows; *Work With Me Annie* by the Midnighters; and *Sincerely* by the Moonglows. By the start of 1955 it looked as though rock'n'roll fever was set to sweep the States ... all it needed was a white popularizer to demonstrate its universal appeal. He arrived in the unlikely shape of Bill Haley.

With his fixed grin and kiss-curl trademark, Haley became the first rock'n'roll idol, the first white guy to mix black R&B into white country music and come up with a mass-marketable teenage product.

Haley began playing guitar and singing the songs of his hero, Gene Autry, and became a professional musician as an alternative to factory work. After a spell as a disc jockey he formed his own group, the Four Aces of Western Swing, but soon disbanded them to form the Saddlemen, playing a blend of hard-edged country music and western swing.

In 1951 Haley dropped his yodelling hillbilly style to cover an R&B record that David Miller, a record producer, had heard on a trip south – *Rocket 88* by Jackie Brenston (often cited as the first rock'n'roll record). In 1952 he cut *Rock The Joint*, copped from a 'race' record heard on a radio show. With a prominent slap bass, a teen lyric, a hot guitar and a stomping beat, it became a sizeable hit and over the next two years Haley adapted his image to enlarge his teenage following.

The cowboy gear was discarded along with the group's name, and as Bill Haley and his Comets, they cut *Crazy Man Crazy*, which again met favourable response, leading to them signing for Decca, one of the USA's leading record companies, in early 1954. *Rock Around The Clock*, a popular rabble rouser from their stage act, was their first effort. Initial sales were healthy and the follow-up, a cover of Joe Turner's *Shake Rattle And Roll*, with all sexual innuendo removed to prevent either criticism or airplay restriction, was a huge international hit ... but nobody was prepared for what was to come.

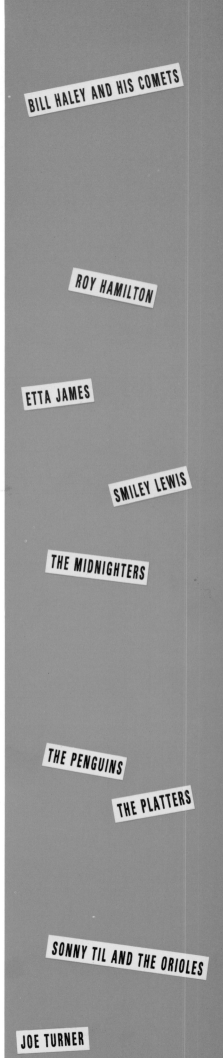

Jim Myers, the co-author of *Rock Around The Clock*, arranged for Haley's recording to play under the credits of *The Blackboard Jungle*, a generation gap/juvenile delinquency film on which he was technical adviser. Released in February 1955, it instantly became mandatory viewing for every youth with even the slightest streak of rebellion. The snare rim-shots, the slapping bass, the driving guitar solo, the whopping beat, the live-for-today lyric and that hoarse shouting vocal were to influence a generation.

The record shot back into the charts, selling millions and remaining at number one for eight weeks. Hit followed hit, Haley was big news. Sam Katzman, a film producer, saw the celluloid potential and signed him to star in *Rock Around The Clock*, a thin storyline bolstered by nine Haley tunes and appearances by Alan Freed and the Platters. Aisle dancing, seat slashing, cinema wrecking and authority flouting soon became *de rigueur* at screenings across America and Europe as the media encouraged a link between teen vandalism and rock'n'roll.

Refuting the critics who saw this mild-mannered man as the leader of a rebellion intent on destroying the fabric of society Haley remained buoyant with a second film, *Don't Knock The Rock* (also featuring Little Richard) and record-breaking tours of America and Australia. The most successful

7

rock'n'roll star in the world, he had racked up 12 top 20 hits in Britain, including *See You Later Alligator, Rockin' Through The Rye, Rip It Up* and the chart-topping *Rock Around The Clock,* by February 1957 when his first UK tour began. All shows had sold out in minutes, with fans queuing for days to ensure good seats, but when Haley left for home a few weeks later he was all but washed-up by a combination of failures and shortcomings. He was seen to be old (one of them, not one of us!) and keen to emphasize how tame and non-violent rock'n'roll was. The quality of his records dwindled alarmingly. In America he regained brief popularity with *Skinny Minnie,* but, apart from re-issues of *Rock Around The Clock,* he never saw the British chart again!

Bill Haley, the original king of rock'n'roll, died from a heart ailment, exacerbated by bouts of serious drinking, in February 1981. He was 55 years old. His influence remains incalculable.

Haley's version of *Shake Rattle And Roll,* originally recorded specifically for black

audiences by Joe Turner, heralded the 'white cover version'. To make it palatable to white radio stations, he moved the setting of the song from the bedroom to the kitchen. Among those who followed in his footsteps were the Crew Cuts, a wholesome quartet from Canada, who made a killing with *Sh-boom* (originally by the Chords) and *Earth Angel* (originally by the Penguins) and Georgia Gibbs, who converted to rock with versions of LaVern Baker's *Tweedle Dee* and Etta James' sexual romp *Roll With Me Henry* – summarily doctored into the innocuous *Dance With Me Henry*!

Because black acts were usually denied airplay these weaker, sanitized versions, although scorned by the hardcore R&B fan for their lack of originality, easily outsold the originals during this first transitional year of rock'n'roll – and no one benefited from this more than Pat Boone.

For those who considered rock too coarse, violent and threatening, Pat Boone was the perfect antidote. He was charming, neat, clean-cut, happily married, a devout Christian, and 21 years old ... almost too good to be true! After signing to Dot Records, Boone cut a string of songs unashamedly appropriated from black sources. His version of Fats Domino's *Ain't That A Shame*, a top 10 hit on both sides of the Atlantic, was followed by re-makes of *I'll Be Home* (the Flamingos), *Tutti Frutti*, *Long Tall Sally* (both Little Richard), and *I Almost Lost My Mind* (Ivory Joe Hunter), and these served as a solid foundation for a more creative phase. He became the first rock star to achieve that elusive 'all round appeal', gathering over 30 chart entries, including *Friendly Persuasion*, *Love Letters*

Below: Clean-cut family man Pat Boone provided the acceptable face of rock'n'roll. During the late fifties, only Elvis Presley sold more records.

Above: The Platters were one of the most successful black vocal groups of the rock'n'roll era. Left to right: Herb Reed, David Lynch, Zola Taylor, Paul Robi and Tony Williams.

Right: One of the first in a long line of winners discovered by the Atlantic label – Ray Charles. Soon to be hailed as a soul giant, he was a hot R&B singer in 1955.

In The Sand and *Speedy Gonzales*.

When the hits began to wane, Boone focused on religious work, recording sacred songs, while his children (Debbie, in particular) kept alive the family name in the recording field.

Despite the attentions of white predators some black acts were able to make considerable headway during 1955. Rhythm and blues moved out of the ghetto to make a dramatic crossover into white markets: the percentage of black acts in the Billboard top 50 chart rose from 3 per cent in 1954 to 10 per cent a year later. Among these were several vocal groups, including the Nutmegs (*A Story Untold*), the El Dorados (*At My Front Door*) and the Cadillacs (*Speedo*). Since they usually relied on a single lead voice backed by three or four harmony singers, these came to be known as 'doo wop' groups – 'doo wop' being a favourite background chant. The most successful of these groups were the Platters, who came to international prominence with their recording of *Only You*.

Formed in Los Angeles in 1953, the Platters' major strengths lay in the magnificent tenor of Tony Williams, the magnetic appeal of 15-year-old Zola Taylor and the songwriting skills of their mentor and manager Buck Ram, who provided them with two chart toppers in *The Great Pretender* and *Twilight Time*. One of the most innovative and consistent groups of the fifties, they scored more than 15 top 40 hits, including two more number ones in *My Prayer* and *Smoke Gets In Your Eyes*, before Williams left the group in 1960.

Johnny Ace's soulful recording of *Pledging My Love* became one of the year's biggest sellers. The song was to be his epitaph, however: he died playing Russian roulette, becoming the genre's first and most dramatic fatality.

Roy Hamilton who had triumphed with *You'll Never Walk Alone* two years earlier, also made his mark in 1955 with the film theme *Unchained Melody*, as did Smiley Lewis with *I Hear You Knocking* – a song also recorded by one of the era's greatest stars, Fats Domino.

Born in New Orleans in 1928, Antoine 'Fats' Domino had become a local celebrity at 21 when his recording of *The Fat Man* first captured the idiosyncratic vocal and percussive piano style which would characterize over 20 million-sellers. *I'm In Love Again* took him into the national top 10 and he returned with *Blue Monday*, *I'm Walking*, *Be My Guest*, *Walking To New Orleans* and

Blueberry Hill – also a smash in Britain.

Fats is still active today, as are several of his peers, including Chuck Berry and Bo Diddley, and the legendary Ray Charles from Georgia.

Blind and orphaned, Charles taught himself the piano and began touring as a professional musician in his teens. Signed by Atlantic Records as an R&B act in 1952, he had a clutch of hits including *I Got A Woman* and the much covered *What'd I Say*, but by the turn of the sixties he was being hailed as 'the genius of soul' for such inspired performances as *Georgia On My Mind*, *I Can't Stop Loving You*, *Hit The Road Jack* and *Take These Chains From My Heart*. His consistency kept him in the charts until well into the seventies.

Chuck Berry and Bo Diddley both travelled north to record for Chess Records,

12

based in Chicago. Singers, songwriters, guitarists and charismatic showmen, their output was inspirational for hordes of starry-eyed kids, including the Beatles and the Rolling Stones.

Beating out a staccato rhythm on his exotically shaped custom-built guitar, the ebullient Diddley charted with *Bo Diddley* in early 1955, establishing the maracas-based R&B style which pervaded most of his subsequent works, including *Road Runner* and *You Can't Judge A Book By Its Cover*, and became a foundation stone in the early sixties' R&B boom in Britain.

Chuck Berry originated a guitar style which was emulated by almost every aspiring rock musician over the next 20 years. He sprang to fame with *Maybellene*, following up with a string of hits which were to become rock'n'roll standards. Although almost 30 he had an intuitive comprehension of the teenage condition, which enabled him to write such durable epics as *Roll Over Beethoven*, *School Day*, *Sweet Little Sixteen*, *Rock And Roll Music* and *Johnny B.Goode* – but it was some 15 years later that he peaked commercially with the chart-topping novelty *My Ding-A-Ling*. He remains

a hardworking headliner at almost 60.

One of Berry's main supporters was disc jockey Alan Freed, one of the few white men playing black records for a white teenage audience. He had moved from Cleveland to New York in September 1954 and did more to popularize rock'n'roll – a term he claimed to have invented – than any other disc jockey. As well as featuring in several rock movies, Freed presented some of the most memorable package shows, before his career came to an abrupt end in late 1959, when he was made the principal scapegoat in the 'payola scandal', where several DJs were charged with accepting money to push certain records. He died six years later, a broken and humiliated man.

Apart from Decca, who had Bill Haley, the major labels were slow to pick up on rock'n'roll, leaving independents like Chess, Imperial and Atlantic to clean up, but towards the end of the year, RCA Victor made a deal with Sun Records of Memphis, signing their rising star, Elvis Presley. 'He may be unknown up north,' said his manager, Colonel Tom Parker, 'but in Georgia and Florida, the girls are tearing off his clothes!'

Left: One of the most colourful rockers to emerge was Bo Diddley, whose customized guitars were a distinctive trademark.

27 January: The UK bank rate is raised from 3 per cent to 3½ per cent.

8 February: Malenkov, Soviet premier since the death of Stalin in March 1953, resigns. Marshal Bulganin succeeds him.

5 April: Sir Winston Churchill resigns as Prime Minister of the United Kingdom. Sir Anthony Eden takes over.

10 April: South Africa withdraws from UNESCO rather than modify racialist policies. African families are compulsorily moved out of Johannesburg to a black settlement 11 miles away.

12 April: Researchers announce that Jonas Salk's polio vaccine is safe and effective. Mass vaccination of school children is scheduled.

16 April: President Eisenhower states that he may use nuclear weapons if America is drawn into another war. Foreign Minister Molotov warns of Soviet strength, claiming superiority in hydrogen weapons.

31 May: The US Supreme Court orders that schools must be racially integrated by local authorities within 'a reasonable time'.

18 September: The Foreign Office states its belief that Burgess and Maclean, the former diplomats who disappeared in 1951, had been long-term Soviet agents. Kim Philby denies being the 'third man'.

19 September: After nine years of dictatorship General Peron resigns as President of Argentina after civil uprising and flees to Paraguay.

22 September: Commercial television begins broadcasting in the UK.

26 September: America and the UK are linked by a submarine telephone cable.

26 October: Ngo Dinh Diem proclaims South Vietnam a republic and declares himself President.

26 November: An IRA group crosses the border into Roslea, County Fermanagh, and attacks a Royal Ulster Constabulary station.

22 December: The French government sends 60,000 more troops to Algeria to suppress revolutionary elements.

Quiz shows, with big prizes, are introduced to American television.

Astronomers announce that an area of Mars has turned a bluey-green colour – possibly the result of plant life. There follows a spate of speculation about the possibility of extra-terrestrial life forms.

America begins supplying direct financial aid to Vietnam.

Big American crazes are the mambo, Davy Crockett hats . . . and rock'n'roll!

Blackboard Jungle
The Colditz Story
The Dam Busters
East Of Eden
Guys And Dolls
The Lady And The Tramp
Love Is A Many Splendoured Thing
The Man With The Golden Arm
Marty
Oklahoma
Rebel Without A Cause
The Rose Tattoo
The Seven-Year Itch
A Star Is Born
To Catch A Thief

Ruby M. Ayres, novelist
Theda Bara, silent movie star
James Dean, film star
Dr Albert Einstein, physicist
Sir Alexander Fleming, bacteriologist
Carmen Miranda, Brazilian actress
Charlie Parker, jazz musician

Left: James Dean defends his honour in Rebel Without A Cause *(Warner, 1955).*

USA CHART TOPPERS

TITLE	ARTIST	LABEL	WEEKS AT NO. 1
Mr Sandman	The Chordettes	Cadence	2
Let Me Go Lover	Joan Weber	Columbia	2
Hearts Of Stone	Fontane Sisters	Dot	1
Sincerely	McGuire Sisters	Coral	6
The Ballad Of Davy Crockett	Bill Hayes	Cadence	5
Cherry Pink And Apple Blossom White	Perez Prado	Victor	10
Rock Around The Clock	Bill Haley and his Comets	Decca	8
The Yellow Rose Of Texas	Mitch Miller	Columbia	6
Love Is A Many Splendoured Thing	The Four Aces	Decca	5
Autumn Leaves	Roger Williams	Kapp	2
Sixteen Tons	Tennessee Ernie Ford	Capitol	5

UK CHART TOPPERS

TITLE	ARTIST	LABEL	WEEKS AT NO. 1
Finger Of Suspicion	Dickie Valentine	Decca	1
Mambo Italiano	Rosemary Clooney	Philips	3
I Need You Now	Eddie Fisher	HMV	2
Softly Softly	Ruby Murray	Columbia	3
Give Me Your Word	Tennessee Ernie Ford	Capitol	7
Cherry Pink And Apple Blossom White	Perez Prado	HMV	2
Stranger In Paradise	Tony Bennett	Philips	2
Cherry Pink And Apple Blossom White	Eddie Calvert	Columbia	4
Unchained Melody	Jimmy Young	Decca	3
Dreamboat	Alma Cogan	HMV	2
Rose Marie	Slim Whitman	London	11
The Man From Laramie	Jimmy Young	Decca	4
Hernando's Hideaway	The Johnston Brothers	Decca	2
Rock Around The Clock	Bill Haley and his Comets	Brunswick	3
Christmas Alphabet	Dickie Valentine	Decca	3

Made in England

1955

SIDE ONE
45 RPM
STEREO

Rock Around The Clock

ALL RIGHTS OF THE MANUFACTURER AND OF THE OWNER OF THE RECORDED WORK RESERVED. UNAUTHORISED PUBLIC PERFORMANCE, BROADCASTING AND COPYING OF THIS RECORD PROHIBITED

1956

SIDE ONE
45 RPM
STEREO

Let The Good Times Roll

HARRY BELAFONTE

FREDDIE BELL AND THE BELL BOYS

JAMES BROWN

JOHNNY CASH

SANFORD CLARK

BILL DOGGETT

LONNIE DONEGAN

THE FIVE SATINS

IVORY JOE HUNTER

TAB HUNTER

LITTLE RICHARD

As Bill Haley cut a swath through the British charts, the music establishment began to realize that rock'n'roll was more than just a brief aberration – although they did their best to ignore it.

Ballroom managers banned teddy boys, jeans and jiving in an attempt to 'raise the standards of dress and dancing' and the head of BBC radio's Light Programme denounced rock'n'roll as 'a passing phase' – a stance his successors maintained for another 11 years! Members of Parliament condemned the barbarism of fans, clergymen made idiotic generalizations from the pulpit, cinemas banned *Rock Around The Clock* and the popular press continued to link the music with crime and anti-social behaviour generally – even though juvenile delinquency decreased, having peaked in 1951! No longer a curiosity, but a menace, rock'n'roll was endowed with even more teen appeal.

Radio Luxembourg (featuring Alan Freed's syndicated show) played all the American hits, but the few home-grown bands were pretty tame compared with the real thing. Rock'n'roll tended to be the province of teddy boys while their more conservative counterparts preferred traditional jazz, as dispensed by Chris Barber and Humphrey Lyttleton and their bands – and the first teenage idol to emerge from this mêlée played a hybrid known as 'skiffle'. He was Lonnie Donegan.

Donegan, a Glaswegian, picked up the

rudiments of guitar and banjo and joined Chris Barber's pioneering jazz band – where he was allowed to give rein to his particular passion during a skiffle interlude within their show. As he interpreted it, skiffle was basically folk and blues, as popularized by Woody Guthrie and Huddie Ledbetter, rocked up a little and accompanied by acoustic guitar, washboard and string bass ... and his first recorded effort, *Rock Island Line*, hit the top 10 in both Britain and America – allowing Donegan to leave Barber and start his own group. For the next six years he was phenomenally successful, clocking up another 30 hits, including three number ones: *Cumberland Gap*, *Putting On The Style* and *My Old Man's A Dustman* – and in his wake followed many imitators. Reduced to a three-chord strum, skiffle was within reach of even the most primitive musician, and skiffle groups proliferated as guitar sales escalated ... but whereas Donegan was able to modify his act into a long career, most of his competitors came and went with the craze.

Above: The emotional 'prince of wails', Johnnie Ray, whose female fans were rabid in their devotion.

Previous page top: Teenager Tommy Steele, discovered in a Soho coffee bar, became Britain's first rock'n'roll idol . . . his maritime days behind him.

Previous page bottom: Lonnie Donegan gave up traditional jazz to become the 'king of skiffle'. Beryl Bryden demonstrates her virtuosity on the washboard!

Among these were the Vipers, led by Wally Whyton, who were the resident group at London's first rock'n'roll coffee bar, the 2I's in Old Compton Street. Their floating personnel included a merchant seaman called Tommy Hicks, who was 'spotted' by two would-be managers, John Kennedy and Larry Parnes, and turned into Britain's first rock'n'roll star – Tommy Steele.

An unknown ship's cabin boy from Bermondsey in September, Steele was topping the charts with *Singing The Blues* three months later, and starring in his own film, *The Tommy Steele Story,* the following year! It was a meteoric rise to fame that inspired many imitators over the next few years, but Steele saw the limitations of rock and moved towards becoming an 'all-round entertainer'.

Singing The Blues had also topped the charts in America in the hands of Guy Mitchell, a consistent hitmaker in the early fifties, who was now enjoying a renaissance by recording uptempo, quasi rock'n'roll material. He scored again with *Knee Deep In The Blues* and *Rock-A-Billy,* and returned to number one with *Heartaches By The Number* in 1959 before drifting towards cabaret.

Several of his contemporaries enjoyed a similar surge of popularity by employing the same tactics: Frankie Laine, previously noted for cowboy ballads like *Mule Train* and *Cry Of The Wild Goose,* came up with *Moonlight Gambler,* Perry Como bounced back with *Hot Diggity* and Johnnie Ray rode back into favour with a cover of the Prisonaires' *Just Walking In The Rain.* Ray, the most intense and histrionic white singer before Presley, had originally come to prominence in 1951 when his first single, *Cry,* sold over two million copies and the 'nabob of sob', as he became known, consolidated his success with another emotional *tour de force, Such A Night,* in 1954. But his chart appearances were sporadic and after *Yes Tonight, Josephine* in 1957 he was en route for the Las Vegas cabaret circuit.

In 1956 rock'n'roll and teen-orientated pop submerged the old guard. Leading the attack was Elvis Presley who, at the beginning of the year, was just cutting his first sides for RCA.

Elvis, born in Tupelo, Mississippi, on 8 January 1935, left school to drift through various menial jobs. He visited Sun Studios in Memphis, supposedly to record a ballad as a birthday present for his mother, but his presence excited secretary Marion Keisker so much that she persuaded her boss, Sam Phillips, to assess his potential . . . which did not manifest itself until Phillips brought in a couple of other young musicians who hung around the studio: Scotty Moore on electric guitar and Bill Black on string bass. When Elvis began thrashing on his acoustic guitar, singing rocked-up versions of Arthur Crudup's *That's All Right Mama* and Bill Monroe's *Blue Moon Of Kentucky*, Phillips heard the sound of gold!

Phillips was owner of the Sun label, which had tended to concentrate on blues acts but he had no hesitation in signing the 19-year-old Presley, who promptly quit truck driving and began touring with Scotty and Bill. Between August 1954 and August 1955 Sun issued five Presley singles – each with an R&B song on one side and a rocked-up country song on the other. None made the national charts, although airplay and sales snowballed throughout the south. They remain among the finest rock'n'roll records ever made.

On the strength of these RCA bought out Presley's contract for the unprecedentedly large sum of $35,000. By April 1956 *Heartbreak Hotel*, his first RCA release, was number one and by September, when no less than 82 per cent of America's television audience had seen him on the Ed Sullivan Show, *Don't Be Cruel/Hound Dog* was enjoying a seven-week run at the top of the charts. His appeal lay not only in his wild music but also in his totally uninhibited, hip-swivelling, snarling, undisguised sexuality and (to the older generation) incomprehensible lyrics.

Guided by the prudent Colonel Parker, Elvis became the fastest-seller in history. *Love Me Tender*, the title song from his film debut, became the first single with over a million pre-release orders and by the end of the year sales of his records exceeded ten million – almost half RCA's turnover! 'When I found Elvis,' said the Colonel, 'the boy had a million dollars worth of talent. Now, he has a million dollars.'

Left: With a clutch of gold records under his belt, Elvis Presley was soon able to revel in luxury!

19

Above: Raised on an Arkansas farm, Johnny Cash found himself in Memphis after his discharge from the air force. With his backing group, the Tennessee Two, he took rockabilly into the charts.

Sam Phillips, meanwhile, had found Johnny Cash and Carl Perkins – both of whom helped to define 'rockabilly', the rock rhythm particularly associated with Memphis.

Johnny Cash was 24 when *I Walk The Line* took him into the US top 20. He went on to have a string of hits with Sun, including *Ballad Of A Teenage Queen* and *Guess Things Happen That Way*. After signing with Columbia in 1958, however, he reverted from rock to country music, reaching a commercial peak some ten years later with a number two single, *A Boy Named Sue*, and a number one album, *Johnny Cash At San Quentin*. Ever since, his consistent album output has consolidated his position as country music's most illustrious star.

Carl Perkins was less fortunate. After breaking through with *Blue Suede Shoes*, a song destined to become a rock'n'roll standard, he was involved in a car crash which laid him up for almost a year – and subsequent recordings lacked the cachet of his original hit. Nevertheless, his songs and

guitar work were embraced by the British beat merchants of the mid-sixties, when his career was revitalized.

After Elvis upset their apple cart, other record companies worked feverishly to sign their own equivalent – but only Capitol succeeded with Eugene Craddock - better known as Gene Vincent.

A serious motorcycle accident, in which he almost lost a leg, had put paid to Vincent's job as a despatch rider at the US Navy base in his hometown of Norfolk, Virginia – and during his convalescence he began singing with the resident band at a local radio station. It was here that the self-styled Sheriff Tex Davis, a local disc jockey, sensed his potential: 'The first time I saw Gene, his leg was in a cast and he had crutches; his teeth were black; he smelt; he almost looked like a bum at 20 ... but he could sing like a bird!' A three-track demo tape was enough to convince Capitol, and Gene and his newly assembled group, the Blue Caps, went to Nashville, where they cut one of the era's classics – *Be Bop A Lula*.

The cascading runs of Gene's outstanding guitarist, Cliff Gallup, who played on *Be Bop A Lula* and his biggest UK hit, *Blue Jean Bop*, were a source of inspiration to many a sixties' guitarist, including George Harrison and Jeff Beck – and when he left the group at the end of 1956 Gene was lucky enough to find a dynamic replacement in Johnny Meeks, who sparkled on the 1957 hit *Lotta Lovin'*.

For a few years Gene and his Caps toured the States, and appeared in two films, *The Girl Can't Help It* and *Hot Rod Gang*, then Gene moved to England to start the second phase of his career. The early sixties saw him in fine form, on tour and on television if not on record, but a combination of problems led him to alcohol, a contributory cause of his early death in 1971.

Most other newcomers made a rather less permanent impression: rockabilly singer Sanford Clark had the biggest hit of his career with *The Fool*; the demented Nervous Norvus scored with a couple of novelties, *Transfusion* and *Ape Call*; Jim Lowe made number one with *The Green Door*; film star Tab Hunter was flavour of the month with the chart-topping *Young Love*; and Patience and Prudence, schoolgirl sisters who charted with *Tonight You Belong To Me* and *Gonna Get Along Without Ya Now*. Another American group, Freddie Bell and the Bell Boys, reached number four in Britain with *Giddy-Up-A-Ding-Dong*, although they never glimpsed the US chart. But if major white rockers were a little thin on the ground, successful new black acts were legion.

The most electrifying was Little Richard, one of the most exciting performers of all time. Born Richard Penniman in 1932, he spent the early fifties recording gospel songs, but following diminishing sales his RCA contract was terminated. But Specialty signed him and sent him to New Orleans to record with a hot session band. By the end of 1956 he had had five top 50 hits – *Tutti Frutti, Long Tall Sally, Slippin' And Slidin', Rip It Up* and *Ready Teddy.* A string of classics followed, including *Keep A Knockin', Good Golly Miss Molly* and *Lucille,* until, in October 1957, he quit rock'n'roll to dedicate his life to religion. For a few years he studied at a Seventh Day Adventist College but since the early sixties he has been performing again – although his comeback soon slid towards self-parody.

James Brown's 1956 hit *Please Please Please* was the first of over 100! Brown spent the late fifties touring with his band, the Famous Flames, and between 1965 and 1968 he hit the top 10 six times. Still able to fill vast arenas, Brown's consistency has been astonishing, although his later recordings seldom approached the heights of *It's A Man's Man's Man's World, I Got You* or *Say It Loud – I'm Black And I'm Proud.*

Another dazzling showman was Screaming Jay Hawkins, whose manic vocal on *I Put A Spell On You* sounds like the result of a rather heavy drinking binge. Hawkins saw his stage antics adapted by Screaming Lord Sutch, and his record covered with far greater success by both Alan Price and Creedence Clearwater Revival.

The 'doo wop' front was spearheaded by the Five Satins, whose innovative million-seller *In The Still Of The Nite* remains a classic, the Heartbeats (*A Thousand Miles Away*) and the Flamingos (*I'll Be Home*). Clyde McPhatter, former leader of the Drifters, achieved success with *Seven Days* and *Treasure Of Love*; Bill Doggett took the instrumental *Honky Tonk* to number two; Ivory Joe Hunter reached the top 20 with *Since I Met You Baby*; and Shirley and Lee saw action with *Let The Good Times Roll.*

The most precocious of the black entrants, however, was 13-year-old Frankie Lymon, lead singer with a New York vocal group, the Teenagers. Their first record, *Why Do Fools Fall In Love?,* shot into the US top 10 and reached number one in Britain. Other hits followed, they soon split up.

While the Teenagers pressed on, with a female replacement trying to emulate Lymon's lead, the latter went solo – plummeting into obscurity after his voice broke. An involvement with drugs returned him to the headlines, but success eluded him and he died of a heroin overdose in 1968, 12 years after his magnificent entrance.

In 1956 Jamaican-born New York cabaret folksinger Harry Belafonte precipitated 'the calypso boom'. With two number one albums, he enjoyed a phenomenally successful year and a handful of non-Caribbeans also charted with Americanized calypsos. Tin Pan Alley pundits prophesied a massive swing to calypso – but they were deluding themselves. Rock'n'roll was only just getting started!

Left: His wild vocals and frantic piano playing made Little Richard one of the most exciting rockers of the era. Although an inspiration to subsequent generations, he renounced rock'n'roll to serve God.

Below: Fronted by the diminutive but exuberant Frankie Lymon (second from left), the Teenagers devised a vocal style which was adapted by soul groups like the Jackson Five during the early seventies.

CURRENT EVENTS

28 January: Elvis Presley makes his first appearance on national television on The Dorsey Brothers Show.

2 March: France recognizes the independence of Morocco and Tunisia.

18 April: Prince Rainier of Monaco marries film star Grace Kelly.

22 April: The 2 I's coffee bar opens in Old Compton Street, London, and begins to feature skiffle sessions.

27 April: World heavyweight boxing champion Rocky Marciano, undefeated in his 49 professional bouts, renounces the title. Later in the year 21-year-old Floyd Patterson becomes the youngest champion when he knocks out Archie Moore.

29 June: Marilyn Monroe marries playwright Arthur Miller.

25 July: The Italian liner *Andrea Doria* collides with Swedish ship the *Stockholm* about 60 miles south of Massachusetts. The former sinks, but the latter reaches port.

26 July: President Nasser of Egypt announces the nationalization of the Suez Canal, provoking anger in the USA, France and the UK.

17 October: The Queen opens the UK's first atomic power station at Calder Hall, Cumberland.

23 October: The start of the Hungarian crisis: bloodshed and rioting accompany national uprising as the country rejects communism and Soviet domination.

30 October: Start of the Suez crisis: British bombers attack Egyptian airfields and military targets in preparation for full-scale invasion.

4 November: Soviet forces regain control of Hungary after many lives are lost.

6 November: Anglo/French forces gain control of the Suez Canal zone, allowing UN troops to maintain peace.

13 December: The US Supreme Court rules unconstitutional the Alabama state law which requires blacks to travel in the rear of vehicles used for public transport. Reverend Martin Luther King begins his fight for black civil rights.

Coffee bars become the focus of teen life in the UK, and Studio 51, in Great Newport Street, becomes London's first rock'n'roll club.

Howl by Allen Ginsberg is published. The resultant publicity and obscenity trial draws attention to the growing beatnik movement in the States.

DEATHS

Clarence Birdseye, frozen food mogul
Tommy Dorsey, jazz bandleader
Sir Alexander Korda, film producer
Walter de la Mare, poet and novelist
A.A. Milne, author
Robert Newton, film star
Jackson Pollock, painter

FILMS

Around The World In Eighty Days
Baby Doll
Carousel
Giant
The King And I
Love Me Tender
The Magnificent Seven
Moby Dick
Reach For The Sky
Rock Around The Clock
Rock Rock Rock
The Searchers
The Ten Commandments

Below: Within months of his national breakthrough, Elvis Presley was in Hollywood filming his screen debut, Love Me Tender (TCF, 1956).

USA CHART TOPPERS

TITLE	ARTIST	LABEL	WEEKS AT NO. 1
Sixteen Tons	Tennessee Ernie Ford	Capitol	1
Memories Are Made Of This	Dean Martin	Capitol	5
The Great Pretender	The Platters	Mercury	2
Rock And Roll Waltz	Kay Starr	Victor	3
Poor People Of Paris	Les Baxter	Capitol	6
Heartbreak Hotel	Elvis Presley	Victor	6
The Wayward Wind	Cogi Grant	Era	7
I Almost Lost My Mind	Pat Boone	Dot	2
My Prayer	The Platters	Mercury	4
Don't Be Cruel	Elvis Presley	Victor	7
The Green Door	Jim Lowe	Dot	2
Love Me Tender	Elvis Presley	Victor	4
Singing The Blues	Guy Mitchell	Columbia	3

UK CHART TOPPERS

TITLE	ARTIST	LABEL	WEEKS AT NO. 1
Rock Around The Clock	Bill Haley and his Comets	Brunswick	2
Sixteen Tons	Tennessee Ernie Ford	Capitol	4
Memories Are Made Of This	Dean Martin	Capitol	4
It's Almost Tomorrow	The Dream Weavers	Brunswick	3
Rock And Roll Waltz	Kay Starr	HMV	1
Poor People Of Paris	Winifred Atwell	Decca	3
No Other Love	Ronnie Hilton	HMV	6
I'll Be Home	Pat Boone	London	5
Why Do Fools Fall In Love?	Frankie Lymon and the Teenagers		
Que Sera Sera	Doris Day	Columbia	6
Lay Down Your Arms	Anne Shelton	Philips	3
Woman In Love	Frankie Laine	Philips	4
Just Walkin' In The Rain	Johnnie Ray	Philips	4
		Philips	7

Made in England

1956

SIDE ONE
45 RPM
STEREO

Let The Good Times Roll

ALL RIGHTS OF THE MANUFACTURER AND OF THE OWNER OF THE RECORDED WORK RESERVED. UNAUTHORISED PUBLIC PERFORMANCE BROADCASTING AND COPYING OF THIS RECORD PROHIBITED

PAUL ANKA

LAVERN BAKER

JIMMY BOWEN

RUTH BROWN

THE CHANTELS

DICK CLARK

THE COASTERS

EDDIE COCHRAN

SAM COOKE

DANNY AND THE JUNIORS

JIM DALE

THE DELL-VIKINGS

TERRY DENE

THE DIAMONDS

THE EVERLY BROTHERS

Made in England

1957

SIDE ONE
45 RPM
STEREO

Whole Lotta Shakin' Goin' On

ALL RIGHTS OF THE MANUFACTURER AND OF THE OWNER OF THE RECORDED WORK RESERVED. UNAUTHORISED PUBLIC PERFORMANCE, BROADCASTING AND COPYING OF THIS RECORD PROHIBITED

As Bill Haley, the first rocker, faded into oblivion, Elvis stormed on, with his third and last appearance on the Ed Sullivan Show, on which cameramen were instructed to show him from the waist up only, for fear of offending conservative viewers! His first single of the year, *Too Much*, was a comparative failure – it reached number two! – but *All Shook Up*, *Teddy Bear* and *Jailhouse Rock* all topped the charts, while his second and third films, *Loving You* and *Jailhouse Rock* were eminently viewable as well as the expected box-office triumphs.

Other films capitalizing on the music included *Mr Rock'n'roll*, *Rock Rock Rock*, and *The Girl Can't Help It* – possibly the best of all rock movies, with dazzling performances by Little Richard, Fats Domino, Gene Vincent, the Platters, and a newcomer to the charts, Eddie Cochran, singing *Twenty Flight Rock*.

An 18-year-old singer and guitarist, Cochran signed with Liberty Records in Los Angeles. His first release *Sittin' In The Balcony* made the top 20 in 1957, and in the following year he released a series of classics defining American teen life: *Summertime Blues*, *C'mon Everybody* and *Somethin' Else*. His popularity waned in the States, but in Britain he became a massive star, touring (alongside Gene Vincent) in spring 1960.

It was during this tour that the car in which he was travelling spun off the road near Chippenham in Wiltshire, leaving Cochran with multiple head injuries from

which he died a few hours later. *Three Steps To Heaven*, released soon after, topped the British charts, and his songs lived on in (thoroughly inferior) cover versions by artists ranging from T. Rex and Rod Stewart to Sid Vicious and the Flying Lizards.

Other aspiring rock'n'rollers included Dale Hawkins, a Louisiana teenager who scored with *Susie Q*, Sal Mineo, a film star who got in on the action with *Start Movin'*, and Buddy Knox, who had a smash hit with his debut, *Party Doll*.

Knox and his partner Jimmy Bowen were the first rock acts to use the Clovis, New Mexico, studio of Norman Petty – and their success prompted another local lad, Buddy Holly, to see if Petty could work the same magic for him. An earlier quest for stardom had ended in failure, with Holly dropped by Decca after miserable response to his records, but Petty was quick to recognize the potential and it was arranged that recordings would be leased to Coral under the name of Buddy Holly and simultaneously to Brunswick, using the group's name, the Crickets.

Holly's rise to fame was meteoric: *That'll Be The Day*, the Crickets' debut, scorched to number three in the States and number one in Britain, and was followed three months later by another top tenner, *Oh Boy!*, and the equally successful *Peggy Sue* – the latter issued under Holly's name. For a year and a half he wrote and recorded a stream

26

CHARLIE GRACIE

WEE WILLIE HARRIS

DALE HAWKINS

BUDDY HOLLY AND THE CRICKETS

BUDDY KNOX

JERRY LEE LEWIS

MICKEY AND SYLVIA

RICKY NELSON

THE JOHNNY OTIS SHOW

JIM REEVES

THE VIPERS

ANDY WILLIAMS

LARRY WILLIAMS

CHUCK WILLIS

JACKIE WILSON

of classics, including *Maybe Baby*, *Rave On*, *True Love Ways* and *Not Fade Away*. Imaginative arrangements and production techniques complemented Holly's sometimes raucous, sometimes plaintive voice to produce a legacy unique in the rock'n'roll field. Its timeless currency was confirmed 20 years later, when a *Golden Greats* compilation album topped the British charts.

Charlie Gracie from Philadelphia found himself in the right place at the right time when a local TV rock and dance show *American Bandstand* began nationwide transmission. Hosted by Dick Clark, the show quickly became hugely influential, establishing criteria for dress, behaviour, dance steps, music and heroes – and the local Philadelphia-based record companies began to flourish. Gracie, a 20-year-old guitarist of considerable prowess, signed with Cameo Records and was provided with suitable hit material in the shape of *Butterfly*, which floated into the top 10 with the assistance of TV publicity. Although unable to

27

repeat his initial success in America he remained buoyant in Britain, scoring with *Fabulous* and *Wanderin' Eyes*.

Television exposure also launched Ricky Nelson. Since the age of nine he had been featured in his parents' show, *The Adventures Of Ozzie And Harriet*, which soon became a showcase for his latest recording. In 1957 his cover of Fats Domino's *I'm Walking* purred into the top 20, the first of over 50 chart appearances. *Poor Little Fool* and *Travellin' Man* took him to the top, and *Lonesome Town*, *It's Late*, *Just A Little Too Much* and *Hello Mary Lou* kept him in clover. Nelson profited from his producer's knack of providing perfect material, and his superb studio band, fronted by the exceptional guitarist James Burton, always made a Ricky Nelson record worthwhile.

A sudden loss of direction resulted in several wilderness years, but *Garden Party* returned him to the fore in 1972, since when Rick (as he now calls himself) has settled into a comfortable career playing rock revivals and country shows.

The Everly Brothers benefited from similar parental support, first appearing on their Kentucky radio show in 1945, when Don was eight and Phil six. In 1957 they had a landslide hit in *Bye Bye Love*, the first in a series, including *Wake Up Little Susie*, *All I Have To Do Is Dream*, *Bird Dog*, *Cathy's Clown* and *Walk Right Back*. They continued to impress audiences with their smooth harmonies and stylish shows until a feud separated them in 1973, but ten years later they re-united and are recording again.

Destined to become the biggest country

star of the early sixties was Jim Reeves, 33 years old when he scored his first hit, *Four Walls*. His chart career continued even after his death in a plane crash in 1964, especially in Britain, where two-thirds of his 24 hits were posthumous – including his only number one, *Distant Drums*.

Sun Records, still searching for another Elvis, came up with country music's most spectacular convert, a rebellious, uncompromising, 21-year-old piano-pumping whirlwind ... Jerry Lee Lewis. He exploded on to the scene with two of 1957's most dramatic singles, *Whole Lotta Shakin' Goin' On* and *Great Balls Of Fire*, smashes on both sides of the Atlantic, and was on course for superstardom until he arrived in Britain to tour in May 1958. When it was discovered that his wife was his 13-year-old cousin he was submerged by a deluge of press and public indignation from which he never recovered, and, after a string of excellent singles failed to reinstate him, he retreated to the country field where he built a new career. He has remained true to his rock-'n'roll ideals, however, and although almost 50 seems unlikely to tone down his act.

Other new arrivals included Andy Williams, whose chart-topping *Butterfly* was the first in a series of teen market hits; Bill Justis, with his sax instrumental *Raunchy* and Paul Anka, a 16-year-old Canadian who had a massive hit with *Diana*. Anka went on to specialize in emotional ballads like *Lonely Boy* and *Puppy Love*, before concentrating on a songwriting career capped by *My Way*.

There were several white vocal groups, including Danny and the Juniors, who took *At The Hop* to number one, and the Diamonds, who successfully covered the Gladiolas' original of *Little Darlin'* before introducing *The Stroll* to dance floors across America. There was one racially integrated group, the Dell-Vikings, who delivered two classics in *Come Go With Me* and *Whispering Bells*, plus a multitude of black groups, most of whom delivered only one cracker each: the Rays (*Silhouettes*), the Hollywood Flames (*Buzz-Buzz-Buzz*), the Dubs (*Could This Be Magic*), the Tune Weavers (*Happy, Happy Birthday Baby*), Lee Andrews and the Hearts (*Teardrops*), Mickey and Sylvia (*Love Is Strange*) and Thurston Harris and the Sharps (*Little Bitty Pretty One*).

Displaying somewhat greater longevity were the all-female Chantels, five New Yorkers led by 15-year-old Arlene Smith, who made the top 20 with *Maybe* and *Look In My Eyes*; Billy Ward and his Dominoes, who had formed in 1950 but hit a commercial peak in 1957 with *Star Dust* and *Deep Purple*; Huey (Piano) Smith and the Clowns, a New Orleans band who scored with *Rockin' Pneumonia And The Boogie Woogie Flu* and *Don't You Just Know It*; and the Johnny Otis Show, a West Coast R&B show-band who reached number two in Britain with *Ma He's Making Eyes At Me* and number nine in the US with *Willie And The Hand Jive*.

The most impressive new black group was the Coasters. As the Robins, they signed with the songwriting/producing team of Leiber and Stoller in Los Angeles and scored a minor hit with *Smokey Joe's Cafe* in late 1955, but friction within the group led to a change of line-up and a change of name ... and in the summer of 1957 both sides of their single *Searchin'/Young Blood* reached the US top 10. Leiber and Stoller produced a mind-boggling variety of hit songs for the group, most of them underpinned by a dazzling sax solo by top session man King Curtis.

Yakety Yak, *Charlie Brown*, *Along Came Jones* and *Poison Ivy* were all top 10 smashes for the Coasters in 1958 and 1959. A break with their mentors, combined with numerous line-up shuffles, resulted in the Coasters' decline and dispersal during the sixties.

On the solo front Sam Cooke, Jackie Wilson, Larry Williams and Chuck Willis were the most influential men to emerge, while LaVern Baker and Ruth Brown were the most energetic women.

Cooke, formerly a gospel singer, moved into the rock arena with *You Send Me*, an American number one at the end of 1957. From then until 1966 he was seldom absent from the chart – even though in December 1964 he was shot dead in a Los Angeles motel. His unique voice inspired many subsequent stars, not least Rod Stewart, and many of his recordings, particularly *Wonderful World*, *Chain Gang*, *Twistin' The Night Away* and *Another Saturday Night*, remain unsurpassed.

The dynamic Jackie Wilson left Billy Ward's Dominoes to score an immediate solo success with *Reet Petite*, written by struggling Detroit songwriter Berry Gordy, later founder of the Tamla Motown empire, and it was Gordy who provided him with his next four hits, including *To Be Loved* and *Lonely Teardrops*, his top 10 breakthrough. Wilson logged over 60 hits, including such classics as *Night*, *Baby Workout* and *Higher And Higher*, before he suffered a heart attack on stage in New Jersey in 1975. He failed to recover, remaining semi-comatose until his death in January 1984.

While Sam Cooke and Jackie Wilson were soul men, Larry Williams was an out and out rocker. His powerhouse run of hits – *Short Fat Fannie*, *Bony Moronie*, *Dizzy Miss Lizzy* and *She Said Yeah* – cast spells during the British beat boom, by which time Williams had disappeared from the scene ... as indeed had Chuck Willis.

An R&B singer from Atlanta, Willis became known as the 'king of the stroll',

Above: Paul Anka's obsession with Diana inspired a multi-million selling debut! Unrequited love does have its compensations!

Left: Jerry Lee Lewis epitomized all that was exciting and dangerous about rock'n'roll.

31

although he saw himself as a latter-day Johnny Ace. A year after *C C Rider* took him to number 12 he died in hospital following an operation. It was ironic that his last two hits, recorded two months earlier, were *What Am I Living For?* and *Hang Up My Rock And Roll Shoes.*

Atlantic's leading women, LaVern Baker and Ruth Brown, both specialized in gospel-based rhythm and blues. Brown had her first major R&B hit with *5-10-15 Hours* in 1952, following up with *Mama, He Treats Your Daughter Mean* a year later. Leiber and Stoller provided her with her first nation-wide hit *Lucky Lips* in 1957 and *This Little Girl's Gone Rockin'* was equally successful – but by 1960 she had left Atlantic and gone into semi-retirement.

Chicago-born LaVern Baker saw her early singles trampled by cover versions, but she triumphed with her stomping tribute to *Jim Dandy* and put the issue beyond doubt with *I Cried A Tear* soon after. *Bumble Bee* and *Saved* saw her through the early sixties after which she retired to Japan.

While America produced an abundance of vital, original rock'n'roll talent, Britain could come up with only a handful of limp imitators. Nevertheless, Terry Dene, Laurie London, Russ Hamilton, Adam Faith, Jim Dale, Wee Willie Harris, and a host of others survived temporarily, their popularity boosted by appearances on Jack Good's weekly television show, *The 6.5 Special*, which, despite its lacklustre content, at least addressed itself to the teenage audience.

The skiffle craze was at its height, but although the Vipers Skiffle Group were consistently interesting, and Johnny Duncan and the Bluegrass Boys (*Last Train To San Fernando*) and the Chas McDevitt Skiffle Group featuring Nancy Whiskey (*Freight Train*) both had hits, Lonnie Donegan's crown at no time looked in any danger of slipping. However, in darkest Enfield, a young credit control clerk sat daydreaming about making it as a rock star. His name was Harry Webb. It wouldn't be until May 1958 that one of his friends would convince him to change it to Cliff Richard.

Right: LaVern Baker graduated from her Baptist church choir to become known as Little Miss Sharecropper on the Detroit night club circuit. During the late fifties, she established herself as one of the finest female rock'n'rollers of all time.

Below: With their fingers glued to the pulse of teenage life, songwriters Leiber and Stoller provided the Coasters with a string of smash hits. In their heyday, no other group could touch the Coasters for originality and invention.

9 January: Sir Anthony Eden resigns as the UK's Prime Minister on grounds of ill-health. Harold MacMillan succeeds him.

18 January: A record non-stop flight of 24,325 miles around the world is completed by three US Air Force Stratofortresses in just under 45½ hours.

8 March: The Suez Canal re-opens for ships following the clearance after Egyptian sabotage, though the last obstructions are not removed for another two months.

11 March: Three witnesses declare that they have seen the Loch Ness monster in Scotland.

21 March: President Eisenhower and Prime Minister MacMillan, meeting in Bermuda, announce that the US will provide the UK with guided missiles.

1 June: The first premium bond draw takes place in the UK.

9 June: The headless body of a frogman, later identified as Commander Lionel Crabbe, who went missing when examining the ship which brought Soviet leaders Bulganin and Krushchev to the UK the previous year, is washed ashore near Chichester Harbour.

19 June: The UK explodes an atomic bomb in the Pacific.

5 August: After local success, Dick Clark's Philadelphia-based TV show *American Bandstand* is broadcast nationally for the first time.

19 August: An American Air Force pilot sets a 19½-mile altitude record in a specially equipped balloon.

4 September: The Wolfenden Report on homosexuality and prostitution in the UK is published, recommending many changes in the existing laws.

24 September: Federal troops are sent to Little Rock, Arkansas, to enforce a school integration order thwarted by Governor Orval Faubus.

4 October: The USSR launches Sputnik 1, the first earth-orbiting satellite.

3 November: The USSR launches a second satellite, Sputnik 2, containing a dog.

18 December: America's first atomic power plant, at Shippingport, Pennsylvania, begins operation.

Ford Motors introduce the Edsel, soon to become the most spectacular commercial failure in the history of the automobile.

DEATHS

Humphrey Bogart, film star
Christian Dior, fashion designer
Oliver Hardy, film star
Louis Mayer, film mogul
Senator Joe McCarthy, US politician
Jan Sibelius, composer

FILMS

The Bridge On The River Kwai (major Academy Award winner)
Disc Jockey Jamboree
Don't Knock The Rock
Funny Face
The Girl Can't Help It
Gunfight At The OK Corral
Jailhouse Rock
Lucky Jim
Paths Of Glory
Peyton Place
The Prince And The Showgirl
Raintree County
Shake Rattle And Rock
Silk Stockings
The Three Faces Of Eve
The Tommy Steele Story
Twelve Angry Men

Left: Tom Ewell protects Jayne Mansfield from a predatory night-club owner in The Girl Can't Help It – one of best rock'n'roll films (TCF, 1956).

USA CHART TOPPERS

TITLE	ARTIST	LABEL	WEEKS AT NO. 1
Singing The Blues	Guy Mitchell	Columbia	5
Don't Forbid Me	Pat Boone	Dot	1
Young Love	Tab Hunter	Dot	6
Butterfly	Andy Williams	Cadence	3
All Shook Up	Elvis Presley	Victor	8
Love Letters In The Sand	Pat Boone	Dot	5
Teddy Bear	Elvis Presley	Victor	7
Tammy	Debbie Reynolds	Coral	4
Honeycomb	Jimmie Rodgers	Roulette	2
Wake Up Little Susie	The Everly Brothers	Cadence	2
Jailhouse Rock	Elvis Presley	Victor	5
You Send Me	Sam Cooke	Keen	3
April Love	Pat Boone	Dot	1

UK CHART TOPPERS

TITLE	ARTIST	LABEL	WEEKS AT NO. 1
Singing The Blues	Guy Mitchell	Philips	2
Singing The Blues	Tommy Steele	Decca	1
Garden Of Eden	Frankie Vaughan	Philips	4
Young Love	Tab Hunter	London	7
Cumberland Gap	Lonnie Donegan	Pye Nixa	5
Rock-A-Billy	Guy Mitchell	Philips	1
Butterfly	Andy Williams	London	2
Yes Tonight Josephine	Johnnie Ray	Philips	3
Putting On The Style	Lonnie Donegan	Pye Nixa	2
All Shook Up	Elvis Presley	HMV	7
Diana	Paul Anka	Columbia	9
That'll Be The Day	The Crickets	Coral	3
Mary's Boy Child	Harry Belafonte	RCA	6

Made in England

1957

SIDE ONE
45 RPM
STEREO

Whole Lotta Shakin' Goin' On

ALL RIGHTS OF THE MANUFACTURER AND OF THE OWNER OF THE RECORDED WORK RESERVED UNAUTHORISED PUBLIC PERFORMANCE BROADCASTING AND COPYING OF THIS RECORD PROHIBITED

35

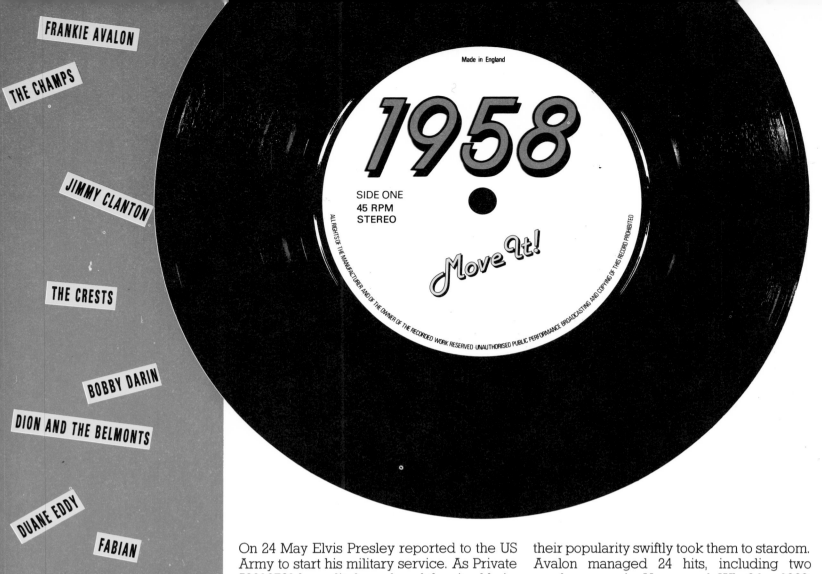

1958

SIDE ONE
45 RPM
STEREO

Made in England

Move It!

On 24 May Elvis Presley reported to the US Army to start his military service. As Private 53310761 he politely endured the ritual hair-shearing ceremony mounted for the media. He'd completed his fourth film *King Creole* and left a stockpile of records – all of which duly climbed the charts: *Don't*, *Wear My Ring Around Your Neck*, *Hard Headed Woman* and *One Night* – so his absence did not impair his popularity. But what happened to Elvis was certainly symbolic of what was happening around him; 1958 saw a distinct trend towards the widespread softening and dilution of rock'n'roll into a more universally palatable product.

Across America for the previous three years the music and its perpetrators had been under attack from the church, the establishment and the press, and resistance appeared to be weakening. In April came the first rumblings of payola, as tax authorities began investigating unreported income. In May a stabbing at a Boston concert led to the arrest of Alan Freed on charges of incitement to riot, giving local authorities an excuse to ban rock shows.

Symptomatic of the changes was the rise of 'Pepsodent pop' whose leading exponents were Frankie Avalon and Fabian. They appeared to have been signed for their looks as much as musical ability, but clever songs and production camouflaged any vocal deficiency. With the benefit of constant exposure on *American Bandstand* (they were, of course, from Philadelphia),

their popularity swiftly took them to stardom. Avalon managed 24 hits, including two number ones in *Venus* and *Why?* by 1962, by which time he had become the star of innumerable beach movies. Fabian's vocal limitations were manifest in much of his output, although *Tiger* and *Hound Dog Man* displayed some redeeming features, and he too moved on to a Hollywood career.

In their wake came the first of the clean-cut, marginally musical brigade, whose insipid love ballads whisked up the charts after television promotion: Johnny Tillotson who would peak with *Poetry In Motion* two years later; Robin Luke, a five-minute wonder with *Susie Darlin'*; the Kalin Twins going top 5 with *When* (a number one in Britain); and Jimmy Clanton striking gold with *Just A Dream* and *Venus In Blue Jeans.*

But there were exceptions to the rule, and some newcomers broke through to reveal substantial talents ... particularly Walden Robert Cassotto from the Bronx and Harold Jenkins from Mississippi, better known as Bobby Darin and Conway Twitty. After plucking a new name from a telephone directory Darin watched several singles disappear before the jaunty rocker *Splish Splash*, which he wrote in ten minutes, took him to national prominence. He remained in the spotlight with *Queen Of The Hop* and *Dream Lover* and then enlarged his audience dramatically to produce the chart-topping *Mack The Knife* and three top 10 albums, after which some 30

Above: A potent mixture of emotional ballads and rockabilly kept Jack Scott buoyant until the sixties.

Opposite top: 19-year-old Duane Eddy roared out of Phoenix Arizona to worldwide acclaim. In Britain, following nine consecutive top 10 hits, he was voted Number One Pop Personality in 1960.

Opposite bottom: Considered by Phil Spector to be one of rock's greatest talents, Dion first found fame as leader of 'doo wop' group the Belmonts.

Previous page top: 17-year-old Frankie Avalon – a careful combination of show-biz elegance and purity.

Previous page bottom left: By 1958 even such an obvious construction as Fabian became a massive pop hero.

Previous page bottom right: Originally a raucous rocker, Bobby Darin modified his style and image to prolong his career.

hits, including *Things* and *If I Were A Carpenter*, were interspersed with film and television roles in a varied career. In 1973 Darin died following heart surgery, at the age of 37.

A reformed country singer out to impress the rock market, Twitty stuck pins in road maps to find Conway, Arkansas, and Twitty, Texas, and also dashed off his first hit in a matter of minutes. *It's Only Make Believe*, featuring a very creditable Presley imper-sonation, hit number one on both sides of the Atlantic and he found a further million-seller in *Lonely Blue Boy*. When his rock-'n'roll career began to fail he reverted to country music where his progress has been unbounded with over three dozen number one country hits.

Don Gibson, another country act, crossed over to the rock chart with *Oh Lonesome Me*, destined to be his biggest hit despite a string of equally attractive follow-ups, in-cluding *Sweet Dreams*, *Sea Of Heartbreak* and the song which provided Ray Charles with his finest hour, *I Can't Stop Loving You*.

The first Canadian to make a significant contribution was Jack Scott whose early singles coupled a fast rocker with a slow ballad – resulting in several double-sided classics, the best of which was his first big hit *My True Love/Leroy*. By 1960 he was concentrating almost entirely on emotional ballads like his last top 5 appearances, *What In The World's Come Over You* and *Burning Bridges*, after which his popularity tapered off.

A great many artists enjoyed isolated moments of glory during 1958, coming up with a winner they would never be able to match again. The Poni-Tails had *Born Too Late*, Jody Reynolds *Endless Sleep*, Tommy Edwards *It's All In The Game* and the Teddy Bears (including subsequent genius producer Phil Spector) had *To Know Him Is To Love Him*. The Four Preps had two smash hits in *26 Miles* and *Big Man*; Jan and Arnie split up after *Jennie Lee*, although Jan found a new partner called Dean in 1959; and Bill Parsons, who had his only hit with *The All American Boy*, resurfaced as country star Bobby Bare in the sixties. Novelty hits abounded too: *Short Shorts* by the Royal Teens, *The Purple People Eater* by Sheb Wooley, *Chantilly Lace* by the Big Bopper and *Dinner With Drac* by John Zacherle.

Tom Dooley, a fluke hit by the Kingston Trio, sparked off a folk music boom. As acoustic guitar sales soared, a deluge of replica groups appeared, and the Trio's debut album topped the charts – as did four more over the next couple of years. The first golden era of rock'n'roll was certainly on its way out but not before a spirited rearguard action.

Into the fray came two excellent vocal groups, the Crests and Dion and the Belmonts. The Belmonts would only be a training ground for Dion, who flowered as a solo star in the sixties, but while he led them they scored two top 5 hits in *A Teenager In Love* and *Where Or When*. Another New York outfit, the Crests, fronted by Johnny Maestro, reached number two with *16 Candles*, returning to the top 20 with *Step By Step* and *Trouble In Paradise*. In 1960 Maestro embarked on a solo career before forming another harmony group, the Brooklyn Bridge, towards the end of the decade.

On the instrumental front Link Wray scored dramatically with *Rumble*, the Champs had their first and biggest success with the chart topper *Tequila* ... but none galvanized the teen world like Duane Eddy, who became an instant favourite with hard-core rockers.

With an idiosyncratic guitar style based almost exclusively on the lower strings, Eddy soon established himself as 'the king of the twangy guitar' and, having evolved a seemingly infallible formula of guitar twanging peppered with sax breaks and yelling from his backing group the Rebels, he stormed into the top 100 26 times between 1958 and 1963. *Rebel-Rouser*, *Forty Miles Of Bad Road* and *Because They're Young* all brought him gold discs but his reign ended in 1964 when he turned his hand to producing.

The year's hottest female singer was also the era's most successful. Connie Francis was only 11 when she begun singing in clubs around New Jersey, where she lived, and by the time she signed with MGM Records six years later she was already a veteran of several radio and television shows. She zoomed to international fame with *Who's Sorry Now*, the first of 16 top 10 hits in under five years. She topped the charts three times, with *Everybody's Somebody's Fool*, *My Heart Has A Mind Of Its Own* and *Don't Break The Heart That Loves You*, but she will always be remembered for her earlier hits *Stupid Cupid* and *Lipstick On Your Collar*.

As a result of growing airplay constrictions the percentage of black acts in the charts dropped for the first time since 1954. Bobby Freeman, a 17-year-old still attending high school in San Francisco, would have several hits, but none as great as his debut, *Do You Want To Dance?* and the Olympics would never find another to rival *Western Movies*. Similarly the Silhouettes would never follow *Get A Job* nor the Monotones *Book Of Love*. The only group to

display any staying power was Little Anthony and the Imperials, who took off with *Tears On My Pillow*. Seventeen more chart appearances included *Goin' Out Of My Head* and *Hurt So Bad*, both top tenners during the mid-sixties, and they remain active today.

Television was having an enormous influence on the charts, not only in America, but in Britain too. After pioneering televised beat music with *The 6.5 Special*, producer Jack Good's next programme was *Oh Boy*. Launched in June 1958, it was to become the best rock show of the fifties, making its predecessor look so archaic that it was taken off the air only weeks later.

Oh Boy's house band was Lord Rockingham's XI, a bunch of jazz musicians and session men who combined to produce an unusually crunchy sound – heard to good effect on their debut single, *Hoots Mon* – but most of the home-grown talent on display was fairly mediocre by American standards ... the Dallas Boys were not Dion and the Belmonts and the Vernons Girls were not the Shirelles. However, Jack Good did have a couple of tricks up his sleeve. The first was Marty Wilde whom he appointed compere.

Managed by Tommy Steele's mentor Larry Parnes, Reg Smith emerged from the same cellar coffee-bar scene with a new name – Marty Wilde – and started covering American hits. After two failures he went top 5 with a duplication of Jody Reynolds' *Endless Sleep*, Ritchie Valens' *Donna*, Dion and the Belmonts' *A Teenager In Love*, and Phil Phillips' *Sea Of Love*. His fifth hit was his own composition *Bad Boy*, which also reached the US top 50 to bring him his sole Stateside success.

Wilde's renditions certainly lacked the cachet of the American originals, but he succeeded because he was the best that Britain had to offer, and as the ringmaster of *Oh Boy* and a subsequent series *Boy Meets Girls* he was able to give full rein to his talents. When the hits trailed off in the early sixties he branched into films and cabaret, before finding his niche as a songwriter, providing hits for Status Quo, the Casuals and his daughter Kim.

Oh Boy's major revelation made his debut on the show transmitted on 13 September 1958. His name was Cliff Richard.

Richard had turned professional the previous month, quitting his job to work a four-

week residency at Butlins in Clacton with his backing group, the Drifters. Before leaving he had cut a single for EMI – a cover of *Schoolboy Crush* by Bobby Helms, an American hit which his producer Norrie Paramor thought had chart potential. Cliff was allowed to slap any old song on the B side (normal practice for the hundreds of hopefuls who turned EMI's treadmill) ... and he chose to record *Move It*, written by his guitarist Ian Samwell.

Jack Good played an advance copy of the single, which he found unimpressive. The B side, however, took him out of his chair! He couldn't believe that an English record could sound so good, and promptly booked Cliff for a series of appearances which would take him to national stardom.

In fact *Move It* was good in every respect. Most previous British attempts had been thin, weedy concoctions rendered even less digestible by the total lack of understanding and interest displayed by every musician involved ... but *Move It* was different. The lyric rang with teenage defiance, Cliff sang with an intuitive authority, the guitar work was stunning and original, and the overall sound was magnificent. It was the first British rock record with any intrinsic merit and it rushed into the top 3 to become the first of many hits.

Modelled on Presley, Cliff attracted criticism for his 'overt sexuality' and 'crude exhibitionism' but he evolved a distinct style of his own. By 1960 he had already released ten top tenners, including three number ones: *Living Doll, Travellin' Light* and *Please Don't Tease.* He had also become the most popular British entertainer since the Second World War.

41

1 January: The European Economic Community comes into being; the UK is not included.

31 January: USA successfully launches a space satellite, Explorer 1.

6 February: A BEA aircraft crashes during take-off from Munich. Among 23 dead are eight Manchester United footballers.

10 February: US broadcaster Walter Cronkite reports that Iran and Egypt have banned rock'n'roll on moral and religious grounds.

24 March: Elvis Presley starts his military service.

27 March: Nikita Krushchev replaces Bulganin as Soviet premier.

6 April: The UK organization Campaign For Nuclear Disarmament launches the first of its annual Aldermaston marches to ban the bomb.

30 April: Vice President Nixon, on a goodwill tour of Latin America, is stoned, spat upon and booed.

24 May: Questions are asked in Parliament after Jerry Lee Lewis arrives in the UK. He is sent home after the discovery that his wife is only 13.

29 May: General de Gaulle becomes new French President.

9 June: The Queen opens Gatwick, London's second airport.

26 July: Prince Charles is created Prince of Wales.

29 July: The National Aeronautics and Space Administration (NASA) is set up in America.

5 August: The US submarine *Nautilus* surfaces after passing under the North Pole.

24 August: Isolated incidents escalate into widespread race riots in Nottingham and London.

20 September: Tommy Steele is first rock'n'roller to be immortalized in wax at Madame Tussauds.

4 October: BOAC inaugurates first transatlantic jet airliner service with the Comet IV. Pan-Am introduce the Boeing 707 a month later.

16 October: The UK's latest unemployment figure of 476,000 is the worst for ten years.

27 December: Last broadcast of BBC TV's *The 6.5 Special*.

In America rock'n'roll records appear in stereo for the first time; in the UK sales of 45 rpm singles eclipse those of the 78 rpm.

The sack dress, designed by Yves Saint-Laurent in Paris, is latest fashion craze, while children go mad for hula-hoops.

The Big Country
Cat On A Hot Tin Roof
The Defiant Ones
Dracula
The Fiend Who Walked The West
Gigi
I Want To Live
King Creole
Mon Oncle
The Revenge Of Frankenstein
Some Came Running
South Pacific

Ronald Colman, film star
Robert Donat, film star
King Faysal of Iraq
W.C. Handy, jazz musician and blues pioneer
Tyrone Power, film star
Marie Stopes, family planning pioneer
Mike Todd, film producer
Ralph Vaughan Williams, composer
Chuck Willis, R&B singer

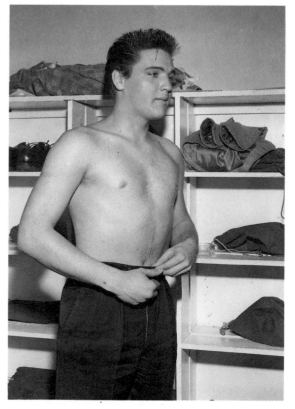

Below: Uncle Sam needs you, boy! When Elvis went into the army, the rock'n'roll scene changed for ever.

42

TITLE	ARTIST	LABEL	WEEKS AT NO. 1
At The Hop	Danny and the Juniors	ABC-Paramount	7
Get A Job	The Silhouettes	Ember	2
Don't	Elvis Presley	Victor	1
Tequila	The Champs	Challenge	5
Twilight Time	The Platters	Mercury	1
Witch Doctor	David Seville	Liberty	3
All I Have To Do Is Dream	The Everly Brothers	Cadence	3
The Purple People Eater	Sheb Wooley	MGM	6
Yakety Yak	The Coasters	Atco	1
Patricia	Perez Prado	Victor	1
Poor Little Fool	Ricky Nelson	Imperial	2
Volare	Domenico Modugno	Decca	5
Little Star	The Elegants	Apt	1
It's All In The Game	Tommy Edwards	MGM	6
It's Only Make Believe	Conway Twitty	MGM	2
Tom Dooley	The Kingston Trio	Capitol	1
To Know Him Is To Love Him	The Teddy Bears	Dore	3
The Chipmunk Song	The Chipmunks	Liberty	2

TITLE	ARTIST	LABEL	WEEKS AT NO. 1
Mary's Boy Child	Harry Belafonte	RCA	1
Great Balls Of Fire	Jerry Lee Lewis	London	2
Jailhouse Rock	Elvis Presley	RCA	3
The Story Of My Life	Michael Holliday	Columbia	2
Magic Moments	Perry Como	RCA	8
Whole Lotta Woman	Marvin Rainwater	MGM	3
Who's Sorry Now	Connie Francis	MGM	6
On The Street Where You Live	Vic Damone	Philips	1
All I Have To Do Is Dream	The Everly Brothers	London	7
When	The Kalin Twins	Brunswick	5
Stupid Cupid	Connie Francis	MGM	6
It's All In The Game	Tommy Edwards	MGM	3
Hoots Mon!	Lord Rockingham's XI	Decca	3
It's Only Make Believe	Conway Twitty	MGM	2

Made in England

1958

SIDE ONE
45 RPM
STEREO

Move It!

1959

SIDE ONE
45 RPM
STEREO

It Doesn't Matter Anymore

THE BROWNS

FREDDY CANNON

DEE CLARK

THE DRIFTERS

ADAM FAITH

THE FLAMINGOS

THE FLEETWOODS

EMILE FORD AND THE CHECKMATES

FRANKIE FORD

RONNIE HAWKINS

JOHNNY HORTON

THE ISLEY BROTHERS

Bad news on the doorstep. On 4 February headlines announced the death of Buddy Holly, killed in a plane crash the previous day during a gruelling package tour. For many this tragedy would come to symbolize the end of an era ... the day the music died.

Two of his new backing group, guitarist Tommy Allsup and bassist Waylon Jennings, would have accompanied him on the flight but at the last minute gave up their seats to the other stars of the show, Ritchie Valens and the Big Bopper. All four occupants, including the pilot, were thought to have died at the moment of impact.

A disc jockey from Beaumont, Texas, J.P. Richardson, or the Big Bopper as he called himself, made records as a sideline, taking leave from his radio station to undertake promotional tours after *Chantilly Lace* became an international smash. A songwriter too, he would never see his greatest success *Running Bear*, recorded by his protégé Johnny Preston, become a worldwide number one later in the year.

Only 17 at the time of his death, Ritchie Valens was riding high on the charts with *Donna*, a song he had written for his high school sweetheart. Coupled with the much-copied Latin rocker *La Bamba*, the record went on to become a million-seller, despite the success of Marty Wilde's version in Britain (which reached number 3). Posthumous releases made considerably less impact, although the growth of a subsequent cult resulted in the 1983 release of a boxed set

containing his entire recorded output.

In New York Holly had dropped his guitar-dominated style to experiment with a full orchestra on four tracks recorded with producer Dick Jacobs. Two of these, *It Doesn't Matter Anymore* and *Raining In My Heart*, were paired for US release before the tour, peaking at number 13 on the day he died. In Britain, where Holly's work was always held in greater esteem, the record swept to number one – and 11 singles charted during the next five years, as old demos and home recordings were unearthed to meet the seemingly insatiable demand for Holly product.

Across America mainstream rock continued to soften. *American Bandstand* devoted more and more time to the more manufactured aspects of the scene. While Jerry Lee Lewis and Chuck Berry found it impossible to penetrate the top 30, stars like Johnny Mathis, Andy Williams, Fabian, Frankie Avalon, Paul Anka and Pat Boone enjoyed an abundance of chart activity, inspiring a glut of newcomers in their mould. Among those to break nationally were James Darren (Philadelphia born), who scored with a song from his movie *Gidget* – although his biggest seller was *Goodbye Cruel World* two years later – Bobby Rydell (also from Philadelphia), whose *Kissin' Time* was the start of a tremendously successful 26-hit career, and Jerry Keller, a one-hit-wonder with *Here Comes Summer*.

Somewhat more consistent, Neil Sedaka's career has lasted longer. A Jewish lad from New York, he had trained as a classical pianist but after writing *Stupid Cupid*, one of Connie Francis' best singles, his fascination with pop music eclipsed any academic aspirations. He joined Aldon Music, a publishing company headed by Al Nevins and Don Kirshner operating from Broadway's famous Brill Building where literally hundreds of music business middlemen leased rooms. Among his colleagues were Carole King and Gerry Goffin, and Barry Mann and Cynthia Weil – songwriting teams who turned out dozens of hits during their very

productive time working at Aldon Music.

With his partner Howard Greenfield Sedaka wrote some 500 songs, recording dozens of them himself – including *Oh! Carol*, addressed to Carole King. *Calendar Girl* and *Happy Birthday, Sweet Sixteen* continued a long chart run distinguished by the number one hit *Breaking Up Is Hard To Do*. He had some difficulty during the Beatles-led British invasion of the mid-sixties, when the hits began to thin out, but he bounced back with another chart topper, *Laughter In The Rain*, in 1974, since when his lasting appeal has never seemed in jeopardy.

Rockers abounded, but most visited the charts only fleetingly. Frankie Ford, from Louisiana, was never able to equal his powerhouse performance on *Sea Cruise*, made with the help of Huey Smith, and Ronnie Hawkins saw the top 40 for the first and last time with *Mary Lou*. Freddy Cannon, however, was here to stay ... until 1966, anyway!

Eighteen-year-old Cannon was able to quit his truck-driving job when *Tallahassee Lassie* zoomed into the top 10, to be followed by the even more successful *Way Down Yonder In New Orleans* and *Palisades Park*. Raucous, rowdy and coloured by much 'whooping', his records were produced by Frank Slay and Bob Crewe, who later catapulted the Four Seasons into the charts.

On the instrumental front there were

JAN AND DEAN

JOHNNY AND THE HURRICANES

MARV JOHNSON

SANDY NELSON

LLOYD PRICE

MARTY ROBBINS

BOBBY RYDELL

NEIL SEDAKA

SAMMY TURNER

RITCHIE VALENS

have been the blueprint for the Mamas and the Papas in the mid-sixties.

The year's most significant new group, however, was a duo. Jan Berry and Dean Torrance, better known as Jan and Dean, teamed up at high school in west Los Angeles and on graduation set about making it in the music business. Their first songwriting attempt was inspired by a burlesque dancer, and their recording of the song, *Jennie Lee*, on primitive equipment in Jan's garage, was hot enough for Arwin, a small local independent label, to release. Despite the muffled, jumbled sound, it caught the public's imagination, to become the first of many 'garage' hits.

Since Dean had started his military service by the time the record came out, the label credited Jan and Arnie – Arnie being a third participant, Arnie Ginsberg, who dropped out of the picture on Dean's return, when they signed with the Dore label. There they conspired with Lou Adler and Herb Alpert (record company fledglings who would later become millionaires) to produce *Baby Talk*, another top tenner, but a relatively barren period followed until they moved to Liberty and struck gold with *Surf City* in summer 1963. Co-written with their friend Brian Wilson, who was riding high with his own group the Beach Boys, it was the first of a series of hits exalting surfing, hot rod racing, skateboarding and girls ... records like *Dead Man's Curve* and *Ride The Wild Surf*, which were supercharged with exciting arrangements, innovative production techniques, and the abundant use of a secret ingredient, California. Very little white rock'n'roll had come out of Los Angeles during the fifties, but as the new decade opened the music industry began to gravitate towards the West Coast – and a slice of Californian sun, fun and romance became the nation's dream.

Jan and Dean's highly successful career came to an abrupt halt in early 1966 after Jan was involved in a car crash. He survived, but suffered brain damage which kept him in hospital for many years, although recently the duo have been able to re-form and are now recreating their hits in a revitalized club act.

Top country group the Browns crossed into the pop charts, going to number one with *The Three Bells*, and Stonewall Jackson broke out of Nashville with *Waterloo*, but they were both outsold by Johnny Horton and Marty Robbins. Lonnie Donegan's British version could not prevent Horton's *The Battle Of New Orleans* from becoming the year's biggest-selling single, opening the door for two further top 5 entries, *Sink The Bismarck* and *North To Alaska*. As the latter was careering up the charts in November 1960, however, Horton died in a car accident in Texas.

many one-off hits, the best of which were *Teen Beat* by Sandy Nelson, *The Happy Organ* by Dave 'Baby' Cortez and *Guitar Boogie Shuffle* by the Virtues. All returned to the chart with lesser hits, but none had the staying power of Johnny and the Hurricanes, a blaring outfit from Toledo, Ohio, who crashed into the charts three times during the year – with *Crossfire*, *Red River Rock* and *Reveille Rock*. With a distinctive sax/organ combination, they had six other hits over the next two years and leader Johnny Paris still fronts a group of Hurricanes, touring on the strength of his success 20 years ago.

Of the white vocal groups to appear the best were the Tempos with *See You In September*, the Skyliners with *Since I Don't Have You*, the Bell Notes with *I've Had It* and the Fleetwoods with two number one smashes, *Come Softly To Me* and *Mr Blue*. A boy and two girls from Seattle, the Fleetwoods' polished harmonies and inventive productions kept them buoyant for five years and many consider their sound to

Marty Robbins had reached the top 3 with *A White Sport Coat* in 1957, since when he'd dropped his teen romance image to become 'the gunfighter balladeer'. *El Paso*, his 1959 number one, was the most popular of several cowboy efforts, however, and he subsequently reverted to poppier material to score top 20 hits with *Devil Woman* and *Ruby Ann.*

For the second year running new black acts were less than profuse. Among those shining through were the Impalas with *Sorry (I Ran All The Way Home)*, Phil Phillips with *Sea Of Love*, Wilbert Harrison with *Kansas City*, the Flamingos with *I Only Have Eyes For You* and the Clovers with *Love Potion No. 9* – all of whom had the biggest hits of their careers.

Marv Johnson was able to quit his job in a Detroit record store after having the good fortune to run into Berry Gordy: *You Got What It Takes* gave him a top 10 hit, which he was able to equal with *I Love The Way You Love*. Sammy Turner benefited from an alliance with Leiber and Stoller, who produced his biggest hits, *Lavender-Blue* and *Always* – records which would inspire Cilla Black to start singing – and another strong Merseybeat influence, the Isley Brothers, got off and running with *Shout*. Dee Clark, who had taken over Little Richard's band when the latter joined the ministry, reached the top 20 twice during the year, with *Just Keep It Up* and *Hey Little Girl* – although his greatest success *Raindrops* would follow two years later.

Making a spectacular national breakout were two acts who had been around for a long time ... Lloyd Price, a raucous rocker from New Orleans, and the Drifters, a New

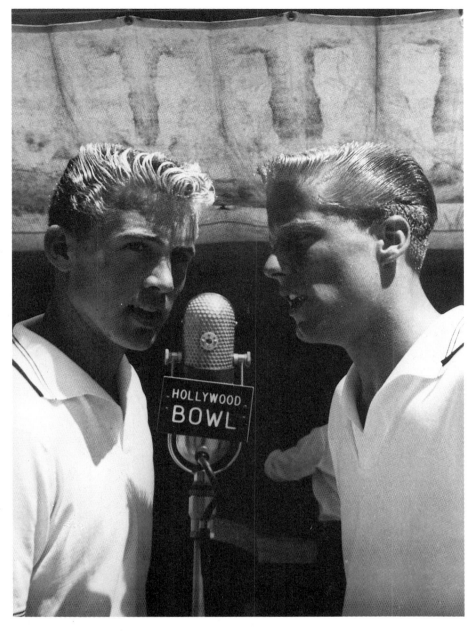

Above: Jan (left) and Dean documented the Californian teen-scene, uniting with the Beach Boys to popularize 'surf music'.

Left: The archetypal fifties instrumental group, Johnny and the Hurricanes specialized in dramatic re-workings of familiar tunes. Strangely, their popularity was greater in Britain than in America.

York vocal quintet of extraordinary pedi-
gree. Price's 1952 recording of *Lawdy Miss
Clawdy* had brought him a gold record, but
his next major success came when *Stagger
Lee* stormed to number one. *Personality*
and *I'm Gonna Get Married* returned him to
the top 3 later in the year but a succession of
lesser hits then presaged a move to cabaret.

The Drifters had been going since 1953,
and there had been a constant turnover of
personnel. With Clyde McPhatter at the
helm, they'd scored huge R&B hits with
Money Honey and *Honey Love* but after
McPhatter's induction into the army, David
Baughan was considerably less successful.
His replacement Johnny Moore put them
back on course with *Ruby Baby* and *Soldier
Of Fortune* and when he left Bobby Hen-
dricks led them on *Drip Drop*, their biggest
seller for some years.

In 1958 the group disbanded completely,
but rather than lose the popularity they had
built up manager George Treadwell signed
up a similar outfit called the Five Crowns
and re-christened them the Drifters. With
Ben E. King on lead vocals and the ubiquitous Leiber and Stoller in the control room
(they also engineered smashes by the
Coasters, the Clovers and Sammy Turner
during the year), they soared to number two
with *There Goes My Baby*. Four more top 20
entries followed, including the number one
Save The Last Dance For Me, before King
went solo at the end of 1960. Rudy Lewis
subsequently sang lead on such hits as *Up
On The Roof* and *On Broadway*, before
Johnny Moore returned in 1964 to maintain
their chart tenure with *Under The Board-
walk* and *Saturday Night At The Movies*. By

1968, however, they were struggling to
survive – which is not to say they were
finished, as will later be revealed.

The Drifters' international success convinced Cliff Richard's group to change their
name. As the Shadows, they began recording instrumentals while their boss was
working on his movie debut *Serious Charge*.
It had become *de rigueur* for British rockers
to get into films as quickly as possible.
Tommy Steele was already on his third,
Tommy The Toreador, while Terry Dene,
despite nervous breakdowns, court appearances and national service rejection, starred
in *The Golden Disc*. Cliff won another role in
Expresso Bongo, Marty Wilde played in
Jetstorm, and Adam Faith had a leading part
in *Beat Girl*, stabilizing a shaky start in show
business.

Following the failure of his first efforts in
1957 Faith had returned to his day job but
his selection as anchorman of *Drumbeat* put
him on the road to fame. Although as dismal
and short-lived as its predecessor *Dig This*,
BBC's answer to *Oh Boy* at least brought
Faith into contact with John Barry, who was
instrumental, literally and figuratively, in his
instant rise. It was Barry's distinctive orches-
tration, combined with Faith's nasal deli-
very, which took *What Do You Want?* to
number one at the end of the year. *Poor Me*
was equally effective and Faith had nine
more top 10 hits (including *Someone Else's
Baby* and *How About That*) before the mid-
sixties. Then he concentrated on acting,
winning approval for his performances in
the David Essex film *Stardust* and the television series *Budgie*, in which he played the
leading role.

The BBC did finally find a successful pop-orientated TV show in *Juke Box Jury*, while ITV dropped *Oh Boy* to launch *Boy Meets Girls*, featuring Marty Wilde and a young guitarist called Joe Brown – but rock fans found little to interest them in such chart newcomers as Russ Conway, Anthony Newley and Craig Douglas. The year's most successful local discovery was Emile Ford. A Bahamian immigrant, Ford and his group the Checkmates specialized in beaty revivals of popular oldies, and *What Do You Want To Make Those Eyes At Me For?* sped to the top of the charts to provide temporary stardom. *Slow Boat To China* was another winner but *Counting Teardrops* a year later proved to be his swan song.

As Adam Faith was taking off, Alan Freed was taking his leave. American newspapers were filled with the revelations of tribunals investigating payola – when disc jockeys were paid to plug records – and the furore was having serious repercussions in the rock'n'roll world. On the face of it, payola did seem corrupt and iniquitous, but it did bring many great records, usually on small labels, to the public's attention, breaking the stranglehold of the major companies, who had previously monopolized the record business. Numerous suspected culprits were interrogated and, although several, who had managed to divest themselves of any conflicting business interests, managed to escape unscathed, Freed, who had been one of rock's most sincere and important popularizers, was finished. His radio contract was terminated, and a suspended prison sentence ensured that he would never regain his prominence.

It was an unsavoury note on which to end the decade.

Above: Emile Ford was the biggest star to emerge from the London coffee bar scene in 1959. His backing group, the Checkmates, included his brother George – later in Cockney Rebel.

Left: When his skiffle group, the Worried Men, failed to make a significant impact, Adam Faith feared that his show-biz career was over . . . but two years later he was topping the charts!

1 January: The Cuban government falls; President Battista flees.

3 January: Alaska becomes America's 49th state.

8 February: Fidel Castro, leader of the Cuban revolution and now President, makes a triumphant entry into Havana with his right-hand man Che Guevara.

30 March: 10,000 CND marchers congregate in Trafalgar Square, London.

8 April: NASA tells Congress they will have a man on the moon within ten years. The first seven astronauts are chosen.

8 August: The first picture of the world from outer space is transmitted from US satellite Explorer 6 and broadcast on television.

21 August: Hawaii becomes America's 50th state.

27 August: A Polaris missile is fired at sea – meaning that intercontinental ballistic missiles need no longer be land-based.

13 September: A Soviet rocket, Lunik 2, hits the moon.

15 September: During a working holiday to the States, Soviet Premier Krushchev is angered when security officials deny him entry to Disneyland.

2 November: The first section of the UK's M1 motorway is opened.

3 November: Charles Van Doren, questioned about winning $129,000 on a US television quiz show, tells a congressional committee that he was given the answers in advance.

14 December: Archbishop Makarios is elected first President of Cyprus.

20 December: The cross-channel hovercraft comes into service.

Cramming as many people as possible into a phone booth, car, or other confined space, is a short-lived American craze.

To counter poor sales, US car manufacturers introduce more functional, economical models after a fad for excess. In the UK, BMC introduce the Mini – a snip at just under £500.

Ben Hur (winner of eleven Oscars)
I'm Alright Jack
Inn Of The Sixth Happiness
Look Back In Anger
North By Northwest
Pillow Talk
Porgy And Bess
Rio Bravo
Room At The Top
Some Like It Hot

Sydney Bechet, jazz musician
The Big Bopper, rock star
Raymond Chandler, author
Lou Costello, film star
Cecil B. DeMille, film director
Errol Flynn, film star
Billie Holliday, jazz singer
Buddy Holly, rock star
Kay Kendall, actress
Mario Lanza, singer
Ritchie Valens, rock star
Frank Lloyd Wright, architect

Left: Cliff Richard throws himself into the part of Bongo Herbert, a pop star manipulated by manager Laurence Harvey in the film Expresso Bongo *(Britannia, 1959).*

TITLE	ARTIST	LABEL	WEEKS AT NO. 1
The Chipmunk Song	The Chipmunks	Liberty	2
Smoke Gets In Your Eyes	The Platters	Mercury	3
Stagger Lee	Lloyd Price	ABC Paramount	4
Venus	Frankie Avalon	Chancellor	5
Come Softly To Me	The Fleetwoods	Dolphin	4
The Happy Organ	Dave 'Baby' Cortez	Clock	1
Kansas City	Wilbert Harrison	Fury	2
The Battle Of New Orleans	Johnny Horton	Columbia	6
Lonely Boy	Paul Anka	ABC Paramount	4
A Big Hunk Of Love	Elvis Presley	Victor	2
The Three Bells	The Browns	Victor	4
Sleep Walk	Santo & Johnny	Can-Am	2
Mack The Knife	Bobby Darin	Atco	9
Mr Blue	The Fleetwoods	Dolton	1
Heartaches By The Number	Guy Mitchell	Columbia	2
Why	Frankie Avalon	Chancellor	1

UK CHART TOPPERS

TITLE	ARTIST	LABEL	WEEKS AT NO. 1
It's Only Make Believe	Conway Twitty	MGM	3
I Got Stung/One Night	Elvis Presley	RCA	4
Smoke Gets In Your Eyes	The Platters	Mercury	6
Side Saddle	Russ Conway	Columbia	2
It Doesn't Matter Anymore	Buddy Holly	Coral	2
A Fool Such As I	Elvis Presley	RCA	7
Roulette	Russ Conway	Columbia	1
Dream Lover	Bobby Darin	London	5
Living Doll	Cliff Richard	Columbia	4
Only Sixteen	Craig Douglas	Top Rank	7
Travellin' Light	Cliff Richard	Columbia	4
What Do You Want?	Adam Faith	Parlophone	4

Made in England

1959

SIDE ONE
45 RPM
STEREO

It Doesn't Matter Anymore

Made in England

1960

SIDE ONE
45 RPM
STEREO

Let's Do The Twist!

ALL RIGHTS OF THE MANUFACTURER AND OF THE OWNER OF THE RECORDED WORK RESERVED. UNAUTHORISED PUBLIC PERFORMANCE BROADCASTING AND COPYING OF THIS RECORD PROHIBITED

The sixties started without a bang! If rock fans expected the new decade to bring fresh excitement they were in for a big disappointment because we were waist deep in the soggy middle ground between rock'n'roll and the Beatles, who at this point were about to visit Hamburg for the first time, having just completed a lacklustre tour of Scotland backing Johnny Gentle.

In the company of Vince Eager, Dickie Pride, Duffy Power and his biggest acts Tommy Steele and Marty Wilde, Johnny Gentle was a transitory inmate of Larry Parnes' 'stable of stars' – all of whose names were said to have been selected as an indication of their sexual characteristics! Gentle was destined to remain in obscurity, but another Parnes discovery was making a big splash.

Ronald Wycherley, alias Billy Fury, soon became one of the best British rockers. He wrote his own songs and benefited from un-usually skilful and sympathetic production. *Maybe Tomorrow*, *Margot* and *Colette* catapulted him to prominence in spring 1960. A run of 26 top 40 entries including *Halfway To Paradise*, *Jealousy* and *Like I've Never Been Gone* kept him in the spotlight until 1966. During the seventies his career was dogged by ill-health, but after a cameo role in the David Essex film *That'll Be The Day* he returned to the fray with two minor hits in 1982. In January of the following year he died of a heart attack, aged 41.

Even more convincing was Johnny Kidd – born Fred Heath! – an uncompromising rocker from Willesden, who also avoided covering US hits and scored with original material. By the late fifties his skiffle group had evolved into a Gene Vincent-inspired rock group, Johnny Kidd and the Pirates, who developed into the best and most exciting outfit in Britain. Kidd's stage act saw him wearing an eye patch and wielding a cutlass, while his Pirates sported colourful swashbuckling gear and played in front of a galleon backdrop, but he was able to cut it in the studio too, as his records attested.

After breaking through with *Please Don't Touch* he sliced his way into the top 3 with *Shakin' All Over*. Ranking with Cliff Richard's *Move It* as one of the few genu-inely exhilarating early British rock'n'roll records, it raised Kidd to a level he could not sustain. Subsequent singles, good as they were, failed to grip the public to the same extent and although *I'll Never Get Over You* returned him to the top 5 three years later, his career was distinctly patchy, finding him playing the northern cabaret circuit with his seventh group of Pirates by summer 1966. In October that year he was killed in a car crash.

Cliff Richard, meanwhile, could do no wrong. His audience was now expanding to encompass all ages. His next two films *The Young Ones* and *Summer Holiday* were box-office smashes and both soundtrack albums topped the charts. During the next two decades he continued to be amazingly successful in Britain, scoring over 70 consecutive hits – an unapproachable record. His 1979 chart topper *We Don't Talk Anymore* confirmed his undiminished excellence and the number one album *Love Songs* two years later put him well beyond the reach of any competitors. The Rolling Stones, his closest rivals, need eight more hit albums and 48 more hit singles to catch him!

His backing group the Shadows were also successful in their own right in 1960 when *Apache* took them to number one. The mainstays of the group Hank Marvin and Bruce Welch had joined Cliff for his first package tour. Quickly developing their own sound and identity the Shads became the most successful and most copied British instrumental group of the era, reaching the top again with *Kon-Tiki*, *Wonderful Land*, *Dance On!* and *Foot Tapper*. Their bespectacled lead guitarist Hank Marvin precipitated the most widespread guitar-buying epidemic since the days of skiffle. They split up in 1969, but re-formed in 1977 when a hits compilation became the second biggest selling album of that year.

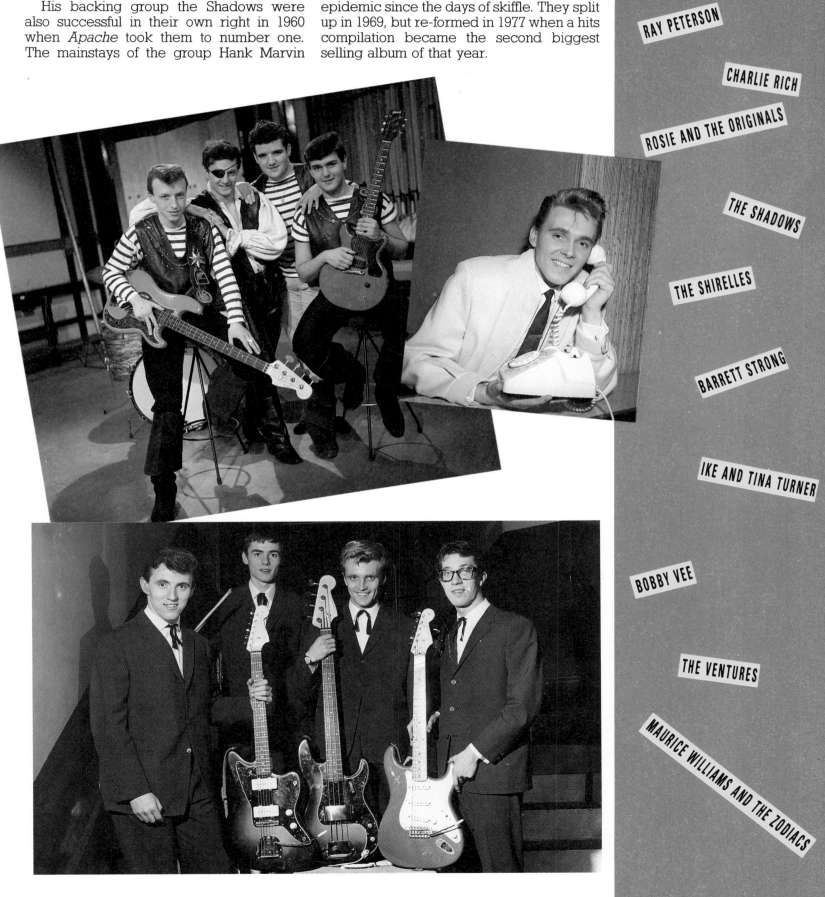

JOHNNY KIDD AND THE PIRATES

BRENDA LEE

RAY PETERSON

CHARLIE RICH

ROSIE AND THE ORIGINALS

THE SHADOWS

THE SHIRELLES

BARRETT STRONG

IKE AND TINA TURNER

BOBBY VEE

THE VENTURES

MAURICE WILLIAMS AND THE ZODIACS

In America no pretenders had threatened Presley's position as king. The month after his army release in March *Stuck On You* bolted to number one, to be followed by *It's Now Or Never* and *Are You Lonesome Tonight?* later in the year. By the time *Surrender* had achieved similar status in February 1961 Elvis already had a dozen chart-toppers under his belt; but he was concentrating all his activities in the recording and film studios, making no personal appearances.

Over the next decade he starred in a succession of woeful song-vehicles with films like *Tickle Me* and *Clambake*, and the low standard of his records was reflected in his failure to achieve more than one US top 10 entry between 1964 and mid-1969, when *In The Ghetto* and *Suspicious Minds* showed a rally.

As the Drifters, Sam Cooke and Ray Charles entered their most productive period other black challengers were just starting out. Although their debuts were superb, some, like Maurice Williams and the Zodiacs (*Stay*), Jessie Hill (*Ooh Poo Pah Doo*), Jimmy Jones (*Handy Man* and *Good Timin'*), Barrett Strong (*Money*) and Billy Bland (*Let The Little Girl Dance*) returned to the backwoods almost immediately. Ike and Tina Turner and Gary 'US' Bonds, on the other hand, began careers which would extend into the eighties.

Ike, a respected R&B bandleader and producer, met Annie Mae Bullock in 1956, when she was 16. He invited her to join his band – not long after which they married and Annie Mae became Tina Turner. *A Fool In Love* brought their first chart success, followed by *It's Gonna Work Out Fine*, a top 20 hit in 1961 – but it was mainly on their stage act, one of the raunchiest and most powerful ever seen, that their sixties' reputation was based.

Gary Anderson, a 20-year-old from Norfolk, Virginia, changed his name to 'US' Bonds at the suggestion of Frank Guida – soon to become his manager, songwriter, producer and record label owner! Bonds rocketed to number six with *New Orleans*, featuring the most muffled 'garage' sound since Jan and Arnie's *Jennie Lee*. Using the same formula he followed up with *Quarter To Three*, which reached number one. But despite three more hits his career was in decline in 1962 and not until 1981, when Bruce Springsteen resuscitated him with songs/production/patronage, did he return to prominence.

Bonds was one of many artists capitalizing on the twist, a dance craze originated by Hank Ballard, one of four acts whose careers were flowering after considerable dues-paying – the others being Bobby Bland, Jerry Butler and the Shirelles.

Born in 1930, Bobby Bland served his apprenticeship with the Beale Streeters,

whose personnel also included B. B. King, Johnny Ace, Rosco Gordon and Junior Parker. In 1960 *I'll Take Care Of You* started a long string of solo hits, the biggest of which were *Turn On Your Love Light* and *Call On Me*. Jerry Butler had set out in the Impressions, which he formed with Curtis Mayfield in Chicago during 1957. After reaching number 11 with *For Your Precious Love* the following year Butler left to go solo with *He Will Break Your Heart*. He went on to score over 30 hits although it was not until 1969 that *Only The Strong Survive* brought another top tenner.

Four black teenagers from New Jersey, the Shirelles were one of the earliest and best of the sixties female groups. Powered by the emotional voice of Shirley Allston (from whom they had taken their name), they were responsible for the magnificent

Above: Child prodigy Brenda Lee, whose age, diminutive stature and powerpack voice earned her the nickname Little Miss Dynamite.

Previous page top left: Johnny Kidd and his most famous set of Pirates. Left to right: Johnny Spence, Johnny Kidd, Frank Farley and Mick Green.

Previous page top right: After inveigling his way backstage on a Marty Wilde tour, Billy Fury impressed so much that he was soon on the show!

Previous page bottom: When his own group was unable to make the transition from local gigs, Cliff Richard assembled a supergroup ... the Shadows. Left to right: Bruce Welch, Tony Meehan, Jet Harris and Hank Marvin.

and much-copied singles stretching from *Tonight's The Night* (1960) to *Soldier Boy* (1962), and taking in such classics as *Will You Love Me Tomorrow?* and *Dedicated To The One I Love.* They continued to record for several years, achieving minor hits until 1967.

Hank Ballard had been without a substantial hit since 1954, when a trio of suggestive songs, *Work With Me Annie*, *Sexy Ways* and *Annie Had A Baby*, sold well despite restricted airplay. His greatest claim to fame was as the inventor of the twist. Originally a 1959 B side, the record was revived on *American Bandstand*, inspiring the studio dancers to twist along ... and an apocryphal story has Ballard failing to honour Dick Clark's invitation to perform the song on the show, leading the latter to suggest that Chubby Checker record a note-for-note copy.

Checker – originally Ernest Evans, but re-named because of his resemblance to a young Fats Domino! – had scored a minor hit with *The Class*, but his recording of *The Twist* took off like a whirlwind after prime time TV exposure. It became the biggest dance craze since the Charleston. The steps were so easy that anyone could do it, and everybody did!

Checker spent the next few years achieving more hit records based on further dances ... the hucklebuck, the limbo and the hitchhike among them. None succeeded like the original, however, and after *Let's*

Above: Gary 'US' Bonds, originally a sixties 'garage' sound protagonist, who re-emerged much more recently under the patronage of Bruce Springsteen and 'Miami' Steve Van Zandt.

Right: Two of Philadelphia's dance-era stars – Chubby Checker and Bobby Rydell. Their only recorded collaboration was Jingle Bell Rock.

Twist Again rekindled the fire, a re-issue of *The Twist* returned to number one at the end of 1961! By the end of 1965 Checker was running out of ideas.

The twist, however, turned into an industry. Perhaps the best variation was *Twistin' The Night Away* by Sam Cooke, the worst was a spin-off film, the appalling potboiler *Twist Around The Clock.* The most influential was undoubtedly *Twist And Shout* by the Isley Brothers, which provided the Beatles with their wildest show stopper, and the most commercial adaptation was by Joey Dee and the Starliters, who reached number one with *Peppermint Twist.* The house band at the ultra-fashionable Peppermint Lounge, a New York niterie, they faded fast, but Dee can boast that the Ronettes and three of the Young Rascals passed through his Starliters on their way to fame.

Apart from the twist, it was business as usual. Rosie and the Originals had the year's best one-off in *Angel Baby.* What happened to Rosie remains unclear, but several other women were around a little longer, including Wanda Jackson who opened up with the raving *Let's Have A Party. Sweet Nothin's* introduced Brenda Lee, who went on to have two chart toppers in 1960 – *I'm Sorry* and *I Want To Be Wanted.*

Brenda had signed her first recording contract in 1956, aged 11! After several rockers, notably *Let's Jump The Broomstick* (a hit only in Britain), she reverted to a country career and can still be persuaded to perform at the odd country festival.

Another Nashville native, Floyd Cramer was a studio pianist who broke into the charts with three top tenners, *Last Date, On The Rebound* and *San Antonio Rose,* although the year's hottest instrumentalist was another of Presley's ex-sidemen, Bill Black. Now leading Bill Black's Combo, he also relied on session work, but a succession of 18 hits, including *White Silver Sands* and *Don't Be Cruel* (which he had previously cut with Elvis), allowed him to tour successfully until 1965, when he died from a brain tumour.

Charlie Rich also started his career in the Sun studios. A talented singer/pianist/songwriter, he had spent years in the shadows of the label's stars – like Jerry Lee Lewis and Johnny Cash, for both of whom he had written hits. In 1960 *Lonely Weekends* brushed the top 20 ... but it was another five years before *Mohair Sam* reminded rock fans of his existence. Another bleak period ended in 1973 when *Behind Closed Doors* and the subsequent number one *The Most Beautiful Girl* finally revealed his full potential. He'd found superstardom at 41.

Also passing through the charts in 1960 were Bob Luman with *Let's Think About Living,* the Fendermen with *Mule Skinner Blues,* the Hollywood Argyles with *Alley-Oop* and Ray Peterson with the year's big 'death disc' *Tell Laura I Love Her.* None would find another winner except Peterson with *Corinna Corinna* – Phil Spector's first independent production after learning the ropes with Leiber and Stoller.

Below: Bobby Vee's American success was equalled in Britain, where he toured (backed by the Crickets) and starred in two films – Just For Fun *and* Play It Cool.

The Ventures started out with the biggest hit of their career, *Walk Don't Run*, and Brian Hyland did likewise with *Itsy Bitsy Teenie Weenie Yellow Polka Dot Bikini*, although he sustained his popularity throughout the decade with *Ginny Come Lately* and *Sealed With A Kiss*, among 22 chart appearances. Appealing to the same teen romance market was Bobby Vee, who at 15 had been called to his local ballroom in Fargo, North Dakota, the day Buddy Holly died. Because he was familiar with Holly's songs he helped to make up the depleted bill. A year and a half later he was in the top 10 with *Devil Or Angel*, the first of five million-sellers, including *Take Good Care Of My Baby* and *The Night Has A Thousand Eyes*.

Johnny Burnette, who attended the same school as Elvis Presley, began as one of the wildest rockabilly boppers around, and records by his Rock'n'Roll Trio remain highly prized items today. However, their true worth was barely recognized at the time and Johnny turned to songwriting to get his foot in the door. After penning three million-sellers for Ricky Nelson, he stowed his untamed youth and plugged into the Frankie Avalon scene for his triumphant return, racking up immediate winners in *Dreamin'* and *You're Sixteen*. *Little Boy Sad* showed evidence of his earlier abandon, but preceded a dry spell from which he had not recovered when a boating accident took his life in 1964.

All in all it was a pretty desperate year. Not only were innovation and genius pretty thin on the ground, rock was suddenly no longer the exclusive province of the young. Old people were twisting and going to see Elvis films! Something was going to have to be done about it!

Above: Johnny Burnette, from Memphis, Tennessee, attempted to emulate Elvis Presley in the rock'n'roll stakes but ultimately found success as a balladeer.

TITLE	ARTIST	LABEL	WEEKS AT NO. 1
El Paso	Marty Robbins	Columbia	2
Running Bear	Johnny Preston	Mercury	3
Teen Angel	Mark Dinning	MGM	2
A Summer Place	Percy Faith	Columbia	9
Stuck On You	Elvis Presley	Victor	4
Cathy's Clown	The Everly Brothers	Warner Bros	5
Everybody's Somebody's Fool	Connie Francis	MGM	2
Alley Oop	Hollywood Argyles	Lute	1
I'm Sorry	Brenda Lee	Decca	3
Itsy Bitsy Teenie Weenie Yellow Polka Dot Bikini	Brian Hyland	Leader	1
It's Now Or Never	Elvis Presley	Victor	5
The Twist	Chubby Checker	Parkway	1
My Heart Has A Mind Of Its Own	Connie Francis	MGM	2
Mr Custer	Larry Verne	Era	1
Save The Last Dance For Me	The Drifters	Atlantic	3
I Want To Be Wanted	Brenda Lee	Decca	1
Georgia On My Mind	Ray Charles	ABC Paramount	1
Stay	Maurice Williams and the Zodiacs	Herald	1
Are You Lonesome Tonight?	Elvis Presley	Victor	5

TITLE	ARTIST	LABEL	WEEKS AT NO. 1
What Do You Want?	Adam Faith	Parlophone	1
What Do You Want To Make Those Eyes At Me For?	Emile Ford	Pye	1
Why?	Anthony Newley	Decca	6
Poor Me	Adam Faith	Parlophone	1
Running Bear	Johnny Preston	Mercury	2
My Old Man's A Dustman	Lonnie Donegan	Pye	5
Cathy's Clown	The Everly Brothers	Warner Bros	9
Good Timing	Jimmy Jones	MGM	4
Please Don't Tease	Cliff Richard	Columbia	3
Apache	The Shadows	Columbia	6
Tell Laura I Love Her	Ricky Valance	Columbia	2
Only The Lonely	Roy Orbison	London	3
It's Now Or Never	Elvis Presley	RCA	8
Poetry In Motion	Johnny Tillotson	London	1

Right: On 16 April 1960 21-year-old Eddie Cochran died when the car taking him to London Airport skidded off the road. The other passengers, his fiancée Sharon Sheeley and singer Gene Vincent recovered from their injuries.

DEATHS

Jesse Belvin, soul singer
Albert Camus, French writer
Eddie Cochran, rock singer
Clark Gable, film star
Oscar Hammerstein III, songwriter
Johnny Horton, country singer
Mack Sennett, film producer
Nevil Shute, author

CURRENT EVENTS

1 February: At Greensboro, North Carolina, four black students defy a whites-only rule and sit in at a Woolworth's lunch counter. The sit-in tactic spreads as the civil rights movement gathers pace.

13 February: An atomic bomb is exploded by France, the fourth nation to have one.

19 February: Prince Andrew is born to the Queen and Prince Philip.

29 February: The Agadir earthquake in Morocco kills over 10,000 people.

5 March: Elvis is discharged from the US army.

21 March: South African police open fire on crowds at Sharpeville killing over 70.

4 April: USA launches its first weather satellite, transmitting pictures of the earth's cloud cover.

22 April: Fidel Castro accuses USA of plotting to overthrow his newly established government.

1 May: US pilot Francis Gary Powers, flying a U2 high altitude plane, is shot down by Soviet missiles over Soviet territory. Powers is captured, confesses he was on a photo-reconnaissance flight for the CIA, and is sentenced to ten years for espionage.

2 May: Convicted US murderer Caryl Chessman is executed after 12 years on death row.

9 May: The US Federal Drug Administration approves the public sale of birth control pills.

23 June: The Cavern Club in Liverpool relaxes its jazz-only policy and allows rock groups to play.

25 August: Cassius Clay wins the gold medal in the light heavyweight boxing class at the seventeenth Olympic Games in Rome.

19 September: Parking meter wardens start duties in London.

12 October: The twenty-fifth anniversary meeting of the United Nations breaks up in pandemonium after Krushchev pounds the table with his shoe, before making a dramatic exit.

8 November: 43-year-old John Kennedy becomes the youngest US President.

2 December: Pope John XXIII meets the Archbishop of Canterbury, Dr Fisher – the first such meeting since the Anglican/Catholic split of 1534.

FILMS

The Alamo
The Apartment (Oscars for Best Film and Best Director)
Butterfield 8
Can Can
Elmer Gantry
Exodus
The Millionairess
Never On A Sunday
North To Alaska
Psycho
Saturday Night And Sunday Morning
Sons And Lovers
Spartacus
The Sundowners

Made in England

1960

SIDE ONE
45 RPM
STEREO

Let's Do The Twist!

ALL RIGHTS OF THE MANUFACTURER AND OF THE OWNER OF THE RECORDED WORK RESERVED UNAUTHORISED PUBLIC PERFORMANCE BROADCASTING AND COPYING OF THIS RECORD PROHIBITED

1961

SIDE ONE
45 RPM
STEREO

Running Scared

THE ALLISONS

MIKE BERRY AND THE OUTLAWS

SOLOMON BURKE

THE CRYSTALS

JIMMY DEAN

DION

RAL DONNER

LEE DORSEY

SHANE FENTON AND THE FENTONES

BERRY GORDY

CLARENCE FROGMAN HENRY

THE HIGHWAYMEN

THE IMPRESSIONS

EDEN KANE

BEN E. KING

At the beginning of the year 19-year-old Bob Dylan arrived in Greenwich Village, New York, to try to establish himself on the folk scene, having temporarily divested himself of any rock'n'roll urges. He was not alone in feeling that most white rock music now seemed to be aimed at the lowest common denominator.

Folk music had been trivialized too, with a million clean-cut college boys trying to emulate the success of the Kingston Trio. The Highwaymen and the Tokens both reached number one, with *Michael* and *The Lion Sleeps Tonight* respectively, and old-timer Burl Ives even came out of the woodwork with a run of ersatz folk hits.

In 1961 much of the best American popular music came from the Tamla Motown group of labels in Detroit, owned and masterminded by Berry Gordy, who had worked on the Ford assembly line before practising his songwriting and production skills with Jackie Wilson, Marv Johnson and Barrett Strong. The intention was to promote local black talent – and within 18 months of the label's inception, three of their acts were national stars.

The first to break out were the Miracles, formed in 1957 and led by one of the chief architects behind the company's astonishing growth, William 'Smokey' Robinson. They rose to number two with the eighth release on Tamla, *Shop Around*, during February – at which point the fourth release on Motown, *Bye Bye Baby*, written and recorded by

17-year-old Mary Wells, began to climb the charts. By the end of the year the Miracles had returned to the chart four times and Mary Wells once ... but, more significantly, the debut by the Marvelettes, *Please Mr Postman*, had provided Tamla with their first number one. It was an auspicious start.

Robinson's exceptional songwriting ability combined with his extraordinarily expressive falsetto voice made each Miracles' release an occasion. During the next ten years some 36 singles hit the charts – among them such classics as *You've Really Got A Hold On Me*, *What's So Good About Goodby?*, *The Tracks Of My Tears*, *I Second That Emotion* and the chart-topping *Tears Of A Clown*. Many people were upset when Robinson split from the Miracles in 1972 – but his solo career was not without interest, as will be seen.

So prolific was Smokey Robinson during the sixties that he was able to provide colleagues with equally powerful songs: the Temptations and Marvin Gaye both benefited from his writing, as did Mary Wells, whose trio of Robinson epics, *The One Who Really Loves You*, *You Beat Me To The Punch* and *Two Lovers*, were all top tenners during 1962. Robinson also penned *My Guy*, a number one hit for Wells, but also her Motown swan song. After leaving the label her chart career declined alarmingly.

The five 17-year-old girls who came together as the Marvelettes were introduced to Gordy after winning a high school talent

ERNIE K-DOE

GLADYS KNIGHT AND THE PIPS

JOHN LEYTON

BARRY MANN

THE MARCELS

THE MARVELETTES

JOE MEEK

ROY ORBISON

TONY ORLANDO

GENE PITNEY

SMOKEY ROBINSON AND THE MIRACLES

DEL SHANNON

HELEN SHAPIRO

PHIL SPECTOR

LEROY VAN DYKE

MARY WELLS

contest. Led by the raspy-voiced Gladys Horton, they followed their initial hit with 20 more, including *Beechwood 4-5789*, *The Hunter Gets Captured By The Game* and *My Baby Must Be A Magician* – the last two written by the ubiquitous Smokey Robinson, but when Horton was replaced in 1968 it was just a matter of time before they ran out of magic.

Gladys Knight, then on Fury Records but later to sign with Motown, also struck gold in 1961 when *Every Beat Of My Heart* began a

chart career which has yet to fade. Seventeen at the time, she sang lead in front of three members of her family, collectively known as the Pips, and they returned to the chart with *Letter Full Of Tears* at the end of the year. After a relatively thin spell a move to the Gordy empire in 1966 resulted in two top tenners, *I Heard It Through The Grapevine* and *If I Were Your Woman*, and the hits continued on Buddah, where she crowned her impressive career with the spine-tingling *Midnight Train To Georgia*.

61

Right: From Atlanta, Georgia, came Gladys Knight and the Pips – comprising her brother Merald Knight, and two cousins, William Guest and Edward Patten.

Previous page top: Soul star Mary Wells rehearses with Sounds Incorporated in preparation for her first British tour.

Previous page bottom: On hearing early records by the Miracles, many listeners assumed that Claudette Rogers was the lead singer. In fact, the pleading falsetto voice belonged to Smokey Robinson (bottom right).

Equally significant soul acts could be found on other labels, like Atlantic, who had pioneered and popularized R&B and soul in the fifties. They lost the current king, Ray Charles (who moved to Paramount), but came up with two new winners in Solomon Burke and Ben E. King. Burke's *Just Out Of Reach* was the first of over 20 hits for the label, some of which found their way into the early repertoire of the Rolling Stones.

Even more influential was Ben E. King, former leader of the Drifters, who cruised into the top 10 with his solo debut *Spanish Harlem* – a song written by the rare partnership of Jerry Leiber and Phil Spector. *Stand By Me* consolidated his position and the hits continued until 1967. His style mellowed considerably, and he rejoined the Drifters in the early eighties.

If Detroit was humming with talent, New Orleans was not doing badly either. Ernie K-Doe had a number one hit with *Mother-In-Law* and Chris Kenner reached number two with *I Like It Like That*, while the Showmen (*It Will Stand*) and Clarence 'Frogman' Henry (*But I Do* and *You Always Hurt The One You Love*), made a strong, if temporary, impression. Also working in the city was Kid Chocolate, an ex-prizefighter who reverted to his real name, Lee Dorsey, to cut *Ya Ya* – his first and biggest hit. Of eight subsequent chart entries *Working In The Coal Mine* and *Holy Cow* brought him greatest international recognition.

The Impressions found a formula which turned them into one of the greatest soul groups ever. Now led by Curtis Mayfield, they reached the top 20 with *Gypsy Woman*,

Left: As lead singer of the Drifters, Ben E. King topped the US chart with Save The Last Dance For Me. *Within weeks, he'd embarked on a solo career.*

Below: After four years of only localized success as a rockabilly singer, Roy Orbison found fame and fortune with Only The Lonely.

the first of well over 30 hits, including such classics as *It's All Right, Keep On Pushing, Amen* and *People Get Ready*. Although they struggled into the early seventies it was never the same after Mayfield left in 1968.

Other black groups were transiently successful, most notably Shep and the Limelites with *Daddy's Home* (a huge hit for Cliff Richard 20 years later), the Marcels with *Blue Moon*, the Flares with *Foot Stomping* and Little Caesar and the Romans with *Those Oldies But Goodies*.

Other black hits were provided by Slim Harpo (*Rainin' In My Heart*), Freddy King (*Hide Away*), James Ray (*If You Gotta Make A Fool of Somebody*), Roy Hamilton (*You Can Have Her*) and Bobby Lewis (*Tossin' and Turnin'* – the year's best-selling single). Gene McDaniels had three hits – *A Hundred Pounds Of Clay, Tower Of Strength* and *Chip Chip* – only to drop from view soon after.

The same fate befell many of the white entrants: Joe Dowell came and went with his chart-topping *Wooden Heart*, Troy Shondell with *This Time* and Barry Mann with *Who Put The Bomp*. Little was heard of Ral Donner after his impressive brace *Girl Of My Best Friend* and *You Don't Know What You've Got*, or of Tony Orlando after *Halfway To Paradise* and *Bless You* – although he was to re-surface nine years later as the leader of Dawn.

Displaying somewhat greater tenacity were four guys specializing in upbeat ballads: Gene Pitney, Del Shannon, Dion and Roy Orbison. A 24-year-old from Texas, Orbison had sprung to prominence in 1960 when *Only The Lonely* reached number two. In summer 1961 *Running Scared* topped the chart, and Orbison went on to accumulate the remarkable total of 12 million-sellers in four years. Even as Beatlemania was sweeping all before it he reached the top again with *Oh Pretty Woman*, also a number one (his third) in Britain, where he toured consistently during the sixties.

Ill-health ultimately brought his career to a standstill, but he returned to the stage in 1980 just in time to see Don McLean take his song *Crying* to the top of the British charts.

Although the Belmonts were never able to recover from his departure in 1960 Dion Di Mucci became enormously successful. *Runaround Sue* and *The Wanderer* brought him gold discs the following year and *Lovers Who Wander, Ruby Baby* and *Drip Drop* were among the dozen hits which kept him hot until the middle of 1964. Four years later he made a dramatic comeback with *Abraham, Martin And John* but although critical acclaim greeted much of his subsequent work changing taste denied him any widespread re-acceptance.

Runaway shot Del Shannon to number

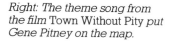

Right: The theme song from the film Town Without Pity *put Gene Pitney on the map.*

one on both sides of the Atlantic. It was to be his greatest achievement, although he managed to keep the hits coming: *Hats Off To Larry*, *Swiss Maid*, *Little Town Flirt* and *Keep Searchin'* all became firm international favourites. Since his golden period his appearances have been sporadic, but his *Greatest Hits* compilation album remains a consistent seller.

After *Town Without Pity* Gene Pitney, a 20-year-old from Connecticut, followed up with *(The Man Who Shot) Liberty Valance* and *Only Love Can Break A Heart*. Over the next five years he was seldom absent from the chart, either in America or Britain, where he had ten top 10 hits. New singles found their way into the UK chart until well into the seventies, although the continued success of his stage act hinged on his rendition of such memory-joggers as *Twenty Four Hours From Tulsa* and *I'm Gonna Be Strong*.

As a songwriter Pitney had provided others with ideal material: Ricky Nelson made the top 10 with *Hello Mary Lou* and *He's A Rebel* would soon carry the Crystals to number one.

Five black schoolgirls from New York, the Crystals were chosen by Phil Spector to launch his Philles label in late 1961. Spector was also a New Yorker, whose family moved to Los Angeles in 1953. His introduction

to the record business came five years later when his high school trio, the Teddy Bears, sped to the top of the charts on both sides of the Atlantic with *To Know Him Is To Love Him* – a song written by Spector. For the next two years he studied production techniques, working with Lee Hazlewood and Lester Sill (Duane Eddy's producers) and then Leiber and Stoller, before testing his newly acquired skills on Ray Peterson, Curtis Lee and the Paris Sisters – scoring top tenners with *Corinna Corinna*, *Pretty Little Angel Eyes* and *I Love How You Love Me* respectively.

The Crystals' debut *There's No Other* was followed into the top 20 by *Uptown*, paving the way for the million-selling *He's A Rebel* in 1962. A couple more classics, *Da Doo Ron Ron* and *Then He Kissed Me*, scored heavily but then their success rate fell away sharply as Spector began to concentrate on the Ronettes, who were more suited to the 'wall of sound' he had evolved.

Switching labels failed to reactivate their career, and they re-formed only for the periodic revival show. The Crystals, however, will never be forgotten – and nor too will some of 1961's fluke hits like *Big Bad John* by Jimmy Dean, *Wheels* by the String-A-Longs and *Walk On By* by Leroy Van Dyke.

Among the instrumental hits were *Last Night* by the Mar-Keys and *You Can't Sit*

Above: Having covered his office walls with gold discs, Phil Spector can afford to take it easy once in a while.

Above: By the time the Crystals visited London to appear on Ready Steady Go, *one of their number, Mary Thomas, had departed – leaving (left to right) Lala Brooks, Barbara Alston, Pat Wright and Dee Dee Kennibrew.*

Down by Phil Upchurch, which convinced Georgie Fame to buy a Hammond organ and turn the Flamingo Club's 'twist sessions' into rhythm and blues sessions – adding impetus to an underground movement started up by Alexis Korner.

In London the first rock groups were appearing, but most of them sounded pretty weak and unimaginative compared with the Americans. Some even had hits: Nero and the Gladiators experienced five-minute stardom with *Entry Of The Gladiators* and *In The Hall Of The Mountain King*, Shane Fenton and the Fentones scored with *I'm A Moody Guy* and Mike Berry and the Outlaws found favour with *Tribute To Buddy Holly* – an early success for independent producer Joe Meek.

Meek had built his own studio in a flat above a shop in Holloway Road, in north London, and there he experimented with echo, overdubs and various other effects to achieve a sound unique on the British scene. A tune he had written for his studio group the Tornados would soon bring him world-wide acclaim, but in 1961 he was riding high with John Leyton.

Leyton was really an actor, but *Johnny Remember Me* zoomed to number one. During the next two years he scored nine more hits, including *Wild Wind, Son This Is She* and *Lone Rider* – all bearing the distinctive Meek stamp. When his time ran out he reverted to films and theatre – as did Hayley Mills, who had a freak hit with *Let's Get Together*.

Leyton's only rival was Eden Kane. *Well I Ask You* was the first of five top 10 hits, but he went out of style quite quickly, as did yodelling country singer Karl Denver. Both outlasted the Allisons, however. They are still looking for a follow-up to their Eurovision Song Contest hit, *Are You Sure?*

'Will trad jazz kill rock?' wondered a music press headline. Well, rock seemed to be dying on its feet anyway, but the 'trad boom' certainly was not helping matters. Sparked off by Chris Barber's *Petite Fleur* in 1959 and fed by a series of lightweight confections by Acker Bilk, Kenny Ball and the Temperance Seven, the boom had succeeded in diluting traditional jazz for mass consumption.

While Acker tootled on his clarinet and

the Temperance Seven warbled through their megaphone, the year's brightest new discovery was being groomed for stardom. East Ender Helen Shapiro was only 14 when she cut the specially conceived *Don't Treat Me Like A Child*, a surefire hit. Her unusually deep voice, extreme youth and bubbly personality hypnotized the media and her next two singles, *You Don't Know* and *Walkin' Back To Happiness*, both tore to number one. But the hits trailed off and, despite a starring role in the execrable film *It's Trad Dad*, by her 18th birthday she had forever vanished from the charts – laid waste by the Beatles, who at the end of 1961 were on their way down to London to audition for Decca ... who would see no commercial potential and turn them down.

Above: 'Please don't treat me like a child,' begged schoolgirl Helen Shapiro (left), whose girl-next-door image attracted a huge following. Two years later, when she headlined a package tour over the Beatles, she would see the writing on the wall.

Left: John Leyton was one of Joe Meek's early protégés, relying heavily on the producer's artistry to keep his name in the charts.

USA CHART TOPPERS

TITLE	ARTIST	LABEL	WEEKS AT NO. 1
Wonderland By Night	Bert Kaempfert	Decca	3
Will You Love Me Tomorrow?	The Shirelles	Scepter	2
Calcutta	Lawrence Welk	Dot	2
Pony Time	Chubby Checker	Parkway	3
Surrender	Elvis Presley	Victor	2
Blue Moon	The Marcels	Colpix	3
Runaway	Del Shannon	Big Top	4
Mother-In-Law	Ernie K-Doe	Minit	1
Travellin' Man	Ricky Nelson	Imperial	2
Running Scared	Roy Orbison	Monument	1
Moody River	Pat Boone	Dot	1
Quarter To Three	'US' Bonds	Legrand	2
Tossin' And Turnin'	Bobby Lewis	Belton	7
Wooden Heart	Joe Dowell	Smash	1
Michael	The Highwaymen	UA	2
Take Good Care Of My Baby	Bobby Vee	Liberty	3
Hit The Road, Jack	Ray Charles	ABC Paramount	2
Runaround Sue	Dion	Laurie	2
Big Bad John	Jimmy Dean	Columbia	5
Please Mr Postman	The Marvelettes	Tamla	1
The Lion Sleeps Tonight	The Tokens	Victor	3

UK CHART TOPPERS

TITLE	ARTIST	LABEL	WEEKS AT NO. 1
Poetry In Motion	Johnny Tillotson	London	1
Are You Lonesome Tonight?	Elvis Presley	RCA	4
Walk Right Back	The Everly Brothers	Warner Bros	4
Wooden Heart	Elvis Presley	RCA	4
Are You Sure?	The Allisons	Fontana	2
You're Driving Me Crazy	The Temperance Seven	Parlophone	2
Blue Moon	The Marcels	Pye Int	2
Runaway	Del Shannon	London	2
Surrender	Elvis Presley	RCA	5
Temptation	The Everly Brothers	Warner Bros	4
Well I Ask You	Eden Kane	Decca	1
You Don't Know	Helen Shapiro	Columbia	2
Johnny Remember Me	John Leyton	Top Rank	5
Kon Tiki	The Shadows	Columbia	1
Michael	The Highwaymen	HMV	1
Walkin' Back To Happiness	Helen Shapiro	Columbia	4
His Latest Flame	Elvis Presley	RCA	3
Take Good Care Of My Baby	Bobby Vee	London	1
Tower Of Strength	Frankie Vaughan	Philips	2
Stranger On The Shore	Acker Bilk	Columbia	2

FILMS

Breakfast At Tiffany's
El Cid
La Dolce Vita
The Guns Of Navarone
The Hustler
The Misfits
One Eyed Jacks
101 Dalmations
Splendor In The Grass
The Young Ones
West Side Story (winning 11 Oscars)

Right: Twisting the night away! Not since rock'n'roll had any one dance received so much publicity!

20 January: President Kennedy takes office. 'Ask not what your country can do for you . . . ask what you can do for your country.'

12 February: Fierce fighting in Katanga, Congolese Republic, between UN forces and supporters of Patrice Lumumba, results in the latter's assassination.

18 February: Bertrand Russell leads a demonstration in protest against basing Polaris missiles in Scotland. The first American nuclear submarine arrives a month later.

19 March: Large-scale attacks on Europeans by African terrorists in Angola leave many dead.

12 April: Major Yuri Gagarin becomes the first man in space; he orbits the earth in a Soviet spaceship.

17 April: 1500 Cuban exiles, equipped and trained by the CIA, invade Cuba's south coast at the Bay of Pigs. After brief success they are overpowered and surrender. President Kennedy accepts 'sole responsibility'.

4 May: A bi-racial group sponsored by the Congress of Racial Equality leaves by interstate bus from Washington DC to force the integration of bus terminals in the south. The 'Freedom Riders' are met by hostile mobs.

5 May: Commander Alan Shepard makes a sub-orbital space flight lasting 15 minutes, as America tries to catch the USSR in the space race.

8 May: Lord Stansgate (Anthony Wedgwood Benn) is refused admission to the House of Commons and renounces his peerage.

16 June: Soviet ballet star Rudolf Nureyev defects at Paris airport.

21 July: A second US astronaut, Captain Virgil Grissom, makes a sub-orbital space flight.

5 August: A Soviet astronaut, Major Titov, orbits the earth 17 times.

13 August: The East German government closes the border between East and West Berlin and begins erecting a concrete barrier – the Berlin Wall.

1 September: USSR explodes a nuclear bomb, ending a 34-month test silence. America retaliates with a series of heavy tests.

1 November: The UK government publishes a bill designed to curb immigration, after a long tradition of free entry for all Commonwealth citizens.

10 November: The Mecca ballroom chain reveal plans to introduce 'disc sessions' with disc jockeys throughout the country, instead of all-live music.

11 December: President Kennedy sends 400 helicopter crewmen to Vietnam, to assist the 2000 'military advisers and technicians' already there.

The Twist starts a dancing craze, which also sees the introduction of the Fish, the Pony, the Madison, the Bird, the Mess Around, the Watusi, the Bristol Stomp, the Surfer's Stomp and various others!

Gary Cooper, film star
Dag Hammarskjold, UN General Secretary
Ernest Hemingway, author
Cisco Houston, folk singer
Chico Marx, film star

Made in England

1961

SIDE ONE
45 RPM
STEREO

Running Scared

ALL RIGHTS OF THE MANUFACTURER AND OF THE OWNER OF THE RECORDED WORK RESERVED UNAUTHORISED PUBLIC PERFORMANCE BROADCASTING AND COPYING OF THIS RECORD PROHIBITED

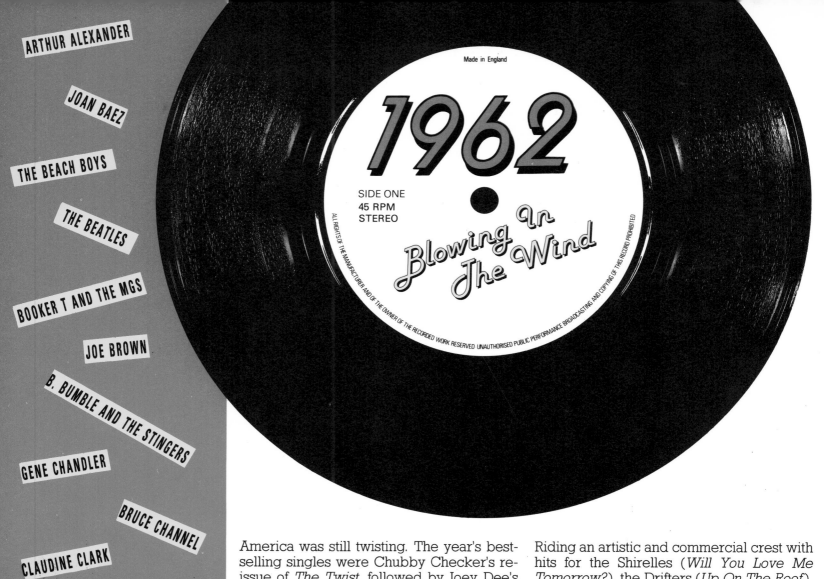

1962

SIDE ONE
45 RPM
STEREO

Made in England

Blowing In The Wind

ARTHUR ALEXANDER

JOAN BAEZ

THE BEACH BOYS

THE BEATLES

BOOKER T AND THE MGS

JOE BROWN

B. BUMBLE AND THE STINGERS

GENE CHANDLER

BRUCE CHANNEL

CLAUDINE CLARK

THE CONTOURS

THE COOKIES

BOB DYLAN

THE FOUR SEASONS

MARVIN GAYE

America was still twisting. The year's best-selling singles were Chubby Checker's re-issue of *The Twist*, followed by Joey Dee's *Peppermint Twist* ... but close behind them at number four on the sales list was *Mashed Potato Time* by Dee Dee Sharp, a record reflecting the popularity of dancing songs.

Sixteen-year-old Dee Dee answered a small ad placed by Cameo Parkway Records for a girl who could read music, play the piano and sing. Within months she had two records in the top 3 – *Slow Twistin'*, a duet with Chubby Checker, and her own *Mashed Potato Time* – but her chart career was short. *Gravy* and *Ride!* followed and *Do The Bird* saw the energetic Dee Dee in the top 10 for the last time. She later married the noted producer Kenny Gamble, the gener-ator of 'Philly soul'.

R&B pioneer Etta James came back with *Something's Got A Hold On Me* and the Ikettes temporarily left the shadows of Ike and Tina to score with *I'm Blue*. Patti LaBelle and the Blue Belles made their debut with *I Sold My Heart To The Junkman*, ten years before they returned as Labelle. Among those who fell by the wayside after deliver-ing one classic were Claudine Clark with *Party Lights*, Little Esther Phillips, who put *Release Me* into the top 10 and Ketty Lester, whose smouldering *Love Letters* reached the top 5 on both sides of the Atlantic.

Both the Cookies and Little Eva enjoyed the patronage of Carole King and her song-writing partner and husband Gerry Goffin.

Riding an artistic and commercial crest with hits for the Shirelles (*Will You Love Me Tomorrow?*), the Drifters (*Up On The Roof*), Tony Orlando (*Halfway To Paradise*) and Bobby Vee (*Take Good Care Of My Baby*), they capitalized on the dance craze by creating *The Loco-Motion* for Eva Boyd, a black teenager who was earning pocket money as their babysitter. Little Eva reached number one, and her fame was largely to rest on that song, despite a couple of interesting follow-ups. The background singers on *The Loco-Motion* took another Goffin/King song, *Chains*, into the top 20 as the Cookies – hitting again with *Don't Say Nothin' Bad (About My Baby)* before revert-ing to anonymous session work.

Carole King's own release *It Might As Well Rain Until September* reached number three in Britain in 1962. It was to be her only move out of the songwriting booth, however, until her dramatic re-emergence in the early seventies.

Black guys had a very productive year. Chubby Checker put four albums into the top 20, and Ray Charles had three in the top 5, while in the singles market black acts accounted for over 40 per cent of sales. Gene Chandler found a memorable debut in *Duke Of Earl*, a chart topper, and Chuck Jackson broke through with *Any Day Now* ... and, although Arthur Alexander came with *You Better Move On* and went with *Anna*, his songs lived on in versions by the Rolling Stones and the Beatles respectively.

70

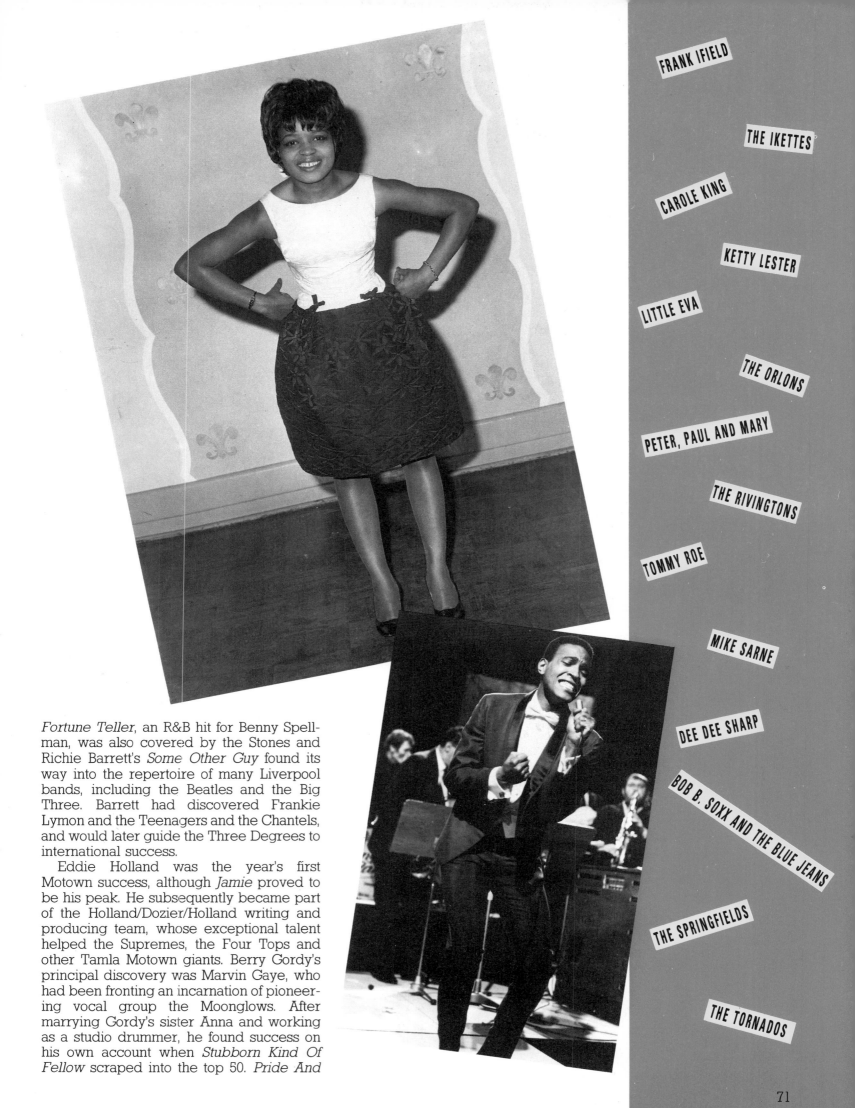

Fortune Teller, an R&B hit for Benny Spellman, was also covered by the Stones and Richie Barrett's *Some Other Guy* found its way into the repertoire of many Liverpool bands, including the Beatles and the Big Three. Barrett had discovered Frankie Lymon and the Teenagers and the Chantels, and would later guide the Three Degrees to international success.

Eddie Holland was the year's first Motown success, although *Jamie* proved to be his peak. He subsequently became part of the Holland/Dozier/Holland writing and producing team, whose exceptional talent helped the Supremes, the Four Tops and other Tamla Motown giants. Berry Gordy's principal discovery was Marvin Gaye, who had been fronting an incarnation of pioneering vocal group the Moonglows. After marrying Gordy's sister Anna and working as a studio drummer, he found success on his own account when *Stubborn Kind Of Fellow* scraped into the top 50. *Pride And*

71

Joy and *Can I Get A Witness* consolidated his position and his career really took off in the mid-sixties with a run of hits leading up to his epic chart topper *I Heard It Through The Grapevine*. Despite upheavals in his personal life he maintained his consistency through the seventies with classics like *What's Going On* and *Let's Get It On* and the quality of his work did not suffer when in 1982 he left Tamla after 20 years. *Sexual Healing* won him renewed acclaim, but the life of one of the greatest soul singers of all time ended in April 1984, when, on the eve of his 45th birthday, he was shot by his father during a family argument.

Gordy's latest group, the Contours, had a well deserved but solitary smash with their raucous debut, *Do You Love Me?* But most new black groups foundered after initial success including the Valentinos, who got little response after *Looking For A Love* – although lead singers Bobby and Cecil Womack are high in the charts in the 1980s. The Orlons did better, with three top tenners including the dance hit *The Wah Watusi*, while the Rivingtons had two minor but unforgettable hits, *Papa Oom Mow Mow* and *The Bird's The Word*.

Although concentrating on the Crystals, Phil Spector shot the strangely named Bob B. Soxx and the Blue Jeans into the top 10 with *Zip-A-Dee-Doo-Dah* – and although their excellent follow-up *Why Do Lovers Break Each Other's Hearts?*, had comparatively little impact one of the Blue Jeans, Darlene Love, went on to make three great singles for Spector the following year.

The hottest new instrumentalists were Booker T and the MGs. Two blacks and two whites, they were the studio band for Stax Records, but their own hit *Green Onions* was as original and influential as any others they had played on. While they continued to back Otis Redding, Wilson Pickett, Eddie Floyd and many other soul stars, they kept their identity with hits like *Hang 'Em High* and *Time Is Tight*, and became one of the most respected instrumental units.

Imitated by scores of R&B hopefuls, *Green Onions* made a great impression in Britain – but not as great as that made by the Routers whose hand-clapping rhythm and chant *Let's Go!* has reverberated around football terraces ever since. 1962's other significant instrumentals were *Nut Rocker*, a scorching mutilation of Tchaikovsky's *Nutcracker Suite*, by B. Bumble and the Stingers and *Surfer's Stomp* by the Marketts, which heralded a new craze – surf music!

The genre's popularizers were the Beach Boys – three brothers, a cousin and a schoolfriend who sang the praises of their idealistic Californian life style in songs such as *Surfin'*, *Surfin' Safari*, *Surfin' USA* and *Surfer Girl*. Many of their early ideas were derived from sources as varied as Jan and Dean, Chuck Berry, the Four Freshmen and Dick Dale, but as leader Brian Wilson

Previous page top: With fists clenched and elbows bent, Little Eva prepares to demonstrate the latest dance craze, the Turkey Trot.

Previous page bottom: The son of a minister from Washington, DC, Marvin Gaye received his musical grounding in the church choir before becoming a prime soul contender on the fledgling Tamla label.

Below: With his local two-tone group the MGs, Booker T put Memphis on the soul map.

refined his songwriting they began to evolve a distinctive vocal and instrumental style, which shone through on *I Get Around*, their first number one.

By the time *Help Me Rhonda* topped the charts in summer 1965 they had become one of the world's biggest groups. As an American group they were unapproachable between 1963 and 1966: 13 top 10 singles and 10 top 10 albums. *Good Vibrations*, a late 1966 chart topper on both sides of the Atlantic, was seen as Wilson's crowning glory and the album *Pet Sounds* was widely described as the group's masterpiece.

The hits continued, although their supremacy grew shaky after drugs and meditation affected some of their work. Their old magic occasionally reappeared during the seventies and several compilation albums returned them to the charts.

Their principal rivals in 1962 were the Four Seasons who came from the other side of the continent, Newark, New Jersey, and as the Four Lovers had been struggling for recognition since 1956. Their break came after Bob Crewe (Freddie Cannon's mentor) convinced them to adopt a vocal style similar to Maurice Williams and the Zodiacs'; whereupon *Sherry* reached number one. *Big Girls Don't Cry*, *Walk Like A Man* and *Rag Doll* followed it to the top, and the magical formula lasted well into the seventies, with hits like *Who Loves You?* and

December 1963 (Oh What A Night). *Can't Take My Eyes Off You* and *My Eyes Adored You* were two of several solo hits by leader Frankie Valli.

Other new white groups included Jay and the Americans with *She Cried* and the Earls with *Remember Then*, while Paul Revere and the Raiders had a pre-fame skirmish with *Like Long Hair*, a bridge between the 'garage' and 'punk' styles, and the Crickets came back with *Don't Ever Change*.

Buddy Holly's influence was also discernible on Tommy Roe's chart-topping debut *Sheila* – the first of over 20 hits including *Everybody* and *Sweet Pea*. His 1969 hit *Dizzy* reached number one on both sides of the Atlantic.

His challengers made little progress. Chris Montez had to wait four years for another substantial hit after *Let's Dance* and Bruce Channel never got back into the reckoning after his classic *Hey Baby*.

In New York's Greenwich Village and in student communities across America folk clubs and record labels were proliferating and singers had little trouble securing gigs. Inevitably new heroes began to emerge. Pete Seeger, an established folk singer and writer, soon found himself with a new audience eager to listen to his songs and stories, and he became the father-figure of the movement. The first new star was Joan Baez, whose intensity and charisma propelled her first three albums into the charts.

Below left: The Beach Boys arrive in the UK. Back row: Carl Wilson and Dennis Wilson; front row: Mike Love, Al Jardine and Brian Wilson.

Below right: American stars Tommy Roe (left) and Chris Montez were among those touring Britain to promote their hits.

Above: Bob Dylan was one of many young people drawn to New York's Greenwich Village during the early sixties.

Opposite top: Peter, Paul and Mary (or Paul, Mary and Peter, as they appear here) were folkies whose material transcended the commercial superficiality of the current boom.

Opposite bottom left: Frank Ifield was the first artist to appear on television in Australia, when transmission began in Sydney. I Remember You brought him instant global stardom.

Opposite bottom right: The Springfields were voted Britain's top vocal group in 1962 – but Dusty would go on to greater success when she went solo the following year.

Political awareness was growing in colleges and folk music soon became the authorized soundtrack for activist meetings from civil rights demonstrations to anti-nuclear marches and rallies denouncing US involvement in Vietnam – and the movement's principal musical innovator was Bob Dylan. While most singers continued the folk process singing traditional material, Dylan and a handful of others wrote 'contemporary folk songs' and soon a strong political vein began to permeate his lyrics. His first album showed little evidence of 'protest music', but within weeks he had defined the style with *Blowing In The Wind* – soon to become the anthem of the civil rights movement. Over the years it would be covered by literally hundreds of artists, but it was Peter, Paul and Mary who carried it to the world.

Led by the soulful Mary Travers, they had already put protest music into the charts with a version of Pete Seeger's *If I Had A Hammer*, but they were able to balance their commercial success with their espousal of worthy causes. In August 1963 their performance of *Blowing In The Wind* to an army of black freedom marchers in Washington who had just heard Martin Luther King deliver his 'I have a dream' speech was the high point of their career.

Meanwhile Dylan saw his popularity spread with three more albums, although it was not until 1965 when he put aside his acoustic guitar and moved into 'folk rock' that he really took off.

Britain's Peter, Paul and Mary equivalent were the Springfields, a folksy trio fronted by Dusty Springfield. They reached the top 5 with *Island Of Dreams* and *Say I Won't Be There* before Dusty left to go solo in 1963.

A guitarist from the *Boy Meets Girls* TV show, Joe Brown adopted a folksy, Cockney persona which pervaded *A Picture Of You*, the biggest of a dozen hits, and provided for a long television career in succeeding years.

The most successful new British act was an instrumental group, the Tornados. They started their career as Joe Meek studio musicians, backing John Leyton among others, before working as Billy Fury's band. Their breakthrough came with *Telstar*, which rocketed them to number one in Britain and America, showering both group and producer with praise. Unfortunately they never delivered anything as contagious again and several original members left. Bassist Heinz found solo stardom, while Clem Cattini became Britain's hottest session drummer.

Frank Ifield, an Australian country and western specialist, topped the charts for seven weeks with *I Remember You*. He returned to number one with *Lovesick Blues*, *The Wayward Wind* and *Confessin'*, but subsequent releases were less successful although his cabaret career still thrives.

Apart from the rare exceptions like Screaming Lord Sutch and the Savages, most groups working the southern clubs were limp Elvis and Shadows impersonators. Meanwhile, unknown beyond Merseyside, some 350 rock groups were shaking the streets of Liverpool – but so far, any advances on London had been repelled, although current hopes were pinned on the Beatles, whose local reputation was second to none.

John Lennon, George Harrison and Paul McCartney had been performing together since the late fifties, but the group had only stabilized with the addition of drummer Pete Best. Since then, they had attained a degree of proficiency that compelled Brian Epstein, a local record shop owner, to take on their management – but his attempts to secure them a recording contract met with failure.

Eventually Parlophone agreed to record them – although not before Best had been dropped in favour of Ringo Starr, the drummer with another popular Liverpool group, Rory Storme and the Hurricanes. Their extensive repertoire was almost entirely made up of US rock and R&B covers, but when they came to record they had a number of impressive songs of their own, and two of these, *Love Me Do* and *PS I Love You*, were coupled for their first single release in November 1962.

It made the charts, but only reached number 17. Nobody had any idea that within 18 months the Beatles would be the most famous musical group in history.

CURRENT EVENTS

29 January: Nuclear test ban talks between America, the USSR and the UK, held in Geneva, break down after three years.

10 February: Spy plane pilot Gary Powers is exchanged for Soviet spy Colonel Rudolf Abel.

20 February: Astronaut John Glenn becomes the first American to orbit the earth. Launched from Cape Canaveral on Friendship 7, he completes three orbits before splashdown into the Atlantic.

9 March: The Pentagon verifies reports that US pilots are flying combat missions in Vietnam.

28 May: American share prices suffer their worst slump since 1929.

31 May: Adolf Eichmann, former Gestapo officer convicted of a major role in the extermination of Jews during the Second World War, is hanged in Tel Aviv.

9 July: America explodes a massive nuclear device 250 miles in space above the Pacific. The blast is seen in New Zealand, 4000 miles away.

10 July: Telstar, the first US communications satellite, is launched. Live TV pictures are transmitted from America to the UK a week later.

18 August: Rebuffed by American doctors, Sherri Finkbine goes to Sweden for the abortion of a baby deformed by the drug thalidomide. New safety regulations are introduced for testing drugs after further congenital deformities are attributed to thalidomide.

10 September: The US Supreme Court upholds that James Meredith, a black student, is to be admitted to the University of Mississippi. Two are killed in ensuing riots.

3 October: After Walter Schirra makes a six-orbit space flight, the Americans claim supremacy over the USSR – reaffirming their promise to have a man on the moon before the decade ends.

22 October: President Kennedy reveals that the Soviets have missile bases in Cuba. He announces a partial blockade to prevent further military equipment being installed.

6 November: The United Nations condemns apartheid and recommends that its members break off diplomatic relations with South Africa.

7 November: Richard Nixon loses the governorship of California . . . 'You won't have Nixon to kick around anymore.'

17 November: Dulles Airport, the first to be designed for jets, opens in America.

20 November: America lifts the Cuban blockade after Krushchev agrees to remove Soviet installations.

Pop Art receives media saturation. Andy Warhol, one of the first to introduce such techniques as the use of commercial silk screen reproduction, supersize blow-ups of familiar items, and multiple image portraits, emerges as the leading light.

In America home owners are encouraged by civil defence authorities to build fall-out shelters in case of Soviet nuclear attack.

In the UK the government undertakes to initiate a campaign of public education about the dangers of smoking.

FILMS

The Birdman Of Alcatraz
Days Of Wine And Roses
How The West Was Won
It's Trad Dad
Lawrence Of Arabia (Oscars for Best Film and Best Director)
The Longest Day
The Manchurian Candidate
The Man Who Shot Liberty Valance
Mutiny On The Bounty
Summer Holiday
A Taste Of Honey
To Kill A Mockingbird
Victim

DEATHS

Hoot Gibson, silent movie star
Charles Laughton, film star
Marilyn Monroe, actress film star
Eleanor Roosevelt, wife of former President
John Steinbeck, author
Stuart Sutcliffe, former Beatle

Below: We're all going on a summer holiday! Cliff Richard swings into action on the set of his latest film, Summer Holiday *(Ivy, 1962).*

USA CHART TOPPERS

TITLE	ARTIST	LABEL	WEEKS AT NO. 1
The Lion Sleeps Tonight	The Tokens	Victor	2
The Twist	Chubby Checker	Parkway	2
The Peppermint Twist	Joey Dee and the Starliters	Roulette	3
Duke Of Earl	Gene Chandler	Vee Jay	3
Hey Baby	Bruce Channel	Smash	3
Don't Break The Heart That Loves You	Connie Francis	MGM	1
Johnny Angel	Shelley Fabares	Colpix	2
Good Luck Charm	Elvis Presley	RCA	2
Soldier Boy	The Shirelles	Scepter	3
Stranger On The Shore	Acker Bilk	Atco	1
I Can't Stop Loving You	Ray Charles	ABC Paramount	5
The Stripper	David Rose	MGM	1
Roses Are Red	Bobby Vinton	Epic	4
Breaking Up Is Hard To Do	Neil Sedaka	RCA	2
The Locomotion	Little Eva	Dimension	1
Sheila	Tommy Roe	ABC Paramount	2
Sherry	The Four Seasons	Vee Jay	5
Monster Mash	Bobby 'Boris' Pickett	Garpax	2
He's A Rebel	The Crystals	Philles	2
Big Girls Don't Cry	The Four Seasons	Vee Jay	5
Telstar	The Tornados	London	1

UK CHART TOPPERS

TITLE	ARTIST	LABEL	WEEKS AT NO. 1
Stranger On The Shore	Acker Bilk	Columbia	2
The Young Ones	Cliff Richard	Columbia	5
Rock-A-Hula Baby	Elvis Presley	RCA	4
Wonderful Land	The Shadows	Columbia	8
Nut Rocker	B. Bumble and the Stingers	Top Rank	1
Good Luck Charm	Elvis Presley	RCA	5
Come Outside	Mike Sarne	Parlophone	2
I Can't Stop Loving You	Ray Charles	HMV	2
I Remember You	Frank Ifield	Columbia	7
She's Not You	Elvis Presley	RCA	3
Telstar	The Tornados	Decca	5
Lovesick Blues	Frank Ifield	Columbia	5
Return To Sender	Elvis Presley	RCA	3

Made in England

1962

SIDE ONE
45 RPM
STEREO

Blowing In The Wind

ALL RIGHTS OF THE MANUFACTURER AND OF THE OWNER OF THE RECORDED WORK RESERVED. UNAUTHORISED PUBLIC PERFORMANCE BROADCASTING AND COPYING OF THIS RECORD PROHIBITED

Made in England

1963

SIDE ONE
45 RPM
STEREO

With The Beatles

ALL RIGHTS OF THE MANUFACTURER AND OF THE OWNER OF THE RECORDED WORK RESERVED. UNAUTHORISED PUBLIC PERFORMANCE BROADCASTING AND COPYING OF THIS RECORD PROHIBITED

As the year opened things seemed normal enough on the British charts: the best-selling album was *The Black And White Minstrel Show* and Cliff Richard had the number one single . . . but by May the writing was on the wall.

Down the bill on package tours headed by Helen Shapiro and Tommy Roe the Beatles were stealing the show every night, and while their second single *Please Please Me* was held off the top spot, the next one, *From Me To You*, monopolized it for seven weeks. The same month *Please Please Me* reached the top of the album chart – and stayed there for the next 30 weeks! The Beatles had arrived! Establishing a pattern which would be repeated throughout the sixties, *She Loves You* and *I Want To Hold Your Hand* moved swiftly to number one within days of release, as did their second album *With The Beatles*, which dislodged its predecessor to remain the best seller for 21 weeks.

Fearful of losing out on similar talent, the record companies swooped on Liverpool, signing up anything that moved. Two other Brian Epstein-managed groups, Gerry and the Pacemakers and Billy J. Kramer and the Dakotas, were immediately successful. Gerry and the Pacemakers had been popular on Merseyside for years and once brought to national attention, they went into the record books as *How Do You Do It?*, *I Like It* and *You'll Never Walk Alone* all zoomed to number one! Never before had

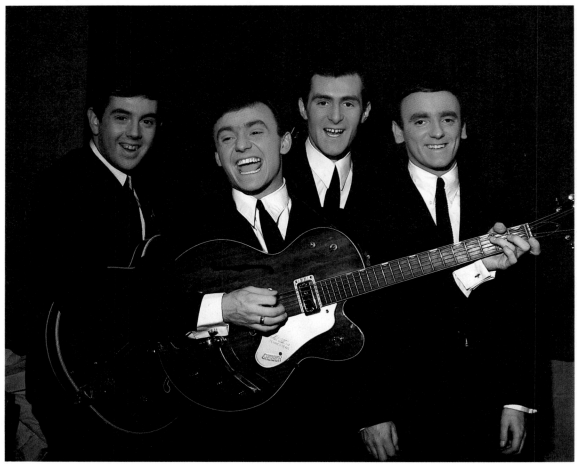

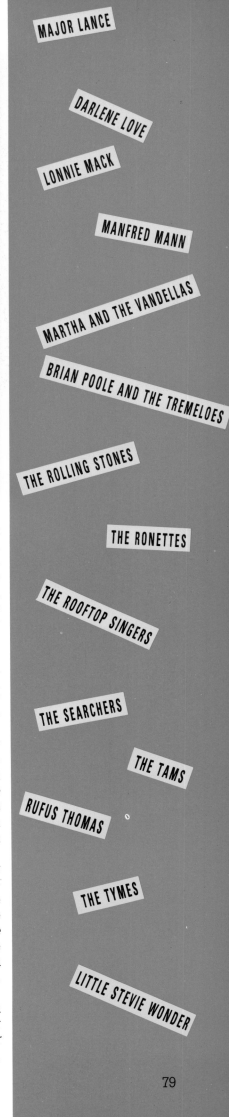

MAJOR LANCE

DARLENE LOVE

LONNIE MACK

MANFRED MANN

MARTHA AND THE VANDELLAS

BRIAN POOLE AND THE TREMELOES

THE ROLLING STONES

THE RONETTES

THE ROOFTOP SINGERS

THE SEARCHERS

THE TAMS

RUFUS THOMAS

THE TYMES

LITTLE STEVIE WONDER

any act achieved such results with its first three releases – and the feat would remain unequalled for over 20 years. Further hits like *I'm The One* and *Ferry Cross The Mersey* draw warm response in a club and cabaret act which flourishes today, but it is for *You'll Never Walk Alone*, subsequently adopted by Liverpool Football Club fans, that Gerry is best remembered.

Billy J. Kramer's local success enabled him to quit his day job, but it was not until Epstein signed him that he achieved wider acclaim. After replacing his backing group with a Manchester group, the Dakotas, Epstein persuaded Lennon and McCartney to give him a couple of their latest compositions. *Do You Want To Know A Secret?* and *Bad To Me* were instant hits and *Little Children*, a 1964 chart topper, increased his celebrity, but Kramer was unable to sustain the course and dropped from view soon after.

Suddenly the hottest manager in popular music, Brian Epstein had the record companies feeding from his hand, and two more of his charges made a speedy impact. The hard-rocking Big Three found it in *Some Other Guy* and the Four Jays became the Fourmost to achieve their breakthrough with another Lennon and McCartney song, *Hello Little Girl*.

The only non-Epstein act to smash through were the Searchers, who took their name from a John Wayne film. *Sweets For My Sweet*, their cover of an old Drifters' hit,

carried them to number one, a position they regained with *Needles And Pins* and *Don't Throw Your Love Away*, establishing them as one of the strongest Merseyside groups. Their trademarks, the 12-string jangle and polished harmonies (a formula soon to be adopted by the Byrds), stood them in good stead for a long and illustrious career, which thrives today.

Having plundered Liverpool, the music business fixed its stare on Manchester, and found Freddie and the Dreamers and the Hollies. Freddie Garrity managed to propel himself to stardom by mixing large doses of comedy into his act. His version of *If You Gotta Make A Fool Of Somebody* was tepid compared with James Ray's original, but the demand for Merseybeat had reached epidemic proportions and it hit the top 3 – as did his next two singles, *I'm Telling You Now* and *You Were Made For Me*. His chart success was limited but his stage act

enabled him to make a smooth transition to children's television and pantomime.

The Hollies, too, started out with resuscitated US hits and tailor-made publishers' demos, but soon evolved their own distinctive sound and identity on *I'm Alive*, *Carrie-Anne* and *Jennifer Eccles*. After a long chart career which saw 17 singles reach the top 10, they settled into the carabet circuit, where they continue to operate.

Heinz, the blond-haired Tornados' bassist, had solo success with *Just Like Eddie* and two ex-Shadows, Jet Harris and Tony Meehan, topped the chart with *Diamonds*. But if you were not Beatles-influenced you did not stand much chance of survival – and among the first to realize were Dave Berry and the Cruisers from Sheffield, Brian Poole and the Tremeloes from Essex and the Dave Clark Five from London, all of whom adjusted their repertoire and image to some degree. *The Crying Game* became Berry's

done by Alexis Korner and Cyril Davies, leaders of Blues Incorporated and the founders of London's first R&B club, and Georgie Fame, whose Blue Flames were transforming the jazz-dominated Flamingo into an R&B stronghold. Close behind came John Mayall's Bluesbreakers, but the first disciples to find commercial acceptance were the Rolling Stones and Manfred Mann.

By summer 1963, a year after their inception, the Stones had stabilized as a quintet: Mick Jagger, Keith Richard, Brian Jones, Charlie Watts and Bill Wyman. They had also acquired a dynamic manager in Andrew Loog Oldham, and a recording contract with Decca, who were trying to atone for passing over the Beatles. Although their songwriting skills took longer to emerge, their musical talents were immediately obvious. *Come On* (written by Chuck Berry), *I Wanna Be Your Man* (Lennon and McCartney) and *Not Fade Away* (Buddy Holly) climbed the charts and *It's All Over*

Left: The Hollies (left to right): Graham Nash, Tony Hicks, Eric Haydock, Allan Clarke and Bobby Elliott.

Below: Street credibility? Freddie impresses the Dreamers with his antics.

first of three top 5 hits, and Brian Poole shot to prominence with *Twist And Shout* and *Do You Love Me?* (his first and last number one), after which he saw his career dwindle alarmingly and, although his group revived their fortunes in 1967, Poole left the business.

After seeing their version of *Do You Love Me?* left at the post the Dave Clark Five contrived to write their own winners, which they did in *Glad All Over* and *Bits And Pieces*, reaching number one and two respectively. However, their British success was dwarfed by their progress in America, where they concentrated their efforts throughout the sixties. Following their 1964 breakthrough they scored no fewer than 24 hits before breaking up.

Running parallel to the Beatles-inspired 'beat group boom' was a rhythm and blues movement which had been growing in London. Much of the pioneering work was

Right: The Dave Clark Five were led by their drummer, but organist Mike Smith did most of the singing.

Below: Manfred Mann (left to right): Manfred himself, Paul Jones, Mike Hugg, Mike Vickers and Tom McGuinness.

Now (the Valentinos) made number one ... the first of eight chart toppers during the sixties. Their writing flowered on songs like *Satisfaction*, *Get Off Of My Cloud*, *Paint It Black* and *Honky Tonk Women* (also US number ones), and the hits continued throughout the seventies. Now in their forties and touring less frequently, they still survive as the world's biggest and most enduring rock group.

Manfred Mann is still around too, although his current band bears no relation to that which bore his name and sprang to fame with *5-4-3-2-1* at the tail end of 1963. Previously the Mann Hugg Blues Brothers, they dropped their jazzy orientation to succeed with a mixed bag of American hits like *Do Wah Diddy Diddy*, specially concocted Tin Pan Alley efforts like *Pretty Flamingo*, and obscure Dylan songs like *Mighty Quinn* – all chart toppers. Since the group folded at the end of the sixties Manfred has commanded a series of bands, still managing to come up with the occasional hit to boost his considerable live following.

What a turnaround! Whereas previously little of any artistic merit had ever emerged from the British rock scene, there was now a gold mine opening up ... none of this was making the slightest impression on the American market, where things were much the same as 1962: soul, surf and folk.

Meanwhile Chuck Berry, just released from prison and all but forgotten in America, found a whole new generation of British rockers singing his songs! Mention here too of Del Shannon – one of the first Americans

to acknowledge the Beatles; his version of *From Me To You* reached number 77 on the US chart – which is higher than any of the Beatles' own early records, none of which got anywhere!

The surf scene was burgeoning, with everybody from Bo Diddley to Chubby Checker riding the wave. Jan and Dean reached number one with *Surf City*, while several instrumentals employed surfing vernacular like *Pipeline* by the Chantays and *Wipe Out* by the Surfaris.

Three of the year's top four albums were in the folk field, two by Peter, Paul and Mary and one by Joan Baez, but most of the singles were either fairly plastic like *Green, Green* by the New Christy Minstrels, or aimed at the cabaret market like *If I Had A Hammer* by Trini Lopez. The most popular was *Walk Right In*, a jug band tune commercially souped-up by the Rooftop Singers.

The hottest new rock group was Jimmy Gilmer and the Fireballs, who had the year's

best-selling single, *Sugar Shack*. The Cascades found their only winner in *Rhythm Of The Rain*, and special mention must be made of *Louie Louie* by the Kingsmen, the seminal 'garage' hit which was instantly added to the repertoire of almost every beat group in Britain. It was subsequently covered by literally scores of artists, ranging from Frank Zappa to Motorhead, and seems to have been the Kinks' major inspirational source.

Female groups were very popular, none more so than the Ronettes, a trio of New York Puerto Ricans led by Veronica (Ronnie) Bennett who had been working as back-up singers. It was in this capacity that Phil Spector first hired them, but sensing their potential he signed them up, ensuring that their debut *Be My Baby* would be one of his best creations. The Ronettes' adept singing made *Baby I Love You*, *The Best Part Of Breaking Up* and *Walking In The Rain* among the finest records ever

Above: Hardly looking like the wildest bunch of tearaways on the scene! The Rolling Stones (left to right): Bill Wyman, Brian Jones, Mick Jagger, Keith Richard and Charlie Watts.

83

Right: Little Stevie Wonder plays his harmonica while the Supremes sway in the background.

recorded by a female group. During this time Spector (who later married Ronnie) was perfecting his 'wall of sound' – simultaneously recording the voices, four guitars, three pianos, two basses, a drummer, three other percussionists and four horn players. By now the most respected producer in the world, he put all his acts and all his skills into an imposing Christmas album, but its release coincided with President Kennedy's assassination, and nobody was in any mood for celebration.

Among non-Spector groups were the Chiffons, four black teenagers from the Bronx who took *He's So Fine* to number one. *One Fine Day* and *Sweet Talkin' Guy* won them more honours, but they did not make it beyond 1966. Martha and the Vandellas stayed hot throughout the sixties, scoring six top tenners including *Heat Wave, Quicksand, Dancing In The Street* and *Nowhere To Run.* After working for Tamla Motown as a secretary Martha Reeves joined two friends to add backing vocals to early recordings by Mary Wells and Marvin Gaye. Their own career got under way when the Holland/Dozier/Holland team furnished them with a string of perfect soul rockers, which kept them bubbling for eight years – but neither party was able to recapture the magic after Martha split with the Vandellas in 1971.

Motown's real find was Stevie Wonder. Blind from birth, Wonder was only 11 when Ronnie White of the Miracles brought him to the label's attention, and had just turned 13 when *Fingertips – Part 2* swept to the top of the charts. A concurrent album prophetically titled *The 12-Year-Old Genius* also made number one. Eleven more top 10 singles including *Uptight, I Was Made To Love Her* and *For Once In My Life* led to another chart topper, *Superstition,* in 1972, by which time his genius was in no doubt. His super-

stardom continued through the seventies with hit albums like *Songs In The Key Of Life* and *Hotter Than July,* and his 1984 chart-topping single *I Just Called To Say I Love You* shows undiminished strength.

The year's other soul acts pale in comparison. Rufus Thomas climaxed a long recording career with *Walking The Dog.* Garnett Mimms and the Enchanters hit with *Cry Baby,* Freddie Scott with *Hey, Girl,* Inez and Charlie Foxx with *Mocking Bird* and Bob and Earl with *Harlem Shuffle.* The Tams started a long run with *What Kind Of Fool,* as did the Tymes with *So Much In Love.* Both groups would top the UK chart during the 1970s.

Major Lance found fame with a Curtis Mayfield song, *The Monkey Time,* but after *Um Um Um Um Um Um* the following year he began a chart decline. Jimmy Soul topped the chart with *If You Wanna Be Happy* and was never seen again.

Shirley Ellis and Barbara Lewis were the principal women of soul. Her husband Lincoln Chase, provided Shirley Ellis with three nursery rhyme novelties, *The Nitty Gritty, The Name Game* and *The Clapping Song* – all of which reached the top 10, as did *Hello Stranger,* the debut by Barbara Lewis. Two years later *Baby I'm Yours* reinstated her near the top of the charts. Betty Harris did well with *Cry To Me* and Doris Troy went top 10 with *Just One Look,* while Darlene Love, once a third of Bob B. Soxx and the Blue Jeans, continued her alliance with Phil Spector on *(Today I Met) The Boy I'm Gonna Marry* and *Wait Til' My Bobby Gets Home.*

It was a white girl who made the most headway – Lesley Gore, a 17-year-old from New Jersey, who hit the top with *It's My Party.* Pure pop, comprising strong songs and impassioned vocals, was her forte. *Judy's Turn To Cry, She's A Fool* and *You Don't Own Me* were all top 5 hits but by 1967 the formula had lost its potency.

White guys were scarce. Lonnie Mack and Boots Randolph had instrumental hits in *Memphis* and *Yakety Sax;* Dave Dudley and Bobby Bare started impressive country & western careers with *Six Days On The Road* and *Detroit City;* and two Pennsylvanians, Bobby Vinton and Lou Christie, were very successful.

Vinton was a balladeer specializing in songs like *Roses Are Red* and *Blue Velvet,* chart-topping foundation stones for a 50-hit career which continues today. Christie was a falsetto merchant of the Frankie Valli school. *Two Faces Have I* attracted national attention, which peaked in 1965 when *Lightnin' Strikes* topped the charts.

As the year ended British groups prepared to invade America and transform the face of popular music. It would not be difficult.

USA CHART TOPPERS

TITLE	ARTIST	LABEL	WEEKS AT NO. 1
Telstar	The Tornados	London	2
Go Away Little Girl	Steve Lawrence	Columbia	2
Walk Right In	The Rooftop Singers	Vanguard	2
Hey Paula	Paul and Paula	Philips	3
Walk Like A Man	The Four Seasons	Vee Jay	3
Our Day Will Come	Ruby and the Romantics	Kapp	1
He's So Fine	The Chiffons	Laurie	4
I Will Follow Him	Little Peggy March	RCA	3
If You Wanna Be Happy	Jimmy Soul	SPQR	2
It's My Party	Lesley Gore	Mercury	2
Sukiyaki	Kyu Sakamoto	Capitol	3
Easier Said Than Done	The Essex	Roulette	2
Surf City	Jan and Dean	Liberty	2
So Much In Love	The Tymes	Parkway	1
Fingertips Pt II	Little Stevie Wonder	Tamla	3
My Boyfriend's Back	The Angels	Smash	3
Blue Velvet	Bobby Vinton	Epic	3
Sugar Shack	Jimmy Gilmer and the Fireballs	Dot	5
Deep Purple	Nino Tempo and April Stevens	Atco	1
I'm Leaving It Up To You	Dale and Grace	Montol Michele	2
Dominique	The Singing Nun	Philips	3

UK CHART TOPPERS

TITLE	ARTIST	LABEL	WEEKS AT NO. 1
The Next Time	Cliff Richard	Columbia	3
Dance On	The Shadows	Columbia	1
Diamonds	Jet Harris and Tony Meehan	Decca	3
The Wayward Wind	Frank Ifield	Columbia	3
Summer Holiday	Cliff Richard	Columbia	2
Foot Tapper	The Shadows	Columbia	1
How Do You Do It?	Gerry and the Pacemakers	Columbia	4
From Me To You	The Beatles	Parlophone	7
I Like It	Gerry and the Pacemakers	Columbia	4
Confessin'	Frank Ifield	Columbia	2
Devil In Disguise	Elvis Presley	RCA	1
Sweets For My Sweet	The Searchers	Pye	2
Bad To Me	Billy J. Kramer and the Dakotas	Parlophone	3
She Loves You	The Beatles	Parlophone	6
Do You Love Me?	Brian Poole and the Tremeloes	Decca	3
You'll Never Walk Alone	Gerry and the Pacemakers	Columbia	4
I Want To Hold Your Hand	The Beatles	Parlophone	3

DEATHS

Patsy Cline, country singer
Jean Cocteau, French author
Cowboy Copas, country singer
Robert Frost, American poet
Hugh Gaitskill, politician
Jack Hobbs, cricketer
Michael Holliday, pop singer
Elmore James, blues singer
Max Miller, comedian
Edith Piaf, chanteuse
Dinah Washington, jazz singer

FILMS

Cleopatra
Dr No
Hud
Just For Fun
Lilies Of The Field
Love With A Proper Stranger
The L-Shaped Room
This Sporting Life
Tom Jones (Academy Awards for Best Film and Best Director)
The VIPs

CURRENT EVENTS

2 January: UPI reports that 30 Americans have died in Vietnam combat to date.

14 January: President de Gaulle says Britain is not yet ready to join the EEC.

21 March: Rumours link UK Minister of War John Profumo with Christine Keeler, a call girl. He denies the allegations, but subsequently admits the affair and resigns.

21 March: Alcatraz prison is closed down.

3 April: After civil rights groups co-ordinate voter registration drives in black areas of Mississippi, Martin Luther King spearheads a massive demonstration in Birmingham, Alabama. The use of dogs and fire hoses by police arouses national indignation.

5 April: A telephone hot-line is established between the White House and the Kremlin.

10 April: The US nuclear submarine *Thresher* fails to re-surface after deep-diving trials in the North Atlantic.

27 May: Harvard lecturers Richard Alpert and Timothy Leary are fired after experiments with LSD.

3 June: Pope John XXIII dies at the age of 81.

11 June: A Buddhist monk burns himself to death in Saigon in protest against Vietnam's religious persecution.

12 June: *Cleopatra*, the most expensive film ever made, opens in New York. Critics doubt that the $35 million will be recouped.

26 June: President Kennedy visits the Berlin Wall to deliver his 'Ich bin ein Berliner' freedom speech.

8 August: The Great Train Robbery takes place in Buckinghamshire; some £2½ million are stolen.

9 August: First broadcast of TV show *Ready Steady Go*.

28 August: More than 20,000 participate in a black freedom march on Washington. Martin Luther King makes his 'I have a dream' speech.

27 September: Joe Valachi tells the Senate crime hearings all about the Cosa Nostra.

18 October: Harold MacMillan resigns as UK Prime Minister; Sir Alec Douglas-Home succeeds him.

1 November: A military coup in Vietnam overthrows the government; President Ngo Dinh Diem is killed.

22 November: President Kennedy is assassinated in Dallas, Texas. Vice President Lyndon B. Johnson is sworn in as replacement. Lee Harvey Oswald is arrested and charged with the murder, but is shot dead by club owner Jack Ruby two days later – in full view of a nationwide television audience.

29 November: President Johnson appoints the Warren Commission to investigate Kennedy's death.

Elephant jokes are fashionable.

The Campaign For Nuclear Disarmament begins to dissolve after the USA, the USSR, the UK and 100 other countries enter a nuclear test ban treaty, banning all nuclear tests except those underground.

Above: French visitor Françoise Hardy (left) with Ready Steady Go presenter Cathy McGowan.

Made in England

1963

SIDE ONE
45 RPM
STEREO

With The Beatles

ALL RIGHTS OF THE MANUFACTURER AND OF THE OWNER OF THE RECORDED WORK RESERVED. UNAUTHORISED PUBLIC PERFORMANCE BROADCASTING AND COPYING OF THIS RECORD PROHIBITED

Made in England

1964

SIDE ONE
45 RPM
STEREO

Everything's Alright!

ALL RIGHTS OF THE MANUFACTURER AND OF THE OWNER OF THE RECORDED WORK RESERVED· UNAUTHORISED PUBLIC PERFORMANCE BROADCASTING AND COPYING OF THIS RECORD PROHIBITED

THE ANIMALS

THE APPLEJACKS

CLIFF BENNETT AND THE REBEL ROUSERS

CILLA BLACK

PETULA CLARK

THE DIXIE CUPS

MARIANNE FAITHFULL

GEORGIE FAME

WAYNE FONTANA AND THE MINDBENDERS

THE FOUR PENNIES

THE FOUR TOPS

HERMAN'S HERMITS

THE HONEYCOMBS

B.B. KING

THE KINKS

THE MERSEYBEATS

For the first time in rock history America was looking up to Britain.

Rampant Beatlemania was at Kennedy Airport to greet the Beatles when they arrived in February for a triumphant appearance on the Ed Sullivan Show. *I Want To Hold Your Hand* was already in the US charts, having sold half a million in ten days, and for the next 14 weeks the Beatles monopolized the pole position.

By this time Capitol, EMI's American arm, who had passed up their initial option a year earlier, were distributing Beatle products as fast as possible. So too were Swan, Tollie and Vee-Jay, labels which had been fortunate enough to do short-term deals on early singles rejected by Capitol. In Britain they had three chart-topping singles – *Can't Buy Me Love*, *A Hard Day's Night* and *I Feel Fine* – and two number one albums – *A Hard Day's Night* and *Beatles For Sale*. But in America product dissemination was such that 31 Beatles' tracks made the top 100, including six number ones! At one point in April the week's top 5 sellers were all by the Beatles! After the premiere of *A Hard Day's Night* the Beatles made their first coast-to-coast tour of America.

During the year numerous British acts made inroads into the US charts, although some had only just taken off in Britain. The Kinks, for instance, were all but unknown before August, when *You Really Got Me* suddenly shot them to the top of the charts, as were the Zombies, who arrived with *She's Not There*. A quartet from North London, the Kinks were led by Ray Davies, an exceptional songwriter, whose prolific output provided ten more top tenners, including such classics as *Dedicated Follower Of Fashion*, *Sunny Afternoon* and *Waterloo Sunset*. A relatively barren spell ended when *Lola* and *Apeman* returned them to prominence in 1970, since when they have become an institution, celebrating their twentieth year with their umpteenth hit, *Come Dancing*.

The Zombies, from St Albans, came and went rather more quickly, although their consistent level of excellence deserved wider recognition. Their British swansong *Tell Her No* was a smash in America, where they concentrated their efforts until their album *Odyssey And Oracle*, released in 1968, was largely ignored. Ironically a single from the album, *Time Of The Season*, began to attract airplay and rose to the US top 3 in 1969 – by which time the Zombies were no more: Rod Argent had formed a new group and Colin Blunstone had gone solo.

Few of the other new beat groups were able to sustain their success beyond a significant debut: the Nashville Teens never equalled *Tobacco Road*, an early Mickie Most production; the Applejacks, from Birmingham, are remembered only for *Tell Me When*; and the Honeycombs sank without trace after stomping to number one with *Have I The Right?* – the last of producer Joe Meek's many chart busters.

Peter and Gordon, a singing duo strumming acoustic guitars, topped the UK chart first time out, courtesy of Paul McCartney. When he presented them with an unreleased Lennon/McCartney song *World Without Love* international success was assured.

Despite more Beatles songs they never made it quite that high again, but accumulated ten hits by 1967, many appealing more to the American market, which they exploited until parting in 1968. While Gordon drifted into the unknown, Peter Asher used his show-biz know-how to become a respected manager and producer, orchestrating the rise of Linda Ronstadt and James Taylor.

Up on Merseyside the Merseybeats and the Mojos had something original to offer. *It's Love That Really Counts* established the Merseybeats, who did even better with *I Think Of You*. Melodic beatsters with frilly shirts, they were a direct contrast to most Liverpool groups, including the Swinging Blue Jeans, a trad-jazz outfit who converted to raucous rock'n'roll, and scored with frenzied versions of old American hits like *Hippy Hippy Shake* and *Good Golly Miss Molly*. The Mojos' only substantial hit *Everything's Alright* was as innovative as it was intense, but they never recaptured that initial magic – and nor did the Four Pennies, from Blackburn, who reached number one with *Juliet*.

The brightest new Manchester acts were Wayne Fontana and the Mindbenders and

Herman's Hermits. The former's version of *Um Um Um Um Um Um*, a US hit by Major Lance, took them into the top 5 and they managed four other top 40 entries, including the worldwide hit *Game Of Love*. While Fontana moved into cabaret, the Mindbenders had a huge hit of their own, *Groovy Kind Of Love*, after which guitarist Eric Stewart popped back with 10 cc.

I'm Into Something Good warbled Peter Noone, the personable singer with Herman's Hermits, whose all-round appeal garnered nine more top 10 hits, including *No Milk Today* and *There's A Kind Of Hush*, but the group's UK success pales beside their American fame. There audiences found Noone's Englishness so appealing that he took music hall novelties like *Mrs Brown You've Got a Lovely Daughter* and *I'm Henry VIII I Am* to the top of the charts.

MILLIE

THE MOJOS

THE NASHVILLE TEENS

PETER AND GORDON

THE PRETTY THINGS

P.J. PROBY

JOHNNY RIVERS

THE SHANGRI-LAS

SANDIE SHAW

DUSTY SPRINGFIELD

THE SUPREMES

THE SWINGING BLUE JEANS

TOMMY TUCKER

TWINKLE

DIONNE WARWICK

THE ZOMBIES

Above: The Animals on Ready Steady Go. *Left to right: Alan Price, Chas Chandler, John Steel, Eric Burdon and Hilton Valentine.*

In his first year as a producer Mickie Most scored heavily with Herman's Hermits, but he received greater acclaim for his work with the Animals, the hottest R&B band to emerge in 1964. Made up of the best musicians in Newcastle, the Animals, initially inspired by Chicago blues, began to experiment with electrified versions of American folk songs, thus originating the 'folk rock' style which would erupt the following year in the hands of Bob Dylan and his disciples. In fact, adaptations of two songs from Dylan's debut album, *Baby Let Me Take You Home* and *House Of The Rising Sun*, were issued as the Animals' first singles, the latter becoming one of the year's most powerful releases, reaching number one on both sides of the Atlantic.

Brilliant material and ingenious execution continued until they split up in September 1966. Lead singer Eric Burdon then formed the New Animals, and led them to success for another two years, scoring well with hits like *San Franciscan Nights* and *Monterey*. Burdon re-appeared as vocalist with War, before embarking on an erratic solo career, but the original Animals' 1983 world tour was a remarkably successful reunion.

Other breakthroughs were effected by the Pretty Things and Cliff Bennett. The Pretties surfaced from the R&B club scene. *Don't Bring Me Down*, their only top 10 hit, marked a departure from their Bo Diddley background, which receded further as they began to experiment with drug-orientated ideas. Frustrated by the reaction to this interesting phase, they disbanded ... but a strong cult following applauded subsequent reunions.

Cliff Bennett and the Rebel Rousers started out in 1959 playing rock'n'roll, but added saxes in the early sixties, when they were one of the first British bands playing soul. Merseybeat all but drowned them, but they survived to chart with *One Way Love*. Their music became more fashionable, and when Paul McCartney provided them with *Got To Get You Into My Life* they returned to the top 10. Bennett's early career paralleled that of Georgie Fame, whose break came when *Yeh Yeh* suddenly lifted him to number one. *Get Away* and *Ballad Of Bonnie & Clyde* were equally popular, establishing a long and comfortable career.

Fame's interest in blue beat fuelled a boom in Caribbean music, but the only real hit to come out of the bluebeat/ska scene (from which reggae would soon develop) was *My Boy Lollipop* by Millie Small, a 15-year-old Jamaican. The song eventually sold more than three million copies, reaching number two in both Britain and America, and Millie's mentor Chris Blackwell was able to plan his next move – the formation of Island Records.

Millie was one of several British female singers enjoying their first taste of the charts. Dusty Springfield's first solo outing won her a gold disc too: *I Only Want To Be With You* opened the door for a long run of superb, soulful performances including *I Just Don't Know What To Do With Myself* and *Son Of A Preacher Man*, which maintained her commanding position throughout the decade. At the turn of the seventies, however, following her classic album *Dusty In Memphis*, her success declined, but occasional concerts reveal why many consider her to be the finest female singer Britain has ever produced.

Twinkle burst on the scene with her never-to-be-equalled motorcycle drama *Terry*, while Sandie Shaw's *Always Something There To Remind Me* brought instant

Previous page top: The Kinks ... frilly shirts and hunting pinks. Left to right: Ray Davies, Dave Davies, Mick Avory and Pete Quaife.

Previous page bottom: Untroubled by besieging fans, Herman's Hermits and Brian Poole and the Tremeloes watch the birdie while Dusty Springfield ponders the lyrics of I Just Don't Know What To Do With Myself.

fame, which she consolidated with *Long Live Love*, another chart topper. In 1967 she represented Britain in the Eurovision Song Contest, and 50 million viewers saw her sweep to victory with *Puppet On A String*, but two years later she dropped from view until the eighties, when she returned for collaborations with Heaven 17 and the Smiths.

Lulu's version of the Isley Brothers' *Shout* marked her chart entrance (the only hit with her sidemen the Luvvers). A series of tailor-made hits culminated in her sweet and innocent US chart topper *To Sir With Love*. After 15 chart appearances her gentle smile is now most frequently seen in advertisements for mail order catalogues.

Cilla Black and Marianne Faithfull had the right connections. Cilla was a Liverpool lass, the first to be signed by Brian Epstein, who arranged for an unknown Beatles song to be her debut – but while the ruse worked for Billy J. Kramer and Peter and Gordon, Cilla's *Love Of The Loved* was only a minor hit. Abandoning that tactic she covered a Dionne Warwick hit, *Anyone Who Had A Heart*, which reached number one, as did the follow-up *You're My World*. With her help Liverpool acts topped the charts for a total of 20 weeks during the year! By the end of the sixties, with a dozen top 20 hits to her credit, Cilla was able to concentrate on her own television series.

Marianne Faithfull, spotted at a party by Rolling Stones manager Andrew Oldham, had her first single written by Mick Jagger

Right: Radio and TV
personality Keith Fordyce
welcomes the Four Tops to
Britain.

Below right: After years of
scuffling in Los Angeles, P.J.
Proby was an instant smash in
Britain – until his trousers
disintegrated on stage!

and Keith Richard – *As Tears Go By* – which
reached the top 10. *Come And Stay With
Me* and *This Little Bird* proved she was no
flash-in-the-pan. After a lull she returned to
recording in the late seventies when she
began an album career with Island.

Petula Clark had been in and out of the
charts since 1954. In British eyes, she was
hardly a rock artist but after *Downtown*
topped the US chart she found herself on TV
rock shows with the rest of them.

In America Tamla Motown unveiled their
latest models ... the Four Tops and the
Supremes. The Four Tops had been playing
the Detroit club circuit since the mid-fifties,
but after signing with Motown their *Baby I
Need Your Loving* was a smash in America.
It was the start of a five-year harvest which
provided a dozen top 20 hits, including such
soul-stirring epics as *I Can't Help Myself, It's
The Same Old Song* and *Reach Out I'll Be
There* – a worldwide number one. However, their luck walked out with Holland/
Dozier/Holland, who left the Gordy empire
after a heated disagreement, and the Tops
began to slide, until they moved to Casa-
blanca in 1981, when they made an impressive comeback with *When She Was My
Girl.*

The Primettes – Diana Ross, Mary Wilson
and Florence Ballard – joined Motown
straight from school in 1961, when they
changed their name to the Supremes. After
the poor showing of their first six singles,
Berry Gordy's faith was vindicated when
their next five releases all went to number
one! Another product of the Holland/Dozier/
Holland hit factory, they found the right
formula with *Where Did Our Love Go?* and
milked it until December 1969, when Diana
Ross left for a solo career; but by this time
they had racked up 12 number ones!

The Dixie Cups, three students from New
Orleans, were the only other black female
group to make an impact – when their debut
Chapel Of Love reached number one. They
never saw the top 10 again, however, and
after their label, Red Bird, folded in 1966
they disappeared without trace.

Sharing the same label were the Shangri-
Las, one of the best ever female groups.
Two pairs of New York sisters, they created
a series of brilliantly theatrical singles masterminded by madcap producer Shadow
Morton. *Remember (Walkin' In The Sand)*, a
teenage heartbreaker, made the top 5 and
sold a million, as did the even more melo-
dramatic *Leader Of The Pack*, a sure-fire
number one and a top 20 hit in Britain on
three separate occasions! The quality and
imagination remained consistently high
during the next two years, but only *I Can
Never Go Home Anymore* reinstated them
in the top 10.

Other contenders in 1964 included Tamla's
first West Coast act Brenda Holloway,

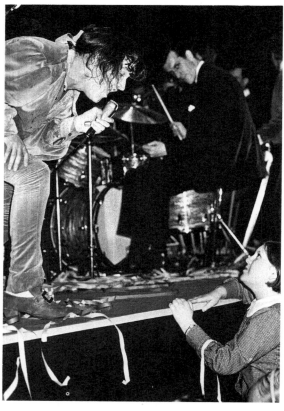

who scored with *Every Little Bit Hurts*; soul
singer Betty Everett, a top tenner with *It's In
His Kiss* and Tommy Tucker, who had an
R&B hit with *Hi-Heel Sneakers*.

A regular on the R&B charts since 1951,
B.B. King scored a big pop chart hit in 1964
and Chuck Berry had five hits after four
barren years. Dionne Warwick cracked the
top 10 with *Anyone Who Had A Heart* and
Walk On By, the first of many Burt
Bacharach/Hal David compositions she recorded, and she continued her run with
such classics as *I Say A Little Prayer* and *Do*

You Know The Way To San Jose?

Johnny Rivers and P.J. Proby were the only significant white guys. A New Yorker, Rivers broke through with a cover version of *Memphis*, although his biggest hit was a song he had written with Lou Adler, *Poor Side Of Town* – his only number one. In the late sixties he formed his own label, Soul City, but his own success centred around live work, bolstered by a scattering of hits.

P.J. Proby became an overnight sensation in Britain when Jack Good brought him in to appear on a TV special. His specialities were re-vamped old show tunes like *Hold Me* and mutilations of screen hits like *Somewhere* and *Maria*, but he eventually disappeared into ignominy and bankruptcy.

As the year ended record sales in Britain were up by 60 per cent on 1960 ... the rock scene was vibrant, boosted among other things by the arrival of the pirate radio stations. By Christmas six stations including Radio Caroline were operating from boats or wartime defence forts in the Thames estuary, offering infinitely more interest than the BBC. It was great to be alive!

Above: The Supremes, led by Diana Ross (left), were soon able to graduate to rather larger stages!

TITLE	ARTIST	LABEL	WEEKS AT NO. 1
There I've Said It Again	Bobby Vinton	Epic	4
I Want To Hold Your Hand	The Beatles	Capitol	7
She Loves You	The Beatles	Swan	2
Can't Buy Me Love	The Beatles	Capitol	5
Hello Dolly	Louis Armstrong	Kapp	1
My Guy	Mary Wells	Motown	2
Love Me Do	The Beatles	Tollie	1
Chapel Of Love	The Dixie Cups	Red Bird	3
A World Without Love	Peter and Gordon	Capitol	1
I Get Around	The Beach Boys	Capitol	2
Rag Doll	The Four Seasons	Philips	2
A Hard Day's Night	The Beatles	Capitol	2
Everybody Loves Somebody	Dean Martin	Reprise	1
Where Did Our Love Go?	The Supremes	Motown	2
House Of The Rising Sun	The Animals	MGM	3
Oh Pretty Woman	Roy Orbison	Monument	3
Do Wah Diddy Diddy	Manfred Mann	Ascot	2
Baby Love	The Supremes	Motown	4
Leader Of The Pack	Shangri Las	Red Bird	1
Ringo	Lorne Greene	RCA	1
Mr Lonely	Bobby Vinton	Epic	1
Come See About Me	The Supremes	Motown	2

UK CHART TOPPERS

I Want To Hold Your Hand	The Beatles	Parlophone	2
Glad All Over	The Dave Clark Five	Columbia	2
Needles And Pins	The Searchers	Pye	3
Diane	The Bachelors	Decca	1
Anyone Who Had A Heart	Cilla Black	Parlophone	3
Little Children	Billy J. Kramer and the Dakotas	Parlophone	2
Can't Buy Me Love	The Beatles	Parlophone	3
A World Without Love	Peter and Gordon	Columbia	2
Don't Throw Your Love Away	The Searchers	Pye	2
Juliet	The Four Pennies	Philips	1
You're My World	Cilla Black	Parlophone	4
It's Over	Roy Orbison	London	2
House Of The Rising Sun	The Animals	Columbia	1
It's All Over Now	The Rolling Stones	Decca	1
A Hard Day's Night	The Beatles	Parlophone	3
Do Wah Diddy Diddy	Manfred Mann	HMV	2
Have I The Right?	The Honeycombs	Pye	2
You Really Got Me	The Kinks	Pye	2
I'm Into Something Good	Herman's Hermits	Columbia	2
Oh Pretty Woman	Roy Orbison	London	3
There's Always Something There To Remind Me	Sandie Shaw	Pye	3
Baby Love	The Supremes	Stateside	2
Little Red Rooster	The Rolling Stones	Decca	1
I Feel Fine	The Beatles	Parlophone	3

FILMS

Becket
The Carpetbaggers
Dr Strangelove
Goldfinger (out-grossing all others, making Sean Connery top box-office star)
A Hard Day's Night
Mary Poppins
My Fair Lady (eight Oscars)
Night Of The Iguana
The Pink Panther
The Pumpkin Eater
The Servant
Topkapi
Zorba The Greek

DEATHS

Brendan Behan, writer
Johnny Burnette, pop singer
Sean O'Casey, playwright
Sam Cooke, soul singer
Cyril Davies, British blues pioneer
Ian Fleming, author
Alan Ladd, film star
Peter Lorre, film star
Harpo Marx, film star
Jawaharlal Nehru, Indian statesman
Cole Porter, songwriter
Jim Reeves, country star

11 January: A report by the US Surgeon General concludes that cigarette smoking is the principal cause of lung cancer.

6 February: A Channel tunnel project is officially announced by the UK and France.

25 February: Cassius Clay becomes world heavyweight boxing champion when Sonny Liston refuses to leave his stool for the seventh round. Two weeks later Clay reveals his membership of the Black Muslim sect and changes his name to Muhammad Ali.

10 March: The Queen gives birth to her fourth child, Prince Edward.

14 March: Jack Ruby, murderer of Lee Harvey Oswald, is sentenced to death in Dallas.

26 March: 30-year sentences are handed out to seven of the Great Train Robbers in Aylesbury.

1 April: François Duvalier officially makes himself President of Haiti for life.

13 April: Ian Smith becomes Prime Minister of Southern Rhodesia.

20 April: BBC-2 begins transmission; the 625-line signal greatly increases screen clarity.

19 May: Some 40 microphones are found hidden in the walls of the American Embassy in Moscow.

23 May: The first issue of The Los Angeles Free Press sparks a spate of 'underground' newspapers.

30 May: Armies of Mods and Rockers clash on holiday beaches – a fad which continues off and on all year. The press exposes 'the drug menace' that has instigated this behaviour.

3 June: President Johnson claims that US military strength is greater than 'the combined might of all nations in the history of the world'.

19 June: In America Carol Doda makes entertainment history by dancing topless.

2 July: President Johnson signs the Civil Rights Bill, designed to give the Federal government more power to protect the constitutional rights of black citizens. Meanwhile Georgia's governor, Lester Maddox, urges the use of axe handles against blacks entering restaurants.

18 July: Black riots in Harlem, New Jersey, and Philadelphia punctuate 'the long hot summer'.

15 September: Krushchev claims weapons which could annihilate all life on earth.

27 September: The Warren Commission concludes that Lee Harvey Oswald acted alone in Kennedy's assassination.

15 October: In the UK general election, the Labour Party win with a majority of only five. Harold Wilson becomes Prime Minister.

15 October: Shakedown in USSR; Krushchev, undisputed ruler of the Soviet Union since March 1958, is suddenly stripped of his power and replaced by Kosygin and Brezhnev.

15 October: Martin Luther King wins the Nobel Peace Prize.

11 December: Kenya becomes a republic within the Commonwealth, with Jomo Kenyatta its first President.

Made in England

1964

SIDE ONE
45 RPM
STEREO

Everything's Alright!

ALL RIGHTS OF THE MANUFACTURER AND OF THE OWNER OF THE RECORDED WORK RESERVED. UNAUTHORISED PUBLIC PERFORMANCE BROADCASTING AND COPYING OF THIS RECORD PROHIBITED

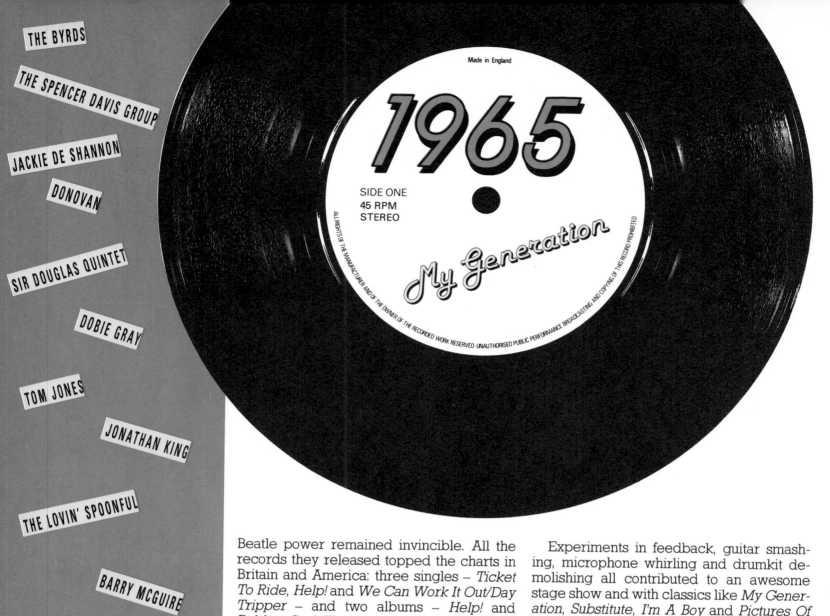

THE BYRDS

THE SPENCER DAVIS GROUP

JACKIE DE SHANNON

DONOVAN

SIR DOUGLAS QUINTET

DOBIE GRAY

TOM JONES

JONATHAN KING

THE LOVIN' SPOONFUL

BARRY MCGUIRE

ROGER MILLER

THE MOODY BLUES

WILSON PICKETT

THE RIGHTEOUS BROTHERS

Made in England

1965

SIDE ONE
45 RPM
STEREO

ALL RIGHTS OF THE MANUFACTURER AND OF THE OWNER OF THE RECORDED WORK RESERVED. UNAUTHORISED PUBLIC PERFORMANCE BROADCASTING AND COPYING OF THIS RECORD PROHIBITED

My Generation

Beatle power remained invincible. All the records they released topped the charts in Britain and America: three singles – *Ticket To Ride, Help!* and *We Can Work It Out/Day Tripper* – and two albums – *Help!* and *Rubber Soul.* Their second film *Help!* was a global box-office smash, and their efforts to restore Britain's international prestige were rewarded in June when the Queen presented them with MBEs.

Liverpool was now the focus of a thriving tourist industry, as fans from all over the world converged on the Cavern to see 'where it all began', but the music scene was dying fast. Record companies were still signing new groups but by the end of the year several of the pioneers, including Gerry and the Pacemakers and Billy J. Kramer and the Dakotas, had kissed the hit parade goodbye.

If Merseybeat was slumping, it was boomtime on the R&B front, where many newcomers emerged, the Who being the most innovative and exciting. They had burst out of the West London mod clubs, dressed in tomorrow's street fashion and playing a hard, fast mixture of R&B, soul and surf, with Beatles and Stones influences thrown in. By the beginning of 1965 their style was completely their own. All four members radiated charisma and when *I Can't Explain* hurtled into the charts no one doubted that the Who were going to be around for many years to come ... although few would have gambled on 18!

Experiments in feedback, guitar smashing, microphone whirling and drumkit demolishing all contributed to an awesome stage show and with classics like *My Generation, Substitute, I'm A Boy* and *Pictures Of Lily*, they remained hot throughout the sixties. Their monumental rock opera *Tommy,*

followed by *Live At Leeds* and *Who's Next*, gave them the respect which would keep them on the top until they finally broke up in 1983. Pete Townshend, their leader, songwriter and guitarist, and one of the most articulate rock musicians, had by this time laid the foundation for a solo career.

Battling with the Who for chart honours was a bunch from Richmond, Surrey, the Yardbirds, who had succeeded the Stones in local clubs after they left for larger venues. They too were rooted in rhythm and blues – as their first two singles, neither widely appreciated, showed. At the instigation of their manager they went 'commercial'

for their next effort, which was a more conventional pop song, *For Your Love*. As a result they lost their purist guitarist Eric Clapton, but were soon in the top 3!

Successive releases were increasingly adventurous, featuring fledgling guitarist Jeff Beck, who soon stamped his mark on *Heart Full Of Soul*, *Shapes Of Things* and *Over Under Sideways Down*. In Britain they were very popular, hitting the top 10 five times, but in America they were worshipped, putting five albums into the charts. The Yardbirds' flight was spectacular but short; in the middle of 1968 they split up, whereupon their latest guitarist Jimmy Page

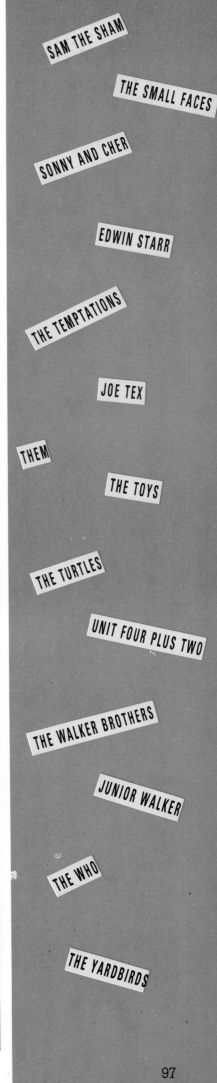

SAM THE SHAM

THE SMALL FACES

SONNY AND CHER

EDWIN STARR

THE TEMPTATIONS

JOE TEX

THEM

THE TOYS

THE TURTLES

UNIT FOUR PLUS TWO

THE WALKER BROTHERS

JUNIOR WALKER

THE WHO

THE YARDBIRDS

Right: The Spencer Davis Group was powered by the extraordinary voice and instrumental prowess of Stevie Winwood (far left).

formed a new group ... Led Zeppelin.

Birmingham's hottest bands the Moody Blues and the Spencer Davis Group both made a national splash in 1965. *Go Now*, the Moody Blues' version of an obscure American song, took them to number one. Then two members departed, including singer/guitarist Denny Laine (later to join Wings), and the Moodies regrouped to spring back with *Nights In White Satin* at the end of 1967. Six top 5 albums attested to the popularity of their revised style, known as 'pomp rock'.

Most of the acclaim showered on the Spencer Davis Group focused on the soulful voice of 16-year-old singer/guitarist/keyboard player Steve Winwood, whose astonishing talents flowered on two chart toppers – *Keep On Running* and *Somebody Help Me* – and three more mighty hits. However, in spring 1967 he left to start Traffic, who thrived while the reconstituted Spencer Davis Group soon disappeared.

Two other R&B combos hit the big time: the Small Faces from the East End of London and Them from Belfast. The former were mods, breaking through with *Whatcha Gonna Do About It?* before settling into a more creative phase fuelled by the songwriting talents of Steve Marriott and Ronnie Lane. *All Or Nothing* reached number one, while *My Mind's Eye* and *Itchycoo Park* came close, and in 1968 *Lazy Sunday* reached number two. Marriott eventually left to form Humble Pie, but the others returned to fame as the Faces when Rod Stewart and Ron Wood arrived.

Blues-bawling Van Morrison was the only constant factor in an ever-changing line-up of Them, but it was his authority which made *Baby Please Don't Go* and *Here Comes The Night* unforgettable. They broke up after two precarious years and Morrison began

Previous page top: Mod heroes the Who became national favourites after appearing on Ready Steady Go. Left to right: John Entwistle, Keith Moon, Roger Daltrey and Pete Townshend.

Previous page bottom: The Yardbirds were regular visitors on the Tops Of The Pops set during 1965. Left to right: Jeff Beck, Chris Dreja, Keith Relf, Jim McCarty and Paul Samwell Smith.

his arduous solo climb, but Them's original recording of *Gloria* still stands as an icon of sixties' punk rock.

In direct contrast to the brash rhythm and blues outfits was a rash of acts with a soft-rock orientation. Unit Four Plus Two topped the charts with *Concrete And Clay*, Paul and Barry Ryan started an eight-hit run with *Don't Bring Me Your Heartaches*, the Seekers arrived from Australia to reach the top with *I'll Never Find Another You* and the Ivy League scored with *Funny How Love Can Be*. None would have been out of place in cabaret, where many of them soon went. Hedgehoppers Anonymous, five RAF recruits, charted with *It's Good News Week* – a tongue-in-cheek protest song written by the year's wonderboy, Jonathan King.

Having established himself with *Everyone's Gone To The Moon*, King proceeded to become singer, songwriter, producer, TV personality, talent spotter, disc jockey and record company owner. Among his subsequent discoveries were Genesis, the Bay City Rollers and 10 cc.

Three unrelated Americans moved to England and scored immediately. The Walker Brothers specialized in heavily orchestrated cover versions like *Make It Easy On Yourself* and *The Sun Ain't Gonna Shine Anymore*, both of which reached number one. Although they remained immensely popular growing tensions prompted their separation in 1967, but a devoted following kept Scott Walker's name in lights. A brief reunion saw *No Regrets* climb to number seven in 1976.

Scott Walker's following was matched only by Tom Jones's, when *It's Not Unusual* streaked to number one. In the next ten years he had more than two dozen hits, enabling him to thrive as a Las Vegas bill-topper.

Bob Dylan and Joan Baez had climbed both the singles and album charts since America's folk boom crossed the Atlantic, but the only British manifestation to make any real headway was Donovan. His debut, *Catch The Wind*, launched on TV, flew into the top 5, as did its successor *Colours*. His Woody Guthrie/Dylan influence was all but gone when *Sunshine Superman* established him in the rock market and throughout the late sixties he experimented with a range of styles on *Mellow Yellow*, *Hurdy Gurdy Man*, *Atlantis* and *Goo Goo Barabajagal*, a collaboration with Jeff Beck.

Bob Dylan's influence was widespread in America, but folk purists were horrified when electric musicians backed him on his 1965 album *Bringing It All Back Home* and his performance at the Newport Folk Festival, where he fronted a rock band, was booed. However, not only did he pursue his new brand of 'folk rock' successfully (his next eight albums were all top tenners and *Like A Rolling Stone* reached number two on the singles chart) but many others began to explore similar territory, none with greater aplomb than the Byrds.

Five folkies from Los Angeles, they saw the possibilities of combining folk with rock music, and their electric version of Dylan's *Mr Tambourine Man*, with its guitars and close harmonies, set the pattern for a long career. Leader Jim McGuinn, whose 12-string Rickenbacker guitar jangled through their 16 hits, was the only Byrd to stay the course, but the group's groundwork in folk rock was matched by their pioneering in the country rock field: Chris Hillman and Gram Parsons formed the Flying Burrito Brothers, while David Crosby started Crosby, Stills and Nash.

Mr Tambourine Man and *Turn! Turn! Turn!* both topped the charts, while such classics as *Eight Miles High*, *So You Want To Be A Rock'n'Roll Star* and *Chestnut Mare* confirmed their status as one of the most innovative groups of the sixties.

Equally imaginative were the Lovin' Spoonful, a New York quartet whose folk rock style was rooted in blues and jug band music rather than the current Dylan vogue. Their first seven singles, all top tenners, revealed the breadth of leader John Sebastian's expertise as a performer and songwriter. They included *Do You Believe In Magic?*, *You Didn't Have To Be So Nice*, *Daydream*, *Summer In The City* and *Nashville Cats*. But when Sebastian left to start a solo career their magic left with him.

Within weeks of the Byrds' breakthrough another group from Los Angeles the Turtles also hit the charts with a souped-up Dylan song *It Ain't Me Babe* but their full potential was realized only in 1967 when their exemplary *Happy Together* reached number one. *She'd Rather Be With Me* and *Elenore* also reached the top 10 before the group fell apart at the start of the seventies. Their ebullient frontmen Mark Volman and Howard Kaylan then joined Frank Zappa's group before establishing themselves as the wildly eccentric Flo and Eddie.

Eve Of Destruction, a protest piece especially devised by Californian P. F. Sloan, provided Barry McGuire with a hit ... but the shrewdest implementation of social protest was by a married couple from Los Angeles. As Caesar and Cleo their early efforts evoked little response, but as Sonny and Cher they zoomed to number one with *I Got You Babe*. They reached the top 10, both together (*The Beat Goes On* and *All I Ever Need Is You*) and separately: Sonny stepped back after *Laugh At Me*, but Cher

pushed on with *Bang Bang* and the chart-topping *Gypsys, Tramps And Thieves*. Before too long their aspirations to entertain in places like Las Vegas surfaced but they separated in 1974.

Other new groups followed a more traditional, albeit Beatles-influenced, line. The Beau Brummels from San Francisco scored five hits, Sam The Sham and the Pharaohs had a monumental hit with *Wooly Bully*, and the Sir Douglas Quintet broke out of Texas with a very Anglicized image and a memorable hit, *She's About A Mover*.

One-off hits were scored by Roy Head, who made number two with *Treat Her Right*; Len Barry with *1-2-3* and songwriter

Above: The Byrds were folksingers until A Hard Day's Night *inspired them to change course. Left to right: David Crosby, Michael Clarke, Chris Hillman, Jim (later Roger) McGuinn and Gene Clark.*

Below: Sonny met Cher at a recording session for Phil Spector, where they were both hired to sing background vocals on a Ronettes track. Soon they were married and launching their own career.

Jackie DeShannon, whose singing career flourished with *What The World Needs Now Is Love*. The Statler Brothers hit with *Flowers On The Wall*, the Vogues with *Five O'Clock World*, the Ad Libs with *The Boy From New York City* and the Tradewinds with *New York's A Lonely Town* ... but the hottest new white vocal group was a duo, the Righteous Brothers.

Like the Walkers, they were not brothers at all. Bill Medley and Bobby Hatfield were a club act popular in southern California, but they attracted national attention when Phil Spector provided them with the soulful classic *You've Lost That Lovin' Feelin'* – his and their finest hour, according to many. It became an instant worldwide number one, but by the end of the year their relationship with Spector had clouded, and they left his label.

(You're My) Soul And Inspiration re-instated them at the top of the charts, but from then on, it was downhill all the way, leading to their parting in 1968. Solo success was not forthcoming, however, and six years later they reunited for a top 10 return, *Rock And Roll Heaven*.

The soul scene was still very much alive, introducing Dobie Gray with *The In Crowd* (soon revived instrumentally by Ramsey Lewis) and Edwin Starr with *Agent Double-O-Soul*, the first of several hits which would lead him to Berry Gordy and a 1970 chart topper, *War*. There were two major new Motown acts: Junior Walker and the Temptations. A sax-dominated dance band, Junior Walker and the All Stars romped to prominence with *Shotgun*, building their following with *Road Runner* and *How Sweet It Is* – the best of over 20 hits.

Above: The Righteous Brothers. Bobby Hatfield wonders whether Bill Medley may have lost that lovin' feeling!

Right: Innumerable line-up changes did little to impair the chart success of the Temptations.

The Temptations were regulars on the Detroit circuit when Berry Gordy signed them. They finally reached the charts with *The Way You Do The Things You Do*, paving the way for another Smokey Robinson song, *My Girl*, to carry them all the way to the top. The Temptations went on to score over 40 hits, including three more number ones: *I Can't Get Next To You*, *Just My Imagination* and *Papa Was A Rolling Stone*.

Another veteran of the Detroit clubs was Wilson Pickett, who moved to Memphis to record *In The Midnight Hour*. One of the biggest soul stars of the sixties, he shared the stage with Joe Tex, whose preaching, home-spun philosophies were first explored in *Hold What You've Got*. His long run of idiosyncratic hits included two more massive sellers, *Skinny Legs And All* and *I Gotcha*, and he remained an active performer until his death in 1982.

The soul/R&B fray also saw Fontella Bass doing well with *Rescue Me* and New York trio the Toys had a million-seller with *A Lover's Concerto*.

Once again it was Britain's year. 'Swinging London' was at its height, with Carnaby Street and Kings Road crowded and Roger Miller, Nashville's offbeat country star, who had recently been *King Of The Road*, itemized further British attractions in his latest timely offering, *England Swings*.

Left: I'm gonna wait 'til the midnight hour! Wilson Pickett emerged as one of the major soul stars of the sixties.

USA CHART TOPPERS

TITLE	ARTIST	LABEL	WEEKS AT NO. 1
I Feel Fine	The Beatles	Capitol	2
Come See About Me	The Supremes	Motown	1
Downtown	Petula Clark	Warner Bros	2
You've Lost That Lovin' Feeling	The Righteous Brothers	Philles	2
This Diamond Ring	Gary Lewis and the Playboys	Liberty	1
My Girl	The Temptations	Gordy	2
Eight Days A Week	The Beatles	Capitol	2
Stop In The Name Of Love	The Supremes	Motown	2
I'm Telling You Now	Freddie and the Dreamers	Tower	
The Game Of Love	Wayne Fontana and the Mindbenders	Fontana	1
Mrs Brown You've Got A Lovely Daughter	Herman's Hermits	MGM	3
Ticket To Ride	The Beatles	Capitol	1
Help Me Rhonda	The Beach Boys	Capitol	2
Back In My Arms Again	The Supremes	Motown	1
I Can't Help Myself	The Four Tops	Motown	2
Mr Tambourine Man	The Byrds	Columbia	1
Satisfaction	The Rolling Stones	London	4
I'm Henry VIII, I Am	Herman's Hermits	MGM	1
I Got You Babe	Sonny and Cher	Atco	3
Help!	The Beatles	Capitol	3
Eve Of Destruction	Barry McGuire	Dunhill	1
Hang On Sloopy	The McCoys	Bang	1
Yesterday	The Beatles	Capitol	4
Get Off My Cloud	The Rolling Stones	London	2
I Hear A Symphony	The Supremes	Motown	2
Turn Turn Turn	The Byrds	Columbia	3
Over And Over	The Dave Clark Five	Epic	1

UK CHART TOPPERS

TITLE	ARTIST	LABEL	WEEKS AT NO. 1
I Feel Fine	The Beatles	Parlophone	2
Yeh Yeh	Georgie Fame	Columbia	2
Go Now	The Moody Blues	Decca	1
You've Lost That Lovin' Feeling	The Righteous Brothers	London	2
Tired Of Waiting For You	The Kinks	Pye	1
I'll Never Find Another You	The Seekers	Columbia	2
It's Not Unusual	Tom Jones	Decca	1
The Last Time	The Rolling Stones	Decca	3
Concrete And Clay	Unit 4 Plus 2	Decca	1
The Minute You're Gone	Cliff Richard	Columbia	1
Ticket To Ride	The Beatles	Parlophone	3
King Of The Road	Roger Miller	Philips	1
Where Are You Now My Love?	Jackie Trent	Pye	1
Long Live Love	Sandie Shaw	Pye	3
Crying In The Chapel	Elvis Presley	RCA	2
I'm Alive	The Hollies	Parlophone	3
Mr Tambourine Man	The Byrds	CBS	2
Help!	The Beatles	Parlophone	3
I Got You Babe	Sonny and Cher	Atlantic	2
Satisfaction	The Rolling Stones	Decca	2
Make It Easy On Yourself	The Walker Brothers	Philips	1
Tears	Ken Dodd	Columbia	5
Get Off My Cloud	The Rolling Stones	Decca	3
The Carnival Is Over	The Seekers	Columbia	3
Day Tripper/We Can Work It Out	The Beatles	Parlophone	2

DEATHS

Bill Black, rock musician
Earl Bostic, rock musician
Clara Bow, film actress
Nat King Cole, popular singer
Alan Freed, rock'n'roll disc jockey
Stan Laurel, film star
Albert Schweitzer, philosopher
Malcolm X, Black Muslim leader

FILMS

Alphaville
Cat Ballou
The Collector
Darling
Dr Zhivago
Ferry Cross The Mersey
The Great Race
Help!
The Sandpiper
The Sound Of Music
The Spy Who Came In From The Cold
Thunderball

4 January: President Johnson, in his State of The Union message, outlines his programme to make America 'The Great Society'.

7 February: American aircraft begin bombing targets in North Vietnam. The bombing escalates during the year.

20 February: The US spacecraft Ranger 8 relays 7000 pictures of the moon before crashing, on target, into the Sea of Tranquillity.

8 March: LBJ sends the first ground combat troops to Vietnam, raising US military personnel to 27,000.

21 March: A 54-mile civil rights march from Selma to Montgomery begins with 3200 marchers and ends with over 25,000, led by Martin Luther King. LBJ sends 4000 troops to protect the participants from hostile rednecks after Governor Wallace refuses to mobilize the National Guard.

6 April: Early Bird, the world's first commercial communications satellite, is launched from Cape Kennedy.

3 June: Astronaut Edward White leaves his Gemini capsule during a four-day/two-man orbital flight and becomes the first man to walk in space.

11 June: The Beatles are awarded MBEs in a ceremony at Buckingham Palace.

28 July: Edward Heath succeeds Sir Alec Douglas-Home as leader of the Conservative party.

3 August: The US Defense Department announces sharply increased draft quotas, as more and more troops are assigned to Vietnam.

12 August: Race riots break out in Watts, Los Angeles. Curfew is imposed after 35 die and $200 million worth of damage is done to property.

31 August: It becomes illegal for Americans to burn draft cards.

19 October: During a House of Unamerican Activities Committee investigation into the Ku Klux Klan, Imperial Wizard Robert Shelton refuses on constitutional grounds to produce records or answer questions.

11 November: Ian Smith makes a Unilateral Declaration of Independence in Rhodesia.

27 November: Ken Kesey hosts his first 'acid test'.

27 November: Over 20,000 take part in a 'March On Washington for Peace In Vietnam'. John Lennon publishes his second book *A Spaniard In The Works*

Left: The appeal of the loveable mop-tops was so universal that even royalty was moved! The Beatles display their MBEs.

Made in England

1965

SIDE ONE
45 RPM
STEREO

My Generation

ALL RIGHTS OF THE MANUFACTURER AND OF THE OWNER OF THE RECORDED WORK RESERVED UNAUTHORISED PUBLIC PERFORMANCE BROADCASTING AND COPYING OF THIS RECORD PROHIBITED

THE ASSOCIATION

THE PAUL BUTTERFIELD
BLUES BAND

COUNT FIVE

DAVE DEE, DOZY, BEAKY,
MICK AND TICH

NEIL DIAMOND

THE EASYBEATS

THE ELECTRIC PRUNES

EDDIE FLOYD

THE BOBBY FULLER FOUR

TOMMY JAMES AND THE SHONDELLS

PAUL JONES

THE LEFT BANKE

LOVE

THE MAMAS AND THE PAPAS

JOHN MAYALL

THE MONKEES

Made in England

1966

SIDE ONE
45 RPM
STEREO

The Sounds of Silence

With more new chart acts than ever before, America's retaliation was comprehensive. They could do little to stop either the Beatles or the Rolling Stones, but they managed to stamp out most of the British competition with a wide variety of home-grown talent, ranging from the sublime to the ridiculous.

Most people saw the Monkees in the latter category, but their millions of screaming, worshipping fans thought differently – as four chart-topping albums confirmed! The world's first completely contrived rock group, the Monkees were chosen from thousands of applicants after auditions, and since the primary object was a television series, looks and acting ability were more important than musical talents; session men could compensate for any shortcomings in the studio. Disclosures that the group had little to do with early recordings had no adverse effect on sales: the TV series was an immediate hit, and the highly polished records shot up the charts - *Last Train To Clarksville*, *I'm A Believer* and *Daydream Believer* all reaching number one. The Monkees remained omnipotent throughout 1967, and their integrity strengthened before they split up in 1970.

Hooking the same age group were Tommy James and the Shondells, pioneering a style which was known as 'bubble gum'. After *Hanky Panky* reached the top, two years after it was recorded, a series of clever pop songs kept them bubbling – some, like *I Think We're Alone Now* and *Crimson And Clover*, were quite innovative. They were seldom out of the reckoning until 1970, when James went on to carve a respectable solo career, returning to the top 20 as recently as 1980 with *Three Times In Love*.

Other successful studio-orientated pop groups included the Left Banke who never eclipsed their magnificent debut, *Walk Away Renee*, the underrated Critters and the Association, who began a career which continues today. A West Coast six-piece relying on intricate vocal arrangements, they made the top 10 with *Along Comes Mary* and followed with the year's best-selling single, *Cherish*. *Windy* became their second number one, and *Never My Love* almost made it three in a row.

Interest in folk rock continued to grow: Bob Lind scored with *Elusive Butterfly* and the Cyrkle with *Red Rubber Ball* ... but the genre's brightest stars were Simon and Garfunkel and the Mamas and Papas. Paul Simon was bumming around Europe with his guitar and Art Garfunkel was away at college when staff producers added folk rock instrumentation to *The Sounds Of Silence*, an acoustic track they had cut two years earlier. It rocketed to number one, whereupon the duo reunited to make some of the best albums of the decade. *Bookends* and *The Graduate* both made number one, as did the single *Mrs Robinson*, but by far their most successful work was the multi-million-selling *Bridge Over Troubled Water*, as we shall see. During the seventies they pursued separate careers – Garfunkel interspersing movies and albums with massive singles like *I Only Have Eyes For You* and *Bright Eyes* and Simon refining his singer/songwriter craft in several platinum albums and hit singles like *50 Ways To Leave Your Lover* and *Mother And Child Reunion*. They reunited successfully for a concert in New York's Central Park in 1982.

Four refugees from the withering folk scene, the Mamas and the Papas arrived in Los Angeles after living in the Virgin Isles.

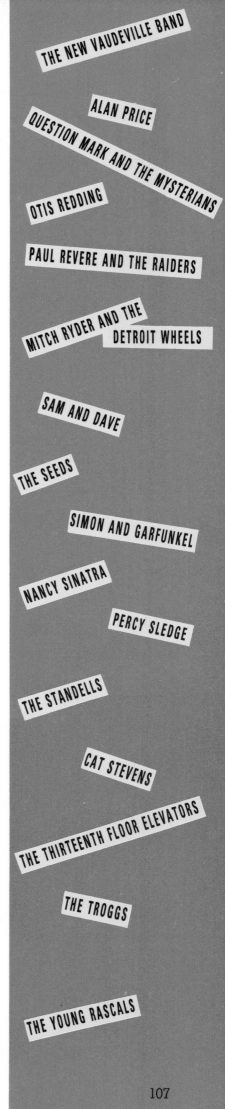

THE NEW VAUDEVILLE BAND

ALAN PRICE

QUESTION MARK AND THE MYSTERIANS

OTIS REDDING

PAUL REVERE AND THE RAIDERS

MITCH RYDER AND THE DETROIT WHEELS

SAM AND DAVE

THE SEEDS

SIMON AND GARFUNKEL

NANCY SINATRA

PERCY SLEDGE

THE STANDELLS

CAT STEVENS

THE THIRTEENTH FLOOR ELEVATORS

THE TROGGS

THE YOUNG RASCALS

Above: Paul Revere and the Raiders were one of the most colourful groups of the era.

Previous page left: In 1957 as schoolboy rock'n'rollers Tom and Jerry, they scored a minor hit. Eight years later, as Simon and Garfunkel, their impact was somewhat greater!

Previous page right: The songs of the Mamas and Papas captured the essence of sixties' California.

Producer Lou Adler framed their material in a folk rock setting and within weeks *California Dreamin'* had become reality. *Monday Monday* topped the charts, as did their debut album *If You Can Believe Your Eyes And Ears* and they continued to burn the candle at both ends for two years, topping the bill at the Monterey Festival and scoring more smash hits like *Dedicated To The One I Love* and *Creeque Alley*.

Punk continued to proliferate across the continent, although most groups disappeared after one or two choice cuts ... like *Little Girl* by the Syndicate Of Sound, *96 Tears* by Question Mark and the Mysterians, *Psychotic Reaction* by the Count Five, *I Fought The Law* and *Love's Made A Fool Of You* by the Bobby Fuller Four, *Gloria* by the Shadows of Knight, *Dirty Water* by the Standells and *Talk Talk* by the Music Machine.

One group managed to stick around a little longer: Paul Revere and the Raiders. Resplendent in American colonial military uniforms, their image matched their colourful records, which were far more polished than those of their contemporaries. *Kicks, Hungry, Good Thing* and *Him Or Me – What's It Gonna Be?* were top 10 singles to complement three top 10 albums, but they were unable to meet changing tastes and went out of style with the onslaught of progressive/underground music. A surprise rally took *Indian Reservation* to number one in 1971, but it was to be their final fling.

Several of the new punk groups were evolving a psychedelic style. The Seeds,

who claimed to have originated the description 'flower power', were in the forefront of this experimentation, scoring with *Pushin' Too Hard* and the Thirteenth Floor Elevators from Texas charted with *You're Gonna Miss Me* before exploring extremely bizarre territory on several albums. The Leaves hit with *Hey Joe*, and the Electric Prunes with *I Had Too Much To Dream (Last Night)*, while Love from Los Angeles started their extraordinary career with *My Little Red Book*. Led by the enigmatic Arthur Lee and originally influenced by the Byrds, Love ultimately found a style all their own on the album *Forever Changes*, blending surreal imagery into a background of acoustic guitars, strings and brass. However, their refusal to play outside California probably contributed to their remaining a cult group.

The year's finest female performances were *Stay With Me* by Lorraine Ellison, and *River Deep Mountain High* by Tina Turner. Ike and Tina had been out of the top 30 since 1961, but their fortunes were expected to change when Phil Spector signed them. He spared no effort to ensure that their Philles debut would be his masterpiece, but although it reached number three in Britain, it peaked at number 88 in

America. Spector was crushed; he went into a hibernation from which he has rarely emerged since ... but Ike and Tina pressed on, relying on their explosive live shows, until *Proud Mary* and *Nutbush City Limits* restored their reputation in the early seventies. Frank Sinatra's daughter Nancy stomped her way to the top with *These Boots Are Made For Walkin'*. *How Does That Grab You, Darlin'?* and *Sugar Town* were almost as successful, and collaborations with Lee Hazlewood and her father provided further hits in *Jackson* and *Somethin' Stupid* – another number one.

The only male singer to make a lasting impression was Neil Diamond, who had started out as a songwriter – giving the Monkees their monumental hit *I'm A Believer* among others. His own top 10 hit *Cherry Cherry* put him on course for seventies superstardom, when his soundtrack album *Jonathan Livingston Seagull* grossed more than the film itself! Since then an unbroken run of gold albums has confirmed his undiminished appeal.

Above: After singing with her father and Elvis Presley on a television show in 1959, Nancy Sinatra had to wait seven years before her vocal talents were fully appreciated.

Left: A hot R&B act since 1960, Ike and Tina Turner combined with Phil Spector to produce the classic River Deep Mountain High *before bringing their supercharged stage show to Britain.*

Following the Righteous Brothers into the white soul field were the Young Rascals from New Jersey and Mitch Ryder and the Detroit Wheels from ... where else? The Rascals, formerly part of Joey Dee and the Starliters, were the first white group signed by Atlantic and they dispelled any doubts about their potency when *Good Lovin'* stormed to number one. *Groovin'* and *People Got To Be Free* also topped the charts, while their live act continued to draw rapturous acclaim until the turn of the seventies, when they split to pursue other projects.

Mitch Ryder's idea of coupling two old hits into a medley paid off when *Jenny Take A Ride!* and *Devil With A Blue Dress On/Good Golly Miss Molly* both penetrated the top 10. *Sock It To Me Baby!* continued his run, but a throat infection affected his voice and he was employed for a spell in a car factory, although he later returned to the club circuit, where he remains popular.

The black soul scene was thriving too. Percy Sledge established himself forever with his sublime chart topper *When A Man Loves A Woman*, James and Bobby Purify amassed huge sales with *I'm Your Puppet*, Bobby Hebb reached number two with *Sunny*, the Capitols had a dance smash in *Cool Jerk* and Eddie Floyd's *Knock On Wood* was his calling card for years to come.

A number of old hands came through too. Sam and Dave, who had been trying since 1960, found the formula in Memphis with *Hold On! I'm A Comin'*, following it with such hits as *Soul Man* and *I Thank You*. Former gospel singer Billy Stewart had the biggest hit of his career when his startling version of Gershwin's *Summertime* took him into the top 10 and Jimmy Ruffin, recording without success for five years, made a sensational breakthrough with *What Becomes Of The Brokenhearted?* on Berry Gordy's Soul label. But towering above them all was one of the greatest soul singers of all time, Otis Redding.

The son of a Baptist minister, Redding left school to tour with his own group, basing his singing style on that of Little Richard. By 1962 he had evolved a more emotional, soulful feel – partly as a result of his role as part-time singer in Johnny Jenkins' band – and this was demonstrated on *These Arms Of Mine*, which he cut at the end of a Jenkins recording session. When the single crept into the top 100 in May 1963 Redding's own career was established. A series of fine records, including *Mr Pitiful*, *I've Been Loving You Too Long*, *Respect* and *Try A Little Tenderness*, increased his standing and his appearance at the Monterey Pop

Below: Otis Redding, probably the most influential soul singer of the late sixties.

Festival in 1967 brought massive acceptance by rock fans. He was poised to conquer the world.

In December 1967, he was killed when a plane carrying him and his band the Bar-Kays, crashed in Wisconsin, just a month before *(Sittin' On) The Dock Of The Bay* began its climb to number one, providing Otis with a memorable epitaph.

Blues music, previously the province of black musicians, was beginning to attract white players, and the first to succeed commercially was the Paul Butterfield Blues Band from Chicago. Their first two albums inspired a spate of imitators – particularly impressed by Butterfield's singing and harmonica playing and by Mike Bloomfield's scorching guitar work – and a 'blues boom' was soon under way.

Equally influential was Butterfield's British counterpart John Mayall whose album *Blues Breakers* reached number six. He had moved down from Manchester to establish himself as London's premier bluesman, his constantly changing band a training ground for such illustrious players as Eric Clapton, Peter Green, John McVie, Mick Taylor and Jack Bruce. After his uncompromising dedication won widespread acclaim he moved to Los Angeles, continuing to form new bands whenever he recorded and toured.

Alan Price and Paul Jones, fugitives from the Animals and Manfred Mann respectively, started solo careers with hit singles. Price took *I Put A Spell On You* into the top 10 and maintained consistent form, graduating from one night-stands to television,

Above: Double dynamite! Samuel Moore and David Prater ... better known as Sam and Dave.

Left: The Young Rascals were one of the first white groups to play soul music with any authority.

111

cabaret and theatre work, while Jones hit with *High Time* and *I've Been A Bad Bad Boy* before devoting practically all his time to acting.

But most new British rock had a soft edge. The New Vaudeville Band's singalong hit *Winchester Cathedral* was a surprise US number one. Crispian St Peters had two folky top fivers, *You Were On My Mind* and *Pied Piper*, and *I Love My Dog* got Cat

Stevens under way. *Matthew And Son* and *I'm Gonna Get Me A Gun* were the biggest of his four hits in 1967, but then ill-health kept him out of the picture until his dramatic re-emergence at the beginning of the seventies. One of the better singer/songwriters, Stevens scored huge worldwide hits with a series of albums including *Teaser And The Firecat*, *Catch Bull At Four* and *Buddah And The Chocolate Box* before

becoming a muslim and assuming a relatively low profile.

The Easybeats from Australia arrived to set up shop in the wake of their smash *Friday On My Mind* and Los Bravos came over from Spain to capitalize on *Black Is Black* – but neither generated a lasting response. Roy C, an R&B singer from New York, had a UK-only hit with *Shotgun Wedding* – a top tenner in 1966 and again in 1972!

Overall there were few newcomers of any real substance to challenge the existing order – and even the year's two most successful groups seemed to be little more than novelty items. The Troggs from Wiltshire were fortunate to have Larry Page behind them. His astute song selection and production ideas kept them in the public eye from spring 1966, when *Wild Thing* crashed into the charts, until autumn 1967, when *Love Is All Around* dropped out, taking the Troggs with it. In between *With A Girl Like You* reached number one and *I Can't Control Myself* number two, as singer

Reg Presley developed his songwriting flair – but attempts to establish a serious musical base were unsuccessful. Nevertheless, their records rang with a naive enthusiasm which allowed the group to build a respectable following on the club scene, where they continue to recreate the good old days.

From the same region were Dave Dee, Dozy, Beaky, Mick and Tich, who came seeking the gold-paved streets of London. They fell into the hands of Ken Howard and Alan Blaikley, a songwriting/production team who provided eight custom-built top tenners, including the chart-topping *Legend Of Xanadu*. They were enormously popular in Britain, but were unable to impress the US market, and in 1969 they ran out of steam. Dave Dee moved to the administrative side of the business when his solo career failed to take off, while his old mates pressed on in cabaret.

A pretty interesting year ... and what's more there was plenty bubbling below the surface, ready to break loose in 1967.

Above: Led by the boisterous Reg Presley (right), the Troggs found overnight stardom when Wild Thing *sold a million.*

USA CHART TOPPERS

TITLE	ARTIST	LABEL	WEEKS AT NO. 1
The Sounds Of Silence	Simon and Garfunkel	Columbia	2
We Can Work It Out	The Beatles	Capitol	3
My Love	Petula Clark	Warner Bros	
Lightnin' Strikes	Lou Christie	MGM	2
These Boots Are Made For Walkin'	Nancy Sinatra	Reprise	1
The Ballad Of The Green Berets	Sgt Barry Sadler	RCA	5
(You're My) Soul And Inspiration	The Righteous Brothers	Verve	3
Good Lovin'	The Young Rascals	Atlantic	1
Monday Monday	The Mamas and the Papas	Dunhill	3
When A Man Loves A Woman	Percy Sledge	Atlantic	2
Paint It Black	The Rolling Stones	London	2
Paperback Writer	The Beatles	Capitol	2
Strangers In The Night	Frank Sinatra	Reprise	1
Hanky Panky	Tommy James and the Shondells	Roulette	2
Wild Thing	The Troggs	Atco	2
Summer In The City	The Lovin' Spoonful	Kama Sutra	3
Sunshine Superman	Donovan	Epic	1
You Can't Hurry Love	The Supremes	Motown	2
Cherish	The Association	Warner Bros	
Reach Out I'll Be There	The Four Tops	Motown	2
96 Tears	? and the Mysterians	Cameo	3
Last Train To Clarksville	The Monkees	Colgems	2
Poor Side Of Town	Johnny Rivers	Imperial	1
You Keep Me Hangin' On	The Supremes	Motown	1
Winchester Cathedral	New Vaudeville Band	Fontana	3
Good Vibrations	The Beach Boys	Capitol	1

UK CHART TOPPERS

TITLE	ARTIST	LABEL	WEEKS AT NO. 1
Day Tripper/We Can Work It Out	The Beatles	Parlophone	3
Keep On Runnin'	The Spencer Davis Group	Fontana	1
Michelle	The Overlanders	Pye	3
These Boots Are Made For Walkin'	Nancy Sinatra	Reprise	4
The Sun Ain't Gonna Shine Anymore	The Walker Brothers	Philips	4
Somebody Help Me	The Spencer Davis Group	Fontana	2
You Don't Have To Say You Love Me	Dusty Springfield	Philips	1
Pretty Flamingo	Manfred Mann	HMV	3
Paint It Black	The Rolling Stones	Decca	1
Strangers In The Night	Frank Sinatra	Reprise	3
Paperback Writer	The Beatles	Parlophone	2
Sunny Afternoon	The Kinks	Pye	2
Get Away	Georgie Fame	Columbia	1
Out Of Time	Chris Farlowe	Immediate	1
With A Girl Like You	The Troggs	Fontana	2
Eleanor Rigby/Yellow Submarine	The Beatles	Parlophone	4
All Or Nothing	The Small Faces	Decca	1
Distant Drums	Jim Reeves	RCA	5
Reach Out I'll Be There	The Four Tops	Tamla Motown	3
Good Vibrations	The Beach Boys	Capitol	2
Green Green Grass Of Home	Tom Jones	Decca	4

DEATHS

Lenny Bruce, comedian
Montgomery Clift, film star
Walt Disney, film mogul
Richard Farina, novelist/folk singer
Bobby Fuller, rock singer
Mississippi John Hurt, blues musician
Buster Keaton, film star
Johnny Kidd, rock singer

CURRENT EVENTS

17 January: A US B-52 bomber, carrying four hydrogen bombs, crashes off the coast of Spain. Three are recovered quickly, the fourth only after four months' searching.

1 February: The drug LSD comes under Federal regulation in America.

10 February: Conviction of first draft card burner, as authorities try to suppress growing opposition to the Vietnam War.

1 March: A Soviet spacecraft lands on Venus – the first man-made object to touch another planet.

8 March: The IRA blow up the Nelson monument in Dublin.

21 April: The US combat toll in Vietnam reaches 3047.

1 June: US spacecraft Surveyor 1 makes a soft landing on the moon and begins to relay photographs to earth.

1 July: Riots start in black ghettos across America.

14 July: Police in Chicago discover the bodies of eight nurses who have been brutally murdered. Richard Speck is subsequently arrested and convicted.

1 August: Former marine Charles Whitman uses a high-powered rifle to kill 15 and wound 31 before being shot by police in a tower at the University of Texas.

29 August: The Beatles' last live appearance, in San Francisco.

1 October: Nazi war criminal Albert Speer is released from Spandau Prison after 20 years.

21 October: 144 are killed in the Aberfan slag tip disaster in Wales.

29 October: Pope Paul VI refuses to review the Roman Catholic birth control prohibition.

4 November: Floods cause immense damage to art treasures in Italy.

8 November: Film actor Ronald Reagan is elected Governor of California.

4 December: Harold Wilson and Ian Smith meet on board HMS *Tiger* to discuss the future of Rhodesia.

12 December: Lone yachtsman Francis Chichester arrives in Sydney after the first half of his global navigation in *Gypsy Moth IV*.

31 December: US troops in Vietnam now exceed 340,000, with the death toll up to 6450.

Transcendental meditation becomes very voguish, but the Beatles lose favour in the Southern bible belt after John Lennon declares them to be 'more popular than Jesus'.

FILMS

Alfie
The Bible
Blow Up
The Blue Max
Born Free
The Fantastic Voyage
The Fortune Cookie
Georgy Girl
Grand Prix
A Man And A Woman
A Man For All Seasons (Oscars for Best Film and Best Actor – Paul Schofield)
Morgan
Nevada Smith
Who's Afraid Of Virginia Woolf?

Left: An advertisement for 'four insane boys, aged 17 to 21' resulted in the Monkees, who soon proved that musical dexterity was not a prerequisite to becoming a hit group.

Made in England

1966

SIDE ONE
45 RPM
STEREO

The Sounds of Silence

ALL RIGHTS OF THE MANUFACTURER AND OF THE OWNER OF THE RECORDED WORK RESERVED. UNAUTHORISED PUBLIC PERFORMANCE, BROADCASTING AND COPYING OF THIS RECORD PROHIBITED

Made in England

1967

SIDE ONE
45 RPM
STEREO

Hi Ho Silver Lining

ALL RIGHTS OF THE MANUFACTURER AND OF THE OWNER OF THE RECORDED WORK RESERVED. UNAUTHORISED PUBLIC PERFORMANCE BROADCASTING AND COPYING OF THIS RECORD PROHIBITED

BOBBIE GENTRY

THE GRATEFUL DEAD

JIMI HENDRIX

THE HERD

JEFFERSON AIRPLANE

SCOTT MCKENZIE

MOBY GRAPE

THE MOVE

PINK FLOYD

PROCOL HARUM

TRAFFIC

VANILLA FUDGE

THE VELVET UNDERGROUND

FRANK ZAPPA

1967 was rock's best year. The music was more exciting, better in every way than ever before ... and a spectacular array of newcomers added even more spice and colour. .

In Britain the most original contenders were the 'underground' bands, who surfaced from London's psychedelic clubs with records so powerful that they were soon known nationally. Regular headliners at UFO, the first and best of these clubs, were the Pink Floyd, who signed a very advantageous record deal before they had even played outside London. Two classic singles, *Arnold Layne* and *See Emily Play*, put them into the charts – but the next two flopped, and when Syd Barrett, their leader and

principal songwriter, left the group many considered them washed up. However, the Floyd regained their pre-eminence with a series of phenomenally popular albums: *Atom Heart Mother* and *Wish You Were Here* both reached number one, while *Dark Side Of The Moon* was on the Billboard charts for several years. In the early eighties they disbanded to pursue solo careers, but not before topping the charts with their first single for ten years, *Another Brick In The Wall.*

Sharing the stage at UFO and the Roundhouse, also in London, were the Soft Machine, whose 12-year history was to survive many personnel changes; the Crazy World of Arthur Brown, who briefly set the

117

world alight with *Fire*; and Jimi Hendrix, the most incandescent of them all.

After spotting him in a New York club, Chas Chandler left the Animals to manage Hendrix, basing his operation in London where he recruited as sidemen drummer Mitch Mitchell and bassist Noel Redding. *Hey Joe*, the Jimi Hendrix Experience's debut, was an ample display of their potency. His double album *Electric Lady-land* topped the US chart after his breathtaking performance at Monterey, but a heavy touring schedule was not eased by drug and management problems, and by summer 1970, when he played the Isle of Wight Festival, he was in poor shape, musically and physically. It was to be his last set; not long afterwards, he died in his hotel bed, and *Voodoo Chile*, which was released a few weeks later, became his only British chart topper.

Many bands abandoned their old paths and went psychedelic. (Definition: suggesting experience of hallucinatory drugs, giving the illusion of freedom from the limitations of reality.) Quick off the mark

were Tomorrow, featuring guitarist Steve Howe (later a pillar of Yes and Asia), whose records made something less than musical history, but whose leader Keith West went solo to make one of the year's biggest selling singles *Excerpt From A Teenage Opera*.

Stevie Winwood from the Spencer Davis Group together with three Midlands mates formed Traffic, whose first two top 10 albums showcased their ingenuity and dexterity. They also produced several notable singles, including *Paper Sun* and *Hole In My Shoe*, but disagreements and diversions prevented them from reaching their full potential.

Another early convert was Gary Brooker, former leader of R&B band the Paramounts. Within days of unveiling his new group, Procol Harum, they were topping the charts with the exceptionally arresting *A Whiter Shade Of Pale*. They never recaptured the splendour of their debut, although they cut several fine albums and enjoyed a solid following until their demise ten years later.

Hi Ho Silver Lining, a record so popular

that even now no local disco can afford to be without it, got Jeff Beck's solo career off to a good start, but although a masterful guitarist, he realized his vocal limitations. Rod Stewart, who had been vainly trying to increase his cult following since the early sixties, accepted his invitation to join, and the Jeff Beck Group, including also Ron Wood on bass, became one of the heaviest rock bands of the sixties. But as Led Zeppelin were heading for superstardom on the formula he had devised, Beck allowed his group to disintegrate – whereupon Stewart and Wood joined the Faces. Throughout the seventies Beck led groups of varying quality, but, although his ideas seemed too idiosyncratic for British tastes, albums like *Wired* and *There And Back* were huge sellers in America.

Eric Clapton, Beck's predecessor in the Yardbirds, had been performing for some time with John Mayall working up a reputation as Britain's finest blues guitarist – but after conspiratorial huddles with virtuoso bassist Jack Bruce and fiery drummer Ginger Baker, he handed in his notice. All three resurfaced as Cream, one of the decade's most successful enterprises and the first outfit to draw the description 'supergroup'. Their whimsical debut *Wrapping Paper* gave little indication of their real penchant, which was for fast-flowing, blues-based improvization, which was fully explored on their double album *Wheels Of Fire* – a US number one. *Sunshine Of Your Love* and *White Room* took them into the US top 10 and their potential seemed boundless, but internal friction caused a parting of the ways after just two years. *Goodbye*, their

final studio album, topped the British chart as Clapton, by now the most influential guitarist of his generation, was rehearsing his next supergroup Blind Faith.

The BBC launched a pop music station, Radio One, basing its format on pirate radio. When Parliament passed legislation outlawing the pirates, the latter were forced to withdraw. Radio One opened in September . . . and the first record they played was *Flowers In The Rain* by the Move, which followed *Night Of Fear* and *I Can Hear The Grass Grow* into the top 5.

The Move from Birmingham, were one of the most creative groups around, and their

Left: The Cream was one of the most powerful blues groups ever seen in Britain. Left to right: Jack Bruce (bass/ vocals), Eric Clapton (guitar/ vocals) and Ginger Baker (drums).

Below: Born and raised in Texas, Janis Joplin was one of many young people drawn to San Francisco during the mid-sixties . . . and it was there that her prodigious vocal talent was first recognized.

string of singles were as innovative as they were successful. *Fire Brigade, Blackberry Way, Brontosaurus* and *California Man* kept them constantly hot, but they were unable to penetrate the album chart or the American market, which contributed to their dissolution in 1972 ... by which time their metamorphosis into the Electric Light Orchestra was complete.

Other mainstreamers included the Tremeloes, who left Brian Poole to start an impressive 13-hit phase, starting with *Here Comes My Baby* and the chart-topping *Silence Is Golden*; the Herd, who had two top tenners but burned out when Peter Frampton left to start Humble Pie; Amen Corner, whose three-year run was climaxed by their number one smash *Half As Nice*; Engelbert Humperdinck, who secured two of the year's million-sellers, *Release Me* and *The Last Waltz*; and the Bee Gees, who cracked the British market with *Massachusetts*.

The Gibb brothers – Barry, Maurice and Robin – had emigrated as children and enjoyed success in Australia. Within a year of returning to Britain, the Bee Gees, as they were known, were internationally famous; *I've Gotta Get A Message To You* returned them to the top of the chart and, despite ups and downs, they were seldom out of the reckoning for the next decade. During the mid-seventies' disco explosion they dropped their emotional love ballads to concentrate on dance-floor material, and became millionaires as a result! An astonishing run of eight hits – *Jive Talkin', You Should Be Dancing, How Deep Is Your Love?, Stayin'*
Alive, Night Fever, Too Much Heaven, Tragedy and *Love You Inside Out* – all reached number one in America! Everything they touched turned platinum!

P.P Arnold, a former Ikette, also benefited from a move to London to start a solo career with *First Cut Is The Deepest*. With her flamboyant backing group the Nice she was one of the attractions at the annual Jazz and Blues (sic) festival, where the duffle coats and scarves of yesteryear had been replaced by kaftans, beads, bells, velvet loons, incense, bright military uniforms, Afro hairstyles and flowers ... hippies! Flower power! Its effect was all pervasive in the music industry. Symptomatic of the commercialization was the immediate spread of flower power styles and bands – crystallized in one record: *Let's Go To San Francisco* by the Flowerpot Men, a studio group who would probably have been laughed out of the city they were eulogizing.

The psychedelic scene had originated in San Francisco and as a result many excellent groups established themselves there. First and foremost were the Grateful Dead, whose slow chart progress belied their importance. They had provided music for the 'acid tests', when author Ken Kesey and 'his merry pranksters' toured California in a converted bus inviting interested parties to sample the hallucinogenic drug LSD (which was legal until 1966) – and it was around them that the city's drug/hippie culture began to grow. Before long the terms 'psychedelic' and 'acid rock' were part of the pop vernacular.

While early outfits like the Charlatans

Below: The Bee Gees first performed together as children in Manchester, but it was in Australia that their show-biz career took off.

were destined to remain local heroes, the Sopwith Camel had a national hit with *Hello Hello* – but it was the Jefferson Airplane who turned America on to 'the San Francisco sound'. Their top 10 hits *Somebody To Love* and *White Rabbit* remain classics of the era, highlighting Grace Slick's clear, soaring voice and Jorma Kaukonen's fluid guitar work. Eight top 20 albums kept them airborne until 1973, when they took off again as the modified Jefferson Starship. Close on their heels were Country Joe and the Fish, whose debut album *Electric Music For The Mind And Body* was hailed as the perfect accompaniment to an acid trip. Although patchy in quality, four subsequent albums made the charts and the group was able to make an impact at the festival at Woodstock, where they were filmed for posterity.

By the middle of 1967 *Newsweek* magazine estimated that some 300 bands were operating in and around San Francisco, though few achieved much. Among those who did were Moby Grape, whose simultaneous release of an album and five singles had the desired effect; the Grateful Dead, who went on to achieve massive international popularity in the 1970s, and Big Brother and the Holding Company, fronted by the raunchy-voiced Janis Joplin.

Initially she was not given star billing, but by the time *Cheap Thrills* topped the album chart in 1968 it was obvious that the others were functioning as her backing band – and incessant adulation soon convinced her to go solo. Despite spectacular success, her personal life was wretchedly unhappy and in October 1970 a heroin overdose took her life. A few months later her final studio album *Pearl* outstripped all competition to reach number one.

The city's euphoric atmosphere induced many visiting musicians – including Boz Scaggs and Steve Miller – to make San Francisco their permanent residence, while Kaleidoscope from Los Angeles and the Thirteenth Floor Elevators from Texas made it their second home ... but musical activity in the San Francisco area peaked in June 1967 when a wealth of international talent converged on Monterey to mount America's first rock festival. Among the performers was Scott McKenzie, whose single *San Francisco (Be Sure To Wear Some Flowers In Your Hair)* was riding high in the charts.

Above: The Move first attracted attention through their wild stage act, in which television sets were axed to pieces and effigies destroyed.

Left: Jefferson Airplane: (left to right) Paul Kantner, Spencer Dryden, Grace Slick, Jorma Kaukonen, Jack Casady and Marty Balin.

Above: The Doors: (left to right) John Densmore, Ray Manzarek, Jim Morrison and Robbie Krieger. Morrison's death only increased their charismatic appeal.

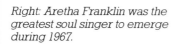

Right: Aretha Franklin was the greatest soul singer to emerge during 1967.

spun to the top of the charts with *Light My Fire*, returning a year later with *Hello, I Love You.* Seven albums made the top 10 before Morrison put the group on ice and moved to Paris, where he expected to find an environment suitable for creative writing. But it was there, in July 1971, that he died – reportedly of a heart attack while taking a bath.

New York's premier drug rockers were the Velvet Underground, with sinister creations like *Heroin* and *I'm Waiting For The Man.* Their artistic aspirations attracted the patronage of Andy Warhol but their albums were too perverse for mass acceptance, and only after their break-up did their strong influence on the likes of Bowie, Mott the Hoople, Patti Smith and the British punks become known. Nico, John Cale and Lou Reed, all refugees from the group, went on to varied solo success.

Also from New York were Vanilla Fudge, specialists in slow, dramatic versions of pop classics like *You Keep Me Hangin' On.* Together with the Velvets, they were a source of fascination for the emerging heavy metal bands.

Extremely weird, even without the use of drugs, were Frank Zappa and Captain

Meanwhile the tentacles of the drug culture were affecting the bands and the music coming out of Los Angeles too, like the Doors whose 1980 *Greatest Hits* LP went platinum, even though singer Jim Morrison had died nine years earlier. Taking their name from Aldous Huxley's psychedelic exploration *The Doors Of Perception* they

Beefheart, both from Los Angeles. Albums like *Safe As Milk* and *Trout Mask Replica* won a limited but fanatical following for Beefheart, whose devotees have remained loyal ever since. Throughout the seventies he continued to make idiosyncratic albums with a succession of puzzled musicians, though recent appearances have been rare. Frank Zappa disguised his serious musical intent with parody and satire. After entering the arena with *Freak Out* his constantly fluctuating group the Mothers of Invention consolidated their success with *Absolutely Free* and *We're Only In It For The Money*. A prolific writer and compulsive worker, Frank Zappa has become one of rock's most respected musicians – but he has never dropped his tongue-in-cheek facade.

Also from Los Angeles were the hottest new white blues band, Canned Heat, and the most imaginative new folk-rockers, the Buffalo Springfield. Canned Heat faded fast after hitting the big time with *On The Road Again*, *Going Up The Country* and *Let's Work Together*, while the Springfield never really found the acclaim their brilliance deserved. *For What It's Worth* was their only top 10 hit and after three albums failed commercially they split and Stephen Stills and Neil Young went off to find immediate superstardom in Crosby, Stills, Nash and Young!

Also hot in 1967 were the Box Tops from Memphis, who started with the year's biggest single *The Letter*; the 5th Dimension, a black vocal group whose *Up-Up And Away* was a Grammy winner; Bobby Gentry, whose murder mystery *Ode To Billie Joe* was a smash; and Van Morrison, formerly of Them and now resident in the States, who returned with *Brown Eyed Girl*.

On the soul scene the Bar-Kays hit with *Soul Finger*, Brenton Wood with *Gimme Little Sign* and Arthur Conley with *Sweet Soul Music* ... but all were overshadowed by Aretha Franklin.

A minister's daughter from Memphis, she began recording after an apprenticeship in her father's choir, but was unsuccessful until she signed with Atlantic and found a sympathetic producer in Jerry Wexler. *I Never Loved A Man* reached the top 10, followed by her chart-topping version of Otis Redding's *Respect* and seven more top tenners within one year! In 1971 she began another series of huge hits and her supremacy seemed assured.

As usual the year's honours went to the Beatles, who maintained their excellence with *Penny Lane/Strawberry Fields Forever*, *All You Need Is Love*, *Hello Goodbye* and their *Magical Mystery Tour* soundtrack ... but it was their album *Sgt Pepper's Lonely Hearts Club Band* that attracted most praise. Hailed as their masterwork, it elevated rock music to an art form in many people's eyes. It also marked the point where for the first time, albums had begun to outsell singles – and the subsequent emphasis on albums saw the swift decline of many singles-orientated groups.

123

CURRENT EVENTS

18 January: Jeremy Thorpe becomes leader of the Liberal party.

27 January: Three astronauts, Chaffee, Grissom and White, die in a Cape Kennedy fire as their spacecraft is prepared for take-off.

18 March: A Liberian tanker, the *Torrey Canyon*, runs aground on Seven Stones Reef and spews oil all over south coast of England beaches.

28 April: Muhammad Ali is stripped of his boxing title for refusing induction into the US Army.

30 April: Political troubles in Greece culminate in an Army coup d'état. King Constantine is placed under house arrest.

1 May: Expo 67 opens in Montreal.

5 May: General Westmoreland, Commander of US Forces, assures Congress that the US 'will prevail over the Communist aggressor in Vietnam'.

5 June: Start of the Six-Day War between Egypt and Israel.

23 June: LBJ and Kosygin confer in abortive peace talks.

24 July: President de Gaulle calls for 'Free Quebec' in a speech in Montreal.

1 August: As rioting sweeps through black ghettos for the third year running, FBI chief J. Edgar Hoover concludes that 'outside agitators' are responsible.

9 August: Rebel forces seize control of Biafra, a province of Nigeria.

14 August: The Marine Offences Act becomes law, closing down pirate radio.

17 August: Stokeley Carmichael, broadcasting from Cuba, calls for American blacks to arm for 'violent revolution'.

6 October: As sightseeing coach tours turn Haight Ashbury into a commercial parody, San Franciscan longhairs stage 'the funeral of the hippie'.

21 October: Norman Mailer is among many arrested as marchers storm the Pentagon during a peace rally.

18 November: Harold Wilson devalues the pound by 14.3 per cent.

3 December: Dr Christian Barnard performs the world's first human heart transplant.

5 December: Allen Ginsberg and Dr Spock are among 264 arrested during a Stop The Draft week in New York. US troops in Vietnam now number 475,000 with over 14,000 dead.

Twiggy is fashion leader as 'swinging' London continues to draw American tourists. Flower power is the fashion and drugs abound: Mick Jagger, Brian Jones and Keith Richard are all convicted of cannabis possession, and Paul McCartney causes a furore by admitting that he's taken LSD.

FILMS

Accident
Barefoot In The Park
Bonnie And Clyde
Camelot
Cool Hand Luke
The Dirty Dozen
Don't Look Back
Dr Doolittle
El Dorado
Far From The Madding Crowd
The Graduate
Guess Who's Coming To Dinner
In The Heat Of The Night
Privilege
Thoroughly Modern Millie

Below: Not only was The Graduate *one of the most popular films ever made, but the soundtrack album, featuring Simon and Garfunkel, was also a worldwide hit (Embassy, 1967).*

DEATHS

The Bar-Kays, R&B band
John Coltrane, jazz musician
Nelson Eddy, screen singer
Brian Epstein, Beatles' manager
Che Guevara, revolutionary
Woody Guthrie, folk singer
Vivien Leigh, film star
Jayne Mansfield, film star
Joe Meek, rock producer
Joe Orton, playwright
Otis Redding, R&B singer
Carl Sandburg, historian/poet
Spencer Tracy, film star

JOSEPH E. LEVINE PRESENTS A MIKE NICHOLS · LAWRENCE TURMAN PRODUCTION

This is Benjamin

He's a little worried about his future

THE G

STARRING

ANNE BANCROFT AND **DUSTIN**

SCREENPLAY BY
CALDER WILLINGHAM AND **BUCK HENRY**

SONGS BY
PAUL SIM

PRODUCED BY
LAWRENCE TURMAN

DIRECTED BY
MIKE NICHOLS

TECHNIC

USA CHART TOPPERS

TITLE	ARTIST	LABEL	WEEKS AT NO. 1
I'm A Believer	The Monkees	Colgems	6
Kind Of A Drag	The Buckinghams	Columbia	2
Ruby Tuesday	The Rolling Stones	London	1
Love Is Here And Now You're Gone	The Supremes	Motown	1
Penny Lane	The Beatles	Capitol	1
Happy Together	The Turtles	White Whale	3
Something Stupid	Nancy and Frank Sinatra	Reprise	4
The Happening	The Supremes	Motown	1
Groovin'	The Young Rascals	Atlantic	4
Respect	Aretha Franklin	Atlantic	2
Windy	The Association	Warner Bros	4
Light My Fire	The Doors	Elektra	3
All You Need Is Love	The Beatles	Capitol	1
Ode To Billie Joe	Bobbie Gentry	Capitol	4
The Letter	The Box Tops	Mala	4
To Sir With Love	Lulu	Epic	5
Incense And Peppermints	Strawberry Alarm Clock	Uni	1
Daydream Believer	The Monkees	Colgems	4
Hello Goodbye	The Beatles	Capitol	1

UK CHART TOPPERS

TITLE	ARTIST	LABEL	WEEKS AT NO. 1
Green Green Grass Of Home	Tom Jones	Decca	2
I'm A Believer	The Monkees	RCA	4
This Is My Song	Petula Clark	Pye	2
Release Me	Engelbert Humperdinck	Decca	6
Something Stupid	Nancy and Frank Sinatra	Reprise	2
Puppet On A String	Sandie Shaw	Pye	3
Silence Is Golden	The Tremeloes	CBS	3
A Whiter Shade Of Pale	Procol Harum	Deram	6
All You Need Is Love	The Beatles	Parlophone	3
San Francisco	Scott McKenzie	CBS	4
The Last Waltz	Engelbert Humperdinck	Decca	5
Massachusetts	The Bee Gees	Polydor	4
Baby Now That I've Found You	The Foundations	Pye	2
Let The Heartaches Begin	Long John Baldry	Pye	2
Hello Goodbye	The Beatles	Parlophone	4

THE BAND

ARCHIE BELL AND THE DRELLS

BLUE CHEER

BONZO DOG DOO DAH BAND

TIM BUCKLEY

GLEN CAMPBELL

CLARENCE CARTER

CHICKEN SHACK

JOE COCKER

LEONARD COHEN

THE DELFONICS

JULIE DRISCOLL

THE EQUALS

FLEETWOOD MAC

ARLO GUTHRIE

MARY HOPKIN

THE INTRUDERS

IRON BUTTERFLY

Flower Power was still blooming in Britain. Every new band had to adopt appropriate uniform – and a parade came and went through the charts: the Casuals with *Jesamine*, the Plastic Penny with *Everything I Am*, the Marbles with *Only One Woman*, the Honeybus with *I Can't Let Maggie Go* and the Gun with *Race With The Devil*. None were able to sustain their early promise, but other pop-orientated acts had rather more success.

The Equals, featuring a young Eddy Grant, reached number one with *Baby Come Back*, and kept current with *Viva Bobby Joe* and *Black Skin Blue Eyed Boys*; Scotland's Marmalade also found the top with *Ob-La-Di Ob-La-Da*, the biggest of eight top tenners which maintained their popularity for almost a decade; and the Love Affair were also chart toppers with *Everlasting Love*. They returned with three more big sellers.

One group that eventually found lasting popularity was an unlikely looking quintet from South London – Status Quo. When they popped into the charts with an ephemeral period piece called *Pictures Of Matchstick Men*, few could have imagined that a massive following would be mourning their decision to cease touring in 1984 . . . 16 years later! Formed at school, they had already been going for six years when they made their breakthrough, but after the inevitable follow-up hit *Ice In The Sun* their popularity dwindled and, although *Down The Dustpipe*

revived their fortunes they seemed to be well and truly washed up by the end of 1972. Nothing could have been further from the truth.

Elsewhere on the scene Esther and Abi Ofarim waltzed *Cinderella Rockefella* to number one and pop satirists the Bonzo Dog Doo-Dah Band had a freaky smash with *I'm The Urban Spaceman* – produced by Paul McCartney, who was also a catalyst in Mary Hopkin's remarkable rise to fame. After the angelic Welsh folksinger had delighted the viewers of *Opportunity Knocks* (a television talent contest) McCartney wrote and produced *Those Were The Days*, which as the second release on the Beatles' Apple label took her to number one. She would never repeat her initial feat, but three more top tenners paved the way for a lasting career.

If Mary Hopkin represented the demure end of the spectrum, Christine Perfect was plying the earthy end, playing the hippie clubs and going for the 'underground' market. As singer and pianist with Chicken Shack, it was her plaintive touch which sent *I'd Rather Go Blind* up the charts to establish them as one of the better new blues bands. She quit the boards but public acclaim prompted her return – first as a solo act and then as a member of John McVie's (her husband) band Fleetwood Mac.

Refugees from John Mayall's Blues Breakers, Fleetwood Mac were immediately successful on the club scene, pounding out a mixture of brash and soulful blues – but it

was a dreamy instrumental *Albatross* which floated to number one. Further hits like *Man Of The World*, *Oh Well* and *The Green Manalishi* saw them headlining around the world, but their stability took a severe knock when founder/guitar hero/leader Peter Green suddenly left the band in 1970. A core of John McVie, Christine McVie and Mick Fleetwood tried to maintain consistency, despite a constantly changing line-up, but their fortunes declined steadily until a magical renaissance in 1975.

A blues boom, created by Cream and John Mayall, and fuelled by the likes of Fleetwood Mac and Chicken Shack, saw the emergence of two more hot groups, Ten Years After and Jethro Tull. The former, from Nottingham, scored with four top 10 albums in Britain – despite their concentration on audiences in America, where a spectacular display at Woodstock and 23 saturation tours propelled 11 albums into the charts. They finally ran out of steam in 1975, since when demon guitarist Alvin Lee has fronted numerous outfits, including one named Ten Years Later!

Jethro Tull, under the leadership of

JETHRO TULL

LED ZEPPELIN

LOVE AFFAIR

MARMALADE

THE STEVE MILLER BAND

JONI MITCHELL

JOHNNY NASH

RANDY NEWMAN

THE NICE

LAURA NYRO

GARY PUCKETT AND THE UNION GAP

QUICKSILVER MESSENGER SERVICE

KENNY ROGERS

SLY AND THE FAMILY STONE

SPIRIT

STATUS QUO

STEPPENWOLF

TEN YEARS AFTER

JIMMY WEBB

127

Right: Led Zeppelin's take off
was swift and sure . . .
everything they touched
turned to platinum.

Below right: I'll get by with a
little help from my friends! Joe
Cocker supercharged a
Beatles song to find
international success.

former soul singer Ian Anderson, became
the most exciting and innovative blues band
of the year. Within months *Living In The
Past* made number three in the singles chart
and *Stand Up* became a number one album.
Anderson's domination resulted in some 14
personnel changes over the next 15 years,
but his unerring vision saw a dozen albums
reach the US top 20, including two chart
toppers in *Thick As A Brick* and *Passion
Play*.

Also using blues as a departure point was
Led Zeppelin – formed by guitarist Jimmy
Page after the dissolution of the Yardbirds.
With the aid of three comparative unknowns
– singer Robert Plant, drummer John
Bonham and bassist John Paul Jones – he
created one of the most successful groups
the world has ever known! After their debut
album reached number six the next eight hit
the top – influencing a whole generation of
'progressive rock' and 'heavy metal' practitioners. In America, too, their supremacy
was unassailable once *Led Zeppelin II* had
become the fastest-selling album in Atlantic's history, and although tours became
increasingly infrequent, their position at the
top of the rock ladder remained unques-
tioned until Bonham's death in 1980, when
the three survivors disbanded the group to
pursue solo projects.

The Rolling Stones returned to top form
during the year, with the single *Jumping
Jack Flash* and the album *Beggers Banquet*,
Jimi Hendrix and Cream were at their peak,
and the Beatles showed no signs of deterioration as *Lady Madonna*, *Hey Jude* and *The
White Album* all topped the charts.

It was a Beatles song *With A Little Help
From My Friends* which took Joe Cocker to
number one. His inventive adaptation
allowed him to escape the Sheffield pub
circuit after several abortive attempts, and
his first American tour took him to Woodstock, where his performance (captured for
posterity in the movie) confirmed that his
was one of the finest soul voices ever to
come out of England. An alliance with Leon
Russell resulted in *Mad Dogs And Englishmen* reaching number two on the US album
charts – but the genial Cocker had no
defences for the pressures of the business,
which effectively nobbled his progress
through the seventies. However, his duet
with Jennifer Warnes, *Up Where We
Belong*, saw him enjoying a three-week run
at the top of the US charts many years later,
as we shall see.

The Nice, formerly P.P. Arnold's backing
group, evolved into a classically based trio
enlivened by Keith Emerson's keyboard
pyrotechnics. *Nice*, *Five Bridges* and *Elegy*
all reached the top 5 in Britain's album chart,
but transatlantic success eluded them after
their on-stage burning of an American flag
precipitated a press furore. Three groups

came out of their 1970 split, but only Emerson, Lake and Palmer eclipsed the achievements of the Nice.

Julie Driscoll, formerly in Steampacket
with Rod Stewart, was the featured vocalist
with the Brian Auger Trinity, who stormed
into the top 5 with their only hit, *This
Wheel's On Fire* – a previously unheard
Dylan song. Meanwhile Dylan himself re-
commenced activities after a motorcycle
accident – releasing *John Wesley Harding*,
his first album in 18 months. His erstwhile

Previous page top: Fleetwood
Mac had ten different line-ups
. . ., this was the third: (left to
right) Jeremy Spencer, Mick
Fleetwood, Peter Green,
Danny Kirwan and John McVie
(standing).

Previous page bottom: Jethro
Tull frontman, Ian Anderson, in
characteristic pose.

backing group, now called the Band, emerged with a debut album, *Music From Big Pink*, which was voted one of the year's finest. Audiences were quick to respond, putting *The Band*, *Stage Fright* and *Rock Of Ages* into the top 10. Interspersing more highly acclaimed albums with Dylan reunions, they worked steadily until November 1977, when their final concert was filmed as *The Last Waltz*. A star-spangled affair, it featured cameo appearances by Neil Young, Eric Clapton, Ronnie Hawkins (in whose band the Hawks they had originally come together), Van Morrison and Joni Mitchell – who had also made her debut LP in 1968.

Like the Band, she was from Canada, but had moved to New York to make a considerable impact on the folk scene, where her songs were recorded by established stars like Judy Collins (who took *Both Sides Now* into the top 10) and Tom Rush. Two of her albums, *Court And Spark* and *Miles Of Aisles*, reached number two during 1974. Since then releases have been less frequent and increasingly esoteric.

Singer/songwriter activity was about to sweep through the music business, but in 1968 the trend was only beginning, and the quality had yet to be diluted. Tim Buckley, Randy Newman, Laura Nyro and Leonard Cohen all turned out excellent albums which attracted praise rather than sales – although all saw their songs reach the charts in the hands of more commercial interpreters. Newman had to wait until 1977 before *Short People* convinced the masses of his talents, whereas Arlo Guthrie, son of folk pioneer Woody, struck a popular vein immediately with *Alice's Restaurant*.

Kenny Rogers had his first taste of the charts with the pseudo-psychedelic *Just Dropped In (To See What Condition My Condition Was In)*, which together with *Ruby, Don't Take Your Love To Town* prepared his way to becoming the biggest country star of the seventies with hits like *Lucille*, *Don't Fall In Love With A Dreamer* and *Lady*.

Below left: Joni Mitchell, one of the freshest and brightest singer/songwriters.

Below right: His backing group emerged from Bob Dylan's shadow to score as The Band.

Above: Glen Campbell played in the Champs and the Beach Boys before establishing his own career.

Right: 'A dance and concert fusion of psychedelia and rhythm and blues' was how Sylvester Stewart described his group, Sly and the Family Stone.

Mason Williams had a huge instrumental hit with *Classical Gas*, Herb Alpert had a number one with *This Guy's In Love With You* and actor Richard Harris became a pop star with the Jim Webb song *MacArthur Park*. Webb also provided former session guitarist and Beach Boy Glen Campbell with solo hits in the shape of *By The Time I Get To Phoenix* and *Wichita Lineman*.

Monkeemania was already declining dramatically, but teenyboppers found new interest in the hits of such groups as the Ohio Express and the 1910 Fruitgum Co – the creations of New York producers Jerry Kasenetz and Jeff Katz. They had the 'bubble gum' market securely sewn up with hits like *Simon Says*, *1, 2, 3, Red Light* and *Yummy Yummy Yummy*, but the most successful new pop act was Gary Puckett and the Union Gap from southern California. Their gimmicks were Civil War uniforms and pop-soul soundalikes – five of which reached the top 10, including *Young Girl* (also a number one in Britain) and *Lady Willpower*.

Black soul flourished in the hands of Clarence Carter, who broke into the top 10 with *Slip Away* and returned two years later with *Patches*; O.C. Smith, who scored with *The Son Of Hickory Holler's Tramp* and *Little Green Apples*; Judy Clay and William Bell, who cut a classic in *Private Number*; Johnny Nash, who broke through with *Hold Me Tight* (and reached the top four years later with *I Can See Clearly Now*) and Tammi Terrell, whose *You're All I Need To Get By* was the last of four top 10 duets with Marvin Gaye.

The soul focus switched from Detroit to Philadelphia where the producing team of Gamble and Huff assisted Cliff Nobles and Co to number two with *The Horse* and

Archie Bell and the Drells to number one with *Tighten Up* – the first of ten hits. The Intruders, more Gamble and Huff protégés, reached the top 10 with *Cowboys To Girls* – their biggest hit – while the unconnected Delfonics established the sweet, soft Philly sound with *La-la Means I Love You*.

Two other black groups, Sly and the Family Stone from San Francisco and the Chambers Brothers from Los Angeles, gained popularity after experimenting with a psychedelic/soul hybrid. A modernized gospel group, the Chambers Brothers were stalwarts of the folk scene, but crossed into the rock charts with their powerful *Time Has Come Today*. As the spearhead of seventies' funk Sly and his crew influenced both black and white music over the next few years. Sly Stone, formerly Sylvester Stewart, had been a successful disc jockey and producer, but early attempts to launch his seven-strong group were thwarted.

Dance To The Music provided their breakthrough, followed by three number one singles – *Everyday People*, *Thank You (Falettinme Be Mice Elf Agin)* and *Family Affair* – and the chart-topping album *There's A Riot Going On*. They cruised into self-imposed limbo during the mid-seventies, only to see their ideas pervading records by groups like Earth, Wind and Fire and Funkadelic.

A second wave of innovative San Franciscan groups emerged – notably Quicksilver Messenger Service and the Steve Miller Band. After their acid-rock masterpiece *Happy Trails* Quicksilver were hampered by personality clashes and line-up changes, although they still managed three more top 30 albums.

Steve Miller, a Texan, finally settled in San Francisco after abortive meanderings in Chicago and the city's ambience convinced him to drop the blues in favour of more experimental music. In collaboration with producer Glyn Johns he made some of the finest albums to come out of the West Coast, starting with *Children Of The Future* and *Sailor*. A dry spell ended in 1973 when *The Joker* took him to the top of the US charts, since when sporadic hits like *Rock 'n Me* and *Abracadabra* have kept his popularity and credibility intact.

Also from San Francisco were Blue Cheer – loud, unsubtle pioneers of heavy metal, best remembered for their first album *Vincebus Eruptum*, containing a savage distortion of Eddie Cochran's *Summertime Blues*. Exploring similar territory were Iron Butterfly, who scored heavily when its 17-minute title track propelled *In-A-Gadda-Da-Vida* into the top 5 of the album chart. Ted Nugent's 1968 outfit the Amboy Dukes got off to a good start with the raucous psychedelic scorcher *Journey To The Center Of The Mind*.

Other underground groups included Steppenwolf, whose run of overt drug/outlaw hits included *Born To Be Wild* and *Magic Carpet Ride*, and Spirit, whose approach was infinitely more delicate. Combining blues, jazz, classical and rock backgrounds, they cut a succession of fine albums, culminating in their classic *Twelve Dreams Of Dr Sardonicus*. Audience response remained low, however, and they split for pastures new. Subtlety, they realized, was the last element necessary for survival ... rock music was becoming more calculated and obvious. The sparkling sixties had peaked and less exuberant times were ahead.

TITLE	ARTIST	LABEL	WEEKS AT NO. 1
Hello Goodbye	The Beatles	Capitol	2
Judy In Disguise	John Fred and his Playboy Band	Paula	2
Green Tambourine	The Lemon Pipers	Buddah	1
Love Is Blue	Paul Mauriat	Philips	5
(Sittin' On) The Dock Of The Bay	Otis Redding	Volt	4
Honey	Bobby Goldsboro	United Artists	5
Tighten Up	Archie Bell and the Drells	Atlantic	2
Mrs Robinson	Simon and Garfunkel	Columbia	3
This Guy's In Love With You	Herb Alpert	A&M	4
Grazing In The Grass	Hugh Masakela	Uni	2
Hello I Love You	The Doors	Elektra	2
People Got To Be Free	The Rascals	Atlantic	5
Harper Valley PTA	Jeannie C. Riley	Plantation	1
Hey Jude	The Beatles	Apple	9
Love Child	The Supremes	Motown	2
I Heard It Through The Grapevine	Marvin Gaye	Tamla	3

UK CHART TOPPERS

TITLE	ARTIST	LABEL	WEEKS AT NO. 1
Hello Goodbye	The Beatles	Parlophone	3
The Ballad Of Bonnie & Clyde	Georgie Fame	CBS	1
Everlasting Love	The Love Affair	CBS	2
The Mighty Quinn	Manfred Mann	Fontana	2
Cinderella Rockefella	Esther and Abi Ofarim	Philips	3
Legend Of Xanadu	Dave Dee, Dozy, Beaky, Mick and Tich	Fontana	1
Lady Madonna	The Beatles	Parlophone	2
Congratulations	Cliff Richard	Columbia	2
Wonderful World	Louis Armstrong	HMV	4
Young Girl	Gary Puckett and the Union Gap	CBS	4
Jumping Jack Flash	The Rolling Stones	Decca	3
Baby Come Back	The Equals	President	3
I Pretend	Des O'Connor	Columbia	1
Mony Mony	Tommy James and the Shondells	Major Minor	3
Fire	The Crazy World Of Arthur Brown	Track	1
Do It Again	The Beach Boys	Capitol	1
I Gotta Get A Message To You	The Bee Gees	Polydor	1
Hey Jude	The Beatles	Apple	2
Those Were The Days	Mary Hopkin	Apple	6
With A Little Help From My Friends	Joe Cocker	Regal Zonophone	1
The Good, The Bad And The Ugly	Hugo Montenegro	RCA	4
Lily The Pink	The Scaffold	Parlophone	3

FILMS

- Belle De Jour
- Bullitt
- Coogan's Bluff
- Funny Girl
- The Good The Bad And The Ugly
- Hang 'Em High
- Here We Go Round The Mulberry Bush
- Jungle Book
- The Lion In Winter
- Monterey Pop
- Oliver
- Planet Of The Apes
- The Producers
- Rachel Rachel
- Romeo And Juliet
- Rosemary's Baby
- The Thomas Crown Affair
- 2001 – A Space Odyssey
- Yellow Submarine

CURRENT EVENTS

12 January: Soviet writers Alexander Ginsburg and Yuri Galanskov receive labour camp sentences for 'slandering the Soviet state'.

6 March: Three Africans are hanged in Rhodesia, despite having been reprieved by the Queen.

17 March: Outside the US embassy in London 10,000 demonstrate against US involvement in Vietnam.

4 April: Martin Luther King, 39, leader of the non-violent civil rights movement, is shot and killed by a sniper in Memphis.

7 April: Pierre Trudeau succeeds Lester Pearson as leader of the Canadian Liberal party and is sworn in as Prime Minister.

11 April: Rudi Dutschke, West German left-wing student leader, is shot and seriously wounded in Berlin. Student demonstrations ensue.

20 April: In Birmingham Enoch Powell makes an 'inflammatory speech' on race relations in Britain. Edward Heath dismisses him from the Shadow Cabinet.

27 April: The Abortion Law becomes effective in the UK.

4 May: Sorbonne students and teachers go on strike. Police surround the university and arrest 422 during intense fighting. Mayhem persists through the month until the government yields to student demands.

28 May: Student unrest reaches the UK, as they take over Hornsey Art College and, later, the London School of Economics.

5 June: Senator Robert Kennedy is assassinated in Los Angeles by a Jordanian Arab, Sirhan Sirhan.

23 June: Valerie Solanos shoots Andy Warhol, who recovers.

20 August: Soviet troops invade Czechoslovakia to restore 'normality' by curbing freedom of the press, limiting public assembly and banning new political organizations.

26 August: The US Democrat Party convention, nominating Humphrey and Muskie, results in 'the battle of Chicago', where police and national guardsmen attack demonstrators with batons, tear gas and bayonets.

3 September: Governor Reagan declares a State of Civil Disaster at Berkeley following fervent anti-Vietnam War demonstrations.

8 November: Richard Nixon wins the US Presidential election.

25 December: Crewman on Apollo 8 see the far side of the moon for the first time.

DEATHS

Enid Blyton, author
Tony Hancock, comedian
Bobby Hutton, Black Panther
Little Willie John, R&B singer
Robert Kennedy, politician
Martin Luther King, civil rights leader
Frankie Lymon, rock pioneer
Wes Montgomery, jazz guitarist
Mervyn Peake, author
John Steinbeck, writer
Tammi Terrell, soul singer
Little Walter, blues man
Jess Willard, boxer

Left: After starring in A Hard Day's Night *and* Help!, *the Beatles kept cinema audiences happy with their animated* Yellow Submarine *(Apple, 1968).*

Made in England

1968

SIDE ONE
45 RPM
STEREO

Dance To The Music

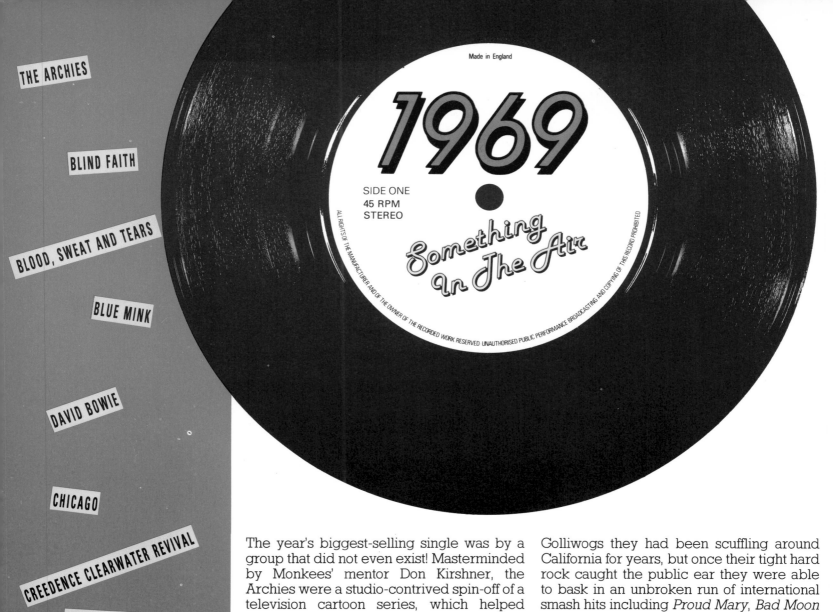

Made in England

1969

SIDE ONE
45 RPM
STEREO

Something In The Air

ALL RIGHTS OF THE MANUFACTURER AND OF THE OWNER OF THE RECORDED WORK RESERVED. UNAUTHORISED PUBLIC PERFORMANCE BROADCASTING AND COPYING OF THIS RECORD PROHIBITED

THE ARCHIES

BLIND FAITH

BLOOD, SWEAT AND TEARS

BLUE MINK

DAVID BOWIE

CHICAGO

CREEDENCE CLEARWATER REVIVAL

CROSBY, STILLS AND NASH

DESMOND DEKKER AND THE ACES

THE FACES

FAIRPORT CONVENTION

FAMILY

THE FLYING BURRITO BROTHERS

GRAND FUNK RAILROAD

The year's biggest-selling single was by a group that did not even exist! Masterminded by Monkees' mentor Don Kirshner, the Archies were a studio-contrived spin-off of a television cartoon series, which helped *Sugar, Sugar* to top the US chart for four weeks. Astonishingly it went on to monopolize the British chart for eight weeks, and attracted sales in excess of six million!

The Archies were never heard of again and neither were Zager and Evans after *In The Year 2525* had been a worldwide chart topper. Steam also dropped from sight after a number one hit, *Na Na Hey Hey Kiss Him Goodbye*, but Bobby Sherman (who meant nothing in Britain) established himself as an American teenybop heart-throb with four top tenners, starting with his biggest, *Little Woman*. His main competition was provided by Three Dog Night, an overtly commercial pop group specializing in snappy cover versions – like Harry Nilsson's *One*, the first of nine million-sellers. Making an asset of their inability to write songs, they took Randy Newman's *Mama Told Me (Not To Come)* and Hoyt Axton's *Joy To The World* to the top of the charts and by the time their magic palled in the mid-seventies they had collected 14 gold albums.

Their cover of Dale Hawkins' *Suzie Q* furnished Creedence Clearwater Revival with their first hit, and leader John Fogerty soon revealed himself to be an exceptional writer – not to mention guitarist, singer and producer. As the Blue Velvets and the

Golliwogs they had been scuffling around California for years, but once their tight hard rock caught the public ear they were able to bask in an unbroken run of international smash hits including *Proud Mary*, *Bad Moon Rising* and *Up Around The Bend*. *Green River* and *Cosmo's Factory* were the biggest of five platinum albums, and their watertight formula seemed inexhaustible until Creedence elected to pack up while they were still on top in late 1972. Fogerty's subsequent seclusion was broken only by occasional solo albums.

His East Coast counterpart John Sebastian, erstwhile brainbox of the Lovin' Spoonful, was the brightest singer/songwriter to emerge, although his concert popularity eclipsed record sales until *Welcome Back* topped the charts in 1976. Tony Joe White from Louisiana had a country-soul hit with *Polk Salad Annie*, and studio guitarist Joe South found his own identity with *Games People Play* and *Walk A Mile In My Shoes*, while country star Merle Haggard succeeded with *Okie From Muskogee*.

Delaney and Bonnie, a white soul group, came out into the open after years working the back streets – as did Johnny Winter, a blues guitarist from Texas, who came to national attention after a *Rolling Stone* article had led to a recording contract. Launched on a massive publicity campaign, an early album made the top 30 and Winter was soon one of the hottest blues acts in the world, but the transition from bar entertainer to superstar created problems, and he was forced to quit the road for a couple of years. His eventual return saw Winter more in control of his future.

Another guitar hero, Mike Bloomfield, was one of the first musicians to incorporate a brass section into a blues band, but the Electric·Flag was not destined to survive. However, 'brass rock' did take off in a big way in the hands of Blood, Sweat and Tears. The eight-piece group was the brainchild of Al Kooper, former Dylan sideman and king-pin of the Blues Project, but he had dropped out by the time *Blood, Sweat and Tears* topped the album chart in spring 1969. Their jazz-rock fusion also found approval in the singles market, where *You've Made Me So Very Happy*, *Spinning Wheel* and *And When I Die* all became million-sellers, and their next album also reached number one. Their success rate trailed off after a few years, but another bunch of pioneer brass rockers showed less sign of decline ... Chicago, whose durability was confirmed by their 1982 chart topper *Hard to Say I'm Sorry*.

Similar to Blood, Sweat and Tears in construction and style, Chicago became a multi-million dollar industry with five consecutive number one albums, although their

HUMBLE PIE

KING CRIMSON

LOVE SCULPTURE

THE MC5

MOTT THE HOOPLE

THE PLASTIC ONO BAND

POCO

SANTANA

BOBBY SHERMAN

THE STOOGES

THREE DOG NIGHT

THUNDERCLAP NEWMAN

TONY JOE WHITE

JOHNNY WINTER

NEIL YOUNG

ZAGER AND EVANS

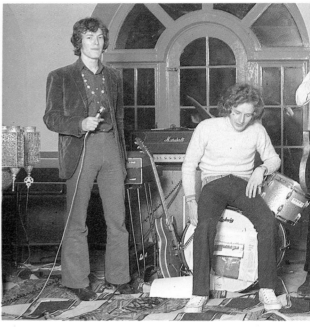

Above: Despite multifarious line-up changes, religious diversions and tangential projects, Santana have maintained their popularity under the resolute leadership of Carlos Santana.

Previous page top: The pre-eminent American singles band of the late sixties, Creedence Clearwater Revival were led by John Fogerty, who, after a decade of hibernation, returned to the spotlight in 1985.

Previous page bottom: The Chicago Transit Authority abbreviated their name to CTA, and then settled for Chicago – which has served them well ever since.

hit single *If You Leave Me Now* remains their most memorable moment. Their 1985 smash *You're The Inspiration* is a tribute to their durability.

Heavy metal was again rampant, particularly in Detroit, where Bob Seger and Ted Nugent were establishing local reputations. Breaking out of the city were three acts whose aberrations won them international acclaim ... the MC5, the Stooges and Grand Funk Railroad. With two chart-topping singles, *We're An American Band* and *The Loco-Motion*, and six top 10 albums, Grand Funk Railroad confirmed their heavy metal supremacy, but individual careers, pursued after their 1977 split, achieved little.

The MC5 rode to fame on a wave of revolutionary hysteria. Their first album *Kick Out The Jams* was an extremely powerful and totally uncompromising live recording which took them into the top 30, but their follow-up, the critically acclaimed *Back In The USA*, sold poorly and they were soon back in the Detroit bars.

Albums by the Stooges were widely regarded as bad jokes until singer Iggy Pop's subsequent emergence led to their being re-examined as a serious musical/

socio-political venture when both he and the MC5 were hailed as gods by the London punk bands of 1977.

The progressive/underground scene saw the arrival of Sea Train and It's A Beautiful Day, who released chart-bound albums – but the year's major new group was Santana. A heady brew of Afro-Cuban rhythms, underscoring Carlos Santana's searing blues guitar, distinguished their eponymous debut album, which took them into the top 5 ... and a dazzling display at Woodstock assisted the passage of their follow-up, *Abraxas*, to number one. Santana continue to assemble for successful tours and albums.

By 1969 folk rock was a dead duck. Country rock was the new trend – but the pioneers were all descendants of the former movement's leading exponents, the Byrds and the Buffalo Springfield. Neither the Flying Burrito Brothers, containing former Byrds Gram Parsons and Chris Hillman, nor Dillard and Clark, led by Byrdman Gene Clark, could attract an audience sufficient for survival, despite consistently inventive albums. And it was touch and go for Poco, initially crewed by ex-Springfielders Richie Furay and Jim Messina, who struggled for ten years before the 1979 top 20 hit *Crazy Love* vindicated their unflagging optimism. While Parsons would die of a drug overdose four years later, his colleagues would go on to bands like Loggins and Messina, Souther, Hillman and Furay and the Eagles ... but in 1969 the hottest country rock supergroup was Crosby, Stills and Nash.

While Neil Young was laying the foundation for a solo career his Buffalo Springfield partner Steve Stills was recording with former Byrd David Crosby and Graham Nash from the Hollies. The resulting album sold over two million copies, but doubts about their ability to duplicate the studio perfection on tour led to the recruitment of

136

Young, together with a bassist and a drummer.

At the peak of popularity, with two number one albums under their belts – *Deja Vu* and *Four Way Street* – Crosby, Stills, Nash and Young split up after only 14 months. Over the next ten years they recorded with various permutations, but Crosby, Stills and Nash came to realize that their original combination was a winner and they regrouped for top 10 albums *CSN* and *Daylight.*

Meanwhile, Neil Young went his own way, following an eccentric path which won a dedicated following. The album *Harvest* and single *Heart Of Gold* both reached the top in 1972, but commercial considerations ranked low in his scale of priorities, and his albums failed to reach the top 20 until *Comes A Time* went gold in 1978. Since then albums like *Rust Never Sleeps* and *Trans* have maintained his uncompromising stance.

Many of the year's newcomers, including Creedence, Santana and Crosby, Stills, Nash and Young, managed to showcase their talents in front of half a million mud-covered fans at the Woodstock Festival, held in August – a couple of months after a similar number witnessed the Hyde Park debut of Britain's most anxiously anticipated supergroup Blind Faith ... formed by Eric Clapton and Ginger Baker from Cream, Steve Winwood from Traffic, and Ric Grech from Family. Advance ballyhoo guaranteed a worldwide chart-topping, platinum album and a sold-out American tour, but the dissatisfaction of the participants led to their dissolving the group in less than a year!

Hyde Park was also the setting for King Crimson's first major gig. Led by charismatic guitarist Robert Fripp, they had quickly earned an underground reputation which led to a record deal with Island, and their first two albums *In The Court Of The*

Crimson King and *In The Wake Of Poseidon* both made the top 5. The next four years saw Fripp directing four completely different line-ups – among a dozen transient members were Greg Lake (ELP), John Wetton (Asia), Ian McDonald (Foreigner), Boz Burrell (Bad Company) and Bill Bruford (Yes) – and after failing to enlarge their modest following he called it a day in October 1974 putting the name on ice until their resurrection in 1981.

Family, an adventurous five-piece from Leicester, made a significant impression with their second album *Family Entertainment*, and remained one of the era's finest live acts until their break-up at the end of 1973. Equally exciting were Mott the Hoople, who had great difficulty transferring their on-stage ebullience on to vinyl. After four albums failed to gather them any commercial momentum they disbanded – only to reform when David Bowie convinced them that success was just a song away. He conjured up *All The Young Dudes* for them and they were soon riding high as overnight stars! *All The Way From Memphis* and *Roll*

Above left: The short-lived supergroup Blind Faith: (left to right) Steve Winwood, Ric Grech, Ginger Baker and Eric Clapton.

Left and above: Two sides of David Bowie: the pensive author of Space Oddity *was soon dazzling audiences with his colourful glam-rock theatrics.*

Right: The Faces provided a perfect setting for Rod Stewart's exuberant personality. Ron Wood (left) and Ronnie Lane admire his tailor's sense of humour.

Right: Mott the Hoople showcased the talents of singer Ian Hunter (hands clasped) as well as guitarist Mick Ralphs (bottom left), who went on to form Bad Company.

Away The Stone consolidated their great popularity, which peaked with a week of sold-out concerts on Broadway. Leader Ian Hunter went on to cement his reputation as a solo star and the extent of his influence was revealed when the next generation of new wavers credited him as a major source of inspiration.

Blind Faith were not the only supergroup around. The Herd's Peter Frampton joined with Steve Marriott from the Small Faces to make Humble Pie, who soon had *Natural Born Bugie* in the top 5. Incompatibility prompted Frampton's early departure, however, and with Colosseum's Clem Clempson on board, they concentrated on America, where their loud, direct, frill-free hard rock coursed through 22 tours and hit albums like

Left: Folk-rockers Fairport
Convention adopt appropriate
French guises to perform their
hit single Si Tu Dois Partir.

Smokin' before their 1975 burnout.

The rest of the Small Faces teamed up with Rod Stewart and Ron Wood from Jeff Beck's group. As the Faces they reached the top 10 on both sides of the Atlantic with their third album *A Nod's As Good As A Wink* and *Ooh-La-La* was a UK number one. But Faces hits like *Stay With Me* and *Cindy Incidentally* were being outsold by Stewart's solo hits like *Maggie May* and *You Wear It Well* – both chart toppers – and although they bent over backwards to stress group democracy it became increasingly obvious that the others were little more than his backing band. The inevitable split came in 1975 when Stewart formed a new band. Ron Wood joined the Rolling Stones and drummer Kenny Jones became the Who's drummer after Keith Moon's death in 1978.

Folk-rock found a wider audience than usual when Fairport Convention hit the charts. By the time they released their masterpiece *Liege And Lief* they had refined their early eclecticism into a style rooted in traditional English music, which they pursued until they split in 1979 ... 15 line-ups, 17 albums and 20 musicians later! Among illustrious Fairporters who continue to convene for annual reunions are Ashley Hutchings, the instigator of the Albion Band, fiddler Dave Swarbrick, Richard Thompson, whose guitar playing leaves other musicians gaping, Ian Matthews, whose *Woodstock* made number one and top session drummer Dave Mattacks. Their gifted singer Sandy Denny, died of a brain haemorrhage in 1978.

Also in the charts were several Caribbean acts including Jimmy Cliff with *Wonderful World Beautiful People* and Desmond Dekker and the Aces with *Israelites* – a chart topper and the biggest of six hits. Tin Pan Alley was represented by Blue Mink, who hit the bull's-eye with *Melting Pot* and other one-off smashes were *Something In The Air* by the wonderfully bizarre Thunderclap Newman and *Je T'Aime ... Moi Non Plus* by Jane Birkin and Serge Gainsbourg, which although banned by the BBC on grounds of 'taste', still got to number one. John Lennon got his Plastic Ono Band airborne with *Give Peace A Chance*, Dave Edmunds made his presence felt in *Sabre Dance*, an instrumental by his trio Love Sculpture and David Bowie reached the top 5 with his eerie *Space Oddity*. Although he had been leading bands since the early sixties any success was localized, and his novel hit was presumed to be a fluke. No one could have guessed what would happen when Bowie returned three years later!

USA CHART TOPPERS

TITLE	ARTIST	LABEL	WEEKS AT NO. 1
I Heard It Through The Grapevine	Marvin Gaye	Tamla	4
Crimson And Clover	Tommy James and the Shondells	Roulette	2
Everyday People	Sly and the Family Stone	Epic	4
Dizzy	Tommy Roe	ABC	4
Aquarius/Let The Sun Shine In	Fifth Dimension	Soul City	6
Get Back	The Beatles	Apple	5
Love Theme From Romeo And Juliet	Henri Mancini	RCA	2
In The Year 2525	Zager and Evans	RCA	6
Honky Tonk Women	The Rolling Stones	London	4
Sugar Sugar	The Archies	Calendar	4
I Can't Get Next To You	The Temptations	Gordy	2
Suspicious Minds	Elvis Presley	RCA	1
Wedding Bell Blues	Fifth Dimension	Soul City	3
Come Together/Something	The Beatles	Apple	1
Na Na Hey Hey Kiss Him Goodbye	Steam	Fontana	2
Leaving On A Jet Plane	Peter, Paul and Mary	Warner Bros	1
Someday We'll Be Together	The Supremes	Motown	1

UK CHART TOPPERS

TITLE	ARTIST	LABEL	WEEKS AT NO. 1
Ob-La-Di Ob-La-Da	Marmalade	CBS	3
Lily The Pink	The Scaffold	Parlophone	1
Albatross	Fleetwood Mac	Blue Horizon	1
Blackberry Way	The Move	Regal Zonophone	1
Half As Nice	Amen Corner	Immediate	2
Where Do You Go To My Lovely?	Peter Sarstedt	United Artists	4
I Heard It Through The Grapevine	Marvin Gaye	Tamla Motown	3
The Israelites	Desmond Dekker and the Aces	Pyramid	1
Get Back	The Beatles	Apple	6
Dizzy	Tommy Roe	Stateside	1
The Ballad Of John and Yoko	The Beatles	Apple	3
Something In The Air	Thunderclap Newman	Track	3
Honky Tonk Women	The Rolling Stones	Decca	5
In The Year 2525	Zager and Evans	RCA	3
Bad Moon Rising	Creedence Clearwater Revival	Liberty	3
Je T'Aime… Moi Non Plus	Jane Birkin and Serge Gainsbourg	Major Minor	1
I'll Never Fall In Love Again	Bobbie Gentry	Capitol	1
Sugar Sugar	The Archies	RCA	8
Two Little Boys	Rolf Harris	Columbia	2

FILMS

Alice's Restaurant
Anne Of A Thousand Days
Butch Cassidy And The Sundance Kid
The Damned
Easy Rider
Hello Dolly
If
The Love Bug
The Magic Christian
Midnight Cowboy
One Plus One
Paint Your Wagon
The Prime Of Miss Jean Brodie
They Shoot Horses Don't They?
True Grit
Where Eagles Dare
The Wild Bunch

3 January: Religious and political factions clash in Londonderry after a 72-mile march from Belfast.

16 January: Jan Palach burns himself to death in Wenceslas Square in protest at Soviet suppresion of Czechoslovak freedom.

16 January: Soviet space capsules, Soyuz 4 and 5, link; two astronauts transfer from one to the other after one hour's walk in space.

5 February: A state of 'extreme emergency' is declared as student protest mounts at the University of California's Berkeley campus.

9 February: Maiden flight of the Boeing 747.

2 March: Maiden flight of the Concorde.

5 March: The Kray brothers are sentenced to 30 years minimum for murder.

10 March: James Earl Ray is sentenced to 99 years' imprisonment for the murder of Martin Luther King.

22 April: The *QE2* makes its first passenger-carrying voyage.

9 May: The Pope removes 200 saints from the church calendar.

15 May: Police use shotguns and tear gas during a battle with 2000 demonstrators at Berkeley. The battle is over the use of parkland! The National Guard, acting on Ronald Reagan's orders, drop CS gas from helicopters.

9 June: Enoch Powell suggests an immigrant repatriation scheme during a speech at Wolverhampton.

20 June: Georges Pompidou replaces De Gaulle as French President.

18 July: Senator Edward Kennedy crashes his car off a bridge at Chappaquiddick Island. His passenger, Mary Jo Kopechne, is drowned.

21 July: Neil Armstrong leaves Apollo 11 to step on to the moon. He is joined by Buzz Aldrin and they explore the surface for over two and a half hours before blasting off for home.

8 August: Sectarian violence flares in Belfast. Troops are called in and their presence becomes necessary full-time from then on.

5 September: Lt Calley is charged with the My Lai massacre of 109 Vietnamese civilians.

9 December: Charles Manson is arrested on charges of killing Sharon Tate and various others in California.

John Lennon marries Yoko Ono and tours the world advocating peace. In December he returns his MBE and says that the Beatles are finished as a group. Meanwhile Paul McCartney marries Linda Eastman and Bee Gee Maurice Gibb marries Lulu.

Meher Baba, religious leader
Billy Cotton, bandleader
Dwight Eisenhower, former US President
Judy Garland, film star
Roy Hamilton, R&B singer
Wynonie Harris, R&B pioneer
Coleman Hawkins, jazz musician
Gabby Hayes, cowboy actor
Brian Jones, former Rolling Stone
Boris Karloff, actor
Sharon Tate, film star
Josh White, folk singer

Left: Swarms of butterflies were released as the Rolling Stones began their free concert in Hyde Park.

Made in England

1969

SIDE ONE
45 RPM
STEREO

Something In The Air

ALL RIGHTS OF THE MANUFACTURER AND OF THE OWNER OF THE RECORDED WORK RESERVED UNAUTHORISED PUBLIC PERFORMANCE BROADCASTING AND COPYING OF THIS RECORD PROHIBITED

141

ALLMAN BROTHERS

BADFINGER

BLACK SABBATH

BREAD

THE CARPENTERS

CLARENCE CARTER

CHAIRMEN OF THE BOARD

DEEP PURPLE

EDISON LIGHTHOUSE

EMERSON, LAKE AND PALMER

FREE

J. GEILS BAND

HOT CHOCOLATE

JACKSON FIVE

Made in England

1970

SIDE ONE
45 RPM
STEREO

Close To You

ALL RIGHTS OF THE MANUFACTURER AND OF THE OWNER OF THE RECORDED WORK RESERVED. UNAUTHORISED PUBLIC PERFORMANCE BROADCASTING AND COPYING OF THIS RECORD PROHIBITED

It has become obvious that the beginning of each decade gives no clue to the enormous musical changes which will occur during a ten-year period, and the start of the 1970s was no exception. The psychedelic era had all but fizzled out. Those who achieved most early success were the bands who would burn out, albeit sometimes coming back in re-formations which would become the life-blood of some areas of the music press.

Deep Purple found initial success in America where *Hush* was a top 5 hit in 1968, but only after a line-up shuffle which saw vocalist Ian Gillan introduced, did they succeed in Britain with top 10 singles *Black Night* and *Strange Kind Of Woman* and early seventies chart-topping LPs *Fireball* and *Machine Head*. However by mid-1973 Gillan had left the band and, although his replacement David Coverdale was able to help the group maintain a portion of its following with a string of top 10 LPs, the group seized up in early 1976. Spin-off bands like Gillan, Whitesnake (featuring Coverdale, organist Jon Lord and drummer Ian Paice) and Rainbow (led by guitarist Ritchie Blackmore and also including bass player Roger Glover) were often over-shadowed in the charts by what seemed to be an endless succession of live recordings by various Purple line-ups.

Another heavy metal act launched at the start of the 1970s, Black Sabbath, made an LP in 1983 which featured as their lead vocalist the very same Ian Gillan. Sabbath enjoyed substantial popularity, particularly in the LP charts, on both sides of the Atlantic – their first six albums made the UK top 10 and *Paranoid* topped the British album chart and made the US top 20 – but business problems affected their output from the mid-1970s. When their non-musical difficulties were resolved singer Ozzy Osbourne opted for solo success and Ian Gillan was one of several who later joined and left the band.

Free were less fortunate. They stormed to the top of the chart with *All Right Now* followed by several highly rated LPs, only to founder during the summer of 1973 when singer Paul Rodgers and drummer Simon Kirke became half of Bad Company. While bass player Andy Fraser went to ground after a few other endeavours, Paul Kossoff, Free's inspirational guitarist, finally succumbed to drug addiction and died in March 1976 on the verge of another come-back attempt.

Emerson, Lake and Palmer, a so-called supergroup formed by keyboard wizard Keith Emerson (ex-the Nice), Greg Lake on bass (ex-King Crimson) and drummer Carl Palmer (ex-Atomic Rooster), in contrast seemed not to die out but to fade away. Their debut at the 1970 Isle of Wight Festival saw them widely praised and their early LPs, particularly *Tarkus*, which topped the British chart in 1971, saw them going from strength to strength as their popularity in America also increased. After a 1974 live album *Welcome Back, My Friends, To The*

Show That Never Ends, which reached the top 5 on both sides of the Atlantic, the trio's inspiration seemed to diminish. They returned successfully in 1977 with the double album *Works*, but after two more albums they disappeared. Palmer, perhaps surprisingly, has since been the most visible – after an abortive attempt at leading a group known as PM he joined Asia, a group composed of his contemporaries, and perhaps even exceeded his fame with ELP. Lake, after a partially successful solo career which peaked when *I Believe In Father Christmas* all but topped the singles charts in 1975, also briefly joined Asia. Emerson seemed to go into hibernation, until in 1985, it was announced that ELP had re-formed, although with drummer Cozy Powell (ex-Rainbow) replacing Carl Palmer, who preferred to remain in Asia.

Above: Marc Bolan (left) and Mickey Finn, who scored numerous hits during the first half of the seventies as T. Rex.

Previous page top: Keith Emerson, Greg Lake and Carl Palmer formed one of the many supergroups of the era and were familiarly known as ELP. In 1985 they announced that a new version of the trio had been launched, but with Cozy Powell replacing Palmer, who preferred to remain with Asia.

Previous page bottom: The highly successful 'Mark 2' line-up of Deep Purple: (left to right) Jon Lord, Roger Glover, Ian Paice, Ian Gillan, Ritchie Blackmore. This version of the group reformed in 1984 and restored Purple to its former glories.

Marc Bolan had recorded solo before forming Tyrannosaurus Rex, a folk/rock duo with a cult following among hippies. Ambitious for greater fame, Bolan recorded simpler pop songs, with a larger group, but an abbreviated group name of T. Rex – Bolan was the only ever-present member. A series of big hits began, which included four UK number ones in Hot Love, Get It On (also Bolan's biggest US hit under the title Bang A Gong), Telegram Sam and Metal Guru. Bolan was also a leading light of 'glitter rock' and enjoyed a dozen consecutive top 10 hits, plus several big-selling albums before relaxing his grip on the charts. In 1977 he had just returned with a TV series and a revamped T.Rex when he was killed in a car accident.

Badfinger, soundalikes and protégés of the Beatles, were dogged by bad luck and two members of the group committed suicide some years later. The most enduring act was Hot Chocolate, who initially had also been signed to Apple Records. Ace talent spotter Mickie Most also spotted the potential in the voice and songs of group leader Errol Brown, and their union produced nearly 30 British hits by the end of 1983, the

biggest of which was the 1977 chart topper So You Win Again.

Among the year's notable newcomers were Hotlegs (who later became 10 cc) and Mungo Jerry, whose In The Summertime topped the chart, and who followed it up with three further top 5 hits including a second number one, Baby Jump. Even a Dutch group, Shocking Blue, topped the US chart and reached the UK top 10 with their biggest hit Venus. Edison Lighthouse, who topped the British chart and reached the American top 5 with Love Grows, were a group of session musicians whose lead singer Tony Burrows also performed the same function for two other hit-making acts of the year, White Plains and Brotherhood of Man.

Soul music was dominated during the year by the latest Motown find, the Jackson Five. The sons of a former musician, the five brothers were fronted by the then 11-year-old Michael Jackson. They began their chart career with four consecutive American number one singles – I Want You Back, ABC, The Love You Save and I'll Be There, which all reached the British top 10. Michael also made the charts as a solo artist.

Left: The Jackson Five at the time of their total domination of the American singles chart, when they scored four consecutive number one hits.

Below: Hot Chocolate, with group leader Errol Brown (left) receiving one of their many awards.

Bottom: The great Curtis Mayfield, who left the Impressions and found major solo fame.

Jimmy Ruffin, another Motown star, scored with *Farewell Is A Lonely Sound*, and stable-mate Edwin Starr topped the US chart with *War*, while Invictus Records, a label formed by ex-Motown hit-makers Holland/Dozier/Holland, began impressively with two hits. *Band Of Gold* by Freda Payne topped the British chart and made the top 3 in America, but her success was fleeting compared with that of the other original Invictus act, the Chairmen of the Board. Starting with their biggest hit *Give Me Just A Little More Time* (number three in Britain and America), the group had another eight hits before Invictus folded a few years later. In addition Clarence Carter scored his biggest hit with *Patches*, which neatly divided his seven-year chart career in two; Eddie Holman had his biggest hit with *Hey There Lonely Girl*; and Curtis Mayfield, having left the Impressions, broke through as a solo artist with the score for the film *Superfly* – the soundtrack album went gold on the day of release, and two big hit singles also resulted in *Freddie's Dead* and the title track. Mayfield remains a highly respected artist.

The Partridge Family, like the Jackson Five (who were portrayed in cartoon form), were promoted via television. Although they were a family only on the screen Shirley Jones, the adult star of the series, was related by marriage to the teenybop star of the show David Cassidy. Cassidy was largely the reason for the 'group' scoring several early 1970s' hits, including an American number one *I Think I Love You*. Even after the series ended, he remained a teen idol until the mid-1970s.

Other pop acts to make an impact during

1970 included B.J. Thomas with *Raindrops Keep Falling On My Head* and Ray Stevens with *Everything Is Beautiful*, but of far greater note were the Carpenters and Bread. The former, a brother and sister duo who played keyboards and drums respectively, owed most to the fact that drummer Karen also possessed a voice of great beauty and clarity which presented melodic songs like *We've Only Just Begun* and *For All We Know* in a way which record buyers found irresistible. Although accused of bland mediocrity, the Carpenters were supreme in their field for most of the 1970s, and their 1973 LP *Now And Then* included an affectionate and accurate rock'n'roll medley. *Now And Then* reached number two on both sides of the Atlantic, but its success was surpassed by *The Singles 1969-1973* which was one of the biggest-selling LPs of the year. Although it wasn't their biggest hit (that accolade belonged jointly to *Close To You*, *Top Of The World* and *Please Mr Postman*, which topped the US charts in 1970, 1973 and 1974 respectively), *Goodbye To Love* – containing a guitar solo of searing intensity – was a near perfect response to their critics. Towards the end of the 1970s the duo lost some of their chart appeal. Karen Carpenter died in early 1983 – a victim of heart trouble aggravated by anorexia.

Bread's chart career was rather more brief, although no less spectacular at their peak, which came in 1977 when a compilation of their biggest hits *The Sound Of Bread* sold two million copies and topped the British LP charts. Ironically this coincided with a brief reunion which followed the group's original dissolution a few years earlier. They comprised seasoned session musician/producer David Gates, who had worked with Leon Russell, Captain Beefheart and Elvis Presley among many others, and James Griffin, who had written *For All We Know*. *Make It With You* topped the US chart in 1970, but later hits like *Baby I'm A Want You* and *Guitar Man* kept the group in the chart until their demise, which followed a conflict over songwriting between Gates and Griffin. Both went on to solo careers, although neither approached their enormous popularity as group members.

Simon and Garfunkel released their biggest selling LP *Bridge Over Troubled Water*, which not only topped the LP charts around the world, but spent almost six years in the UK album listings. This team owed their success to their Everly Brothers-styled harmonies and Paul Simon's evocative songs. A number of similar singer/song-writers began to achieve acclaim, although as solo performers.

James Taylor, who had been briefly signed with the Beatles' Apple label,

resurfaced under the aegis of Peter Asher (of Peter and Gordon). Asher, who had signed him to Apple, now managed him and negotiated a new deal with Warner Brothers. Taylor wrote personal songs like *Fire And Rain*, a big hit included on his platinum LP *Sweet Baby James*, and his relaxed style propelled several subsequent LPs into the chart over succeeding years. He also married Carly Simon, with whom he sometimes recorded before their divorce.

Taylor's guitar-toting troubadour image was mirrored by Kris Kristofferson, whose first LP, originally titled *Kristofferson*, included such classic songs as *Help Me Make It Through The Night* and *Me And Bobby McGee*. Its great success notwithstanding, Kris began to devote more of his time to acting to the detriment of his musical career, although some of his films like *A Star Is Born* with Barbara Streisand incorporated songs. His marriage to Rita Coolidge, herself a notable vocalist, provided several hit LPs, but since their divorce Kristofferson's output has become obscure.

Leon Russell came to prominence after years of studio work when he assembled a huge band for *Mad Dogs And Englishmen*, the tour/film/LP featuring Joe Cocker. Russell was also part of the cast of the *Concert For Bangla Desh*, George Harrison's star-studded attempt to finance famine relief, in which Bob Dylan was one of many star guests. The year also saw the last of the

Right: The successful husband and wife team of Kris Kristofferson and Rita Coolidge, who charted both as solo artists and as a duo.

146

mega-festivals, the two biggest being those at Bath and at the Isle of Wight, but the deaths of Janis Joplin and Jimi Hendrix overshadowed all.

The J. Geils Band, a sextet from Boston, played straight ahead rhythm and blues. Singer Peter Wolf and guitarist Geils led the band, who ploughed through the seventies with occasional success until 1982, when *Centrefold* from their *Freeze Frame* LP was a huge international hit, not long after which Wolf left the band for a solo career. From a similar musical field came the Allman Brothers, guitarist Duane and singer/keyboard player Gregg. Duane had forged a

solid reputation as a session musician working with Aretha Franklin, Wilson Pickett and Boz Scaggs among others, but when he teamed up with his brother to form a six-piece R&B band who specialized in extended improvization they achieved national success with a live double LP *At Fillmore East*. Duane also added distinctive slide guitar to *Layla* by Derek and the Dominoes (Derek being Eric Clapton), but shortly after he was killed in a motorcycle accident. The rest of the Allman Brothers band opted to continue and their next LP *Eat A Peach* reached the top 5, but history repeated itself and almost exactly a year after Duane's death bassist Berry Oakley was killed in a similar accident.

The band again decided to carry on and their next LP *Brothers And Sisters* reached the top of the LP charts, while a single taken from the LP, *Ramblin' Man*, was also a smash hit and featured guitarist Richard Betts, previously very much in Duane's shadow. However, personal conflicts led to unsuccessful solo outings by various band members, while reunions have so far failed to recapture the group's original magic.

Mountain was a quartet fronted by bassist and ex-Cream producer Felix Pappalardi and guitarist Leslie West, whose 1971 LP *Nantucket Sleighride* became their biggest hit. The group reconvened from time to time during the later 1970s but to less effect. Pappalardi was shot dead in 1983.

Death also affected the career of Little Feat, a band much admired by music critics. After four years of struggling *Feats Don't Fail Me Now*, their 1974 LP, rescued the band but subsequent efforts were less spectacular, and by 1979 Lowell George, the group's leader and guitar genius, released a solo album. But he was found dead in a hotel room soon after the start of his first solo tour.

The story of War, a predominantly black rock/funk band, was less tragic. Their introduction to a wider audience came when they worked as the backing band for Eric Burdon. After two albums with Burdon War went their own way and achieved several big-selling LPs and half a dozen top 10 singles in America.

Among those who impressed in the singles chart were Dave Edmunds (who had scored two years before with *Sabre Dance* as leader of Love Sculpture), who topped the UK chart for six weeks with a revival of Smiley Lewis's *I Hear You Knocking* also making the top 5 in America, and R. Dean Taylor, one of the few white Motown acts, who took the atmospheric *Indiana Wants Me* to the upper reaches of the chart.

There was sad news for Beatle fans, when they were informed by Paul McCartney that the Beatles had split up. Hardly the most optimistic year to launch a new decade.

Left and above:
Bread: (left to right)
James Griffin, David Gates,
Mike Botts and Robb Royer.

TITLE	ARTIST	LABEL	WEEKS AT NO. 1
Raindrops Keep Fallin' On My Head	B.J. Thomas	Scepter	4
I Want You Back	Jackson Five	Motown	1
Venus	Shocking Blue	Colossus	1
Thank You	Sly and the Family Stone	Epic	2
Bridge Over Troubled Water	Simon and Garfunkel	Columbia	6
Let It Be	The Beatles	Apple	2
ABC	Jackson Five	Motown	2
American Woman	Guess Who	RCA	3
Everything Is Beautiful	Ray Stevens	Barnaby	2
The Long And Winding Road	The Beatles	Apple	2
The Love You Save	Jackson Five	Motown	2
Mama Told Me Not To Come	Three Dog Night	Dunhill	2
Close To You	The Carpenters	A&M	4
Make It With You	Bread	Elektra	1
War	Edwin Starr	Gordy	3
Ain't No Mountain High Enough	Diana Ross	Motown	3
Cracklin' Rosie	Neil Diamond	Uni	1
I'll Be There	Jackson Five	Motown	5
I Think I Love You	Partridge Family	Bell	3
The Tears Of A Clown	Smokey Robinson and the Miracles	Tamla	2
My Sweet Lord	George Harrison	Apple	1

TITLE	ARTIST	LABEL	WEEKS AT NO. 1
Two Little Boys	Rolf Harris	Columbia	4
Love Grows	Edison Lighthouse	Bell	5
Wand'rin' Star	Lee Marvin	Paramount	4
Bridge Over Troubled Water	Simon and Garfunkel	CBS	2
All Kinds Of Everything	Dana	Rex	2
Spirit In The Sky	Norman Greenbaum	Reprise	2
Back Home	England World Cup Squad	Pye	3
Yellow River	Christie	CBS	1
In The Summertime	Mungo Jerry	Dawn	8
The Wonder Of You	Elvis Presley	RCA	6
The Tears Of A Clown	Smokey Robinson and the Miracles	Tamla Motown	1
Band Of Gold	Freda Payne	Invictus	6
Woodstock	Matthews Southern Comfort	Uni	3
Voodoo Chile	Jimi Hendrix	Track	1
I Hear You Knocking	Dave Edmunds	MAM	4

FILMS

Airport
Catch 22
Five Easy Pieces
Getting Straight
The Great White Hope
Kes
Let It Be
Little Big Man
Love Story
MASH
Patton
Performance
Rio Lobo
Ryan's Daughter
Soldier Blue
There's A Girl In My Soup
Women In Love
Woodstock
Zabriskie Point

21 January: North Vietnam refuses to publish the names of captured American pilots, saying they are 'criminals' and not prisoners of war.

18 February: The 'Chicago Seven' are acquitted of conspiring to incite riot at the Democratic Convention.

2 March: Rhodesia declares itself a republic, dissolving last ties with the British crown.

11 April: Apollo 13's moon mission is aborted when an oxygen tank explodes, ripping the capsule's skin – but a safe splashdown is achieved.

4 May: Four students are killed when National Guardsmen open fire on a group of anti-war demonstrators at Kent State University, Ohio. In the ensuing wave of protest and further demonstrations two more students are killed at Jackson State University, Mississippi.

10 May: 448 American colleges go on strike over the killings and Nixon's decision to invade Cambodia.

19 June: Labour lose the general election. Conservatives under Edward Heath assume power.

23 July: The Northern Ireland government bans street parades after further killings.

2 August: The first Boeing 747 to be hijacked is met by Castro in Havana.

4 September: As Nixon submits to pressure, US troop withdrawals leave fewer than 400,000 in Vietnam.

8 September: Arab commandos hijack three airliners, land them in the Jordanian desert and blow them up. Legislation is introduced to carry Federal armed guards on overseas flights by US airlines.

8 October: Alexander Solzhenitsyn wins the Nobel Peace Prize for literature.

13 November: Cyclones and tidal waves inflict massive damage in East Pakistan.

30 December: Vietnam peace talks held in Paris end their second full year with both sides agreeing there had been no progress.

The Israel/United Arab Republic conflict rages; the Northern Ireland troubles escalate; Nixon becomes even more unpopular after proposals to invade Cambodia; Basque separatists take action; and plane hijacking is rife.

DEATHS

Albert Ayler, jazz musician
General Charles de Gaulle, former French President
George Goldner, early rock'n'roll producer
Jimi Hendrix, rock musician
Janis Joplin, rock singer
Sonny Liston, boxer
President Gamal Abdel Nasser, Egyptian leader
Bertrand Russell, philosopher
Al Wilson, Canned Heat singer/guitarist

Left: A still from Performance, which starred James Fox (left) and Mick Jagger (Goodtimes, 1970).

Made in England

1970

SIDE ONE
45 RPM
STEREO

Close To You

ALL RIGHTS THE MANUFACTURER AND OF THE OWNER OF THE RECORDED WORK RESERVED UNAUTHORISED PUBLIC PERFORMANCE BROADCASTING AND COPYING OF THIS RECORD PROHIBITED

JOHN DENVER

AL GREEN

GUESS WHO

GEORGE HARRISON

ISAAC HAYES

ELTON JOHN

JOHN LENNON

PAUL McCARTNEY

MELANIE

In the wake of the Beatles' disintegration each member of the group had embarked on a solo career during 1970, although it was not until 1971 that the obvious commercial potential of individual efforts would come to light. John Lennon had charted with singles under the banner of the Plastic Ono Band, but his experimental LPs, collaborations with Japanese avant garde artist Yoko Ono, were inaccessible and controversial. In 1971 Lennon confirmed that he could still make comprehensible music with his LP *Imagine*, whose title track was a masterpiece and deservedly a hit in America, although not until some years later in Britain. Lennon continued to produce straightforward albums like *Mind Games* and *Walls And Bridges* and in 1975 released an album of cover versions from his formative years, *Rock'n'Roll*. After this he went into self-imposed exile; he refused to perform or record until his second son Sean was five years old. His return in late 1980 was to herald a major tragedy.

Ringo Starr was fairly active during the first half of the 1970s with hit singles like *Back Off Boogaloo*, *Photograph* and *You're Sixteen*, the last two both topping the US chart, plus the big-selling LP *Ringo* produced by Richard Perry in 1973. Thereafter he appeared to lose direction musically, although he became notable as a film star in *That'll Be The Day* and *The Magic Christian*.

George Harrison had also drifted into relative obscurity by the end of 1970,

although the start of the decade saw him responsible for possibly the finest Beatle solo LP of the early post-group years *All Things Must Pass*, which included an international chart-topping single *My Sweet Lord*. Harrison would later lose a court action over the song for plagiarism brought by the publishers of *He's So Fine*, a 1963 hit by the Chiffons. Even in 1970 he seemed far more concerned with his consuming passion for India, whose music and religion he eagerly espoused. This led to his organization of the 'Concert For Bangla Desh', the proceeds from which were designed to bring relief to a nation suffering deprivation as a result of a civil war. George also became very interested in Grand Prix motor racing during the latter part of the 1970s, and only occasionally found time for recording. His main artistic endeavours revolved around a film company, Hand Made Films, which he launched along with several friends from the *Monty Python* team of comedy actors.

The most consistently active ex-Beatle remains Paul McCartney, who launched his solo career with some mildly successful records before forming Wings, a group which included his wife Linda and ex-Moody Blue, Denny Laine. The pinnacle of the group's career came in 1973 with *Band On The Run*, an album which topped the charts around the world. In the mid-1970s Wings embarked on the most comprehensive world tour ever undertaken by a rock

MIDDLE OF THE ROAD

OLIVIA NEWTON-JOHN

NILSSON

THE OSMONDS

GILBERT O'SULLIVAN

CARLY SIMON

SLADE

RINGO STARR

ROD STEWART

SWEET

YES

band, taking in 11 countries and lasting just over a year. A resulting triple album *Wings Over America*, released in 1977, was McCartney's lowest placed LP in the UK chart since 1971, but still reached the top 10. During the same year Wings released *Mull Of Kintyre*, a single which became a huge seller during its nine-week run at the top of the chart. Wings disbanded towards the end of the 1970s, but in an inspired move Paul invited first Stevie Wonder and later Michael Jackson to record duets with him (*Ebony And Ivory* and *The Girl Is Mine* respectively) which were massive sellers.

By 1985 McCartney was allegedly the richest man in popular music. His records continued to sell, although a feature film in which he starred and which he also partly financed, *Give My Regards To Broad Street*, was savaged by critics on its late 1984 release.

1971 saw a major increase in LP sales with established acts like Led Zeppelin, the Who, Deep Purple and the Rolling Stones all spending time at the top of the LP chart, although with some competition from Elton John and Rod Stewart.

Elton, born Reginald Dwight, was keyboard player in a small-time London R&B group Bluesology who backed visiting Americans on British tours. He then took a job as a tunesmith with Dick James Music

151

Above: Yes: Jon Anderson (vocals), Steve Howe (guitar), Rick Wakeman (keyboards), Chris Squire (bass), Bill Bruford (drums).

Right: Gilbert O'Sullivan, despite the fact that his image and stage name were equally contrived, became enormously successful during the first half of the seventies taking both Clair *and* Get Down *to number one in Britain.*

where he began to collaborate with lyricist Bernie Taupin. Elton made an album of original songs in 1969, but it was not until 1971 that he broke through with a top 10 single on both sides of the Atlantic, *Your Song*, which came from his second LP simply titled *Elton John*. Subsequent early 1970s LPs saw Elton's fame escalate and aside from mega-platinum albums like *Honky Chateau*, *Goodbye Yellow Brick Road* and *Captain Fantastic And The Brown Dirt Cowboy* he topped the US singles chart with *Crocodile Rock*, *Bennie And The Jets*, *Lucy In The Sky With Diamonds*, *Philadelphia Freedom* and *Island Girl* before the end of 1975. A duet with Kiki Dee – who was signed to Elton's Rocket Records – *Don't Go Breaking My Heart*, not only topped the US chart in 1976 but did the same in Britain. Then came a temporary halt in Elton's remarkable rise to fame, although he was indisputably the biggest act in the world during the middle of the decade. Elton retired from live performance for some time, concentrating his energies and money on establishing Watford Football Club as one of the best teams in the country. This enterprise was highly successful, as was a return to performance in 1979 when he became one of the very few Western rock artists to play a concert in Moscow. A gradual increase in his musical output during the first half of the 1980s saw Elton returning to the vast popularity he had enjoyed a decade before.

Rod Stewart suffered less from fluctuations in popularity. After a promising start as a solo artist following a spell as singer with the Jeff Beck Group Stewart became lead singer of the Faces, who became a major live attraction. He released solo albums which seemed musically superior to those by the Faces, and certainly sold more. His breakthrough came in 1971 with *Every Picture Tells A Story*, the first of numerous number one LPs, and a single from it, *Maggie May*, was the first of a clutch of

chart-topping singles which continued into the 1980s.

While Rod and Elton were the two biggest male stars to emerge in Britain a woman from Cambridge, Olivia Newton-John, also first found success during 1971. Olivia returned to England from Australia, where her family had emigrated, and became quarter of a group known as Toomorrow, assembled along the same lines as the Monkees by American publishing entrepreneur Don Kirshner. The scheme was a failure, but led to Shadows' guitarist Bruce Welch producing her debut hit, a cover version of Bob Dylan's *If Not For You*. Several more hits followed and Olivia discovered that she was a rising country music star in America. Her first chart-topping single *I Honestly Love You* came in 1974 and similar successes convinced her to live in America. In 1978 a move into films brought renewed success.

As Olivia kept the female flag flying in Britain American singers who made it big included Carly Simon and Carole King, who began to thrive as a performer and recording artist as well as a long-established and successful songwriter. Carole was best known for her work with her then husband

Previous page: Reginald Kenneth Dwight, who became the biggest star of the early seventies under the name of Elton John.

Gerry Goffin. She had charted back in 1962 with *It Might As Well Rain Until September*, but had rarely pursued her career. By 1971 she had resumed solo recording and her second solo LP *Tapestry* was an immense seller, containing a US number one single *It's Too Late*. Follow-up records were still big sellers, but could not equal such huge success, although she continues to record.

Carly Simon had been launched without success in the mid-1960s by Bob Dylan's manager Albert Grossman as one half of the Simon Sisters with her sister Lucy. By 1971 she was back as a solo performer and her greatest moment came in early 1973 when *You're So Vain* (with Mick Jagger as a backing vocalist) topped the US singles chart and *No Secrets*, the LP which included the hit, made it a double top. She married James Taylor and after several lean years made a triumphant comeback in 1977 with *Nobody Does It Better*, the theme song from the James Bond movie *The Spy Who Loved Me*. Following her divorce she seemed to rediscover a taste for recording with her 1983 LP *Hello Big Man*.

Other women who found some success during the year included Joan Baez, whose excellent cover version of the Band's *The Night They Drove Old Dixie Down* was a top 5 hit; Melanie, who topped the US chart with the rather sickly *Brand New Key*, her biggest ever hit; and Janis Joplin, who topped the US chart posthumously with *Me And Bobby McGee*.

Yes, were a quintet who broke through in 1973 with *The Yes Album*, their third LP, and the first to feature Steve Howe on guitar. Subsequently keyboard wizard Rick Wakeman joined the band and success escalated to include chart-topping LPs like *Tales From Topographic Oceans* and *Going For The One*, but the group members also diversified into solo projects although only those by Wakeman made an impact. By 1978 both Wakeman and founder member/ vocalist Jon Anderson had left. The group's management teamed the remaining members with Geoff Downes and Trevor Horn, who as Buggles had topped the charts with *Video Killed The Radio Star*. This combination cut a final LP *Drama* before splitting – Downes and Howe formed Asia with Carl Palmer and Anderson worked with Greek keyboard star Vangelis. By 1983 Yes had reformed with Anderson, bass player Chris Squire and drummer Alan White from previous line-ups, together with guitarist Trevor Rabin and Tony Kaye, the group's original keyboard man. When a new Yes LP *90125* came out Britain showed little interest, but it became one of the biggest albums of the year in America.

The year's chart debutants included reggae/ska performers Greyhound, the Pioneers and Dave and Ansil Collins, who took *Double Barrel* to number one, a Scots group calling themselves Middle of the Road who had a number one hit with *Chirpy Chirpy Cheep Cheep* and the New Seekers, whose *I'd Like To Teach The World To Sing* topped the chart just after Christmas, no doubt helped by its concurrent use as a Coca Cola TV commercial. Norman Smith, a studio engineer who had worked with the Beatles and Pink Floyd, changed his first name to Hurricane and reached the top 5 twice within ten months, and a young Scottish group called the Bay City Rollers made their chart debut with a remake of the Gentrys' *Keep On Dancing*, supervised by Jonathan King who also masterminded a top 3 hit by the Piglets, *Johnny Reggae*. Ashton,

Below left: Songwriter turned performer Carole King with James Taylor, who took her composition, You've Got a Friend, to the top of the American charts in 1971.

Below right: The Osmonds (pictured here with sister Marie and youngest brother Jimmy) who hit the British singles chart 25 times in various combinations between 1972 and 1976.

Above: The Sweet: Brian Connolly (vocals), Andy Scott (guitar), Steve Priest (bass) and Mick Tucker (drums).

Right: Isaac Hayes helped transform soul music into disco in the early seventies.

Gardner and Dyke and John Kongos scored with a couple of heavily rhythmic singles, but of far greater staying power was Gilbert O'Sullivan, who despite the contrived name had a genuine talent as a piano playing singer/songwriter, and whose major fame lasted for the first half of the 1970s, during which he topped the UK singles chart with both *Clair* and *Get Down*.

The biggest new sound of the year in Britain, despite all these newcomers, was undoubtedly 'glitter rock', the main proponents of which were Slade, the Sweet and Marc Bolan's T. Rex, who spent ten weeks during the year at number one. The Osmonds, from America were not really part of this movement, but appealed to a similar audience in Britain a year later. They opened their US chart account during 1971 with a pair of number ones: *One Bad Apple*, recorded by all five brothers (who had worked on the televised *Andy Williams Show* during the 1960s), and *Go Away Little Girl*, a solo by Donny.

By mid-1976 25 singles by various Osmond family members had reached the British chart, including a trio of number ones for Donny in *Puppy Love*, *The Twelfth Of Never* and *Young Love*, a group chart topper in *Love Me For A Reason* and, worst of all, *Long Haired Lover From Liverpool* by 'Little' Jimmy Osmond, the baby brother of the quintet. Their sister Marie scored both solo and in duet with Donny. The Osmond family fell from popularity almost as fast as they had acquired it. Nevertheless, they

were a remarkable phenomenon of the early 1970s, a description which also seems to apply to the Sweet, an English quartet who had been trying to make it since 1968. When they began working with producer Phil Wainman and songwriters/producers Nicky Chinn and Mike Chapman their luck changed, at virtually the same time as they adopted a glitter rock image, wearing copious amounts of make-up and dressing in somewhat androgynous style. From 1971, when *Co-Co* reached number two until early 1974 when *Teenage Rampage* did likewise the Sweet were rarely absent from the UK chart but following a dispute between the group and Chinn and Chapman their hits became sporadic and then stopped. Vocalist Brian Connolly tried for solo fame without success, and reunions failed to restore the Sweet to their former glory.

A similar fate appeared to have befallen Slade, a quartet who had formed in the 1960s and had gone through at least two name changes before thundering into the chart with a raucous version of a song by Little Richard, *Get Down And Get With It*. This opened the floodgates for a remarkable string of consistent and mostly self-

written hits, six of which topped the chart in Britain – *Coz I Luv You, Take Me Bak 'Ome, Mama Weer All Crazee Now, Cum On Feel The Noize, Skweeze Me Pleeze Me* and possibly the finest of all, *Merry Xmas Everybody*. Three albums also topped the British chart but despite several attempts to conquer the United States the group's studied illiteracy meant nothing to Americans, and by late 1977 even their British fans seemed finally to have deserted them.

It wasn't until Slade were booked as last-minute replacements for the 1980 Reading Festival that the tide changed again, as the crowd demanded to hear *Merry Xmas Everybody* on a sunny summer afternoon. Ever since then the group have charted consistently in Britain, as well as finally making it in America.

Soul music spawned two major newcomers in Isaac Hayes and Al Green, who followed his chart debut *Tired Of Being Alone* with his biggest hit *Let's Stay Together*, an American number one, but by the second half of the decade he had become a preacher. Isaac Hayes, a songwriter turned performer, was never able to equal his US chart-topping success with *Theme From Shaft*, from a black American cops and robbers movie.

Folk and country music provided a few new stars, notably John Denver, whose real name was John Deutschendorf. He had served an apprenticeship during the 1960s with the Chad Mitchell Trio before writing a hit for Peter, Paul and Mary, *Leaving On A Jet Plane*. After that he embarked on a solo career which first bore fruit during 1971 with a huge hit *Take Me Home, Country Roads*. His career peaked in 1974/75 with two US number one singles in each year. The best of these was surely *Annie's Song*, which also topped the British chart but curiously remains Denver's only solo British hit single.

Rather more consistent were Canadian band the Guess Who, whose members included latter-day stars Randy Bachman and Burton Cummings. By 1971 the group had reached the US top 40 ten times, most successfully with *American Woman*, after which Bachman left to launch Bachman-Turner Overdrive. His departure was followed a few years later by Cummings', who began an extremely successful solo career.

Ex-computer programmer Harry Nilsson's 1967 debut LP *Pandemonium Shadow Show* attracted praise from both the media and Nilsson's rivals. The record-buying public seemed less convinced until 1972, when *Without You* provided his only number one, hitting the top on both sides of the Atlantic. Later Nilsson became a good friend of John Lennon, who produced a few later releases, but the spark which made *Without You* so memorable remained elusive.

An interesting direction for British popular music seemed equally elusive during a year dominated by glitter rock, and America, besotted by the Osmonds, came up with less than ever before.

CURRENT EVENTS

25 January: A coup d'état led by Major General Idi Amin deposes Uganda's President Milton Obote.

9 February: An earthquake in the San Fernando Valley, California, results in 62 deaths and $1000 million worth of damage, but house construction work continues along the San Andreas fault.

15 February: The UK adopts a decimal currency.

24 February: The UK government passes legislation restricting the right of Commonwealth citizens to settle in the UK.

25 March: Fighting breaks out between Pakistan and East Pakistan following the collapse of talks on self-rule. The Independence movement is crushed, after 10,000 die in two days.

22 April: The death is announced of Haitian President François Duvalier. His son, Jean-Claude, is 'sworn in for life'.

31 July: Apollo 15's crewmen roam the surface of the moon in a specially designed vehicle.

9 August: Northern Ireland police invoke emergency powers of preventive detention without trial and begin arresting suspected IRA members.

6 September: A young girl caught in a gun battle between troops and snipers in Northern Ireland is the 100th person to die since the 'troubles' began in 1969.

13 September: 28 prisoners are killed in a riot at Attica Prison, New York.

24 September: The UK government orders the permanent expulsion of 105 Soviet representatives, charging them with espionage.

3 November: After 219 IRA suspects have been detained, the Royal Ulster Constabulary announces that guns will be carried on patrol.

5 November: The three editors of *Oz* magazine, sentenced to imprisonment for offences under the Obscene Publications Act, have their convictions and sentences quashed by the Appeal Court, who find that the judge misdirected the jury.

24 November: A hijacker parachutes from a jet airliner over Washington State after collecting a ransom of $200,000.

3 December: India declares that full-scale war has begun with Pakistan, after recognizing the Bangla Desh rebel government as the government of East Pakistan.

FILMS

Beyond The Valley Of The Dolls
A Clockwork Orange
Death In Venice
Fiddler On The Roof
The French Connection
Get Carter
The Go Between
Gumshoe
Kelly's Heroes
Klute
The Last Picture Show
Mad Dogs And Englishmen
McCabe And Mrs Miller
The Railway Children
Shaft
Summer of '42
Sunday Bloody Sunday

DEATHS

Duane Allman, rock guitarist
Louis Armstrong, jazz musician
King Curtis, saxophonist
George Jackson, 'Soledad brother'
Nikita Krushchev, Soviet statesman
Harold Lloyd, film star
Jim Morrison, rock singer
Junior Parker, R&B singer
Gene Vincent, rock'n'roller

Below left: Joe Cocker (left) and Leon Russell (right) in Mad Dogs And Englishmen (A and M/Creative Film Associates, 1971).

Below right: President Richard M. Nixon shakes hands with his loyal supporter, Elvis A. Presley.

USA CHART TOPPERS

TITLE	ARTIST	LABEL	WEEKS AT NO. 1
My Sweet Lord	George Harrison	Apple	3
Knock Three Times	Dawn	Bell	3
One Bad Apple	The Osmonds	MGM	5
Me And Bobby McGee	Janis Joplin	Columbia	2
Just My Imagination	The Temptations	Gordy	2
Joy To The World	Three Dog Night	Dunhill	6
Brown Sugar	The Rolling Stones	Rolling Stones	2
Want Ads	The Honey Cone	Hot Wax	1
It's Too Late	Carole King	Ode	5
Indian Reservation	The Raiders	Columbia	1
You've Got A Friend	James Taylor	Warner Bros	1
How Can You Mend A Broken Heart	The Bee Gees	Atco	4
Uncle Albert/Admiral Halsey	Paul and Linda McCartney	Apple	1
Go Away Little Girl	Donny Osmond	MGM	3
Maggie May	Rod Stewart	Mercury	5
Gypsies, Tramps And Thieves	Cher	Kapp	2
Theme From Shaft	Isaac Hayes	Enterprise	2
Family Affair	Sly and the Family Stone	Epic	3
Brand New Key	Melanie	Neighbourhood	1

UK CHART TOPPERS

TITLE	ARTIST	LABEL	WEEKS AT NO. 1
I Hear You Knocking	Dave Edmunds	MAM	2
Grandad	Clive Dunn	Columbia	3
My Sweet Lord	George Harrison	Apple	5
Baby Jump	Mungo Jerry	Dawn	2
Hot Love	T. Rex	Fly	6
Double Barrel	Dave and Ansell Collins	Technique	2
Knock Three Times	Dawn	Bell	5
Chirpy Chirpy Cheep Cheep	Middle Of The Road	RCA	5
Get It On	T. Rex	Fly	4
I'm Still Waiting	Diana Ross	Tamla Motown	3
Hey Girl Don't Bother Me	The Tams	Probe	3
Maggie May	Rod Stewart	Mercury	5
Cos I Love You	Slade	Polydor	4
Ernie	Benny Hill	Columbia	3

Made in England

1971

SIDE ONE
45 RPM
STEREO

Maggie May

ALL RIGHTS OF THE MANUFACTURER AND OF THE OWNER OF THE RECORDED WORK RESERVED UNAUTHORISED PUBLIC PERFORMANCE BROADCASTING AND COPYING OF THIS RECORD PROHIBITED

Right: The two most famous Americans of the era? President Richard M. Nixon shakes hands with his loyal supporter, Elvis A. Presley.

157

ARGENT

JACKSON BROWNE

DAVID CASSIDY

CHI-LITES

ALICE COOPER

DOOBIE BROTHERS

DR HOOK

EAGLES

ELECTRIC LIGHT ORCHESTRA

ROBERTA FLACK

GENESIS

GARY GLITTER

LINDISFARNE

Made in England

1972

SIDE ONE
45 RPM
STEREO

Take It Easy

ALL RIGHTS OF THE MANUFACTURER AND OF THE OWNER OF THE RECORDED WORK RESERVED. UNAUTHORISED PUBLIC PERFORMANCE BROADCASTING AND COPYING OF THIS RECORD PROHIBITED

158

Novelty records like *Amazing Grace*, played on bagpipes by the Royal Scots Dragoon Guards and a smutty song by Chuck Berry titled *My Ding-A-Ling* topped the UK singles chart for a month each. The number of charismatic new names was substantial. Among them David Cassidy and Gary Glitter joined the ranks of the glitter rockers.

Cassidy enjoyed mass adulation between 1972 and 1975, scoring nine UK top 20 hits to add to his five as singer with the Partridge Family. Although in his native America his solo career was brief Britain sent two solo singles *How Can I Be Sure* and *Daydreamer* to number one.

Gary Glitter was previously known as Paul Raven, whose only distinction was involvement with the original double album of *Jesus Christ Superstar*. His first single as Gary Glitter, *Rock & Roll (Parts One & Two)*, hovered just below the chart for four

months. Part One was virtually completely instrumental. Finally Part Two became the first of 11 UK top 10 hits before mid-1975, including three number ones – *I'm The Leader Of The Gang*, *I Love You Love Me Love* and *Always Yours* – before the 'double G' broke with his mentors and slid back into obscurity at the end of the 1970s. At the start of the 1980s he returned with a few minor hits.

Allied to glitter rock visually but not musically were Roxy Music and David Bowie. Since his 1969 smash with *Space Oddity* Bowie had kept a low profile, but an imaginative new manager Tony De Fries acquired a new recording contract for him and Bowie returned with a new androgynous image. After two transitionary albums he received vast acclaim for his 1972 LP *The Rise And Fall Of Ziggy Stardust And The Spiders From Mars*, which firmly established Bowie as an international star. This

heralded a string of more than 30 hit singles
which continues today. Only a handful have
reached number one, including a reissue of
Space Oddity, a sequel to it in *Ashes To
Ashes* and a one-off collaboration with
Queen titled *Under Pressure* in 1981.

As far as America was concerned Bowie
had even fewer hits, his only transatlantic
number one before a major resurgence in
1983 being with *Fame*, a song co-written
with John Lennon in 1975.

Bowie became by far the most enduring
star of the post-Beatle period by clever
manipulation of the media and by restricting
his output until each fresh direction he
conceives is fully realized. His adoption of
Philadelphia soul in the mid-1970s, followed
by European synthesizer music in the late
1970s and then by white soul again in the
1980s has enabled this chameleon-like
figure to remain ahead of his rivals.

Roxy Music established themselves in
1972 with *Virginia Plain* and a series of
highly successful LPs before announcing a
temporary hiatus in 1976 to allow various

group members to pursue solo projects.
Leader/singer Bryan Ferry cut solo albums
with some success, sax player Andy
Mackay did likewise, but achieved more
commercially by writing the score for a
fictional TV series about popular music
titled *Rock Follies*. Guitarist Phil Manzanera
launched his own group, 801, and synthesist
Brian Eno released a series of obtuse LPs on
his well named Obscure label. By 1978 the
group reconvened for a new LP *Manifesto*,
which spawned two big hit singles in *Dance
Away* and *Angel Eyes*. Subsequent releases
were sporadic and produced such excellent
LPs as *Flesh And Blood* (1980) and *Avalon*
(1982) as well as *Jealous Guy*, their tribute to
John Lennon which was to be their only
number one single. In 1984 it was announced that the group had broken up in
the wake of the formation of a new group
featuring Mackay and Manzanera.

Among the other emerging groups who
probably appealed to the Roxy audience
were Genesis and Electric Light Orchestra.
Formed at their public school, Charterhouse,

towards the end of the 1960s, Genesis were patronized early on by another Old Carthusian Jonathan King who oversaw their debut LP. Its lack of success failed to deter the group, who acquired a new record deal and amassed a formidable following. In 1975 singer and focal point Peter Gabriel left to pursue solo success and drummer Phil Collins, already a member of the group, became the replacement vocalist. The group became even more popular and both *Duke* (1980) and *Abacab* (1981) topped the UK album chart. Since the departure of guitarist Steve Hackett in 1977 the core of Genesis has consisted of guitarist Mike Rutherford, keyboard player Tony Banks and Collins, all of whom have released solo records, the greatest success by far accruing to Collins who captured the public's imagination during the 1980s as a singer/songwriter, as we shall see.

Electric Light Orchestra initially formed as a splinter group from the Move in late 1971 featuring Move members Roy Wood, Bev Bevan and Jeff Lynne. The idea behind ELO was to develop the sound achieved by the Beatles on *I Am The Walrus* from *Magical Mystery Tour*, which mingled string arrangements and a traditional rock rhythm section. Roy Wood left the group after their first album to form Wizzard. While UK success came relatively easily for ELO it took several lengthy tours before America capitulated on the strength of albums like

Eldorado and *A New World Record*. By 1977, when *Out Of The Blue* attracted advance orders worth nearly $50 million they were established as superstars. New albums since then have emerged every two years, the only exception being 1980 when the group were involved in *Xanadu*, the rock fantasy movie starring Olivia Newton-John. ELO combined with her to top the UK chart with the title track. 1984 saw the group in between albums and the apparent restlessness of some members makes the group's future unsure.

The destiny of another British group founded in 1972, 10 cc, is somewhat clearer. Founded by four friends from Manchester – hit songwriter Graham Gouldman, ex-Mindbenders' guitarist Eric Stewart and studio whizkids Kevin Godley and Lol Creme – 10 cc came into being when Gouldman joined the other three, who had scored a freak hit in 1970 with *Neanderthal Man* using the name Hotlegs. The new group's first single *Donna* was turned down by major labels before being signed to Jonathan King's UK Records. After four top 10 hits on UK in Britain they signed with Mercury, for whom they cut a worldwide chart-topping single *I'm Not In Love* in 1976 before Godley and Creme left the band to develop work on an instrument they had named the gizmo. Gouldman and Steward recruited new members, while Godley and Creme recorded as a duo, before becoming notable video makers during the 1980s. Gouldman wrote film scores and also formed a duo with Andrew Gold in 1984, Common Knowledge, while Stewart occasionally worked with Paul McCartney. However, official statements confirm the continued existence of the parent group.

Other groups successful in 1972 have not survived. Argent, whose biggest hit came with *Hold Your Head Up*, broke up in 1976; the Strawbs, whose finest moment came with *Lay Down*, folded although they occasionally re-form and Derek and the Dominoes, the shortlived quartet fronted by Eric Clapton, released only one classic album, *Layla*, before Clapton moved on.

In America some bands like the Raspberries, whose *Overnight Sensation* was their masterpiece and Steely Dan, who produced a string of brilliant LPs like *Can't Buy A Thrill*, *Pretzel Logic* and *The Royal Scam*, simpled folded because they didn't feel like carrying on. But the Doobie Brothers, who were always of more interest in America than Britain, kept going until early 1982.

Country rock developed from the work of the Byrds largely through Gram Parsons, briefly a Byrd and later one of the founders of the Flying Burrito Brothers. The biggest stars, the Eagles, owed much to their pioneering forebears. Ex-Burrito Bernie

Leadon, Randy Meisner, previously with Rick Nelson and Poco, plus relative new-comers Glenn Frey and Don Henley first joined forces to back Linda Ronstadt, but were signed by the recently formed Asylum label and recorded their debut LP in England with producer Glyn Johns. The album spawned several US hit singles but their major breakthrough came in 1975 with a fourth LP, *One Of These Nights*, which included two American number ones in the title track and *Best Of My Love.* By then guitarist Don Felder had been added and after *One Of These Nights* Joe Walsh, previously of the James Gang and Barnstorm, was introduced to replace the departing Bernie Leadon. The first Eagles LP with Walsh, *Hotel California*, was still more successful with two more chart-topping singles in *New Kid In Town* and the title track, but Meisner then left. He was replaced by another ex-Poco member, Tim Schmit, but the group continued to crumble.

The first hit single by the Eagles *Take It Easy* was in fact co-written with singer/songwriter Jackson Browne who was also signed to Asylum. His own debut LP was largely passed over, but by 1976 he had broken through with a top 5 LP, *The Pretender.* He followed it in 1978 with the equally successful *Running On Empty*. The album included a slightly lyrically amended version of Maurice Williams' *Stay*, which took him into the top 20 of the singles chart on both sides of the Atlantic, but his subsequent work has been patchy.

Left: The predominant act of the country/rock genre, the Eagles: (left to right) Randy Meisner, Glenn Frey, Don Henley, Bernie Leadon and Don Felder.

Right: Dr Hook and the Medicine Show achieved their greatest success after moderating the humorous aspects of their highly entertaining live show.

Dr Hook had started their career as a dope-oriented comedy group. Although this type of material brought them hits like *Sylvia's Mother* and *The Cover Of The 'Rolling Stone'*, their popularity was waning until they recorded *A Little Bit More*, featuring the pathos-filled voice of lead singer Dennis Locorriere. Although their hit singles had tapered off by 1981 the group continued to sell LPs in reasonable quantites and can look forward to a comfortable career in cabaret.

Alice Cooper, a name which applied to both the group and its leader/vocalist Vincent Furnier, were signed by Frank Zappa to his record label. Zappa's logic was that anyone that bad (their act had emptied a Hollywood club) must be good, seemed incorrect after the group's first two LPs failed. Eventually in 1971 a top 30 single *Eighteen* was followed by *School's Out*, which reached the top 10 in America and topped the British charts in 1972, heralding several more hits before his backing band left Cooper. After assembling a new group Alice's weakness for alcohol forced him to rest. Ever resourceful, Cooper used the cure he undertook for his drinking problem as the basis of a new album *From The Inside* in 1978.

The New York Dolls were a quintet whose attitude, apparel and approach to music made them reviled by the establishment on both sides of the Atlantic several years before Johnny Rotten first mimed to an Alice Cooper record (ironically) as his audition for the Sex Pistols. The behaviour of the Dolls was mirrored by the Pistols – on their first visit to London, Dolls drummer Billy Murcia died of a drug overdose, but even that didn't prevent the group quickly acquiring a record deal. Their first LP was wrapped in a sleeve guaranteed to outrage but any advantage gained by their visual

image was lost by the poor quality of their music. A second LP, prophetically titled *Too Much Too Soon*, suffered from similar drawbacks and the band exploded into several different factions in 1975. Vocalist David Johansen was the most successful ex-Doll, releasing several critically acclaimed solo LPs, although guitarist Johnny Thunders and replacement drummer Jerry Nolan were active during the late 1970s in the Heartbreakers, a group whose initial promise was never realized.

The most influential soul sounds came from a new label Philadelphia International formed by songwriters/producers Kenny Gamble, Leon Huff and Thom Bell. They built on the openings created by groups like the Delfonics and the Intruders (who became part of their empire) to create a softer, sweeter type of soul music than the previous giants of Stax and early Motown. The best acts attached to Philly (as the label was known) were the O'Jays, who broke through with *Backstabbers* in 1972 and topped the US chart the following year with *Love Train*; Harold Melvin and the Bluenotes, whose *If You Don't Know Me By Now* helped the group's lead singer Teddy Pendergrass to later solo fame and Billy Paul, who topped the US chart in 1972 with *Me And Mrs Jones*.

Thom Bell launched the Spinners (known in Britain as the Detroit Spinners) to a fresh burst of chart activity in the mid-1970s, although not as big as another of his 'clients', the Stylistics. The Chi-Lites enjoyed three great years at the start of the 1970s, particularly with the timeless *Have You Seen Her* and their only US chart topper, *Oh Girl*. Bill Withers reached the top 3 in America three times in the early 1970s with *Ain't No Sunshine*, *Lean On Me* and *Use Me*. Billy Preston topped the US chart twice during this period with *Will It Go Round In Circles*

Opposite top: The charismatic Alice Cooper with one of his many props, a live snake.

Opposite bottom: The soulful Roberta Flack whose haunting version of The First Time Ever I Saw Your Face *was featured in the Clint Eastwood film* Play Misty For Me.

and *Nothing From Nothing* and the gospel-influenced Staple Singers topped the chart in 1972 with *I'll Take You There* and repeated their success with *Let's Do It Again* in 1975.

Roberta Flack's version of the folk song *The First Time Ever I Saw Your Face* topped the US singles chart after being featured in the Clint Eastwood film *Play Misty For Me*. Roberta returned to number one the following year, 1973, with *Killing Me Softly With His Song* and again in 1974 with *Feel Like Makin' Love*, also scoring several hit duets with Donny Hathaway until the latter's death in 1979.

Don McLean succeeded with the brilliant *American Pie*, which he followed with another huge hit *Vincent* (about the painter Van Gogh), while in Britain Lindisfarne's second LP *Fog On The Tyne* topped the UK album chart for four weeks and also included two British top 5 singles. The group split up during the mid-1970s but reunited in their original form at the end of the decade, returning to the top 10 with a new single *Run For Home*.

Van Morrison launched himself to superstardom when he moved to live in the USA after leaving Them. His first hit, *Brown Eyed Girl*, was produced by veteran R&B hitmaker Bert Berns but after Berns died Van moved into a more poetic musical field with *Astral Weeks*, an album acclaimed as a masterpiece by the critics. Nevertheless it sold considerably less than many of his subsequent albums which continue to appear regularly.

Meanwhile American music, which had led the way since the psychedelic era, began to slide downhill.

TITLE	ARTIST	LABEL	WEEKS AT NO. 1
Brand New Key	Melanie	Neighbour-hood	2
American Pie	Don McLean	United Artists	4
Let's Stay Together	Al Green	Hi	1
Without You	Nilsson	RCA	4
Heart Of Gold	Neil Young	Reprise	1
A Horse With No Name	America	Warner Bros	3
The First Time Ever I Saw Your Face	Roberta Flack	Atlantic	6
Oh Girl	The Chi-Lites	Brunswick	1
I'll Take You There	Staple Singers	Stax	1
The Candy Man	Sammy Davis Jr	MGM	3
Song Sung Blue	Neil Diamond	Uni	1
Lean On Me	Bill Withers	Sussex	3
Alone Again (Naturally)	Gilbert O'Sullivan	MAM	6
Brandy	Looking Glass	Epic	1
Black And White	Three Dog Night	Dunhill	1
Baby Don't Get Hooked On Me	Mac Davis	Columbia	3
Ben	Michael Jackson	Motown	1
My Ding-A-Ling	Chuck Berry	Chess	2
I Can See Clearly Now	Johnny Nash	Epic	4
Papa Was A Rolling Stone	The Temptations	Gordy	1
I Am Woman	Helen Reddy	Capitol	1
Me And Mrs Jones	Billy Paul	Philadelphia International	2

TITLE	ARTIST	LABEL	WEEKS AT NO. 1
Ernie	Benny Hill	Columbia	1
I'd Like To Teach The World To Sing	New Seekers	Polydor	4
Telegram Sam	T. Rex	T. Rex	2
Son Of My Father	Chicory Tip	CBS	4
Without You	Nilsson	RCA	4
Amazing Grace	Royal Scots Dragoon Guards	RCA	5
Metal Guru	T.Rex	EMI	4
Vincent	Don McLean	United Artists	2
Take Me Bak 'Ome	Slade	Polydor	1
Puppy Love	Donny Osmond	MGM	5
School's Out	Alice Cooper	Warner Bros	3
You Wear It Well	Rod Stewart	Mercury	1
Mama Weer All Crazee Now	Slade	Polydor	3
How Can I Be Sure?	David Cassidy	Bell	2
Mouldy Old Dough	Lt Pigeon	Decca	4
Clair	Gilbert O'Sullivan	MAM	2
My Ding-A-Ling	Chuck Berry	Chess	4
Long Haired Lover From Liverpool	Little Jimmy Osmond	MGM	1

Dan Blocker, Hoss in the TV show *Bonanza*
Les Harvey, guitarist
J. Edgar Hoover, FBI boss
Mahalia Jackson, gospel singer
Clyde McPhatter, R&B singer
Billy Murcia, New York Doll
Berry Oakley, Allman Brother
J. Arthur Rank, industrialist
Rory Storme, Merseybeat pioneer
Danny Whitten, guitarist

The Concert For Bangla Desh
Deliverance
Diamonds Are Forever
Dirty Harry
Fritz The Cat
The Godfather
The Harder They Come
Junior Bonner
Play It Again Sam
Play Misty For Me
Silent Running
Straw Dogs
Superfly
What's Up Doc?
Young Winston

9 January: The retired ocean liner *Queen Elizabeth* is destroyed by fire in Hong Kong harbour.

9 January: A telephone caller purporting to be millionaire recluse Howard Hughes explains that Clifford Irving's biography of him is a fake.

30 January: Bloody Sunday: 13 civilians are killed by soldiers as violence erupts during an illegal protest march by Catholics in Londonderry.

2 February: The British embassy in Dublin is burned down by protesters.

28 February: British coal miners return to work after a seven-week strike, which crippled the industry and forced large-scale power cuts.

7 April: Joey Gallo, said to have been the leader of the Mafia, is killed in New York.

18 April: Bangla Desh joins the Commonwealth of Nations.

19 May: After bomb disposal experts parachute in, a bomb scare on the *QE2* turns out to have been a hoax.

22 May: Ceylon becomes the Republic of Sri Lanka.

30 May: Three Japanese gunmen employed by Palestinian guerrillas kill 25 and wound 76 at Lod International Airport in Israel.

1 June: Andreas Baader, leader of a West German guerrilla gang, is captured by Frankfurt police after a gun battle. Ulrike Meinhof is arrested in Hanover two weeks later.

21 July: 13 people die when the IRA explode 22 bombs in 80 minutes in Belfast.

5 August: Idi Amin announces that all Asians with UK passports will be expelled within three months.

12 August: US planes make their heaviest bombing raids ever on North Vietnam. US troop strength in South Vietnam is now down to 39,000.

5 September: Palestinian terrorists from the Black September organisation kill Israeli Olympic team members and disrupt the Games in Munich.

10 October: Sir John Betjeman becomes poet laureate.

7 November: Nixon defeats McGovern to retain his Presidency.

10 November: Letter bombs go off in London.

23 December: Severe earthquakes shake Nicaragua.

31 December: Sectarian killings in Northern Ireland now total 676.

Made in England

1972

SIDE ONE
45 RPM
STEREO

Take It Easy

1973

SIDE ONE
45 RPM
STEREO

Tie A Yellow Ribbon

Made in England

The previous year's general lack of substance continued during 1973, with the top position in the UK singles chart occupied for more than half the year by one or other of the Osmonds, Gary Glitter, David Cassidy, Sweet or Slade, none of whom topped the US chart that year. Also several more acts said to be of the glitter persuasion inhabited the upper part of the chart, including Queen, Suzi Quatro, Alvin Stardust, Mud and Wizzard.

Few of these names were really involved in glitter rock other than visually. Wizzard, for instance, were led by Roy Wood, formerly of the Move and briefly of ELO and while Wood had a penchant for lurid make-up, the group's music contained infinitely more depth. Using his knowledge of and love for the work of Phil Spector, Wood constructed a series of hits which still sound credible today. He started with *Ball Park Incident*, which made the top 10, continuing with two number ones, *See My Baby Jive* and *Angel Fingers*, before ending a triumphant year with *I Wish It Could Be Christmas Everyday*. 1974 saw two more top 10 singles by the group, while Wood also made the chart with four smaller solo hits between 1973 and 1975, as well as writing two songs recorded by Elvis Presley and playing on a Beach Boys album. Wizzard broke up in 1975 and Wood has never quite returned to chart glory.

Detroit-born Suzi Quatro was spotted by Mickie Most, who brought her to Britain and

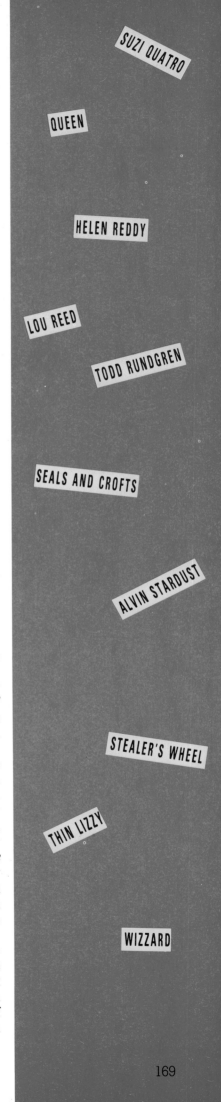

SUZI QUATRO

QUEEN

HELEN REDDY

LOU REED

TODD RUNDGREN

SEALS AND CROFTS

ALVIN STARDUST

STEALER'S WHEEL

THIN LIZZY

WIZZARD

provided a strong image to add to her attacking bass playing and strident singing, but success did not come her way until she was placed in the hands of the songwriting/producing team of Nicky Chinn and Mike Chapman, who were still scoring with the Sweet. The breakthrough came when *Can The Can* topped the chart, the first of six top 20 singles in 18 months including *48 Crash* and another chart topper *Devil Gate Drive*. Thereafter chart success has eluded her apart from sporadic hits including *Stumblin' In*, her duet with Smokie vocalist Chris Norman which reached the top 5 in America in 1979.

Another Chinnichap act who broke through in 1973 were Mud, formerly a cabaret quartet who needed original material to fulfil their promise. During their two years with the Chinnichap team Mud hit the UK top 20 11 times, making number one with *Tiger Feet*, *Lonely This Christmas* and *Oh Boy*. Their decision to write their own material at first seemed to be justified with four top 20 entries in their first year on their own. Ultimately it proved a mistake when they vanished from the chart.

A somewhat similar fate befell Alvin Stardust, although his seven hits in the years from 1973 to 1975 were not his first or last chart placings. As Shane Fenton he had scored in the early 1960s with a handful of minor hits, but ten years later he returned with a new persona based, at least partly,

on that of Gary Glitter but with black leather replacing Glitter's silver paper. Stardust/Fenton teamed up with writer/producer Peter Shelley – who himself took two soft rock hits into the UK top 5 in 1974 and 1975 – and for a year everything they touched succeeded. Stardust's biggest hit came in early 1974 with the chart-topping *Jealous Mind* but when the partnership broke up the hits ceased. However, Stardust re-emerged in 1981 reaching the top 5 with a revival of Carl Mann's late 1950s' rocker *Pretend* and charting again in 1984 with *I Feel Like Buddy Holly*.

Queen emerged in 1973 and went on to become one of the biggest and most popular groups of the 1980s. They went from

Right: The menacing Alvin Stardust, previously a chart star as Shane Fenton, enjoyed a new lease of life with his new name. His real name, incidentally, is Bernard Jewry.

Far right: Lou Reed, who achieved far greater solo fame than with the group which he left, Velvet Underground.

Below: Queen: (left to right), John Deacon, Roger Taylor, Freddie Mercury and Brian May, who survived a shaky start to become one of the most consistent hit-makers of the seventies and eighties.

Above left: Thin Lizzy, fronted by black Irish bass player/singer/songwriter Phil Lynott.

Above: Status Quo: (left to right) Alan Lancaster, John Coghlan, Rick Parfitt and Francis Rossi.

strength to strength, although their early breakthrough came in America where their first LP stayed on the chart for nearly six months despite being largely ignored in Britain. Queen were formed from the remnants of a small-time group, Smile, which included Brian May, an exceptional guitarist, and drummer Roger Taylor, respectively studying astronomy and dentistry at university, who combined with Freddie Mercury, a clothes designer turned singer and John Deacon, a bass-playing electronics graduate. Their crucial first UK hit was *Seven Seas Of Rhye* in 1974, since when the hits have been regular and often immense, like *Bohemian Rhapsody* which topped the chart for nine weeks over the winter of 1975/76, and *Under Pressure*, a collaboration between the group and David Bowie, which rose to number one in Britain at the end of 1981. Queen have frequently topped the British LP charts but solo records by various members have been far less successful. In 1985, with a dozen best-selling LPs and twice as many singles behind them, Queen are one of the top acts in the world, although the imminent release of Mercury's first solo LP in 1985 might signal a change in direction.

David Bowie's one-off single with Queen was by no means his first joint venture and many of his earlier collaborations helped to restore the uncertain fortunes of friends. In 1973 he helped Lou Reed, formerly of the Velvet Underground, to launch his solo career by supervising the recording of *Walk On The Wild Side* and the LP from which it came, *Transformer*. Reed fitted in to glam rock fairly well, although his musical inclinations were often much more interesting, particularly his consistently intriguing LPs especially *Berlin*, which reached the UK top 10 in 1973. Bowie also helped Mott

the Hoople into the charts in 1973, and worked with Iggy Pop, a relationship which would be renewed in the years ahead.

1973 saw a resurgence in heavy metal music which would continue through most of the decade. Three major groups emerged as leaders: Status Quo, Thin Lizzy and from America Lynyrd Skynyrd. Skynyrd, named after school teacher Leonard Skinner who had taught some of the group in Florida, were a bar band in Atlanta, Georgia, before Al Kooper discovered and signed them. They promoted their debut LP on a massive tour supporting the Who and by 1977 had several big-selling LPs including *Gimme Back My Bullets* and *Street Survivors*. Fronted by aggressive vocalist Ronnie Van Zant and including three lead guitarists in their line-up, the band were prime exponents of Southern boogie music, their biggest hits coming with *Free Bird* and *Sweet Home Alabama*, but their progress ended when Van Zant and two other members of the band were killed in a plane crash. Several band members regrouped as the Rossington-Collins Band but were unable to capture the magic of the original group.

Thin Lizzy were an Irish trio who moved to London before making the charts. Led by the charismatic Phil Lynott, a singer/songwriter/bass player, Lizzy first experienced chart life in 1973 with a folk/rock standard *Whisky In The Jar*, which they adapted to their R&B-based format, but failed to equal its success until 1976 when they returned to the top 10 with *The Boys Are Back In Town*, the first of a string of hits which continued until the band finally split up in 1983. Their peak years were probably 1978 and 1979 when both *Live And Dangerous* and *Black Rose* reached number two in the British LP chart, although they were not so successful in America.

171

Above: The dynamic Isley Brothers, whose classic LP, 3 + 3, included the magnificent That Lady.

The same also applied to Status Quo, who had been together for ten years when they found their niche as the premier British head-banging group. They had first attracted attention with a couple of psychedelic hits in 1968, *Pictures Of Matchstick Men* and *Ice In The Sun*, but their popularity slumped despite a return to the top 20 in 1970 with *Down The Dustpipe*. The group then decided to opt for simple guitar-based boogie. While this may have resulted in their lack of chart progress in America after their 1960s' hits, they had their first top 10 single since the psychedelic days in 1973 with *Paper Plane*, which was followed by hit singles in Britain for the next 11 years, including a 1974 chart topper *Down Down* and number one LPs with *Hello* (1973), *On The Level* (1975), *Blue For You* (1976) and *1982* (no prizes). When the group retired from live work in 1984 many saw it as the end of an era, but there seems no reason to suppose that they will also stop recording.

Two American duos made a mark during the year, although only in their own country – neither Loggins and Messina nor Seals and Crofts ever reached the UK album or singles charts. Jim Messina, who had been involved with the Buffalo Springfield and then with Poco, teamed up with singer/songwriter Kenny Loggins, previously a

session player, for what was intended to be a Loggins solo LP, but the two hit it off so well that Messina, originally hired as producer, decided to become part of the act. They stayed together until 1977 turning out eight albums, several of which went gold, and a few hit singles. After their parting Loggins became the more successful. He reached the US top 5 with *Whenever I Call You 'Friend'* and the top 10 with *I'm Alright*, the theme from the film *Caddyshack*. He also had several gold albums but his greatest success came in 1984 with another film theme, *Footloose*. The soundtrack LP topped the US chart for ten weeks just after the title track had relinquished its three-week hold on the top position in the singles chart, and both single and album made the UK top 10s.

Jim Seals and Dash Crofts both worked with a late incarnation of 1950s' hitmakers the Champs (of *Tequila* fame). The two then abandoned music, before re-emerging with a soft folk/rock sound, as opposed to their previous rock'n'roll/bluegrass leanings, and signed to Warner Brothers for whom they cut several successful LPs, as well as making the top 10 with three singles, *Summer Breeze*, *Diamond Girl* and *Get Closer*. Little, however, has been heard of them during the 1980s.

Singer/songwriter Jim Croce was already middle-aged when he scored six US top 20 singles between 1972 and 1974, but a month after *Bad, Bad Leroy Brown* had topped the US chart he was killed in a plane crash in late September 1973. Three subsequent top 10 hits included a posthumous return to number one with *Time In A Bottle*. Songs like *You Don't Mess Around With Jim* and *I'll Have To Say I Love You In A Song* remain much played items on the folk club circuit.

Tony Orlando, 1960s' New York pop star, was now fronting a trio known as Dawn and was halfway through a purple patch which produced more than a dozen US top 40 hits during the first half of the decade, including three number ones in *Knock Three Times* (1970), *Tie A Yellow Ribbon Round The Old Oak Tree* (1973) and *He Don't Love You (Like I Love You)* (1975) – the first two of which also topped the British chart.

In Britain David Essex was forging a successful partnership with producer Jeff Wayne which extended his prowess as an actor (both on stage in *Godspell* and screen in *That'll Be The Day*) into the charts. His first big hit *Rock On* was also his only major American chart voyage but in Britain he has remained consistently popular apart from a brief gap. Of his nine top 10 singles before 1983 *Gonna Make You A Star* and *Hold Me Close* topped the chart, while several more films and plays such as *Stardust* and *Evita* respectively, have kept Essex in the limelight.

Another thespian turned chart star was Helen Reddy, who moved to America after finding insufficient scope for progress in her native Australia. She finally hit the US top 20 in 1971 with *I Don't Know How To Love Him* from *Jesus Christ Superstar*, followed by three US number ones – *I Am Woman* (1972), *Delta Dawn* (1973) and *Angie Baby* (1974). Helen still records occasionally, although with rather less success.

Soul music in 1973 displayed no spectacular changes – the Detroit Emeralds became another Philly sound hit-making act, ex-Temptation Eddie Kendricks topped the US chart with *Keep On Truckin'* in 1973 and reached number two the following year with *Boogie Down*. The Isley Brothers made a welcome re-emergence with their *3 + 3* LP which included *That Lady*, a hit on both sides of the Atlantic, and *Summer Breeze*, written by Seals and Crofts, which was a further UK hit. Also in a soul vein, although he had been regarded previously as a rock artist, was Dr John, a piano-playing ex-session man from Louisiana. He scored his biggest hit single with *Right Place, Wrong Time* from his LP *Gumbo*, but thereafter drifted back into session work.

Of more commercial longevity was Todd Rundgren, a multi-instrumentalist from Philadelphia who had impressed as leader of the Nazz, a highly rated psychedelic band of the late 1960s, and had then become an expert engineer/producer. He continued his own recording career experiencing US chart action with *I Saw The Light* in 1972 and his biggest hit *Hello It's Me* in 1973 and huge critical acclaim for LPs like *Something/Anything* and *A Wizard, A True Star*. Alongside his solo work and productions for such varied acts as Hall and Oates, Grand Funk, Patti Smith and Meat Loaf, Todd also found the time to work with a band he formed, Utopia. Although he enjoys critical support for almost all his undertakings, commercial success as an artist appears to have passed him by.

Others who enjoyed more fleeting stardom included Stories, whose version of Hot Chocolate's *Brother Louie* was an American number one; Nazareth, a Scottish hard rock group, who scored hits throughout the 1970s after first charting in 1973 with *Broken Down Angel* and Stealer's Wheel, a folk rock duo of which one half was Gerry Rafferty, who made the top 10 in both Britain and America with the catchy *Stuck In The Middle With You* before Rafferty embarked on his solo career.

The most unexpected hit LP of an unspectacular year came from Mike Oldfield, a virtually unknown guitarist who almost single-handedly put together an instrumental album *Tubular Bells*, which was rejected by all the big record companies in Britain before the newly launched Virgin label decided to give Oldfield his chance. It sold over five million copies worldwide, not only making Oldfield a major star – his follow-up LP *Hergest Ridge* also topped the UK album chart – but also helping to transform Virgin Records into a larger, more successful organization.

Below: Utopia, led by the multi-talented Todd Rundgren (at microphone), have yet to achieve the success critics have frequently predicted for them.

USA CHART TOPPERS

TITLE	ARTIST	LABEL	WEEKS AT NO. 1
Me And Mrs Jones	Billy Paul	Philadelphia International	1
You're So Vain	Carly Simon	Elektra	3
Superstition	Stevie Wonder	Tamla	1
Crocodile Rock	Elton John	MCA	3
Killing Me Softly With His Song	Roberta Flack	Atlantic	5
Love Train	O'Jays	Philadelphia International	1
The Night The Lights Went Out In Georgia	Vicki Lawrence	Bell	2
Tie A Yellow Ribbon	Dawn with Tony Orlando	Bell	4
You Are The Sunshine Of My Life	Stevie Wonder	Tamla	1
Frankenstein	Edgar Winter	Epic	1
My Love	Paul McCartney and Wings	Apple	3
Give Me Love	George Harrison	Apple	1
Will It Go Round In Circles	Billy Preston	A&M	2
Big Bad Leroy Brown	Jim Croce	ABC	2
The Morning After	Maureen McGovern	20th Century	2
Touch Me In The Morning	Diana Ross	Motown	1
Brother Louie	Stories	Kama Sutra	2
Let's Get It On	Marvin Gaye	Tamla	2
Delta Dawn	Helen Reddy	Capitol	2
We're An American Band	Grand Funk Railroad	Capitol	1
Half Breed	Cher	MCA	1
Angie	The Rolling Stones	Rolling Stones	2
Midnight Train To Georgia	Gladys Knight and the Pips	Buddah	1
Keep On Truckin'	Eddie Kendricks	Tamla	2
Photograph	Ringo Starr	Apple	2
Top Of The World	The Carpenters	A&M	1
The Most Beautiful Girl	Charlie Rich	Epic	2
Time In A Bottle	Jim Croce	ABC	2

UK CHART TOPPERS

TITLE	ARTIST	LABEL	WEEKS
Long Haired Lover From Liverpool	Little Jimmy Osmond	MGM	4
Blockbuster	The Sweet	RCA	5
Cum On Feel The Noize	Slade	Polydor	4
Twelfth Of Never	Donny Osmond	MGM	1
Get Down	Gilbert O'Sullivan	MAM	2
Tie A Yellow Ribbon	Dawn with Tony Orlando	Bell	4
See My Baby Jive	Wizzard	Harvest	4
Can The Can	Suzi Quatro	Rak	1
Rubber Bullets	10 cc	UK	1
Skweeze Me Pleeze Me	Slade	Polydor	3
Welcome Home	Peters and Lee	Philips	1
I'm The Leader Of The Gang	Gary Glitter	Bell	4
Young Love	Donny Osmond	MGM	4
Angel Fingers	Wizzard	Harvest	1
Eye Level	Simon Park Orchestra	Columbia	4
Day Dreamer	David Cassidy	Bell	3
I Love You Love Me Love	Gary Glitter	Bell	4
Merry Xmas Everybody	Slade	Polydor	2

DEATHS

Eddie Condon, jazz musician
Jim Croce, singer
Bobby Darin, singer
Lyndon Johnson, former US President
Gene Krupa, jazz drummer
Bruce Lee, Kung Fu film star
Gram Parsons, country rocker
Pablo Picasso, painter
Edward G. Robinson, film star
J.R. Tolkien, author
Clarence White, Byrds guitarist

FILMS

American Graffiti
The Day Of The Jackal
The Getaway
Jesus Christ Superstar
Last Tango In Paris
Live And Let Die
The Long Goodbye
Mean Streets
Oh Lucky Man
The Paper Chase
Paper Moon
Pat Garrett And Billy The Kid
Sleuth
That'll Be The Day

1 January: The UK becomes a member of the EEC.

27 January: A Vietnam peace agreement is formally signed in Paris.

30 January: Two former officials of Nixon's re-election campaign committee, Liddy and McCord, are found guilty of attempting to spy on the Democratic headquarters in the Watergate Building.

27 February: Wounded Knee, South Dakota, is occupied by the American Indian Movement, demanding an investigation into the Federal treatment of Indians.

29 March: The last American prisoners of war are released from North Vietnam.

14 May: Skylab is launched from Cape Kennedy.

17 May: The Watergate Hearings begin in Washington, after allegations that White House officials knew about the break-in and installation of spying equipment.

7 June: Famine threatens wide areas of Latin America, Asia, Africa and the Middle East following the worst prolonged droughts for 25 years.

25 June: President Nixon becomes implicated in the Watergate affair.

18 August: The IRA sends a series of letter bombs, which disrupts the postal service.

11 September: President Allende is overthrown in a military coup in Chile. General Ugarte succeeds him.

16 September: UNICEF reports that over 50,000 have died in a famine in Ethiopia.

11 October: The Middle East conflict breaks out again. An Israeli tank force breaks through Syrian defences and pushes past 1967 cease-fire lines.

16 October: The Nobel Peace Prize is awarded to Henry Kissinger for his part in the Vietnam peace talks.

3 November: A worldwide oil crisis sees prices raised, and ration books printed up for use in the UK. They are never used.

17 November: During a speech in Florida, Nixon insists 'I am not a crook'.

6 December: Gerald Ford is sworn in as Vice President after Spiro Agnew resigns over tax evasion charges.

Left: A still from That'll Be The Day, *the movie starring David Essex (left) and Ringo Starr which successfully evoked the teddy boy era (Goodtimes, 1973).*

Made in England

1973

SIDE ONE
45 RPM
STEREO

Tie A Yellow Ribbon

ALL RIGHTS OF THE MANUFACTURER AND OF THE OWNER OF THE RECORDED WORK RESERVED. UNAUTHORISED PUBLIC PERFORMANCE BROADCASTING AND COPYING OF THIS RECORD PROHIBITED

Made in England

1974

SIDE ONE
45 RPM
STEREO

Waterloo

As the decade approached halfway it seemed that Britain and America were largely following separate paths. Britain was still gripped by teenybop mania, while in the USA there was no discernible change from the music of the late 1960s. Some of the names were different of course; while in Britain Slade, Mud, Suzi Quatro, Alvin Stardust, Gary Glitter, the Osmonds and David Essex appeared at the top of the chart, joined by new contenders like the Rubettes, Paper Lace and Abba. High chart positions were also achieved by the Bay City Rollers, Showaddywaddy, Pilot and Kenny.

Some of these acts like Kenny, who enjoyed a few months of glory at the end of the year with *The Bump*, and Paper Lace, who topped the UK chart with *Billy Don't Be A Hero* followed by *The Night Chicago Died* (top 3 in Britain and number one in America), were transient in their appeal and neither the Rubettes nor Pilot lived up to their early promise.

The Rubettes were launched with *Sugar Baby Love*, a four-week British chart-topper, and made the top 40 eight more times before disappearing, their best single being *I Can Do It* in 1975. Pilot, whose forebears included the Bay City Rollers, seemed to bring a touch of class to their finest record, *January*, a chart topper in early 1975, but also quickly disappeared. Ex-Bay City Rollers among the band might have wished that they had stayed put in view of the remarkable success of that Edinburgh quintet but, in truth, the Rollers were popular between 1974 and 1976 by virtue of their image and teenybop appeal rather than their music.

Having made the top 10 in 1971 under the aegis of Jonathan King, a series of personnel changes plus a new songwriting and production team of Bill Martin and Phil Coulter brought the Rollers to the top of the teeny-bop tree. Another facet in their run of nine top 10 singles in succession, including chart toppers in Britain with *Bye Bye Baby* and *Give A Little Love* in 1975, was their manager Tam Paton, who not only created a mystique around the group but also master-minded their 'uniform', which included large quantities of tartan material and trousers which were too short. The effect on Britain's pre-teens echoed that of the Beatles a decade before, with platinum LPs following the hit singles, but after 1976 the group concentrated their efforts on America, where they had scored a number one single in 1975 with *Saturday Night*. They did manage a few more hits but, in the wake of punk rock, they were forgotten.

Showaddywaddy, in contrast, rode out the punk era, scoring hits every year from 1974 to 1982 with a style and image derived from the 1950s, an era whose hits they successfully copied to the tune of over 20 UK top 40 entries including *Three Steps To Heaven* and *I Wonder Why*. In 1976 their cover of Curtis Lee's *Under The Moon Of Love* reached number one, while their two *Greatest Hits* albums both went platinum. Their highly visual stage act will no doubt keep them working in cabaret until they decide to retire.

While European acts like Focus and Golden Earring from the Netherlands and Tangerine Dream and Can from Germany also enjoyed chart action, 1974's biggest new European act came from Sweden in the shape of Abba, who swept all before them in the Eurovision Song Contest with their debut hit *Waterloo*. Previously successful elsewhere in Europe, Abba, composed of two married couples, used their Eurovision success to launch an assault on the British charts which made them the most successful act of the decade. Nineteen top 10 singles, including nine number ones, plus eight consecutive chart-topping LPs by the end of 1982, sealed Abba (the name came from the

PAPER LACE

PILOT

MINNIE RIPERTON

LINDA RONSTADT

RUBETTES

LEO SAYER

SHOWADDYWADDY

SPARKS

THREE DEGREES

BARRY WHITE

WOMBLES

initial letters of the quartet's first names) as the Beatles of the 1970s, and, in perhaps similar fashion, the group's hits ended simply because they didn't want to make any more records. This situation was aggravated by the fact that both couples had divorced, and although Agnetha and Anni-Frid released solo records, they were far less successful than Abba had been. Meanwhile their ex-husbands worked with Tim Rice (of *Jesus Christ Superstar* and *Evita* fame) on a musical titled *Chess*, which could turn out to be the theatrical success of the 1980s.

Among Abba's labelmates were one of the most successful novelty acts of the era, the Wombles. Fictitious characters in children's books, the furry litter-collecting creatures made the transition to television, where the theme song for the series was written and sung by Mike Batt. He led the non-existent group to half a dozen top 20 hits in Britain by the end of 1975, then decided to aim for musical credibility, but found himself typecast as the man behind the Wombles and unable to break out of that mould. He became a successful producer/ composer for others like David Essex and Alvin Stardust during the 1980s and even outdid his Womble success when he wrote and produced *Bright Eyes*, a massive hit for Art Garfunkel in 1979.

The mid-1970s saw a tendency for acts to come and go after one or two, often enormous, hits. Among those to whom this applied during the year were Carl Douglas, a Jamaican who topped charts around the world with his ludicrous *Kung Fu Fighting*, Ken Boothe, also a Jamaican but this time of a reggaesque persuasion, who took a cover of Bread's *Everything I Own* to the top in Britain; Blue Swede, a Swedish band who made the US top 10 twice during the year with cover versions, the earlier of which (*Hooked On A Feeling*) was number one. Jim Stafford took a brace of novelty songs *Spiders And Snakes* and *My Girl Bill* into the top 20 on both sides of the Atlantic; Terry Jacks, once of the Poppy Family topped the chart with *Seasons In The Sun*; and Billy Swan, an odd-job man around the Nashville music fraternity wrote and recorded a classic in *I Can Help*.

Philadelphia still produced the most successful soul records underlined by the fact that a session group known as MFSB (Mother, Father, Sister, Brother) took *TSOP* (*The Sound Of Philadelphia*) to number one in America. Singing on that hit were female trio the Three Degrees, who themselves reached the top of the UK chart with *When Will I See You Again*, but neither act was destined for long-term success. This was almost true of George McCrae, who was based in Florida, although he did follow his biggest hit *Rock Your Baby* with several

more hits in Britain when his domestic fame subsided.

The biggest newcomer in soul music was Barry White, a songwriter/producer who also turned performer hitting a purple patch during the year with *Can't Get Enough Of Your Love, Babe* (number one in the US, number eight in the UK) and *You're The First, The Last, My Everything* (number two in the US and number one in the UK) and continued to make the chart with his half-spoken, half-sung love songs until 1978.

Minnie Riperton, ex-lead singer of psychedelic soul group Rotary Connection, emerged as a solo star using her bird-like voice to enormous effect on *Loving You*, but was unable to pursue her promising career due to a serious illness from which she died in 1979. Herbie Hancock, once a keyboard star with Miles Davis, spent nearly a year in the US LP charts with his innovative *Headhunters* album.

Predictably, all the above soulsters were black. America's foremost new white star of 1974 was a part Mexican country rock singer Linda Ronstadt who had first charted with folk rock trio the Stone Poneys in 1967, but whose career had been becalmed until she cut a final LP for Capitol Records to complete her contract before moving to a new label. That album, *Heart Like A Wheel*, topped the US chart and included two massive hit singles in *You're No Good* and *When Will I Be Loved* and made her the top-selling female artist in America. Her success continues into the mid-1980s, taking in numerous platinum LPs and hit singles. Although she remains pre-eminent in the USA Linda's appeal has never been widely accepted in Britain and, where Americans

saw her covers of songs by Elvis Costello and the like as adventurous, the British were less easily convinced. A report in 1984 that she intended to pursue the musical direction of *What's New*, an album on which she performed 'standards' written by George Gershwin and his contemporaries backed by the Nelson Riddle Orchestra, seems likely to be accurate.

From similar musical roots came Gordon Lightfoot, a Canadian folk singer who had recorded with limited success before his breakthrough in 1974 with *Sundown*, an American chart topper which established him as a singer/songwriter with strong appeal for fans of 1960s music.

On the other side of the Atlantic Steve Harley, an ex-journalist, formed a group to perform his adventurous songs. Cockney Rebel, as they were known, broke through with two top 10 hits, *Judy Teen* and *Mr Soft*, before the group fell apart and were replaced by musicians who Harley led to a 1975 British chart topper *Make Me Smile* and a few other hits before his popularity

waned as punk rock took over. A comeback by Harley has so far commercially achieved little.

Another English singer/songwriter, Leo Sayer, has more chart success, after emerging at the start of 1974 with a number two single *The Show Must Go On* taken from his *Silverbird* LP, which also reached number two. Initially assisted by his songwriting partner David Courtney and by his manager, erstwhile singer and actor Adam Faith, Sayer adopted several highly theatrical personae to launch himself, proving that

he had talent in some depth by reaching the top 10 in Britain eight more times before the end of 1980. He also succeeded in America where both *You Make Me Feel Like Dancing* (1976) and *When I Need You* (1977) reached number one, the latter also topping the chart in Britain. Sayer was also a big album seller, his peak coming in 1979 when *The Very Best Of Leo Sayer*, a hits compilation, topped the UK chart for three weeks.

A British act of whom much was expected was Bad Company, composed of Paul Rodgers and Simon Kirke from Free, Mick

Ralphs from Mott the Hoople and Boz Burrell from King Crimson. Their debut LP *Bad Company* and first single *Can't Get Enough* charted strongly in both Britain and America but thereafter it was in America, where supergroups seem more likely to prosper, that the band found most success although each of their first three LPs made the top 5 in Britain as well as the USA. Their 1977 LP *Burning Sky* was rather less popular in a punk-invaded Britain and, perhaps because it was followed by a two-year silence, their eventual comeback LP *Desolation Angels* did little better, although the band retained much of their American following. No one seemed too sure whether or not the band was still extant at the end of 1984.

Another act which enjoyed fluctuating fortunes was Sparks, a duo of brothers, Ron (keyboards and songwriting) and Russell (vocals) Mael, who made their debut LP in their native Los Angeles before trying their luck in Britain where they recruited three British musicians. They started their chart career with their biggest hit *This Town Ain't Big Enough For Both Of Us*, scoring five more UK hits of varying size before disbanding the group, whereupon the Maels, after returning to America and releasing a new LP without success, once again came to Europe where they teamed up with producer Giorgio Moroder. Changing from the quirky rock which had originally brought them fame to an electronic approach, Sparks made three more hits in 1979, the

Below: One of the more successful supergroups of the early seventies, Bad Company: Paul Rodgers (vocals), Mick Ralphs (guitar), Boz Burrell (bass) and Simon Kirke (drums).

182

biggest of them being *Beat The Clock*, before returning once again to the United States from where they have released several more LPs. Thus far they have failed to return to glory.

Also from America came Brownsville Station, a group from Michigan, who had the biggest hit of their career with *Smokin' In The Boys' Room*, and from Canada came Bachman-Turner Overdrive, descendants of the Guess Who, whose *You Ain't Seen Nothin' Yet* topped the US singles chart. If BTO (as they were known) were hardly refined in their neo-heavy metal approach, they seemed tame compared with Ted Nugent, who had previously led the Amboy Dukes, a fiercely loud psychedelic group during the 1960s. Guitarist Nugent's autocracy led to the group falling apart, after which he launched a solo career releasing a new LP each year, most of which reached the US top 30.

On a more sublime level Maria Muldaur, previously of several jug bands in the preceding ten years, scored a memorable hit with *Midnight At The Oasis* and Eric Clapton, whose activity had been sporadic since the short-lived Derek and the Dominos in 1972, re-emerged with a big hit single *I Shot*

The Sheriff and an equally successful LP. Ever since he has delighted his fans with a succession of listenable, if rarely innovative, albums and has assumed his position as an elder statesman of rock.

A far less predictable return came from the Drifters, a much changed group from that which had first charted during the 1950s. Only lead singer Johnny Moore had worked with the numerous previous group line-ups, but with some new recruits the group based themselves in Britain during the mid-1970s adding nine new hits to their already impressive tally of American hits. In a similar, if less pop-oriented, vein Kool and the Gang reached the top 10 in America with *Jungle Boogie* and *Hollywood Swinging*.

At the end of the first half of the decade popular music seemed to have settled into comfortable self-satisfaction and there seemed no reason why this should not continue indefinitely. Warning signals – the rising price of records and the vinyl shortage brought about by oil prices increasing – were ignored as the industry rocked its way through another carefree and commercially successful year. A musical apocalypse was fast approaching!

TITLE	ARTIST	LABEL	WEEKS AT NO. 1
Time In A Bottle	Jim Croce	ABC	1
The Joker	Steve Miller	Capitol	1
Show And Tell	Al Wilson	Rocky Road	1
You're Sixteen	Ringo Starr	Apple	1
The Way We Were	Barbra Streisand	Columbia	3
Love's Theme	Love Unlimited Orchestra	20th Century	1
Seasons In The Sun	Terry Jacks	Bell	3
Dark Lady	Cher	MCA	1
Sunshine On My Shoulder	John Denver	RCA	1
Hooked On A Feeling	Blue Swede	EMI	1
Bennie and The Jets	Elton John	MCA	1
T.S.O.P.	MFSB	Philadelphia International	2
The Loco-Motion	Grand Funk	Capitol	2
The Streak	Ray Stevens	Barnaby	3
Band On The Run	Paul McCartney and Wings	Apple	1
Billy Don't Be A Hero	Bo Donaldson and the Heywoods	ABC	2
Sundown	Gordon Lightfoot	Reprise	1
Rock The Boat	Hues Corporation	RCA	1
Rock Your Baby	George McCrae	TK	2
Annie's Song	John Denver	RCA	2
Feel Like Makin' Love	Roberta Flack	Atlantic	1
The Night Chicago Died	Paper Lace	Mercury	1
You're Having My Baby	Paul Anka	United Artists	3
I Shot The Sheriff	Eric Clapton	RSO	1
Can't Get Enough Of Your Love Baby	Barry White	20th Century	1
Rock Me Gently	Andy Kim	Capitol	1
I Honestly Love You	Olivia Newton-John	MCA	2
Nothing From Nothing	Billy Preston	A&M	1
Then Came You	Dionne Warwick and the Spinners	Atlantic	1
You Haven't Done Nothing	Stevie Wonder	Tamla	1
You Ain't Seen Nothing Yet	Bachman Turner Overdrive	Mercury	1
Whatever Gets You Through The Night	John Lennon	Apple	1
I Can Help	Billy Swan	Monument	2
Kung Fu Fighting	Carl Douglas	20th Century	2
Cat's In The Cradle	Harry Chapin	Elektra	1
Angie Baby	Helen Reddy	Capitol	1

TITLE	ARTIST	LABEL	WEEKS AT NO. 1
Merry Xmas Everybody	Slade	Polydor	2
You Won't Find Another Fool Like Me	The New Seekers	Polydor	1
Tiger Feet	Mud	Rak	4
Devil Gate Drive	Suzi Quatro	Rak	2
Jealous Mind	Alvin Stardust	Magnet	1
Billy Don't Be A Hero	Paper Lace	Bus Stop	3
Seasons In The Sun	Terry Jacks	Bell	4
Waterloo	Abba	Epic	2
Sugar Baby Love	The Rubettes	Polydor	4
The Streak	Ray Stevens	Janus	1
Always Yours	Gary Glitter	Bell	1
She	Charles Aznavour	Barclay	4
Rock Your Baby	George McCrae	Jayboy	3
When Will I See You Again?	The Three Degrees	Philadelphia International	2
Love Me For A Reason	The Osmonds	MGM	3
Kung Fu Fighting	Carl Douglas	Pye	3
Annie's Song	John Denver	RCA	1
Sad Sweet Dreamer	Sweet Sensation	Pye	1
Everything I Own	Ken Boothe	Trojan	3
I'm Gonna Make You A Star	David Essex	CBS	3
You're My First, My Last, My Everything	Barry White	20th Century	2
Lonely This Christmas	Mud	Rak	2

4 January: President Nixon refuses to comply with subpoenas demanding 'the White House tapes'.

9 January: A three-day working week to save electricity and coal follows a go-slow by miners and rail workers in the UK.

18 January: Kissinger negotiates a ceasefire between Israel and Egypt along the Suez Canal.

30 January: In his State of The Union address Nixon urges America not to pursue the Watergate Affair.

4 February: Patty Hearst is kidnapped by the Symbionese Liberation Army.

13 February: USSR deports Solzhenitsyn and strips him of citizenship, in the first forced expulsion since 1929, when Stalin exiled Leon Trotsky.

7 March: With the Labour Party back in power, and the miners accepting a 30 per cent wage increase, the three-day working week is cancelled.

25 April: General Spinola assumes power in Portugal after a bloodless coup.

4 June: Idi Amin is accused of 'a reign of terror' by the International Commission of Jurists.

17 June: The UK Houses of Parliament are bombed by the IRA. 11 people are injured.

5 August: Nixon admits his complicity in the Watergate scandal after months of strenuous denial. He subsequently resigns the Presidency.

9 August: Gerald Ford is sworn in as the 38th President of the United States. He grants Nixon a full pardon.

10 September: Haile Selassie is deposed as Emperor of Ethiopia after ruling since 1930.

21 November: Two crowded pubs in Birmingham are bombed by the IRA, 19 are killed and over 100 wounded.

29 November: The House of Commons approves legislation outlawing the IRA.

FILMS

Airport 1975
Alice Doesn't Live Here Anymore
Badlands
Blazing Saddles
Chinatown
Earthquake
The Godfather
Gold
The Great Gatsby
The Last Detail
Magnum Force
Murder On The Orient Express
The Odessa File
Serpico
The Sting
The Towering Inferno
The Way We Were

DEATHS

Graham Bond, R&B musician
Nick Drake, singer/songwriter
Duke Ellington, jazz musician
Cass Elliott, singer with the Mamas and the Papas
Sam Goldwyn, film tycoon
Ivory Joe Hunter, R&B singer
Robbie McIntosh, drummer with Average White Band
Tex Ritter, singing cowboy
Ed Sullivan, TV show host

Above: The much loved 'Mama' Cass Elliot, who died during July 1974 in London.

Made in England

1974

SIDE ONE
45 RPM
STEREO

Waterloo

ALL RIGHTS OF THE MANUFACTURER AND OF THE OWNER OF THE RECORDED WORK RESERVED UNAUTHORISED PUBLIC PERFORMANCE BROADCASTING AND COPYING OF THIS RECORD PROHIBITED

185

1975

SIDE ONE
45 RPM
STEREO

Love Will Keep Us Together

An indication of how volatile American popular taste had become can be gleaned from the fact that 35 different singles topped the chart during the year, compared with a yearly average of around 20 during the 1960s. With no obvious focus American record buyers were moving in all directions, embracing such diverse forms of music as Elton John, who made number one three times during the year, Neil Sedaka, John Denver and the Eagles, who each scored with two separate chart toppers, as did K.C. and the Sunshine Band and a flurry of newcomers, few of whom would have much future impact. There were exceptions, of course, like Earth, Wind and Fire and Barry Manilow, who would go on to further success. Several acts like Freddy Fender and Silver Convention in America and Typically Tropical and actor Telly Savalas in Britain achieved their greatest chart successes in 1975.

Not that all activity was centred on the singles chart – a major new force in AOR (adult or album oriented rock) emerged when Fleetwood Mac, after struggling for most of the 1970s, recruited new members in guitarist Lindsey Buckingham and singer Stephanie (Stevie) Nicks, who had previously made an obscure LP together. Regarded as a last chance before the band split up, the new group LP, simply titled *Fleetwood Mac*, was an enormous hit, remaining in the US album chart for three years and spawning three hit singles. The group's follow-up LP *Rumours* was still more successful, selling umpteen million copies during several years in the chart, and also including three hit singles. Inevitably subsequent albums were hits, although by the mid-point of the 1980s most of the group were making solo albums more frequently than working as a group.

Supertramp could tell a similar story. After struggling at the start of the decade,

in America, the departure of Hodgson for a solo career in 1984 may mean the end of their golden era.

Events were slightly different for Jefferson Starship, who rose from the ashes of Jefferson Airplane. Having settled into a comfortable rut after their triumphs of the 1960s the group restyled themselves to score with five US top 20 singles during the 1970s, plus several million-selling LPs, before internal wrangles forced leading lights Grace Slick and Marty Balin periodically to leave and rejoin the band, filling their time with occasional solo projects.

While the current state of the Starship remains vague, there is no doubt about the continuing existence of Rush, a heavy metal 'swords and sorcery' trio from Toronto. After financing a debut LP themselves Neil Peart, an ingenious lyricist, replaced the group's original drummer. Then came a succession of million-selling LPs which continue today, despite criticism that Peart's lyrics rely too much on inspiration from J.R.R. Tolkien (who wrote *The Hobbit* and *Lord Of The Rings*) and right-wing authoress Ayn Rand. Similar literary borrowings were undertaken by British group Camel, whose main thrust came with their adaptation of Paul Gallico's novel *The Snow Goose*, which remains their biggest selling LP, although once again the group's continuing existence is a matter for conjecture.

Curiously (or so it seemed at the time) a good deal of easy listening/middle of the

founder members Rick Davies and Roger Hodgson had rebuilt the group before relaunching it in 1974 with *Crime Of The Century*, a million-selling album, after which they were unable to do wrong (at least as far as American record buyers were concerned) for the rest of the decade, which resulted in the group moving to the USA. British success was never automatic and, although the group remain a huge attraction

BARRY MANILOW

BOB MARLEY AND THE WAILERS

GRAHAM PARKER AND THE RUMOUR

RUSH

SENSATIONAL ALEX HARVEY BAND

SILVER CONVENTION

PATTI SMITH

SMOKIE

BRUCE SPRINGSTEEN

SUPERTRAMP

TAMMY WYNETTE

187

Above: Barry Manilow
commands a large following
on both sides of the Atlantic.

Previous page top: Canadian
heavy metal exponents Rush:
Alex Lifeson (guitar), Geddy
Lee (lead vocals, bass), and
Neil Peart (drums and
percussion).

Previous page bottom:
Jefferson Starship, who scored
many more hit singles than the
group from which they
evolved, Jefferson Airplane.

road music achieved major popularity
during 1975. Perhaps it was a case of the
calm before the storm but, for whatever
reasons, professional arranger and musical
director Barry Manilow graduated from
work on TV's *Ed Sullivan Show* to making his
own records. While they have rarely been
innovative, Manilow's well-crafted records
have been extremely successful. His biggest single hits came in America where he
scored three chart toppers during the 1970s,
starting with *Mandy* in 1975. While British
singles were less successful, Manilow's UK
album sales were immense in the period
between 1979 and 1982.

In a similar mould were the Captain and
Tennille, a husband and wife duo. Daryl
Dragon had worked with the Beach Boys,
becoming known as 'Captain Keyboards'
and when he married session singer Toni
Tennille they formed a partnership which
flourished through the second half of the
1970s, topping the US chart with *Love Will
Keep Us Together*, the biggest-selling
single of 1975, and returning to number one
in 1979 with *Do That To Me One More Time*.

The major movement in Britain was
known as pub rock, taking its name from the
venues, generally in London, where groups
like Kokomo, Dr Feelgood and Ace began
to perform. Although several well-known

latter-day musicians served their apprenticeship in the pubs, including Nick Lowe
(in Brinsley Schwarz) and members of Elvis
Costello's Attractions, few big record sellers
emerged from that scene, the only notable
exception being Ace, whose *How Long* was
a bigger hit in America than in Britain, and
Dr Feelgood, an energetic R&B quartet from
Canvey Island who topped the British LP
charts with a live LP titled *Stupidity*. Their
success seemed assured until manic guitarist Wilko Johnson left the band after arguments over material, although his replacement John Mayo helped the group sustain
their impetus through 1979 when they

songwriters, although without achieving much more than in his pub rock days.

Bruce Springsteen was initially regarded as the superior American version of Graham Parker. His first two albums for CBS had seen the creation of a cult following, fuelled by media reports of his dynamic live act and comparisons with Bob Dylan. His breakthrough came in 1975 with his third LP *Born To Run*, a further evocation of his streetwise persona underlined by lyrical ingenuity and catchy melodies, but he was saddled with a publicity campaign which seemed to do the artist himself little justice. When Springsteen and his manager subsequently fell out no new records were released for three years, but this only increased the artist's mystique, fuelled by innumerable live bootleg recordings. When he finally returned to the studio his 'comeback' LP *Darkness On The Edge Of Town* seemed too inhibited, but *The River* (1980), a superb double LP, saw his audience's faith in Bruce restored. His subsequent career has seen some unpredictable moves, like his 1982 LP *Nebraska*, which consisted of his demos for what was intended to be a band LP, but his chart-topping 1984 LP *Born In The USA* confirmed his position as a genuine superstar.

Similarly streetwise although musically less skilled was Patti Smith, a poetess and rock critic from New York who collaborated with another rock critic Lenny Kaye to form a band and procure a recording contract. Her debut LP *Horses* sounded primitive,

Above: Punk godmother Patti Smith, a major source of inspiration for an emergent generation.

Left: Bruce Springsteen who reaffirmed belief in the values of traditional rock'n'roll and continues to grow in popularity.

scored their biggest single hit *Milk And Alcohol*. The band splintered after that until only singer Lee Brilleaux remained with what seemed like an ever-changing selection of backing musicians. Even so the group survived longer than many of their early rivals, the only other major star of the era being Graham Parker, whose early backing group the Rumour was composed of ex-members of pub rock acts like Brinsley Schwarz and Ducks Deluxe. Parker's fine songwriting was much admired, but his albums were never hugely successful and by the first half of the 1980s he had been absorbed into the mainstream of singer/

but perhaps, as several young British musicians were deciding, a change was necessary when smoothness and technical expertise, often at the expense of enthusiasm and spontaneity, were considered vitally important. *Horses* reached the top 50 in the LP chart and three subsequent LPs did reasonably well. *Easter* (1978) which included a hit single in *Because The Night* became her best work, but her most recent LP *Wave* appeared to suffer from a lack of preparation. Five years later nothing new has appeared by Patti, but few would be surprised by her re-emergence.

Blue Oyster Cult were a quintet who used several names before settling on that enigmatic title in the early 1970s. Managed by ex-rock writer Sandy Pearlman, the group initially played heavy metal, but taking their lead from Pearlman's literary aspirations developed a subtlety which few of their genre could equal, resulting in a series of highly commercial albums, but only one classic single, *Don't Fear The Reaper*.

The major new movement in America, which would spread its influence worldwide, was disco music, regarded by many as a somewhat poor substitute for genuine soul music, but as capable of filling dance floors as its artistic antecedent. The disco boom would peak in 1978 with the enormously successful *Saturday Night Fever* movie, whose music was largely provided by the Bee Gees, but beforehand a number of acts, usually from America but sometimes from the unlikely location of Germany, would take disco epics into the chart.

Among those who achieved such distinction were Gloria Gaynor, who had been making records for several years before breaking into the chart with *Never Can Say Goodbye*. Although her output generally had more dance-floor appeal than chart potential, she returned in style in 1979 with *I Will Survive*, a chart topper on both sides of the Atlantic. Her dilemma, like many singers' of the disco genre, seems to have been that any individuality is swamped by the requirement for a rhythmically perfect backing track. This applied particularly to disco records made in Germany, the home base of Silver Convention, a female trio of black American's who had moved to Europe. They sang over often electronically produced backing tracks to front a brief series of hits in 1975 and 1976, the biggest of which was *Fly, Robin Fly* which topped the US chart, closely followed by *Get Up And Boogie*, a top 10 item on both sides of the Atlantic.

Van McCoy, a veteran session musician, was able to take advantage of the disco boom with a chart topper *The Hustle*, but was unable to follow it up successfully before he died in 1979. Labelle, a female trio who had scored during the 1960s as full-blooded soul singers, adapted their output to take in exotic costumes and sexual imagery and made a chart impact with their US chart topper *Lady Marmalade* before splitting into solo acts.

Earth, Wind and Fire, founded by Maurice White – previously drummer with modern jazz pioneer John Coltrane, and who had also backed Muddy Waters and Ramsey Lewis – lasted much longer. Formed in 1970, the seven-piece band topped the US chart in 1975 with *Shining Star*, for once crossing over into the pop chart, after which they seemed guaranteed to have substantial hits until the end of the decade, assisted by a remarkable stage act involving a revolving drummer and a flying bass player.

A new form of music also made its presence felt – reggae, as purveyed by Bob Marley and the Wailers, who remain the only act of the genre to achieve international fame. Born in Jamaica (like most of its practitioners), reggae was often associated with the Jamaican religion Rastafari, and appealed to the underprivileged, initially blacks but later whites, who found both its message and distinctive rhythms infectious. Marley had played as part of a highly talented trio completed by Peter Tosh and Bunny Livingstone during the 1960s, becoming a local star, but a spell working with Johnny Nash, for whom Marley wrote several hits, polished his craft to the point where he and his backing group were signed to Island Records during the early 1970s. Their records thus became widely available for the first time and although he never really broke through in the United States, Marley became the first and only superstar of reggae as a result of several UK top 10 hit singles and a series of chart albums. Unfortunately he died from cancer in 1980. *Legend*, a compilation of his greatest hits, topped the UK album chart in 1984 for three months.

While the usual crop of one-hit wonders made the British chart, including folk acts Ralph McTell and Steeleye Span, comedian Billy Connolly, keyboard session player Pete Wingfield and ex-Amen Corner front man Andy Fairweather-Low, more commercial substance was displayed by such groups as Sailor, who twice hit the top 10, Smokie, another group whose hits were masterminded by the Chinn-Chapman team and Be-Bop Deluxe, a group led by guitar star Bill Nelson. One veteran from the 1960s, Alex Harvey, finally broke through with the modestly titled Sensational Alex Harvey Band, who placed five albums in the UK top 20 in three years before his impetus ran out. Harvey was always presumed capable of a major comeback, but died from a heart attack in 1981.

Kraftwerk, a German electronics duo,

Above: Still the only superstar to emerge from reggae music, Bob Marley, seen here onstage with his band, the Wailers, with backing vocalists the I-Threes (right).

Left: Nashville queen Tammy Wynette receiving an award from CBS (UK) boss Maurice Oberstein for sales of her best known hit, Stand By Your Man.

were normally noted for large sales of albums, but took a catchy instrumental *Autobahn* into the charts all over the world in 1975 and re-emerged as singles chart contenders in 1983 when a re-issued single *The Model* topped the British chart, although by this time their line-up had doubled. Taking a diametrically opposite path musically was country star Tammy Wynette, for some time the queen of the Nashville scene, who found herself at the top of the British charts with *Stand By Your Man*, previously an American hit six years earlier. She was able to follow it with the bizarre *D.I.V.O.R.C.E.*, but soon after returned to the comparatively less competitive country charts.

Business as usual? So everyone thought. But they didn't know about a quartet of unemployed youths who were rehearsing in a shop owned by rag trade entrepreneur Malcolm McLaren. The Sex Pistols were on the move, as the music world would soon find out.

Opposite top: Disco queen, Gloria Gaynor, who certainly did survive – not to mention prosper.

Opposite bottom: Earth, Wind and Fire, led and masterminded by Maurice White, attracted many fans with their highly spectacular live shows.

USA CHART TOPPERS

Title	Artist	Label	Weeks at No. 1
Lucy In The Sky With Diamonds	Elton John	MCA	2
Mandy	Barry Manilow	Bell	1
Please Mr Postman	The Carpenters	A&M	1
Laughter In The Rain	Neil Sedaka	Rocket	1
Fire	Ohio Players	Mercury	1
You're No Good	Linda Ronstadt	Capitol	1
Pick Up The Pieces	Average White Band	Atlantic	1
Best Of My Love	The Eagles	Asylum	1
Have You Never Been Mellow	Olivia Newton-John	MCA	1
Black Water	Doobie Brothers	Warner Bros	1
My Eyes Adored You	Frankie Valli	Private Stock	1
Lady Marmalade	Labelle	Epic	1
Lovin' You	Minnie Riperton	Epic	1
Philadelphia Freedom	Elton John	MCA	2
Another Somebody Done Something Wrong Song	B.J. Thomas	ABC	1
He Don't Love You	Tony Orlando and Dawn	Elektra	3
Shining Star	Earth, Wind and Fire	Columbia	1
Before The Next Teardrop Falls	Freddy Fender	ABC/Dot	1
Thank God I'm A Country Boy	John Denver	RCA	1
Sister Golden Hair	America	Warner Bros	1
Love Will Keep Us Together	Captain and Tenille	A&M	4
Listen To What The Man Said	Paul McCartney and Wings	Capitol	1
The Hustle	Van McCoy	Avco	1
One Of These Nights	The Eagles	Asylum	1
Jive Talkin'	The Bee Gees	RSO	2
Fallin' In Love	Hamilton, Joe Frank and Reynolds	Playboy	1
Get Down Tonight	K.C. and the Sunshine Band	TK	1
Rhinestone Cowboy	Glen Campbell	Capitol	2
Fame	David Bowie	RCA	2
I'm Sorry	John Denver	RCA	1
Bad Blood	Neil Sedaka	Rocket	3
Island Girl	Elton John	MCA	3
That's The Way	K.C. and the Sunshine Band	TK	2
Fly Robin Fly	Silver Convention	Midland International	3
Let's Do It Again	Staple Singers	Curtom	1

UK CHART TOPPERS

Title	Artist	Label	Weeks at No. 1
Lonely This Christmas	Mud	Rak	2
Down Down	Status Quo	Vertigo	1
Ms Grace	The Tymes	RCA	1
January	Pilot	EMI	3
Make Me Smile	Steve Harley and Cockney Rebel	EMI	2
If	Telly Savalas	MCA	2
Bye Bye Baby	Bay City Rollers	Bell	6
Oh Boy!	Mud	Rak	2
Stand By Your Man	Tammy Wynette	Epic	3
Whispering Grass	Windsor Davies and Don Estelle	EMI	3
I'm Not In Love	10 cc	Mercury	2
Tears On My Pillow	Johnny Nash	CBS	1
Give A Little Love	Bay City Rollers	Bell	3
Barbados	Typically Tropical	Gull	1
I Can't Give You Anything	Stylistics	Avco	3
Sailing	Rod Stewart	Warner Bros	4
Hold Me Close	David Essex	CBS	3
I Only Have Eyes For You	Art Garfunkel	CBS	2
Space Oddity	David Bowie	RCA	2
D.I.V.O.R.C.E.	Billy Connolly	Polydor	1
Bohemian Rhapsody	Queen	EMI	5

CURRENT EVENTS

11 February: Margaret Thatcher becomes leader of the Conservative party.

17 April: War in Cambodia ends as the government surrenders to the Communists, and South Vietnam surrenders to Communist forces two weeks later. Saigon is renamed Ho Chi Minh City.

5 June: The Suez Canal opens for the first time since hostilities led to its closure in 1967.

5 June: In a referendum, the UK votes overwhelmingly to stay in the EEC.

11 June: The first North Sea oil is pumped from the sea bed into a tanker.

18 June: Prince Faisal is publicly beheaded for the assassination of his uncle, King Faisal; 10,000 attend.

24 July: Three Apollo astronauts splash down to end manned US space flight for the rest of the decade. The money is considered better spent in other areas.

27 August: Former Ethiopian Emperor Haile Selassie dies after surgery.

5 September: Squeaky Fromme, a follower of Charles Manson, tries to shoot President Ford.

18 September: Patty Hearst, sought since her kidnapping 18 months earlier, is captured by FBI agents in San Francisco.

4 December: South Moluccan terrorists take the Indonesian consulate in Amsterdam, while another group seizes a train, killing two and taking 50 hostage.

16 December: The UK government injects £162 million to save the Chrysler group.

29 December: The Sex Discrimination Act comes into force in the UK.

Civil war continues to rack the Middle East, Angola, Cyprus and Argentina.

FILMS

All Creatures Great And Small
Day Of The Locust
Death Race 2000
Dog Day Afternoon
The Exorcist
The Godfather Part II
Jaws
Lenny
Lisztomania
Love And Death
The Man With The Golden Gun
Monty Python And The Holy Grail
Nashville
Night Moves
Rollerball
Shampoo
Stardust
The Texas Chainsaw Massacre
Tommy

DEATHS

Cannonball Adderley, jazz musician
Tim Buckley, singer/songwriter
General Franco, Spanish President
Ralph Gleason, music critic
Pete Ham, singer in Badfinger
Susan Hayward, film star
Graham Hill, racing driver
Al Jackson, drummer with Booker T and the MGs
Ross McWhirter, writer
Aristotle Onassis, Greek ship owner
James Robertson Justice, actor

Above: A still from Ken Russell's film, Tommy, with (left to right) Oliver Reed, Roger Daltrey and Ann-Margret (Hemdale, 1975).

Made in England

1975

SIDE ONE
45 RPM
STEREO

Love Will Keep Us Together

ALL RIGHTS OF THE MANUFACTURER AND OF THE OWNER OF THE RECORDED WORK RESERVED UNAUTHORISED PUBLIC PERFORMANCE BROADCASTING AND COPYING OF THIS RECORD PROHIBITED

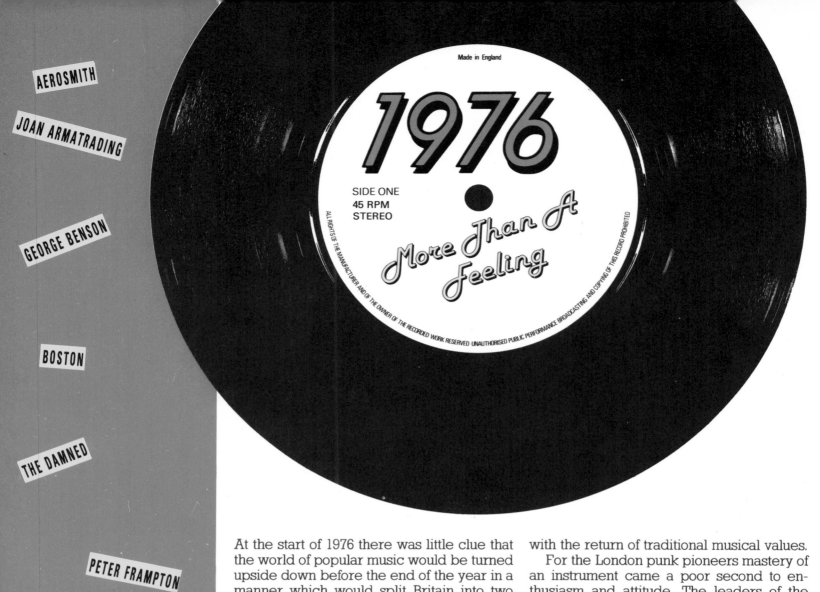

AEROSMITH

JOAN ARMATRADING

GEORGE BENSON

BOSTON

THE DAMNED

PETER FRAMPTON

EMMYLOU HARRIS

HEART

KANSAS

1976

SIDE ONE
45 RPM
STEREO

Made in England

More Than A Feeling

ALL RIGHTS OF THE MANUFACTURER AND OF THE OWNER OF THE RECORDED WORK RESERVED. UNAUTHORISED PUBLIC PERFORMANCE BROADCASTING AND COPYING OF THIS RECORD PROHIBITED

At the start of 1976 there was little clue that the world of popular music would be turned upside down before the end of the year in a manner which would split Britain into two camps – those who appreciated punk rock, and those to whom it was a complete anathema. Even in America the waves from punk would be felt in major cities, although the New Wave took longer to bite, which was curious since all the punk influences came from America – Lou Reed and the Velvet Underground, Iggy Pop and the Stooges, the defunct MC5 and, of more recent vintage, the New York Dolls and Patti Smith. Two emergent American acts, Jonathan Richman and the Modern Lovers and the Ramones also had their admirers.

Richman, from Boston, Massachusetts, was a rabid Velvet Underground fan, if more in his songwriting style than in performance. After a false start in 1973, Richman began to reach a wide audience in America in 1976 and in Britain in 1977, being rather less obnoxious than many of his contemporaries. His classic remains an early single, *Road Runner*, although he scored with other unlikely hits, especially in Britain, before reverting to a virtually acoustic style. In contrast the Ramones, a quartet who pretended to be brothers but were unrelated, adopted a minimalist approach in which few of their songs lasted more than 90 seconds of breakneck simplicity. Despite several changes of drummer the group remain active, although their popularity diminished

with the return of traditional musical values.

For the London punk pioneers mastery of an instrument came a poor second to enthusiasm and attitude. The leaders of the revolution were the Sex Pistols, guided by rag trade entrepreneur Malcolm McLaren, whose visionary genius has permeated British rock music ever since. Having worked in New York where he managed the New York Dolls during their decline, McLaren had absorbed the new trends occurring in the city with special reference to Television, a group whose bass player Richard Hell sported spiky hair and ripped clothes held together with safety pins, styles which McLaren would apply to the Pistols. On his return to London, McLaren ran a clothes shop known as Sex, and a trio of his part-time sales assistants said that they wanted to become a rock group. What was lacking was a singer until John Lydon, a youth who loitered around the shop, agreed to shout above the din created by guitarist Steve Jones, drummer Paul Cook and bass player Glen Matlock. McLaren managed the group, who named themselves after the shop, and helped them to infiltrate gigs headlined by other acts, where they attracted attention by their anti-social behaviour typified by Lydon, who had been dubbed Johnny Rotten. Abusing the audience verbally and physically, the Pistols alienated many who saw them, but their totally unique approach was adopted by their peers.

At the time nothing seemed different – among the chart-topping LPs of the year were glossy items by Abba, Queen, Rod Stewart, Led Zeppelin and Status Quo, while old-timers like the Beach Boys, Glen Campbell, Roy Orbison and even Perry Como, Slim Whitman and guitarist Bert Weedon reached number one. In the singles chart retrogressive acts like folkies the Wurzels, 1976 Eurovision Song Contest winners Brotherhood Of Man, Dutch popsters Pussycat, Greek Demis Roussos and Johnny Mathis reached the top, while America was little different. Disco records ruled, with groups like the Manhattans, the Miracles (now without Smokey Robinson) and Wild Cherry, along with soloists Johnny Taylor and Dorothy Moore, and even a humorous group Rick Dees and his Cast of Idiots scored heavily, although few displayed any staying power.

Equally successful were folk rock/country rock acts like the Bellamy Brothers, the Starland Vocal Band and C. W. McCall, whose *Convoy*, featured in a movie about truck drivers, was a monster hit, while 1960s stars like John Sebastian with *Welcome Back*, the Four Seasons with a new disco sound but still boasting the unique voice of Frankie Valli and Chicago with the dreamy *If You Leave Me Now*, also returned in temporary triumph.

But in Britain something quite new was happening. The American acts who had dominated the early part of the decade were being ignored. The glitter era had passed as its stars had become as remote

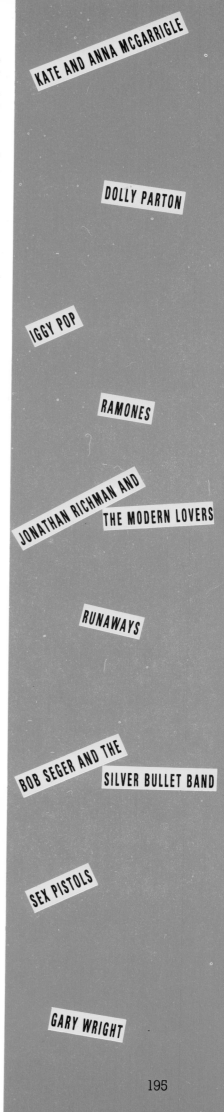

KATE AND ANNA McGARRIGLE

DOLLY PARTON

IGGY POP

RAMONES

JONATHAN RICHMAN AND THE MODERN LOVERS

RUNAWAYS

BOB SEGER AND THE SILVER BULLET BAND

SEX PISTOLS

GARY WRIGHT

195

Above: Boston: (left to right) Barry Goudreau, Sib Hashian, leader and inspiration Tom Scholz, Brad Delp and Fran Sheehan. Their debut album was one of the biggest selling LPs of the decade.

Previous page top: Jonathan Richman, a one-time disciple of the Velvet Underground, became the most unlikely star of the punk rock era.

Previous page bottom: The Sex Pistols, fronted by Johnny Rotten, who became the most reviled, yet most successful act of the punk rock explosion of 1977.

and predictable as American groups. Everyone craved excitement and wanted music they could call their own; not since the 1950s had there been a major musical genre which alienated parents. Punk gave hope to a disaffected youth and the Sex Pistols became the focal point of the new movement.

Fresh rock stars in the traditional mould still rose to prominence. Among them were a number of efficient American groups like Aerosmith, a Massachusetts-based band fronted by Steven Tyler. Loosely basing their hard rock sound on groups like the Yardbirds – guitarist Joe Perry seemed very much in such a mould – the group built up a large following through almost constant touring which finally paid off in 1976 when their *Toys In The Attic* LP went platinum. Subsequent LPs were big hits until 1979, when Perry began to release solo albums, causing rifts in the band from which they have never properly recovered.

The history of another band, Boston, from the same locality was somewhat different. Playing sophisticated hard rock/heavy metal, Boston was formed by Tom Scholz, a successful research technician for the Polaroid Corporation, who made a self-financed LP on which he did everything from songwriting and production to instruments and vocals. He was immediately signed by Epic Records and then formed a five-piece band which he named Boston, re-recording the album to fall in line with union regulations. The eponymous LP was an instant smash hit, selling over six million copies in its first year and remaining in the chart for two years, also spawning a classic top 5 single *More Than A Feeling*, but producing a follow-up was a major problem. Although a new LP *Don't Look Back* did emerge in 1978 and topped the US chart, its longevity was far less than its predecessor's, and by the end of the decade the band had quietly folded,

although 1984 brought news of a forthcoming new LP.

Kansas, named after their home state, were selected as the flagship act on his new label by Don Kirshner, who conceived both the Monkees and the Archies. However, Kansas were neither literally nor even figuratively puppets and attracted the American AOR audience, who bought their albums in huge quantities. Occasionally the group hit the singles charts with, for instance, *Carry On My Wayward Son* in 1976. They remain active and relatively unknown, particularly in Britain.

In a similar vein, although with wider appeal, were Bob Seger and the Silver Bullet Band. From Detroit, Seger had been recording since 1966 with little commercial success, even leaving music to return to college before re-emerging in 1971 with a permanent backing band. His first major success came with a double live LP *Live Bullet*, which demonstrated his powerful sound to a much wider audience. The follow-up LP *Night Moves* was even bigger and its title track was a top 5 single in the US, since when Seger has retained a large American following.

196

A similar approach, the double live LP, also propelled to prominence Peter Frampton, an English singer/guitarist who had first emerged in the late 1960s with the Herd, after which he helped found Humble Pie. After leaving that group, Frampton found himself with a ten-million-seller in *Frampton Comes Alive*, which also included three top 20 American hit singles. In 1977 the title song of his *I'm In You* LP became his biggest hit single, but although he presumably remains active little has been heard of him during the 1980s. This also applies to Gary Wright, formerly of Spooky Tooth, who rose in the wake of Frampton, whom he had supported on tour. After two top 3 singles in America, *Dream Weaver* and *Love Is Alive*, Wright too faded from view.

George Benson appealed to a similar audience, although his route to fame was substantially different. A jazz guitarist during the 1960s, Benson jumped on the disco bandwagon and began to sing, breaking through with *Breezin'*, a double platinum LP which included a hit single *This Masquerade*. While his contemporary output is artistically less challenging than his specialist

work, Benson has released some of the best light funk LPs of recent years, attracting a large easy listening audience.

A number of female acts also made a mark during the year, Joan Armatrading and Kate and Anna McGarrigle approaching the mainstream from folk roots and Dolly Parton and Emmylou Harris from country music.

Dolly Parton had emerged as a featured singer in country star Porter Wagoner's show. Her appealing voice deflected attention from her talent as a songwriter. After leaving Wagoner she quickly established herself as a Nashville star, and by 1977 had reached the top 10 on both sides of the Atlantic, taking *Jolene* into the UK chart and *Here You Come Again* into its US equivalent. Her rise to fame increased as she aimed for a rock audience and moved into films, her peak to date coming in 1980 when *9 To 5*, the title song from a film in which she starred, topped the US singles chart.

Further success for Dolly Parton will surely follow, although the same might not be said of Emmylou Harris, who first came to prominence as Gram Parsons' duet partner on his solo LPs *G.P.* and *Grievous Angel*. After his untimely death in 1973 Emmylou

acquired her own recording contract. She built up a substantial following both by virture of such fine LPs as *Elite Hotel* and *Luxury Liner* and tours with a superb band of well-known musicians, including legendary guitarist James Burton and ex-Cricket Glen D. Hardin on piano, both of whom were also members of Elvis Presley's band. However, Emmylou has since lost her impetus, although LPs have been released regularly delighting the converted without attracting a bigger following.

The McGarrigle Sisters enjoyed brief cult status in the mid-1970s with an endearing amateurism on their eponymous debut LP, but their live shows lacked the charm of their records.

Joan Armatrading, born in the West Indies but brought up in Britain, cut an early solo album which raised few ripples, but

after a two-year hiatus she returned with a stunning LP produced by Glyn Johns, *Back To The Night*, and continued along a similar path with the LP *Joan Armatrading* (1976), which included the notable hit single *Love And Affection*. While more recent releases have been sporadic, Joan has retained an international following, which unfortunately Heart, a rock group led by sisters Ann and Nancy Wilson, cannot claim at the time of writing. Like the McGarrigles, Heart came from Canada and recorded their debut LP *Dreamboat Annie* for a minor Canadian label. Surprisingly it remained in the US chart for two years, leading to a contract with Epic Records and more success, although by the early part of the 1980s things had become much quieter for the group.

Some acts were able to survive the punk onslaught, but even some punks enjoyed only brief popularity, like the Runaways, an all-female quintet whose career was masterminded by Kim Fowley. Eventually the group broke up after several up and down years, the only member to make a subsequent impact being Joan Jett who topped the US chart for seven weeks in 1982 with *I Love Rock'n'Roll*. Punk Godfather Iggy Pop also enjoyed a re-emergence under the patronage of David Bowie but quickly retreated into cult status, which is also true of the first English punk act to record, the Damned. Although they inevitably benefited from their status as pioneers the group were soon eclipsed by the Sex Pistols; their major latter-day claim to fame related to group member Captain Sensible, who unexpectedly topped the UK singles chart in 1982 as we shall see.

The Sex Pistols, on the other hand, were big news. Signed by EMI Records, the group embarked on a national tour to promote the release of their first single *Anarchy In The UK*, which had entered the chart by the time the tour was abandoned after the

Left: The Damned: Dave Vanian (vocals), Brian James (guitar), Captain Sensible (bass), and Rat Scabies (drums). The first British punk group of the seventies to release a single, they seemed unable to build on this distinction.

Below: James Jewel Osterburg, better known as Iggy Pop, seen here performing his notable ostrich impersonation.

majority of the local councils had banned the package from their halls following a TV appearance by Rotten and company in which they had abused interviewer Bill Grundy. Soon EMI, pressured by shareholders and employees, withdrew the single and cancelled the group's contract, after which they signed with A&M Records. They left there after a stay of only a few days due to further pressure from employees. Malcolm McLaren and the group reportedly gained about £75,000 from these two aborted deals. The next label to take on the group, Virgin, profited from the group's prodigious record sales – seven singles by the Pistols made the British top 10, as did three LPs, the first of which *Never Mind The Bollocks – Here's The Sex Pistols* topped the LP chart.

By then bass player Glen Matlock had left the group to be replaced by a friend of Johnny Rotten appropriately named Sid Vicious, whose musical ability came a poor second to his outrageous behaviour. After months of controversy the group embarked on a tour of America, a country which turned out to be unimpressed by punk's primeval protest. During the tour Johnny Rotten left the band, later re-emerging as leader of Public Image Limited, while the remaining trio drifted on, making a documentary style film of the group's history, *The Great Rock-'n'Roll Swindle*, with such guest stars as Tenpole Tudor and fugitive criminal Ronald Biggs. Rotten was never satisfactorily replaced and the group collapsed when Vicious, who was living in New York, apparently murdered his girlfriend and a few days later overdosed on heroin. It was a sad end to an exciting era in British music, but before Sid's death punk had more to contribute, as the following years would prove.

U S A   C H A R T   T O P P E R S

TITLE	ARTIST	LABEL	WEEKS AT NO. 1
Saturday Night	Bay City Rollers	Arista	1
Convoy	C.W. McCall	MGM	1
I Write The Songs	Barry Manilow	Arista	1
Theme From 'Mahogany'	Diana Ross	Motown	1
Love Roller Coaster	Ohio Players	Mercury	3
Fifty Ways To Leave Your Lover	Paul Simon	Columbia	1
Theme From S.W.A.T.	Rhythm Heritage	ABC	1
Love Machine (Part 1)	The Miracles	Tamla	1
December '63	Four Seasons	Warner Bros	
Disco Lady	Johnnie Taylor	Columbia	3
Let Your Love Flow	Bellamy Brothers	Warner Bros	4
Welcome Back	John Sebastian	Reprise	1
Boogie Fever	Sylvers	Capitol	1
Love Hangover	Diana Ross	Motown	2
Silly Love Songs	Wings	Capitol	5
Afternoon Delight	Starland Vocal Group	Windsong	2
Kiss And Say Goodbye	Manhattans	Columbia	2
Don't Go Breaking My Heart	Elton John and Kiki Dee	Rocket	4
You Should Be Dancing	The Bee Gees	RSO	1
Shake Your Booty	K.C. and the Sunshine Band	TK	1
Play That Funky Music	Wild Cherry	Epic	3
A Fifth Of Beethoven	Walter Murphy and the Big Apple Band	Private Stock	
Disco Duck	Rick Dees and his Cast Of Idiots	RSO	1
If You leave Me Now	Chicago	Columbia	2
Rock'n'Me	Steve Miller	Capitol	1
Tonight's The Night	Rod Stewart	Warner Bros	7

U K   C H A R T   T O P P E R S

TITLE	ARTIST	LABEL	WEEKS AT NO. 1
Bohemian Rhapsody	Queen	EMI	4
Mamma Mia	Abba	Epic	2
Forever And Ever	Slik	Bell	1
December '63	Four Seasons	Warner Bros	2
I Love To Love	Tina Charles	CBS	3
Save Your Kisses For Me	Brotherhood Of Man	Pye	6
Fernando	Abba	Epic	4
No Charge	J.J. Barrie	Power Exchange	
Combine Harvester	The Wurzels	EMI	1
You To Me Are Everything	Real Thing	Pye International	2
The Roussos Phenomenon (EP)	Demis Roussos	Philips	3
Don't Go Breaking My Heart	Elton John and Kiki Dee	Rocket	1
Dancing Queen	Abba	Epic	6
Mississippi	Pussycat	Sonet	4
If You Leave Me Now	Chicago	CBS	3
Under The Moon Of Love	Showaddywaddy	Bell	3
When A Child Is Born	Johnny Mathis	CBS	1

D E A T H S

Florence Ballard, former Supreme
Duster Bennett, blues singer
Busby Berkeley, choreographer
Tommy Bolin, guitarist
Agatha Christie, writer
Max Ernst, painter
Howard Hughes, tycoon
Sid James, actor
Freddie King, guitarist
Paul Kossoff, guitarist
L.S. Lowry, painter
The Miami Show Band, IRA bomb victims
Phil Ochs, folk singer
Keith Relf, Yardbirds singer

5 January: Fresh outbreaks of violence in Northern Ireland – with 16 deaths in the first five days of the year – lead to more troops being drafted in.

15 January: The Roman Catholic Church reiterates its condemnation of sex outside marriage and says that homosexuality cannot be condoned under any circumstances.

19 February: Iceland severs ties with the UK over fishing rights disputes.

21 February: Israel withdraws from Sinai, as UN troops move into the buffer zone.

28 February: President Ford denounces Fidel Castro as 'an international outlaw' because of his intervention in the Angolan civil war.

16 March: UK Prime Minister Harold Wilson resigns; James Callaghan succeeds him.

10 May: Jeremy Thorpe resigns his leadership of the Liberal party after allegations of a homosexual affair.

24 May: Concorde service begins between London and Washington.

16 June: Blacks riot in Soweto, South Africa; 175 are killed.

2 July: North and South Vietnam are reunited with Hanoi as capital.

3 July: The Israelis rescue 100 hostages from Entebbe Airport, Uganda.

4 July: America celebrates its bicentenary.

28 July: The UK breaks off relations with Uganda.

9 September: Mao Tse-Tung dies in Peking.

15 September: India fights population growth; sterilization is introduced.

2 November: In US Presidential election Gerald Ford loses to Jimmy Carter.

30 November: The Utah Board of Pardons agrees to execute Gary Gilmore in accordance with his wishes.

FILMS

Airport 77
All The President's Men
Barry Lyndon
Bugsy Malone
Mahogany
The Man Who Fell To Earth
Network
Nickleodeon
The Omen
One Flew Over The Cuckoo's Nest
The Return Of The Pink Panther
Rooster Cogburn
The Shootist
Silent Movie
Taxi Driver

Made in England

1976

SIDE ONE
45 RPM
STEREO

More Than A Feeling

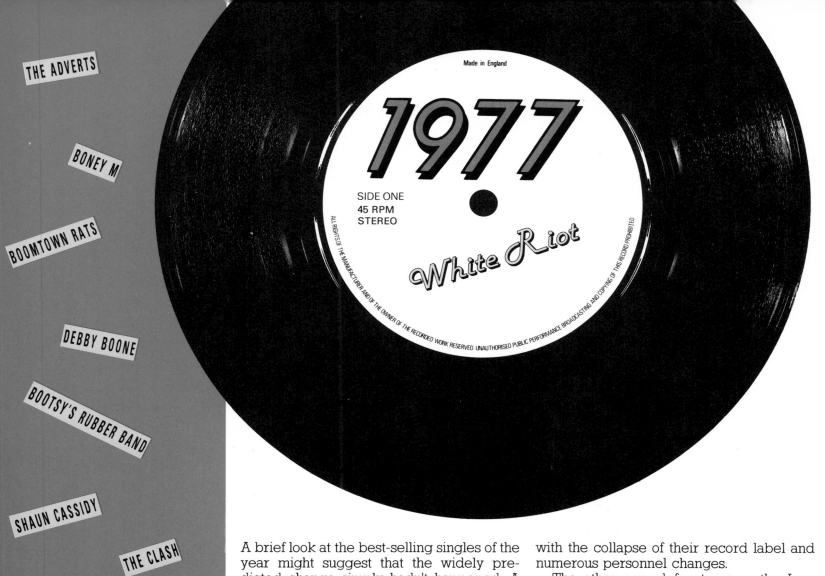

1977

SIDE ONE
45 RPM
STEREO

White Riot

THE ADVERTS

BONEY M

BOOMTOWN RATS

DEBBY BOONE

BOOTSY'S RUBBER BAND

SHAUN CASSIDY

THE CLASH

ELVIS COSTELLO

FIREFALL

FOREIGNER

ANDY GIBB

A brief look at the best-selling singles of the year might suggest that the widely predicted change simply hadn't happened. A few new faces were visible, but many, like Alan O'Day, Meco (the most commercially successful of the many acts to cover the theme music from *Star Wars*, Bill Conti, who took the theme from the film *Rocky*, *Gonna Fly Now*, to the top just before Meco reached the same position, the Floaters, Baccara and several others seemed merely to be experiencing their 15 minutes of fame, while more serious matters were taking place elsewhere.

This was particularly true of Britain, where punk had become a youth cult with cash-in industries working at full power while the boom lasted. Punk fashion was a huge money-spinner – obvious artefacts like posters, T-shirts, jackets and jeans with innumerable zips, specially torn and safety-pinned clothing, bondage gear ... and music, which at times seemed to be forgotten in the rush to make money.

Joining the Pistols and the Damned in the first division of punk popularity were the Clash, the Stranglers and the Jam, while not far behind could be found the Adverts, the Boomtown Rats and some lesser names. Surprisingly the majority of these bands were still active (more or less) in 1984, although few were still punks. The least famous were the Adverts, whose moment of glory came in 1977 with *Gary Gilmore's Eyes*, but who seemed doomed thereafter

with the collapse of their record label and numerous personnel changes.

The other now defunct group, the Jam, were a trio from Woking who spearheaded a brief 'Mod' revival. Leader Paul Weller (vocalist, guitarist, writer of nearly all the group's material) seemed to relate to his audience more than most and sometimes used material from the first 'Mod' era, although his original songs were bigger hits. Every single released by the group (18 between May 1977 and the end of 1982) reached the UK chart, four of them making number one, while their LP sales were equally impressive, although they never reached the top 40 in America. Eventually Weller decided to disband the group and his next endeavour, the Style Council, achieved a good deal of chart action, but his erstwhile Jam colleagues Bruce Foxton and Rick Buckler found life far more of a problem.

The punk group which seemed most likely to implode was the Clash, with whom the majority of the punk audience seemed to empathize. Their history was spotted with controversy and disputes – with their manager, their record company, their drummers – but a central core of singer/guitarist Joe Strummer, guitarist Mick Jones and bass player Paul Simonon remained for five years, during which the group clocked up numerous minor hit singles, starting with *White Riot* in 1977 and peaking in 1979 with *London Calling*, the title track of their third

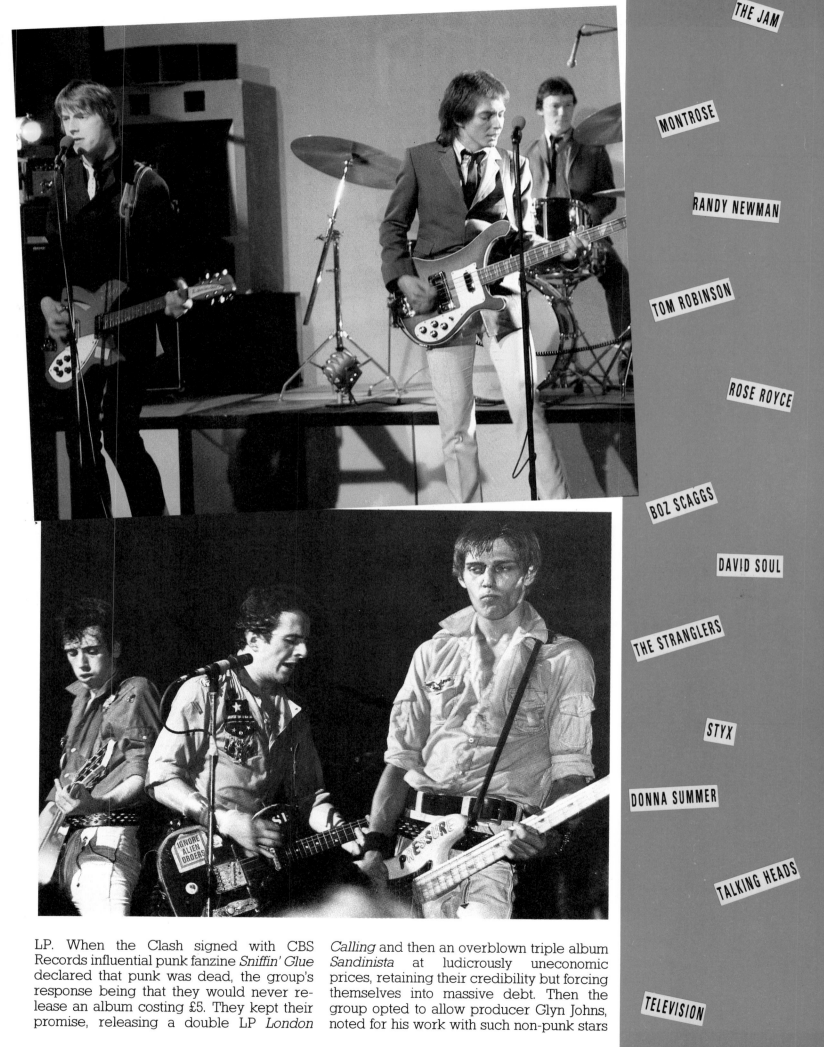

LP. When the Clash signed with CBS Records influential punk fanzine *Sniffin' Glue* declared that punk was dead, the group's response being that they would never release an album costing £5. They kept their promise, releasing a double LP *London* *Calling* and then an overblown triple album *Sandinista* at ludicrously uneconomic prices, retaining their credibility but forcing themselves into massive debt. Then the group opted to allow producer Glyn Johns, noted for his work with such non-punk stars

as the Eagles and the Beatles, to remix their 1982 LP *Combat Rock* and it became the group's first hit album in America, and went platinum. New problems arose and founder member Jones found himself elbowed out because Strummer and Simonon felt his attitude had deteriorated. The lack of subsequent new releases seems to tell its own story.

The Stranglers were perhaps never accepted by hard-line punks. Their musical ability and maturity seemed at odds with the unattainable aims of punk in general. Unlike the Jam, who were associated with 'Mods', the Pistols and the Clash, who were loosely based (although they would have denied it)

on the early Rolling Stones, the Stranglers owed something musically to the Doors. Their singles and particularly their LPs sold well during the 1970s and the group returned in 1982 with their biggest single ever, *Golden Brown*, and have remained in contention ever since.

The Boomtown Rats, a sextet from Dublin, were the first punk (or New Wave – the terms were virtually interchangeable until some acts began to regard the word punk as insulting) act to top the British singles chart, which they did in 1978 with *Rat Trap*, repeating the feat the following year with their masterpiece *I Don't Like Mondays*. After that the group leader Bob Geldof's

growing fame as a media personality, together with the group's unfulfilled desire to conquer America led to a virtual re-run of the situation which afflicted Slade a few years before – British fans stopped buying their records. The Rats may further follow in Slade's footsteps by making a comeback, Geldof's masterminding of Band Aid in 1984 being the first positive step.

Another neo-punk star of 1977, Tom Robinson, did re-emerge in 1984 after a chart absence of several years. Previously his finest hour had come with the classic *2-4-6-8 Motorway* but follow-ups proved to be uncommercial until his return to the upper reaches of the chart in 1984 with *War Baby*.

Connection with the punk/New Wave movement was commercially vital to 1977's newcomers, although a number of credible non-punk performers didn't go out of their way to distance themselves from it. The most notable arrival of this type was Elvis Costello, who was the first representative of the British New Wave to make it in America. After trying for some years to record both in groups and as a solo performer Elvis impressed Stiff Records co-founder Jake Riviera with his remarkable compositions and unequivocal attitude, and Jake supplied a new name (the singer was previously known as Declan McManus) and a recording contract. Early singles were much praised cult items before *Watching The Detectives* reached the UK top 20, alongside Costello's debut LP *My Aim Is True*. Then both Costello and Riviera, along with the former's record producer, Nick Lowe,

Right: Thinking man's punks, Talking Heads: (left to right) Chris Frantz, Jerry Harrison, Tina Weymouth and David Byrne, who survived their uncertain start to become favourites with audiences as well as critics.

left Stiff. After acquiring an American deal Elvis toured with a specially chosen band of seasoned pub rock musicians and found success on both sides of the Atlantic, which has continued, albeit with a slight hiccough in 1981 when he cut an album of country music *Almost Blue* in Nashville.

The ploy of giving Costello the name Elvis seemed inspired when it was first announced, but the unexpected death of the original Elvis (Presley) during the year might have reflected badly on a lesser talent. Presley had been in decline for some years, although a return to live performance and an end to his worthless movies had given hope for a renewal of his early glory. Sadly on 16 August 1977, Presley died from heart failure aggravated by drug abuse at the age of only 42. One observer is said to have remarked that dying was a brilliant

career move and when numerous LPs and 11 singles quickly featured in the UK charts, the accuracy of the statement was confirmed. An avalanche of books followed, many written by erstwhile associates, frequently claiming to tell 'the truth' about the late king of rock'n'roll. The flood of 'tributes' in the form of books and allegedly unreleased records continues.

In America Presleymania was more muted and the top of the singles chart was dominated by relatives of well-known stars. Andy Gibb, brother of the Bee Gees, launched his chart career with three straight number ones in his first year and remained strong in chart terms for several more years. But Shaun Cassidy, half-brother of David, found his career in decline after three top 10 singles in 1977. Debby Boone, daughter of Pat, is viewed as a one-hit wonder, but what

independent single *Little Johnny Jewel.* Their first LP *Marquee Moon* was hailed as a work of genius in Britain but almost ignored in the States, and a similar fate befell the follow-up *Adventure,* after which the group broke up in 1978. Subsequently Verlaine and co-lead guitarist Richard Lloyd opted for solo careers, although neither has achieved much commercially. Another New York group, Talking Heads, took longer to get under way, but continue to thrive despite all four members of the group working on solo projects during inactive periods. Although group leader David Byrne has received acclaim for his solo work, the husband and wife team of bass player Tina Weymouth and drummer Chris Frantz achieved most with their project, Tom Tom Club, whose single *Wordy Rappinghood* made the UK top 10 in 1981 while *Genius Of Love* made the US top 40 in 1982.

New AOR favourites in America included Foreigner, a mostly British band who had previously enjoyed minor fame as backing musicians. Although under-rated in Britain, the group had taken 12 singles into the US top 40 by the end of 1982 from their debut in 1977, while *I Want To Know What Love Is* was a huge hit in early 1985. *Feels Like The First Time* and a series of LPs achieved platinum status despite the fact that individual members of the group remained anonymous. This tendency would recur among American groups, another 1977 candidate for corporate fame but individual anonymity being Styx from Chicago, who regularly reached the US singles chart. Their peak came in 1979 with a chart-topping single *Babe,* but their sales of millions of LPs in America dwarfed their British impact.

More subtle success was achieved by singer/songwriter Randy Newman, who had been recording since the late 1960s, but whose satirical *Short People* peaked at number two in America before Newman returned to cult status and writing film scores. Similarly Boz Scaggs, who had left the Steve Miller Band in the late 1960s, broke into the big time with *Silk Degrees,* a 1977 LP which included three hit singles on both sides of the Atlantic. Unfortunately this inspired streak was brief although a number of aficionados still hope for further masterpieces from Scaggs.

Others who briefly found stardom included country rock group Firefall, who took three LPs into the US top 30 by 1979 but seemed to drift into obscurity; singer/songwriters Jimmy Buffett and Dan Fogelberg, who enjoyed acclaim in their native America but never in Britain; and Montrose, a superior hard rock group led by guitarist Ronnie Montrose. Montrose evolved into the equally promising Gamma, Buffett and Fogelberg appear still to be active, but Firefall's current whereabouts seem uncertain.

a hit! *You Light Up My Life* topped the US chart for an amazing 10 weeks, but Debby then moved into gospel music, following her father's example.

Almost as unexpected was the success of David Soul, star of the very popular *Starsky And Hutch* TV detective show. Soul recorded an easy listening style single *Don't Give Up On Us,* which topped the charts in both Britain and America and while his US chart fame was to end there he managed another chart topper in Britain, *Silver Lady,* before returning to arrest more fictional criminals.

Not all America's emergent stars were so lightweight. A few punks were among them, although they appealed more to Britons than Americans. Television, led by Tom Verlaine, a singer/songwriter/guitarist of note, signed with Elektra after an interesting

The major item of the year among disco music fans was *Saturday Night Fever*, of course, but a strong invasion of dance music created in Germany by American Donna Summer and transplanted Jamaicans Boney M also permeated the world's charts. Donna had first attracted attention in 1975 with her lengthy *Love To Love You Baby* and returned in strength in 1977 with *I Feel Love*, a British number one. Subsequently she scored hits regularly both in Britain and America, where she has several more chart toppers to her credit. By contrast Boney M's fame was brief in America but substantial in Britain, where they made the top 10 nine times before 1980, topping the chart with both *Rivers Of Babylon* and *Mary's Boy Child* before fading away.

American disco group Rose Royce, fronted by Gwen Dickey, topped the US chart with *Car Wash*, the title song to a streetlife film, in early 1977, but thereafter found more chart action in Britain. A different approach came from Bootsy's Rubber Band, a funk group led by William 'Bootsy' Collins, a latter-day Sly Stone-styled figure, who had served his early apprenticeship with James Brown and Parliament/Funkadelic leader George Clinton.

In 1977 it was still widely felt in America that nothing was really changing and with the charts still dominated by familiar names and established musical forms, such doubts were understandable. Even in Britain where the biggest-selling single of the year was *Don't Cry for Me Argentina* by Julie Covington, from the musical *Evita*, things seemed to be slow to change. However, even if punk rock was destined to be a brief phenomenon, its effects would prove to be far-reaching.

Above: William 'Bootsy' Collins who took the soul/funk theatrics of Sly and the Family Stone into a new dimension.

Right: West Indian quartet Boney M, whose German-produced disco anthems provided them with nine consecutive UK top 10 hits.

Opposite: The sultry Donna Summer, the most successful female singer of the disco era.

TITLE	ARTIST	LABEL	WEEKS AT NO. 1
Tonight's The Night	Rod Stewart	Warner Bros	1
You Don't Have To Be A Star	Marilyn McCoo and Billy Davis Jr	ABC	1
You Make Me Feel Like Dancing	Leo Sayer	Warner Bros	1
I Wish	Stevie Wonder	Tamla	1
Car Wash	Rose Royce	MCA	2
Torn Between Two Lovers	Mary McGregor	Ariola	1
Blinded By The Light	Manfred Mann's Earth Band	Warner Bros	1
New Kid In Town	The Eagles	Asylum	1
Evergreen	Barbra Streisand	Columbia	3
Rich Girl	Daryl Hall and John Oates	RCA	2
Dancing Queen	Abba	Atlantic	1
Don't Give Up On Us	David Soul	Private Stock	1
Don't Leave Me This Way	Thelma Houston	Tamla	1
Southern Nights	Glen Campbell	Capitol	1
Hotel California	The Eagles	Asylum	1
When I Need You	Leo Sayer	Warner Bros	3
Sir Duke	Stevie Wonder	Tamla	1
I'm Your Boogie Man	K.C. and the Sunshine Band	TK	1
Dreams	Fleetwood Mac	Warner Bros	1
Got To Give It Up	Marvin Gaye	Tamla	1
Gonna Fly Now	Bill Conti	United Artists	1
Undercover Angel	Alan O'Day	Pacific	1
Da Doo Ron Ron	Shaun Cassidy	Warner/Curb	1
Looks Like We Made It	Barry Manilow	Arista	1
I Just Want To Be Your Everything	Andy Gibb	RSO	4
Best Of My Love	Emotions	Columbia	5
Star Wars Theme	Meco	Millenium	2
You Light Up My Life	Debby Boone	Warner/Curb	10
How Deep Is Your Love	The Bee Gees	RSO	1

TITLE	ARTIST	LABEL	WEEKS AT NO. 1
When A Child Is Born	Johnny Mathis	CBS	2
Don't Give Up On Us	David Soul	Private Stock	4
Don't Cry For Me Argentina	Julie Covington	MCA	1
When I Need You	Leo Sayer	Chrysalis	3
Chanson D'Amour	Manhattan Transfer	Atlantic	3
Knowing Me Knowing You	Abba	Epic	5
Free	Deniece Williams	CBS	2
I Don't Want To Talk About It	Rod Stewart	Riva	4
Lucille	Kenny Rogers	United Artists	1
Show You The Way To Go	The Jacksons	Epic	1
So You Win Again	Hot Chocolate	Rak	3
I Feel Love	Donna Summer	GTO	4
Angelo	Brotherhood Of Man	Pye	1
Float On	The Floaters	ABC	1
Way Down	Elvis Presley	RCA	5
Silver Lady	David Soul	Private Stock	3
Yes Sir I Can Boogie	Baccara	RCA	1
Name Of The Game	Abba	Epic	4
Mull Of Kintyre	Wings	Capitol	4

Right: Elvis Presley, the king of rock'n'roll, who died on 16 August 1977, provoking remarkable scenes of mourning.

29 January: 13 small bombs and incendiary devices planted by the IRA explode in the Oxford Street area of London.

17 February: Three Ugandan leaders being transported to an interrogation centre after plotting to overthrow Idi Amin die in an 'automobile accident'.

9 March: America's Federal Drug Administration bans saccharin as a possible promoter of cancer.

27 March: Two 747 jumbo jets collide on a Tenerife runway, 582 are killed in the worst air disaster in history.

4 May: Former President Nixon admits that he 'let the American people down' in a TV interview with David Frost.

11 July: An 11-month-old dispute at Grunwick photo processing plant in London becomes a national issue when 4000 police clash with 11,000 pickets.

20 July: CIA experiments in behaviour control are revealed.

23 August: The number of unemployed in the UK rises to 1,635,950.

31 August: Ian Smith wins a resounding victory in the Rhodesian national elections.

20 September: Amin bans most Christian churches in Uganda as security risks including Seventh Day Adventists and the Salvation Army.

26 September: Laker Airways start cheap flights between London and New York.

18 October: Three West German terrorists, members of the Baader Meinhof gang, commit suicide in prison.

14 November: Some 30,000 British firemen strike in support of a 30 per cent wage increase.

30 November: Prime Minister Vorster's party win South African elections by an overwhelming majority – only whites are allowed to vote. Three days later an inquest into Steven Biko's death absolves police from any blame.

4 December: Bokassa, of The Central African Republic, crowns himself Emperor in a $20 million ceremony. The country is one of the poorest in the world. .

FILMS

Annie Hall
Black Sunday
A Bridge Too Far
Close Encounters Of The Third Kind
The Enforcer
Julia
King Kong
Marathon Man
New York New York
Rocky
The Spy Who Loved Me
A Star Is Born
Star Wars
Valentino
Victory At Entebbe

DEATHS

Steven Biko, black South African leader
Marc Bolan, rock star
Charlie Chaplin, film star
Bing Crosby, crooner
Cassie Gaines, member of Lynyrd Skynyrd
Steven Gaines, member of Lynyrd Skynyrd
Roland Kirk, jazz saxophonist
Elvis Presley, rock star
Ronnie Van Zant, member of Lynyrd Skynyrd

Made in England

1977

SIDE ONE
45 RPM
STEREO

White Riot

ALL RIGHTS OF THE MANUFACTURER AND OF THE OWNER OF THE RECORDED WORK RESERVED UNAUTHORISED PUBLIC PERFORMANCE BROADCASTING AND COPYING OF THIS RECORD PROHIBITED

211

Made in England

1978

SIDE ONE
45 RPM
STEREO

Three Times A Lady

ALL RIGHTS OF THE MANUFACTURER AND OF THE OWNER OF THE RECORDED WORK RESERVED. UNAUTHORISED PUBLIC PERFORMANCE BROADCASTING AND COPYING OF THIS RECORD PROHIBITED

Somewhat surprisingly punk rock peaked quickly, few joining the punk establishment after 1977. One reason was that most punk music was difficult to enjoy on record because of its practitioners' inexperience and inability to differentiate between a song and a chant. Punk was vital in unsettling the unprogressive self-satisfaction of acts who felt that repetition would continue their success. But it also spurred many newcomers into action, particularly in America, where the term 'New Wave' was used to describe acts like the Cars, a quintet from Boston led by songwriter/guitarist Ric Ocasek whose eponymous debut LP produced by Englishman Roy Thomas Baker was an almost instant success in America.

In Britain, where American music was regarded as bland, it took some assistance from a picture disc of *My Best Friend's Girl* to force them into the chart, where they rarely returned, unlike in America, where each album was a substantial success up to and including 1984's *Heartbeat City*. Devo, a group from Ohio, also hit the headlines with a curious hybrid of techno rock but after the initial impetus of their strange songs and bizarre stage act, they melted quietly into the mainstream.

Something similar could be said of Cheap Trick, seemingly a most interesting and exciting American band with a photogenic vocalist in Robin Zander and an apparently eccentric guitarist, Rick Neilsen. Their early promise was partially fulfilled when they

became overnight superstars in Japan but, apart from occasional LP tracks, the group eventually seemed too shallow for further success.

Of greater long-term note were Tom Petty and the Heartbreakers, a group from Florida who travelled to Los Angeles to get their break. Their initial commercial breakthrough came in Britain with their Byrds-soundalike track *American Girl*. In America

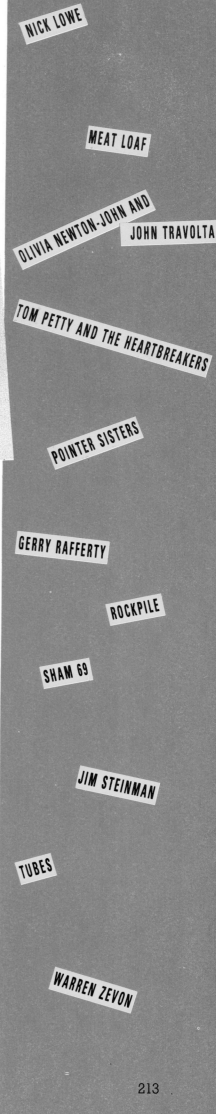

their first hit was *Breakdown*, a track used in the soundtrack of a rock film *FM*, but thereafter business problems and disagreements with his record company hampered Petty's progress, although by 1981 he had recovered sufficiently to approach the top of the US chart with *Stop Draggin' My Heart Around*, a duet with Stevie Nicks of Fleetwood Mac. Petty presumably remains in contention, although the gaps between his albums seem disturbingly lengthy.

Other American acts who flourished in the late 1970s but appear to have fallen from grace include Warren Zevon, a protégé of Jackson Browne who both charted in his own right and also benefited from Linda Ronstadt covering his songs; fluent blues guitarist George Thorogood; and wonder boy Andrew Gold. Gold's first two LPs were superb and he was a vital factor in Linda Ronstadt's success during the mid- to late 1970s. But Gold then seemed to disappear before teaming up in 1984 with 10 cc's Graham Gouldman in Common Knowledge and singer/songwriter Dean Friedman.

One 1977 alumnus who went on to greater things was Billy Joel, who recorded with two New York acts, the Hassles and Attila, before embarking on a solo career in the early 1970s which was initially disastrous and forced him to work as a bar-room pianist for some years. When he returned in 1974, a song he had written about his bar experiences, *Piano Man*, gave him his first big hit, but his real breakthrough came in 1977 with a top 3 US hit *Just The Way You*

Are and a string of sophisticated LPs, which displayed his artistry as both writer and performer to good effect. His first US number one came in 1980 with *It's Still Rock And Roll To Me*, but his 1984 LP *An Innocent Man* provided numerous hit singles on both sides of the Atlantic, including a British number one with *Uptown Girl* and a US chart topper in *Tell Her About It*.

The tail end of the British punk scene

Above: Dave Edmunds (left) and Nick Lowe, co-leaders of Rockpile, a group of whom much was expected, but who, for various reasons, failed to survive.

Previous page left: Ex-boxer Billy Joel who achieved lasting fame as a piano playing singer/songwriter.

Previous page top right: Boston-based quintet the Cars, led by Ric Ocasek (centre), were far more popular in America than Britain.

Previous page bottom right: Jimmy Pursey, leader of Sham 69, a rabble-rousing punk quartet whose so-called fans drove them into retirement as a result of their violent behaviour at concerts.

included two acts who enjoyed early success but failed to follow through. Sham 69, fronted by Jimmy Pursey, enjoyed three hit singles a year in 1978 and 1979, but the fighting in which their so-called fans indulged at gigs forced the band to cease live work and, as their major success was on stage rather than on record, the group fell apart. Pursey's subsequent attempts at a solo career have been far less successful. The same is largely true of the various members of the Buzzcocks, a Manchester band. Their first leader Howard Devoto left to launch Magazine, a group who were only mildly notable, but when Peter Shelley took over as leader the Buzzcocks scored nine mostly minor hits in two and a half years before folding. Shelley's solo career has been almost as patchy as Devoto's.

A pair of comparative veterans of the pub rock scene, Ian Dury and Nick Lowe, both crashed into the charts in 1978. Since the dissolution of Brinsley Schwarz Lowe had worked mostly as a producer for Graham Parker, the Damned, Elvis Costello and Dr Feelgood, among others. He reached the UK top 10 in his own right with the single *I Love The Sound Of Breaking Glass* and his *Jesus Of Cool* LP, before returning to live work with Rockpile, a dynamic four-piece band which he co-led with Dave Edmunds. Although the group could not record under the name Rockpile for contractual reasons, both Edmunds and Lowe enjoyed several hits under their own names which were in fact by Rockpile. Ironically when the group finally made a properly credited group LP they broke up soon afterwards. Neither Lowe nor Edmunds achieved much solo success, although Edmunds also became a successful producer, responsible for huge hits by the Stray Cats plus the comeback LP by the Everly Brothers.

Ian Dury was less fortunate. Having led Kilburn and the High Roads until 1976 he signed with Stiff Records after forming a new band, the Blockheads, who interpreted Dury's quirky songs brilliantly. Dury peaked in early 1978 with a fine LP *New Boots & Panties* and topped the UK singles chart in early 1979 with *Hit Me With Your Rhythm Stick*, but thereafter the only route was

Althia and Donna, popsters Racey and Yellow Dog, and neo-folkies Brian and Michael have either disbanded or vanished and the same is true of US chart toppers Player and A Taste Of Honey. Several groups are still around, like Kiss, a glam rock heavy metal quartet who scored with numerous best-selling LPs and a few singles during the latter half of the 1970s. Their major gimmick was extravagent facial make-up. As their fame dissipated the group took the ultimate step – allowing themselves to be photographed without their warpaint, but it caused little but indifference.

The Tubes, a heavily theatrical group from San Francisco, were a huge live draw during the late 1970s but rarely sold as many records as their fame predicted and seem to have faded away. It would be incorrect to say the same of Meat Loaf despite a sub-stantial loss of weight from his gargantuan size when he first stormed the chart with *Bat Out Of Hell*. This classic hard rock LP was produced by Todd Rundgren, with songs by the remarkable Jim Steinman. In Britain particularly the LP became one of the biggest sellers of all time, and was still featuring in the UK chart almost seven years after its first appearance in early 1978. Meat's next LP took far longer than sched-uled to complete, largely due to disagree-ments with Steinman, who eventually re-corded the songs himself under the title *Bad For Good*. The album reached the top 10 and perhaps detracted from the appeal of Meat Loaf's follow-up LP *Dead Ringer*, which nevertheless remained in the chart for nearly a year. More recent records by Loaf have been comparatively mundane, but Steinman has neglected further solo recording in favour of work as a record producer making hits for Air Supply, Barry Manilow, Barbra Streisand and especially

Above: Marvin Lee Aday, professionally known as Meat Loaf, whose incredible Bat Out Of Hell *album was still in the British album charts more than six years after its initial release.*

Left: Glam rock extremists Kiss: (left to right) Gene Simmons, Peter Criss, Ace Frehley and Paul Stanley. Their unbelievably spectacular live show captured the imagination of thousands of American teenagers.

downhill and the departure of key members of the Blockheads also saw the end of his chart appeal. Both Dury and Nick Lowe, as well as Dave Edmunds, may return, but the passage of time makes new chart fame increasingly remote.

It seems even less likely that a number of those who made the singles chart will ever return there. In Britain, Jamaican schoolgirls

Above: The talented and photogenic Kate Bush, whose debut single, Wuthering Heights, was inspired by the Emily Bronte novel.

by EMI Records after they signed her in 1976. The lack of pressure seemed to work as *Wuthering Heights* topped the UK singles chart and each of her first four LPs reached the top 10 of the album chart, the third, *Never For Ever*, topping it. Thereafter, however, her output dropped dramatically both in quality and quantity and the company are presumably wondering at the end of 1984 whether they should have pushed her harder. Coincidentally another of the year's massive sellers, producer Jeff Wayne's musical version of *War Of The Worlds*, was also based on a novel, this time by H.G. Wells. During its four years in the British LP chart the album spawned a few hit singles, the biggest of which was *Forever Autumn*, performed by moonlighting Moody Blue Justin Hayward. Thus far Wayne has not released a follow-up LP.

1978 was also the year when several of the era's biggest stars reminded their audience that they were still very much alive. Among them were the Rolling Stones, who produced their best album for some time, *Some Girls*, which included *Miss You*, their biggest hit single in five years and underlined their continuing status as the ultimate rock'n'roll band.

David Bowie also demonstrated his ability to stay several months ahead of the opposition with a big-selling live double album *Stage*, but the most spectacular live success was scored by Bob Dylan, who had maintained a fairly low profile since his work with the celebrated Rolling Thunder Revue three years earlier. Film of that touring party had formed part of a movie made by Dylan titled *Renaldo and Clara*, but rumour had it that the commercial failure of the movie had forced the erstwhile king of protest back on the road. The concerts were an outstanding success, but not long afterwards Dylan unexpectedly espoused born-again Christianity and began to make gospel-styled LPs like *Slow Train Coming* and *Saved*. A subsequent tour in which the religious material formed the basis of Dylan's set was disappointing following the magnificent 1978 trek, but by 1984 he seemed to have reverted for the most part to his earlier material and was reported to have reassessed Christianity and reverted to Judaism.

1978 was not a great year for soul music although one of the biggest 1980s' stars, Lionel Richie, at the time fronting the Commodores, first tasted the joy of topping the chart. Having scored four top 10 singles in 1976 and 1977 the group reached number one with the classic *Three Times A Lady*, repeating the feat in 1979 with *Still*. Richie opted for a solo career in 1982, even eclipsing his great success with the group.

Perhaps the only other long-term soul act to hit the top 10 was the Pointer Sisters, a

Bonnie Tyler, as we shall see.

Another huge hitmaker in 1978 was Scottish singer/songwriter Gerry Rafferty, previously Billy Connolly's partner in the Humblebums and later leader of Stealer's Wheel, who charted in both the UK and the US in 1973/74. Rafferty's solo career peaked with *Baker Street*, which reached the top 3 on both sides of the Atlantic in 1978 and, while subsequent releases seemed equal in quality, they obviously failed to catch the public ear.

A similar fate befell Kate Bush, whose career was launched with the highly original *Wuthering Heights*, inspired by Emily Bronte's novel. Patronized by Dave Gilmour of Pink Floyd, Kate was carefully nurtured quartet who became a trio during the year when Bonnie Pointer decided to try for solo success. The remaining trio, Anita, June and Ruth, then signed with producer Richard Perry's newly formed Planet label and by the end of the year had reached the top 5 with *Fire*. They returned to the upper reaches of the chart in 1980 with *He's So Shy* and in 1981 with *Slow Hand*. Renewed success followed in 1984 with *Jump (For My Love)*, although Bonnie has so far failed to equal the chart success of her sisters.

The pop film of the year was undoubtedly *Grease*, which starred *Saturday Night Fever* lead John Travolta opposite Olivia Newton-John. The movie was a huge box-office hit, providing two duets between the principals, *You're The One That I Want* and *Summer Nights*, which between them topped the US singles chart for 16 weeks, while the sound-track LP topped the album chart in Britain for a further three months.

Also of note in Britain were the Darts, a London based group with a front line of four singers who performed an updated version of 1950s 'doo wop'. They had been creating a stir on stage for some time before finding a record label prepared to take them on. Once the plunge had been taken the Darts proved themselves extremely consistent, notching up a dozen hit singles and four hit LPs before internal difficulties forced them out of the limelight around 1981.

In America, Joe Walsh took time out from the Eagles to pick up the strings of his solo career. The resulting album *But Seriously Folks* included a satire on the lifestyle of rock'n'rollers, *Life's Been Good*, which became his biggest hit.

Overall 1978 was a candyfloss year in which little occurred to upset the rock establishment. Record sales continued to increase and already rich rock stars became richer. For most, life certainly was good, but the boom was coming to an end.

Below: After Saturday Night Fever *John Travolta starred in another highly successful rock movie,* Grease, *with Olivia Newton-John (Paramount, 1978).*

USA CHART TOPPERS

TITLE	ARTIST	LABEL	WEEKS AT NO. 1
How Deep Is Your Love?	The Bee Gees	RSO	1
Baby Come Back	Player	RSO	3
Stayin' Alive	The Bee Gees	RSO	4
Love Is Thicker Than Water	Andy Gibb	RSO	2
Night Fever	The Bee Gees	RSO	8
If I Can't Have You	Yvonne Elliman	RSO	1
With A Little Luck	Wings	Capitol	2
Too Much Too Little Too Late	Johnny Mathis and Deniece Williams	Columbia	1
You're The One That I Want	John Travolta and Olivia Newton-John	RSO	1
Shadow Dancing	Andy Gibb	RSO	7
Miss You	The Rolling Stones	Rolling Stones	1
Three Times A Lady	The Commodores	Motown	2
Grease	Frankie Valli	RSO	2
Boogie Oogie Oogie	A Taste Of Honey	Capitol	3
Kiss You All Over	Exile	Warner/Curb	4
Hot Child In The City	Nick Gilder	Chrysalis	1
You Needed Me	Anne Murray	Capitol	1
MacArthur Park	Donna Summer	Casablanca	3
You Don't Bring Me Flowers	Barbra Streisand and Neil Diamond	Columbia	2
Le Freak	Chic	Atlantic	3

UK CHART TOPPERS

TITLE	ARTIST	LABEL	WEEKS AT NO. 1
Mull Of Kintyre	Wings	Capitol	4
Uptown Top Ranking	Althia and Donna	Lightning	1
Figaro	Brotherhood Of Man	Pye	1
Take A Chance On Me	Abba	Epic	3
Wuthering Heights	Kate Bush	EMI	4
Matchstalk Men And Matchstalk Cats And Dogs	Brian and Michael	Pye	3
Night Fever	The Bee Gees	RSO	2
Rivers Of Babylon	Boney M	Atlantic/Hansa	5
You're The One That I Want	John Travolta and Olivia Newton-John	RSO	9
Three Times A Lady	The Commodores	Motown	5
Dreadlock Holiday	10 cc	Mercury	1
Summer Nights	John Travolta and Olivia Newton-John	RSO	7
Rat Trap	Boomtown Rats	Ensign	2
Do Ya Think I'm Sexy?	Rod Stewart	Riva	1
Mary's Boy Child	Boney M	Atlantic/Hansa	4

FILMS

Animal House
The Buddy Holly Story
Death On The Nile
The Eyes Of Laura Mars
Grease
Hooper
The Last Waltz
Lord Of The Rings
Renaldo And Clara
Revenge Of The Pink Panther
Saturday Night Fever
Superman
Watership Down

DEATHS

Sandy Denny, singer
Jim Jones, religious cult leader
Terry Kath, Chicago guitarist
Golda Meir, politician
Keith Moon, drummer
Wilfred Pickles, radio personality
Nancy Spungen, girlfriend of Sid Vicious

15 February: Agreement is reached on black majority rule in Rhodesia.

16 March: His five bodyguards are killed when former Italian premier Aldo Moro is captured by left-wing terrorists of the Red Brigade.

17 March: The huge oil tanker *Amoco Cadiz* breaks in half in heavy seas off Brittany, polluting the Breton coast.

7 April: President Carter announces the deferment of neutron bomb production until circumstances warranted 'the ultimate decision'.

9 May: The bullet-riddled body of Aldo Moro is found in a car boot in the centre of Rome.

25 July: The first test tube baby is born in England.

4 August: Jeremy Thorpe and three others are charged with conspiracy to murder former male model Norman Scott.

6 August: Pope Paul VI dies of a heart attack; John Paul I succeeds him.

17 August: Three American hot air balloonists complete the first transatlantic crossing.

10 September: Martial law is declared in Rhodesia to combat increasing guerrilla activity.

15 September: Muhammad Ali defeats Leon Spinks to become world heavyweight boxing champion for the third time.

29 September: The new Pope, John Paul I, is found dead of a cardiac arrest after a 34-day reign. Karol Wojtyla of Poland becomes John Paul II.

2 November: Soviet cosmonauts Kovalenok and Ivanchenkov descend to earth in Soyuz 31 after a record 139 days in space.

18 November: The murder of a US congressman in Guyana triggers mass suicide by members of a religious cult; 913 die.

Left: The familiar image of the year's most successful musical film, Saturday Night Fever, starring John Travolta (Paramount, 1978).

Made in England

1978

SIDE ONE
45 RPM
STEREO

Three Times A Lady

ALL RIGHTS OF THE MANUFACTURER AND OF THE OWNER OF THE RECORDED WORK RESERVED UNAUTHORISED PUBLIC PERFORMANCE BROADCASTING AND COPYING OF THIS RECORD PROHIBITED

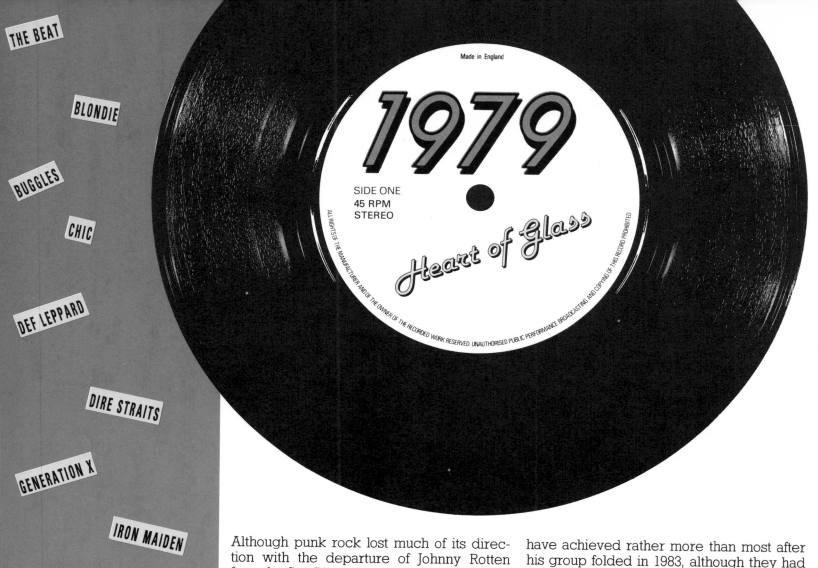

Made in England

1979

SIDE ONE
45 RPM
STEREO

Heart of Glass

ALL RIGHTS OF THE MANUFACTURER AND OF THE OWNER OF THE RECORDED WORK RESERVED. UNAUTHORISED PUBLIC PERFORMANCE BROADCASTING AND COPYING OF THIS RECORD PROHIBITED

Although punk rock lost much of its direction with the departure of Johnny Rotten from the Sex Pistols, the death of Sid Vicious in early February meant the end of an era. Rotten wished henceforward to be known by his real name of John Lydon and formed a new group, Public Image Limited, whose 1978 debut single *Public Image* was their biggest hit until *This Is Not A Love Song* in 1983. Thereafter Lydon was the only ever-present member of a group whose personnel seemed to alter constantly, leading to a considerable loss of influence compared to his years with the Pistols.

Among the final wave of British punk bands were Generation X, the Skids (from Scotland) and two Irish groups the Undertones and Stiff Little Fingers. None of these bands was still functioning by the mid-1980s, although each of their lead singers was either working solo or leading a fresh band by then. Billy Idol of Generation X left the band at the start of 1981 and moved to New York, where he has yet to achieve the stardom predicted for him. Richard Jobson of the Skids, who had ten UK hit singles in just over two years, went on to lead the Armoury Show. Jake Burns of Stiff Little Fingers, a Belfast quartet who impressed with their debut single *Suspect Device* but thereafter promised more than they delivered, has achieved little since leaving the group in early 1983. Along with Billy Idol, Feargal Sharkey, the choirboy-voiced singer of the Undertones, could be said to

have achieved rather more than most after his group folded in 1983, although they had fared better than many of their peers with four UK top 20 singles between 1979 and 1981. Sharkey's solo career began with two hits, the first, *Never Never*, under the name of the Assembly (the alter ego of Vince Clarke, of whom more later) and the second, *Listen To Your Father*, backed by Madness, a North London group who were leading lights of the 2-Tone movement.

2-Tone music, so called because the majority of its practitioners were groups with both black and white members, began in the Midlands of England and owed a musical debt to ska music from Jamaica, which had provided occasional 1960s hits. The leaders and founders of the 2-Tone record label were a Coventry band the Special AKA (later known simply as the Specials, but more recently using their original title), whose first single *Gangsters* was so impressive that Chrysalis Records signed both group and label. The Specials took seven singles into the UK top 10 in two years, including a pair of number ones, *Too Much Too Young* in 1980 and *Ghost Town* in mid-1981, plus two top 5 LPs. After *Ghost Town*'s success, singers Terry Hall and Neville Staples and guitarist Lynval Golding formed a splinter group, Fun Boy Three. Specials leader Jerry Dammers recruited new members and the Special AKA are still well respected (Elvis Costello produces their records) but less commercial

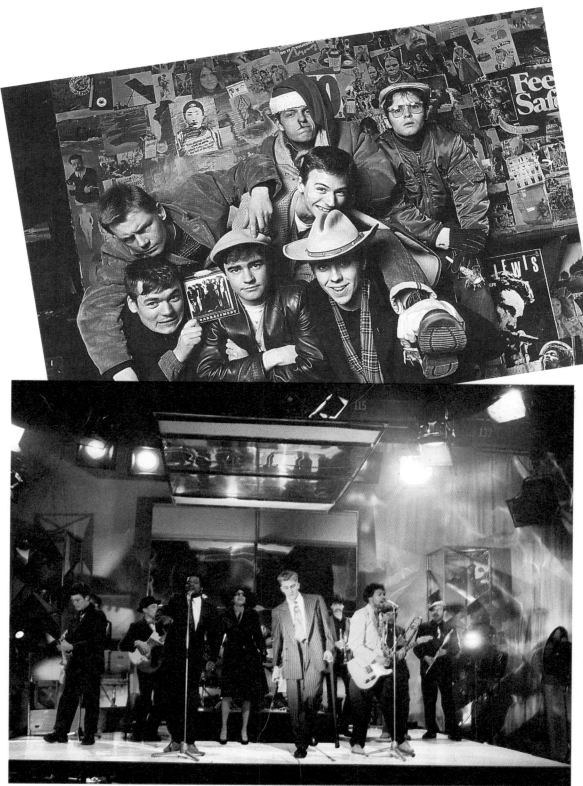

The Selecter, another Coventry group, were the second 2-Tone act. By the end of 1980, singer Pauline Black had achieved some solo success after the group disbanded.

By far the most consistent of the 2-Tone acts was Madness, a seven-piece group from north London who were reviving ska music at the same time as the Specials, but without either knowing of the other group's existence. After reaching the top 20 with their only 2-Tone single the group signed with Stiff Records, for whom they produced a run of nearly 20 British hit singles, most of which made the top 10 and one of which, *House Of Fun*, topped the British chart in 1982 before the group and Stiff fell out. A compilation LP titled *Complete Madness* topped the UK album chart and gave Stiff its biggest ever hit but the decision to leave the label coincided with the departure from the band of its main songwriter, keyboard player and joint founder Mike Barson, and the group's quiet year in 1984 seemed to suggest that fresh inspiration was necessary.

Although several other acts recorded for 2-Tone, the only other notable group on the label was the Beat, whose only 2-Tone single *Tears Of A Clown* was one of their biggest hits. After that they launched their own label Go Feet Records and, although

their first year contained three further top 10 hits, the group's singles became less commercial and by early 1983 they had disbanded. Singers Dave Wakeling and Ranking Roger then formed a new group, General Public, whose eponymous first single suggested that they had regained some of their lost spark. While the 2-Tone movement was comparatively brief, its impact was immense.

Several other British groups were beginning careers which continue to thrive today. They were dubbed the NWOBHM (New Wave Of British Heavy Metal).

Motorhead had started in 1975 after their leader Lemmy Kilmister was fired by his previous band Hawkwind. The group suffered several personnel changes but since their breakthrough in 1979 with their fourth LP *Bomber* have continually returned to the album chart.

Judas Priest, another NWOBHM band, formed in Birmingham in 1973. The group's solid following resulted in a series of chart albums. Their biggest LP in Britain so far has been *British Steel*, which reached the top 5, while their first platinum LP in America came with *Screaming For Vengeance* in 1982.

Saxon, a Yorkshire heavy metal band, scored eight hit singles in 18 months without reaching the top 10, although two of their albums *Wheels Of Steel* and *Denim And Leather* made the upper reaches of the LP chart. Iron Maiden were marginally more successful: *Run To The Hills* climbed to the top 10 of the singles chart in 1982 as their LP *The Number Of The Beast* topped the UK album chart. However, even that paled in comparison with the achievements of Def Leppard, a group from Sheffield whose second LP *High'n'Dry* remained in the US chart for 18 months, while their next album *Pyromania* reached number two in America. British sales were far less spectacular.

American heavy metal also thrived with Los Angeles-based Van Halen, who took their name from two brothers of Dutch extraction, drummer Alex and guitarist Edward Van Halen. Despite the excitement generated by extrovert lead singer David Lee Roth the group found it difficult to acquire a recording contract, but their persistence finally paid off with six platinum LPs in the US. Singles success had been moderate before *Jump* from the group's 1984 LP *1984* topped the charts for five weeks.

The balance between British and American acts in the charts on both sides of the Atlantic became even more pronounced during the year. The new US phenomenon was Blondie, a New York group fronted by Deborah Harry. The group had broken through in Britain in 1978 with four top 20 singles hits and a chart-topping LP *Parallel Lines*, and in 1979 *Heart Of Glass* became the group's first number one single in the USA, just as it had been a few months before in Britain. Blondie's enormous popularity lasted until the end of 1981, encompassing three further chart-topping singles in America and four more in Britain, including *Call Me* and *The Tide Is High*, both of which reached the top in both countries. Their concurrent success in the UK LP chart, where *Eat To The Beat* also reached the top, was not repeated in America. The Blondie bubble finally burst when Debbie Harry made a solo LP *Koo Koo*, produced by Nile Rodgers and Bernard Edwards of Chic. That album was a disappointment and a subsequent Blondie LP fared little better.

Chic themselves were extremely successful during the year, topping the US

Above: Deborah Harry, the focal point and vocalist of Blondie, who topped the British singles chart five times in less than two years.

Left: Chic, led by Nile Rodgers and Bernard Edwards, achieved more hits as producers, with the likes of Diana Ross and David Bowie, than on their own account, after an exceedingly promising start in 1977/78 with Dance, Dance, Dance.

singles chart with both *Le Freak* and *Good Times*. However, their own records seemed to fall out of favour as their production work for others became successful. In 1980 Rodgers and Edwards produced the remarkable *Diana* LP for Diana Ross, which included her first number one single in four years, *Upside Down*. They preceded this triumph with hits for a group of four sisters, Sister Sledge, finding the top 10 on both sides of the Atlantic in 1979 with *He's The Greatest Dancer* and *We Are Family*. The Chic duo also wrote much of the material which they produced as well as playing on it, but their greatest moment so far came in 1984 when Rodgers co-produced David Bowie's *Let's Dance* LP with Edwards playing bass.

The year provided another clutch of one-hit wonders, including ex-teacher Anita Ward's *Ring My Bell*; Amii Stewart, an American girl who scored with German disco producers to take *Knock On Wood* to the top of the US chart; the unlikely duo of Barbra Streisand and Donna Summer, whose sensational *No More Tears (Enough Is Enough)* made number one in the USA and number three in Britain; and Rupert Holmes, who turned from arranging to performing and took *Escape (The Pina Colada Song)* to the top.

Another one-off chart topper was M, in reality Robin Scott, who came up with *Pop Muzik*, an early taste of the synthesizer music which would soon follow, and an American number one. In Britain, too, electronics duo Buggles, previously studio technicians, scored with *Video Killed The Radio Star*. Before long Trevor Horn and Geoff Downes were drafted into Yes, with whom they shared management, and helped that group to make their last LP before a temporary dissolution. A few years later Downes would re-emerge as a member of Asia, while Horn would become one of the architects behind Frankie Goes To Hollywood.

Certainly Siouxsie and the Banshees, early fans of the Sex Pistols and whose first line-up featured Sid Vicious on drums, would not deny their punk connections. They were virtually the last of the original punk bands to be signed, making up for lost time by using their bleak sound to make a dozen medium-sized hit singles and half a dozen hit LPs in Britain by the end of 1982.

Also regarded as part of the punk mainstream before they were properly heard were Gary Numan, the Police, Squeeze and the Pretenders. Numan had functioned under the name of Tubeway Army, which he used for his first hit *Are Friends Electric?*, before assuming a single persona for a second UK chart topper *Cars*, also in 1979. Numan's Bowiesque music, largely produced on synthesizers, seemed a perfect soundtrack for an increasingly electronic

world and he has continued to score hits, albeit smaller ones, to date, topping the UK LP charts with *Replicas*, *The Pleasure Principle* and *Telekon* by late 1980.

The Police were launched in 1977 as a punk band, although this direction was short-lived. Fronted by charismatic singer/writer/bass player Sting (real name Gordon Sumner) and completed by drummer Stewart Copeland and guitarist Andy Summers, both veterans of pre-punk days, the group first charted in 1979 with *Roxanne*, and by the end of the year had taken two further singles, *Message In A Bottle* and *Walking On The Moon*, to the top of the British chart, as well as their *Regatta De Blanc* album. Further Police singles and LPs topped the British chart, but it wasn't until 1983 that the group dominated the US charts, when *Every Breath You Take* topped the singles chart for nine weeks and *Synchronicity* eventually spent 18 weeks at the top of the LP chart.

At the start of their career Squeeze shared management with the Police, despite their talents being somewhat different. Performing the quirky compositions of group leaders Glenn Tilbrook and Chris Difford, the group scored over a dozen hit singles in Britain in less than five years before the two writers decided to go their own way. Their skills will surely re-emerge to great effect in the future.

The Pretenders also appear today in a different form from when they first topped the chart in 1979 with *Brass In Pocket*. Apart from the premature deaths of guitarist James Honeyman-Scott and bass player Pete Farndon, leader/songwriter Chrissie Hynde is (in late 1984) devoting only part of her time to

the group. Joe Jackson, a classically trained keyboard player, had been inspired by the example of Elvis Costello. He scored in both Britain and America with *Is She Really Going Out With Him?*, but thereafter his hits were sporadic. He became much more an album act, cutting *Jumpin' Jive*, a Louis Jordan-styled LP in 1981 and the highly successful *Night And Day*, a jazz-influenced album for which he moved to New York from England in 1982.

Another British act, Dire Straits, first attracted attention in America while they were largely ignored in Britain. The group's leader, Mark Knopfler, is a guitarist and songwriter in the country rock mould. Their lack of acceptance in Britain was brief however and, after three strong-selling LPs along with occasional British single hits, the group's fourth album *Love Over Gold* topped the charts on both sides of the Atlantic. By 1984 the group were among the most popular in the world.

Los Angelean quartet the Knack topped the US singles chart for six weeks with *My Sharona*. Unfortunately they were unable to follow it up with anything as catchy and quietly folded during the early 1980s. The same fate seems to have befallen the Village People, a group of disco singers who appeared to be puppets of producer Jacques Morali. The group reached the top 3 in Britain and America with both *Y.M.C.A.* and *In The Navy* before their magic evaporated.

Two new British names, XTC and Lene Lovich, also made promising debuts. Lene, an American based in Britain, made a huge impact with a top 3 single *Lucky Number*. Her exotic appearance and equally exotic

saxophone playing marked her out as having huge potential, but her extraordinary qualities seemed to evaporate. XTC managed half a dozen hits and several critically acclaimed LPs before fading into the mainstream after their 1982 album *English Settlement* reached the UK top 5. Both seem to be still around, which is more than can be said for Pink Floyd, who re-emerged in 1979 with a conceptual double LP, *The Wall*. This included a number one single, of immense proportions, *Another Brick In The Wall (Part II)*, before the idea behind the record was made into a feature film. After this the group quietly broke up.

1979 ended with a choir of schoolkids singing 'We don't need no education' on the Pink Floyd's hit – few realized how prophetic these words would become.

Top left: Intrepid aviator Gary Numan chortles as disc jockeys Peter Powell (left), Dave Lee Travis (above right) and David 'Kid' Jensen help to start his aeroplane.

Top right: The Police: (left to right) Sting, Andy Summers and Stewart Copeland, who conquered America initially by lengthy low budget touring.

Above: The original line-up of the Pretenders: (left to right) Pete Farndon, Martin Chambers, Chrissie Hynde (now Kerr) and James Honeyman-Scott.

TITLE	ARTIST	LABEL	WEEKS AT NO. 1
Too Much Heaven	The Bee Gees	RSO	2
Le Freak	Chic	Atlantic	3
Do Ya Think I'm Sexy?	Rod Stewart	Warner Bros	4
I Will Survive	Gloria Gaynor	Polydor	3
Tragedy	The Bee Gees	RSO	2
What A Fool Believes	Doobie Brothers	Warner Bros	1
Knock On Wood	Amii Stewart	Ariola	1
Heart Of Glass	Blondie	Chrysalis	4
Reunited	Peaches and Herb	Polydor	3
Hot Stuff	Donna Summer	Casablanca	1
Love You Inside Out	The Bee Gees	RSO	2
Ring My Bell	Anita Ward	Juana/TK	5
Bad Girls	Donna Summer	Casablanca	1
Good Times	Chic	Atlantic	6
My Sharona	The Knack	Capitol	1
Sad Eyes	Robert John	EMI	1
Don't Stop Til You Get Enough	Michael Jackson	Epic	2
Rise	Herb Alpert	A&M	1
Pop Music	M	Sire	1
Heartache Tonight	The Eagles	Asylum	1
Still	The Commodores	Motown	2
No More Tears	Barbra Streisand and Donna Summer	Columbia/Casablanca	2
Babe	Styx	A&M	
Escape	Rupert Holmes	MCA/Infinity	2

TITLE	ARTIST	LABEL	WEEKS AT NO. 1
YMCA	The Village People	Mercury	3
Hit Me With Your Rhythm Stick	Ian Dury and the Blockheads	Stiff	1
Heart Of Glass	Blondie	Chrysalis	4
Tragedy	The Bee Gees	RSO	2
I Will Survive	Gloria Gaynor	Polydor	4
Bright Eyes	Art Garfunkel	CBS	6
Sunday Girl	Blondie	Chrysalis	3
Ring My Bell	Anita Ward	TK	2
Are Friends Electric?	Tubeway Army	Beggars Banquet	4
I Don't Like Mondays	Boomtown Rats	Ensign	4
We Don't Talk Anymore	Cliff Richard	EMI	4
Cars	Gary Numan	Beggars Banquet	1
Message In A Bottle	Police	A&M	3
Video Killed The Radio Star	Buggles	Island	1
One Day At A Time	Lena Martell	Pye	3
When You're In Love With A Beautiful Woman	Dr Hook	Capitol	3
Walking On The Moon	Police	A&M	1
Another Brick In The Wall	Pink Floyd	Harvest	3

DEATHS

- Gracie Fields, singer
- Lester Flatt, bluegrass pioneer
- Lowell George, rock star
- Donny Hathaway, singer
- Stan Kenton, bandleader
- Charlie Mingus, jazz musician
- Mary Pickford, actress
- Jean Renoir, painter
- Minnie Ripperton, singer
- Sid Vicious, punk musician
- John Wayne, film star

FILMS

- Alien
- Apocalypse Now
- Breaking Away
- The China Syndrome
- The Deer Hunter
- The Electric Horseman
- Every Which Way But Loose
- Kramer Vs Kramer
- Manhattan
- Monty Python's Life Of Brian
- Quadrophenia
- Rock'N'Roll High School
- Rocky II
- Tess
- Yanks

1 February: Moslem revolutionary leader Ayatollah Khomeini arrives in Iran after a 15-year exile. Three million supporters line the streets to roar greeting. He takes over the country following the flight of the Shah.

2 March: Home rule for Wales and Scotland is rejected in a referendum.

28 March: An accident at Three Mile Island nuclear power plant in Pennsylvania causes a radioactivity scare.

11 April: The Amin regime is toppled in Uganda, ending eight years of mis-rule.

3 May: The Conservatives win the UK general election, Margaret Thatcher becomes Prime Minister.

22 May: Soviet police are unable to control screaming fans at an Elton John concert in Leningrad.

25 May: All DC10s are grounded after one loses a wing over Chicago airport.

12 June: Bryan Allen pedals a bicycle plane across the English Channel.

26 June: Muhammad Ali, 37, announces his retirement from the ring.

28 June: Chuck Berry plays the White House; is later sentenced to four months in prison for tax evasion.

11 July: The International Whaling Commission bans whale factory ships to save 10,000 creatures a year.

23 July: The Ayatollah bans radio and TV music as remnants of a 'satanic' regime, having already banned alcohol and films from the Western world.

27 August: Earl Mountbatten is killed when his fishing boat is blown up by the IRA. The same day 18 soldiers are killed in an ambush at Warrenpoint, County Down.

3 September: The body of the Yorkshire Ripper's twelfth victim is found in Bradford.

18 September: Following the defection of Alexandr Godunov earlier in the year, two more pincipals of the Bolshoi Ballet defect to USA.

23 September: Jane Fonda is a speaker at a huge anti-nuclear rally in New York City.

18 October: More than 53,000 Kampuchean refugees are driven into Thailand.

4 November: Students occupy the US Embassy in Tehran, taking all US personnel hostage. Their action is fully supported by the Ayatollah.

4 December: 11 people are trampled to death at a Who concert in Cincinnati.

25 December: Soviet forces invade Afghanistan.

29 December: The secret trial of the Gang of Four is announced in Peking.

Made in England

1979

SIDE ONE
45 RPM
STEREO

Heart of Glass

ALL RIGHTS OF THE MANUFACTURER AND OF THE OWNER OF THE RECORDED WORK RESERVED UNAUTHORISED PUBLIC PERFORMANCE BROADCASTING AND COPYING OF THIS RECORD PROHIBITED

227

Made in England

1980

SIDE ONE
45 RPM
STEREO

Just Like Starting Over

ALL RIGHTS OF THE MANUFACTURER AND OF THE OWNER OF THE RECORDED WORK RESERVED UNAUTHORISED PUBLIC PERFORMANCE BROADCASTING AND COPYING OF THIS RECORD PROHIBITED

It became obvious in 1980 that punk rock had not completed its task of clearing away the dead wood of the early 1970s. Among the year's UK chart toppers were Kelly Marie, Odyssey, Johnny Logan and Fern Kinney, all of whom failed to achieve anything as successful again. Even so, they were certainly superior to the sound of a primary school choir intoning *There's No One Quite Like Grandma* another number one.

Fortunately (and inevitably) there were better sounds around, although America had its own crosses to bear in the shape of Lipps Inc and the extremely retrogressive Christopher Cross, whose connection with rock music was tenuous to say the least. Cross had worked with Texan rock band Flash, but left after it became clear that the material he wrote was inappropriate for the band. Several years later, he finally acquired a recording contract and his second single, *Sailing*, topped the US singles chart, a feat which he repeated in 1979 with *Best That You Can Do*, the theme song from the movie *Arthur*.

In Britain the 2-Tone movement was still strong with three newer groups (although none of them were actually signed to the 2-Tone label) joining the Specials and Madness near the top of the charts. Dexy's (short for the stimulant dexedrine) Midnight Runners were the first to break through under the inspired and charismatic leadership of Kevin Rowland. Inclined more towards 1960s soul music than ska, with particular reference to Geno Washington and the Ram Jam Band, Dexy's topped the UK charts with a tribute to their inspiration titled *Geno*. This swift elevation to celebrity perhaps accounted for the internal arguments which soon fragmented the band. Only Rowland and one other member remained to form the nucleus of a second version of the band, but it was fairly shortlived, being supplanted in 1982 by a smaller group featuring two folk-styled fiddle players. The resultant ethnic sound brought a worldwide number one hit in *Come On Eileen* and an accompanying hit LP *Too-Rye-Ay*, but by the end of 1984 Rowland had yet to re-emerge with anything new.

A similar silence has recently pervaded the career of Bad Manners, a nine-piece ska band from north London, who scored nearly a dozen hits in Britain plus four chart LPs before business problems forced them into premature retirement. Nevertheless, their huge singer Douglas Trendle (known as Buster Bloodvessel) will not be easily forgotten.

Of all the 2-Tone style acts the most consistent, along with Madness, have been UB40, who took their name from the infamous unemployment benefit form. Jointly led by the sons of folk singer Ian Campbell,

the group scored eight hits in two and a half years, four of which made the UK top 10 before they went out of fashion for a year. Their return in 1983 produced their biggest hit so far, a cover version of a song written by Neil Diamond, *Red Red Wine*, performed in the style of reggae singer Tony Tribe, who had enjoyed a minor hit with the song in 1969. Taken from a complete LP of reggae cover versions, *Labour Of Love*, which itself topped the British chart, *Red Red Wine* was one of several hits from the album, but following it with an equally commercial original song has so far proved more difficult.

A few more erstwhile punks made the big time like Adam and the Ants, who adopted a new musical direction (suggested by Malcolm McLaren) using two drummers to create an African tribal sound. In a very odd manoeuvre, McLaren convinced the rest of the group to leave Adam and, while they achieved some success as Bow Wow Wow, fronted by a teenage Burmese girl named Annabella Lwin, Adam recruited Marco Pirroni, originally guitarist with Siouxsie and the Banshees, as his new lieutenant and co-writer. During the second half of 1980 he began a run of British hits using the percussive style which included three number ones in *Stand And Deliver*, *Prince Charming* and *Goody Two Shoes*, as well as several big-selling albums of which *Kings Of The Wild Frontier*, also a chart topper, was the biggest. A portion of Adam's success came as a result of several imaginative and colourful videos used to promote his singles. He pursued further fame in America where he became one of the

HAZEL O'CONNOR

ODYSSEY

ORCHESTRAL MANOEUVRES IN THE DARK

OZZY OSBOURNE

EDDIE RABBITT

REO SPEEDWAGON

SHAKIN' STEVENS

PETE TOWNSHEND

UB40

ULTRAVOX

229

Above: The gentle and refined Ozzy Osbourne pictured immediately before attending a recital of chamber music.

Previous page left: Kevin Rowland, leader of Dexy's Midnight Runners.

Previous page right: Adam (front) and the Ants attracted a fervent following as a result of a series of imaginative promotional videos.

earliest stars of MTV, the popular cable television network. Apart from occasional hits, Adam seems to have turned his back on Britain, as has Ozzy Osbourne, erstwhile lead singer of heavy metal band Black Sabbath.

After leaving that band, Ozzy formed his own group, Blizzard of Ozz, in 1980 and his first two LPs with the band, *Blizzard Of Ozz* and *Diary Of A Madman*, both quickly went gold. Despite the death of his guitarist Randy Rhoads in an aviation accident and Ozzie's well-publicized penchant for biting the head off small birds, he remains very popular on both sides of the Atlantic.

Reverting to the punks, Hazel O'Connor launched herself as a singer/songwriter with a starring part in the music business movie, *Breaking Glass*, scoring a top 5 hit single with *Eighth Day*. Her career continued to thrive with several follow-ups, but by 1982 she had fallen out with her manager and her record label and could not record for nearly two years. Her eventual return was unfortunately less notable than her fans had expected. Much more successful were Ultravox, a one-time punk band, albeit of a superior musical quality. After three unsuccessful LPs lead vocalist John Foxx

announced he was leaving the group, as did the latest of their guitarists. The remaining three members, Chris Cross, Billy Currie and Warren Cann, recruited ex-Slik and Rich Kids front man James 'Midge' Ure and adopted a new style using synthesizers, which paid off with two small hits in 1980. By the end of 1984 this total had increased to 15 consecutive hits plus several top 10 albums, the most successful being a double compilation titled *The Collection*, which was close to the top of the British LP chart at the end of 1984. Ultravox's rehabilitation seemed initially secondary to the fortunes of Foxx, who launched his solo career with four small hits in 1980 plus a top 20 album, after which his output slowed to a crawl, while his ex-group went from strength to strength.

The Cure, a group from Crawley in Sussex led by singer/guitarist/writer Robert Smith, had impressed with their debut single *Killing An Arab*, but it failed to reach the chart although five subsequent small hits within the next two and a half years, plus increasingly more successful LPs culminating in *Pornography* reaching the UK top 10 in 1982, redressed the balance in the group's favour. Their future seemed in doubt for a lengthy period when Smith was also working as lead guitarist with Siouxsie and the Banshees, whom he had first joined temporarily when John McKay left the Banshees on the eve of an extensive tour. Smith later devoted his full attention to the Cure, although their chance of megastardom seems to have disappeared.

1980 saw Welsh rock'n'roller Shakin' Stevens becoming an overnight star after more than a decade of recording for a succession of different labels. When he teamed up with record producer Stuart Colman Stevens discovered the vital spark which he had sought for so long and, backed by a seasoned group of session musicians, scored his first top 20 hit *Marie Marie* at the end of 1980. For three years he was rarely out of the British top 10 but, like so many other British discoveries of 1980, failed to take even UK chart toppers like *This Ole House*, *Green Door* and *Oh Julie* anywhere near the top of the US chart. Curiously the single by Stevens which many regarded as his finest, *You Drive Me Crazy*, failed to reach the top. This excellent and catchy record bore at least a certain similarity to a single by American Rocky Burnette, son of Johnny Burnette of *Dreamin'* fame, *Tired Of Toeing The Line*. It had only been a minor hit when it was first released in Britain in 1979 but reached the US top 10 the following year, since when Burnette's recordings have meant little.

John Cougar Mellencamp was more significant. He first emerged during the mid-1970s under the management of Tony De Fries, who had helped to mastermind David Bowie's dramatic rise to fame but then fell out with his star. As a result Cougar (the Mellencamp – his real name – was added later) was regarded erroneously as a potential new Bowie. In fact his talents had more in common with Bruce Springsteen's, but the stigma of De Fries (from whom he quickly split) made progress difficult. In 1980 the streetwise lyrics of *Nothing Matters And What If It Did* took him into the US LP chart. His single *Ain't Even Done With The Night* reached the US top 20 in 1981, but Cougar's major breakthrough came in 1982 when *Jack And Diane* topped the US singles chart three months after *Hurts So Good* had reached number two. The LP from which both songs came, *American Fool*, topped the US chart and went platinum. At the end of 1984 Cougar looked set for a long run.

Another anonymous 'stadium rock' band emerged in America in the shape of REO Speedwagon, a group from Illinois who had formed during the late 1960s and had been making minor chart LPs since 1974. They took off in 1980 with the six-million-selling *Hi-Infidelity* album which topped the US LP chart, along with a single taken from it, *Keep On Loving You*, which was a number one and even made the top 10 in the UK.

Other American acts to create a stir were Steve Forbert, a singer/songwriter who probably suffered from being compared with Bob Dylan but who had a sizeable hit in the USA with *Romeo's Tune*; country music star Eddie Rabbitt, who broke out of his Nashville confines with a string of US pop chart hits, the biggest of which *I Love A Rainy Night* was a chart topper; Rickie Lee

Top: Shakin' Stevens, who made his name in the musical Elvis, *went on to become a consistent hitmaker in Britain during the early 1980s.*

Above: Ultravox: (left to right) Warren Cann, Chris Cross, Billy Currie and Midge Ure during TV's Top of the Pops.

Jones, whose *Chuck E's In Love* was a departure from her usual style (which resembled Tom Waits'), and the somewhat eccentric New Wave quintet from Georgia, the B-52s, who achieved minor fame with *Rock Lobster*, a 1979 single.

British equivalents included Robert Palmer, a veteran of Vinegar Joe, in which he had duetted with Elkie Brooks. Palmer moved to live in the Bahamas and began producing delightfully tasteful LPs. The Tourists, a group featuring Annie Lennox and Dave Stewart, looked set for fame but disbanded in 1981 after a pair of top 10 singles in 1980 after which the two principals went on to form Eurythmics.

Two groups, notable for different reasons, emerged from the north of England – Joy Division from Manchester and Orchestral Manoeuvres In The Dark from Merseyside, who later, for obvious reasons, were known as OMD. Joy Division, a bleak sounding group, had built up a formidable following among disaffected British students, but the cult only translated into chart action after their singer Ian Curtis committed suicide during the first half of 1980. Within a few weeks *Love Will Tear Us Apart* became a top 20 hit in the UK after which the group metamorphosed into New Order. OMD, whose leading lights are synthesists Paul Humphreys and Andy McCluskey (previously members of the oddly named Hitlerz

Underpantz), had enjoyed increasing success since 1979, helped by the patronage of Gary Numan. They released three hit singles and two chart LPs in 1980, but their best year was 1981 with two top 5 singles and a top 3 LP in *Architecture And Morality*. A measure of their wry humour is that even their record company refer to them as 'the boring bank clerks', yet their lack of image and absence from the headlines may have given them a big advantage over their rivals.

A similar, although less extreme, attitude was taken by two British solo performers both named Peter and both from notable groups. Peter Gabriel, once of Genesis, went solo in 1975 but delayed his return to recording until 1977 when he scored with an eponymous debut LP which reached the UK top 10, and a top 20 single *Solsbury Hill*. His output became quirky, infrequent and sometimes political, like his 1980 minor hit *Biko*. During the same year he achieved his greatest success with his third solo LP which, like the previous two and the one which followed, was titled simply *Peter Gabriel*. His refusal to compromise for the sake of commercial considerations is admirable, if perhaps dangerous financially, and his ability to produce interesting ideas should be his ultimate salvation.

Pete Townshend began a solo career in earnest in 1980 with the excellent *Empty Glass* LP. His commitments to the Who were

Below: Synthesizer wizards Orchestral Manoeuvres In The Dark, who, not surprisingly, became better known by their abbreviated name of OMD.

Above: Peter Gabriel fools no-one with his impersonation of a London Transport employee.

to continue until the end of 1982, aside from his personal interest in good causes such as Rock Against Racism and Amnesty International, which sometimes seemed to divert him from his own career. One such event, in which the Who as a whole were involved, was a series of Concerts for Kampuchea, which also featured Wings, Queen, Elvis Costello and the Clash among others. The film and LP of the event were delayed for more than a year by legal problems similar to those experienced by George Harrison's Bangla Desh concerts, but Paul McCartney, who helped to organize the shows, was eventually able to contribute towards relief for the country's people.

The biggest and most tragic Beatle news of the year came on 8 December when John Lennon, who had emerged from a five-year self-imposed exile only a few weeks before, was shot and killed by a schizophrenic 'fan' in New York. Lennon's recently released single *(Just Like) Starting Over* and album *Double Fantasy* had begun to drop in the world's charts and were regarded as disappointing, but his murder produced vast sales of both Beatles' and John's own records. The single and LP returned to the top of the charts on both sides of the Atlantic and the early weeks of 1981 saw the reissued *Imagine* at the top of the UK singles chart after which another track from the new LP *Woman* took its place.

An era had ended with the final realization that the Beatles would never reform. Many considered that rock'n'roll would never be the same again, but it took only a few weeks to return to the familiar routine.

USA CHART TOPPERS

TITLE	ARTIST	LABEL	WEEKS AT NO. 1
Please Don't Go	K.C. and the Sunshine Band	TK	1
Escape	Rupert Holmes	MCA/Infinity	1
Rock With You	Michael Jackson	Epic	4
Do That To Me	The Captain and Tenille	Casablanca	1
Crazy Little Thing Called Love	Queen	Elektra	4
Another Brick In The Wall	Pink Floyd	Columbia	4
Call Me	Blondie	Chrysalis	6
Funky Town	Lipps Inc	Casablanca	4
Coming Up	Paul McCartney and Wings	Columbia	3
Still Rock And Roll To Me	Billy Joel	Columbia	3
Magic	Olivia Newton-John	MCA	3
Sailing	Christopher Cross	Warner Bros	1
All Out Of Love	Air Supply	Arista	2
Upside Down	Diana Ross	Motown	2
Another One Bites The Dust	Queen	Elektra	6
Woman In Love	Barbra Streisand	Columbia	1
Lady	Kenny Rogers	Liberty	5
(Just Like) Starting Over	John Lennon	Geffen	1

UK CHART TOPPERS

TITLE	ARTIST	LABEL	WEEKS AT NO. 1
Another Brick In The Wall	Pink Floyd	Harvest	2
Brass In Pocket	The Pretenders	Real	2
The Special AKA Live (EP)	The Specials	2-Tone	2
Coward Of The County	Kenny Rogers	United Artists	2
Atomic	Blondie	Chrysalis	2
Together We Are Beautiful	Fern Kinney	WEA	1
Going Underground	The Jam	Polydor	3
Working My Way Back To You	Detroit Spinners	Atlantic	2
Call Me	Blondie	Chrysalis	1
Geno	Dexy's Midnight Runners	Parlophone	2
What's Another Year	Johnny Logan	Epic	2
Theme From M.A.S.H.	Mash	CBS	3
Crying	Don McLean	EMI	3
Xanadu	Olivia Newton-John and ELO	Jet	2
Use It Up And Wear It Out	Odyssey	RCA	2
The Winner Takes It All	Abba	Epic	2
Ashes To Ashes	David Bowie	RCA	1
Start	The Jam	Polydor	2
Feels Like I'm In Love	Kelly Marie	Calibre	4
Don't Stand So Close To Me	Police	A&M	3
Woman In Love	Barbra Streisand	CBS	2
The Tide Is High	Blondie	Chrysalis	3
Super Trouper	Abba	Epic	
(Just Like) Starting Over	John Lennon	WEA/Geffen	1
There's No-One Quite Like Grandma	St Winifred's School Choir	MFP	1

DEATHS

John Bonham, drummer with Led Zeppelin
Ian Curtis, singer with Joy Division
Bill Evans, jazz pianist
Tim Hardin, singer/songwriter
Alfred Hitchcock, film director
John Lennon, rock star
Professor Longhair, R&B pioneer
Mantovani, bandleader
Steve McQueen, film star
Amos Milburn, R&B pioneer
Jesse Owens, athlete
Bon Scott, singer with AC/DC
Peter Sellers, film star
Jay Silverheels, Tonto in TV show *The Lone Ranger*
Larry Williams, rock'n'roll singer

15 January: The UN General Assembly, NATO and the European Community call for the immediate withdrawal of Soviet troops from Afghanistan. The USSR remain unmoved.

16 January: Paul McCartney is jailed in Tokyo after half a pound of marijuana is found in his suitcase. He spends ten days in jail, and Wings' tour is cancelled.

18 January: The price of gold rockets to $1000 an ounce.

7 February: Police wind up a £1 million publicity campaign to catch the Yorkshire Ripper, after little useful information has been collected.

3 March: Robert Mugabe's party wins a landslide victory in the Rhodesian elections, ending white rule.

20 March: Radio Caroline, original pirate station and sole survivor, sinks after gales sweep her on to a sandbank in the Thames estuary.

5 April: Castro sanctions the mass exodus of Cuban citizens wishing to escape the Communist regime.

24 April: An attempt to rescue the US hostages in Tehran is bungled by a crack American anti-terrorist squad.

30 April: Terrorists take over the Iranian Embassy in London, threatening to blow up the building and kill 20 hostages if their demands are not met. Four days later an SAS squad liberates the hostages, killing four of the five terrorists.

18 May: Mt St Helens, a volcano in Washington State, erupts with an explosion 2500 times greater than the Hiroshima bomb.

6 June: For the second time in a week US military forces are put on nuclear alert when a computer malfunction reports Soviet missiles heading for America.

12 June: Presidential candidate Ronald Reagan says that if elected he would submit himself to periodic medical examinations and resign if serious evidence of senility or mental deterioration were detected.

19 July: The twenty-second Olympic Games opens in Moscow, where official TV coverage fails to show the extensive boycott due to the USSR's invasion of Afghanistan.

27 August: Unemployment in the UK goes above two million for the first time since 1935.

22 September: The border conflict between Iran and Iraq erupts into a full-scale war.

26 October: The Campaign For Nuclear Disarmament, which all but faded away during the early 1960s, comes back with renewed vigour with a massively supported rally in Trafalgar Square.

4 November: Cowboy actor Ronald Reagan sweeps to victory in the US Presidential election.

10 November: Michael Foot is elected leader of the Parliamentary Labour party.

8 December: John Lennon is shot dead in the courtyard of his apartment building in Manhattan.

FILMS

All That Jazz
Bad Timing
Being There
A Bigger Splash
The Blues Brothers
Bronco Billy
Coal Miner's Daughter
Cruising
Dressed To Kill
The Elephant Man
The Empire Strikes Back
Flash Gordon
The Great Rock'n'roll Swindle
Gregory's Girl
Heaven's Gate
The Jazz Singer
The Long Good Friday
McVicar
Nine To Five
Ordinary People
Popeye
Raging Bull
Rude Boy
The Shining
Urban Cowboy

Left: John Lennon and his second wife Yoko Ono. Lennon's senseless murder occurred only weeks after his re-emergence from a five-year silence.

Made in England

1980

SIDE ONE
45 RPM
STEREO

Just Like Starting Over

ALL RIGHTS OF THE MANUFACTURER AND OF THE OWNER OF THE RECORDED WORK RESERVED. UNAUTHORISED PUBLIC PERFORMANCE BROADCASTING AND COPYING OF THIS RECORD PROHIBITED

235

Made in England

1981

SIDE ONE
45 RPM
STEREO

Tainted Love

ALL RIGHTS OF THE MANUFACTURER AND OF THE OWNER OF THE RECORDED WORK RESERVED UNAUTHORISED PUBLIC PERFORMANCE BROADCASTING AND COPYING OF THIS RECORD PROHIBITED

A good deal changed in 1981 and more newcomers raised their heads than in most years. The move away from punk towards more melodic fare was typified by the medley boom, started by Dutchman Japp Eggermont. He created with the help of studio musicians, a series of medleys of well-known oldies held together by an infectious disco rhythm. Calling his anonymous workers Starsound, Eggermont's first effort, a medley of hits by the Beatles, was an immediate success topping the US chart and reaching number two in Britain under the title *Stars On 45*. The inevitable follow-up LP topped the UK LP chart for five weeks, but that proved to be the peak of the medley craze.

New British acts appeared with increasing frequency like Altered Images, a Scottish band fronted by Clare Grogan, who scored five UK hit singles in just over a year, the biggest of them being *Happy Birthday*. The Stray Cats, a New York trio led by singer/guitarist Brian Setzer, came to Britain to launch themselves and scored with three top 20 singles in six months, while *Rock This Town* hit the US top 10 almost two years after similar British success. The group rarely returned to Britain, but a compilation LP containing tracks from their first two British albums sold over two million copies in America. Their subsequent work was less interesting and the group broke up in 1984.

Similarly short-lived were the Fun Boy Three, a spin-off from the Specials, although

their American impact was minimal compared with the eight top 20 hits they scored in Britain. Their often overtly political material was intoned by the deadpan voice of Terry Hall, but by mid-1983 Hall and his fellow Fun Boys had fallen out and Hall went on to form the Colour Field.

Soft Cell, a duo from Leeds composed of singer Marc Almond and David Ball, who provided synthesized backing, scored a

JAPAN

JOURNEY

KOOL AND THE GANG

SMOKEY ROBINSON

SOFT CELL

SPANDAU BALLET

RICK SPRINGFIELD

STARSOUND

STRAY CATS

THE TEARDROP EXPLODES

TOYAH

U2

VISAGE

WAH!

KIM WILDE

huge international hit with *Tainted Love*, originally recorded by Gloria Jones. Their impact was far greater in Britain than elsewhere and took in four more top 10 hit singles and several major LPs before the duo went their separate ways in 1983. Then Almond worked with a group known as Marc and the Mambas before going solo and Ball formed a group with his wife known as Other People.

Also electronic in their approach were Depeche Mode, a group from Basildon in Essex, who scored with a succession of catchy pop songs. When songwriter Vince Clarke left the group after their first LP to form Yazoo his mantle was assumed by Martin Gore and the hits continued, both in the singles and album charts.

Few of the newcomers apart from Soft Cell actually topped the chart in 1981, although there were exceptions like Dave Stewart and Barbara Gaskin, who took an electronically revamped *It's My Party* to number one in the UK for a month. Eurovision Song Contest winners Bucks Fizz took not only *Making Your Mind Up* (the Eurovision song) but also *The Land Of Make Believe* and *My Camera Never Lies* to the top of the British chart within a year.

Sheena Easton, from Scotland, was featured as an unknown on a TV show, and interest in the show resulted in three top 20 hits in the UK for her during 1980. Even greater acclaim in America was less expected, especially as the title of her biggest UK hit, *9 To 5* had to be altered in the United States to *Morning Train (9 To 5)* before it could reach the top of the charts, because

Dolly Parton had already topped the US chart in early 1981 with a completely different song titled *9 To 5*. Sheena continued to score hits until the end of 1982, including a top 10 item with *For Your Eyes Only*, the title song from a James Bond movie; but in Britain, at least, her time as a major star seems to have ended. This problem also affected Kim Wilde, the daughter of early British rock'n'roller Marty Wilde. With the

237

help of Marty and her brother Ricky, who wrote and produced her records, and Mickie Most, whose Rak label released them, Kim scored half a dozen UK hits in under two years starting with *Kids In America*. After that her material seemed less inspired.

Toyah, an actress/singer from Birmingham, suffered from similar problems after three top 10 singles during 1981 and two top 10 LPs *Anthem* and *The Changeling* in nine months. Her punk styled approach began to lose its appeal, although her acting career continues.

Two American female singers also broke through during the year. Pat Benatar was signed to the same label as Debbie Harry and initially languished in the shadow of Blondie even though her debut LP *In The Heat Of The Night* eventually went platinum. As Blondie dropped from favour, Pat took over as the biggest-selling female singer in America and had sold over 20 million records by the end of 1984, although few of these were in Britain.

Kim Carnes' *Bette Davis Eyes*, the biggest single of 1981, briefly featured in the UK top 10. She had been recording with little success since 1972 apart from reaching the US top 5 in 1980 with *Don't Fall In Love With A Dreamer*, a duet with Kenny Rogers. Kim's subsequent releases have, however, been somewhat less spectacular.

The major new movement in Britain was dubbed 'new romanticism' by the media, who saw as its leaders Spandau Ballet, Duran Duran and Visage. This constantly changing colourful collision of clothing styles caused a minor revolution among British teenagers. After a hesitant start in 1981 Duran Duran had three top 10 singles in the UK in 1982 and two top 3 LPs. A breakthrough in America came in 1983 when two singles made the top 5 and the *Rio* LP reached the top 10, due to some extent to the group's exotic videos, which were heavily rotated on MTV. *Is There Something I Should Know?* became the group's first UK chart-topping single, *Union Of The Snake* made the top 3 of the singles charts on both sides of the Atlantic and the group's third LP *Seven And The Ragged Tiger* topped the UK LP chart before *The Reflex* became the first Duran Duran single to reach the top in both Britain and America in 1984.

Halfway through the 1980s, Duran Duran are among the biggest stars in the world, in stark contrast to Visage, led by Steve Strange, a Welshman who had moved to London during the initial punk rock era. Strange immersed himself in the London night club circuit which grew up around the New Romantics before launching a recording career under the name of Visage. It was never more than an occasional band, as most of its members belonged to other

groups at the same time, particularly Midge Ure and Billy Currie of Ultravox. After half a dozen medium-sized hits Visage stopped recording, albeit perhaps temporarily.

Strange's co-leaders at the forefront of New Romanticism, Spandau Ballet, were granted their own label, Reformation Records, when they became, in 1980, one of the most expensive signings ever undertaken by Chrysalis Records. It was an investment which must have paid off, for everything released by the group in the UK by the end of 1984 had been a hit, particularly *True*, which topped the UK album chart in 1983. The title track, besides becoming a big American hit also became their first UK number one single.

Several new British hits came from Liverpool, which had remained sunk in the shadow of the Merseybeat boom for nearly two decades. After the emergence of OMD in 1980 other groups from the area began to attract attention, including Echo and the Bunnymen, fronted by Ian McCulloch, the Teardrop Explodes, fronted by Julian Cope and Wah!, led by Peter Wylie. Influenced by the music of the Doors and the Velvet Underground, the acts became major live attractions and later sold many records. Eventually Pete Wylie began to operate as

Above: Birmingham based group Duran Duran took their unlikely name from a villain in the film Barbarella.

Previous page left: Marc Almond, front man and vocalist of Soft Cell, pictured here with his spin-off group, Marc and the Mambas.

Previous page top right: 1981 Eurovision Song Contest winners Bucks Fizz: (left to right) Cheryl Baker, Mike Nolan, Jay Aston and Bobby Gee.

Previous page bottom right: Sheena Easton, whose British success has been overshadowed by her achievements in the United States.

the leader of an ever-changing group which seemed to alter its name with monotonous regularity, although always including a variant of Wah in it. Cope disbanded the Teardrop Explodes and went solo with some success and McCulloch placed Echo in suspended animation while he and his colleagues investigated solo projects.

In America the anonymity of Styx and REO Speedwagon was equalled by Journey, originally a Santana spin-off group who had been gradually growing more popular through the previous six years, which had seen a succession of personnel changes. By 1978 the group had achieved their first platinum LP *Infinity*, but it was in 1981, when they were joined by Jonathan Cain, formerly of the Babys, that things really broke out as their ninth LP *Escape* became a number one in America, and three singles reached the US top 10 within six months. The ultimate accolade came when a video game, *Journey Escape*, was launched based on their hit LP.

Equally unknown individually to the general public were Air Supply from Australia who scored seven top 5 hit singles in just over two years, starting with *Lost In Love* in 1980 and peaking with *The One That You Love*, which topped the US chart in 1981.

Kool and the Gang, a New Jersey soul group led by Robert 'Kool' Bell, topped an eight-year chart career by reaching number one in the US chart with *Celebration*, also one of the biggest of their dozen British hits.

Since the move away from Motown by all the Jackson family except Jermaine, who was married to Motown boss Berry Gordy's daughter, the group had changed their name from the Jackson Five to the Jacksons, with a younger brother Randy replacing Jermaine, who had scored his biggest hit since leaving the group with *Let's Get Serious* in 1980. His impact was minor compared with that of his brother Michael. While still a member of the Jacksons Michael cut a solo LP *Off The Wall* in 1979 with Quincy Jones and eclipsed all the competition by taking four tracks from the LP into the US chart, including chart toppers with *Don't Stop 'Till You Get Enough* and *Rock With You*. That was in America.

In the UK four singles from the LP reached the top 10 in 1979 and 1980. Even more surprising, a re-issued Motown single *One Day In Your Life* became Michael's first solo UK chart topper in 1981, replacing another Motown single, Smokey Robinson's *Being With You*, at the top. This was Smokey's first major hit in Britain since

leaving the Miracles in the first half of the 1970s, and it also reached number two in America.

Meanwhile Motown had developed a new star in Lionel Richie, who left the Commodores and got his solo career off to a flying start by topping the US chart with *Endless Love*, a duet with Diana Ross.

The year also saw the emergence of two British groups, Japan and the Human League, both of whom had been recording with little success for several years. Japan, a group fronted by the photogenic David Sylvian, reached the top 20 in 1981 for the first time with *Quiet Life*, ironically an old track issued by the label they had just left. They had six hit singles in 1982 shared equally between their old label and the new one. At the end of 1982 the group announced that they were splitting up with Sylvian and bass player Mick Karn the two members most likely to do well.

Success for the Human League came, in contrast, after a split. The group had been recording with little chart impact for three years when Ian Craig Marsh and Martyn Ware decided to leave the group to work on a new project (to be called the British Electric Foundation and incorporating a group known as Heaven 17). This left Phil Oakey, leader of the Human League, without a group so he recruited a new band, including two girls whom he introduced as vocalists. They had five hit singles in 1981, the last of which *Don't You Want Me* topped the singles chart in the UK and America. The LP on which it was included, *Dare*, topped the UK album chart and made the top 3 in America. Subsequent releases seemed to lack the spark which had made *Dare* such an attraction.

Godley and Creme, former members of

Right: After replacing Peter Gabriel as singer with Genesis, Phil Collins also launched a phenomenally successful solo career alongside the group.

Below: The Human League, from Sheffield, only achieved stardom when group leader Phil Oakey was forced to recruit replacements after the departure of two original group members.

10 cc, scored with two imaginative top 10 singles after several years' absence from the charts, in Britain before moving on to work as one of the most in demand video production teams.

Irish quartet U2 took two LPs into the British chart in 1981, but announced their arrival in the big time in 1983 when *War*, their next LP, entered the UK album chart at number one. Allied to growing success in America U2, fronted by the charismatic Bono Vox (real name Paul Hewson), look certain to be a major force in the future.

Phil Collins of Genesis also achieved much as a solo star, taking *In The Air Tonight* to number two in the UK singles chart and *Face Values* to the top of the LP chart in 1981, before returning to his Genesis duties. At the end of 1982 his cover version of the Supremes' *You Can't Hurry Love* topped the UK singles chart, while his second LP reached the top 10 in both the UK and America. In 1984 his single *Against All Odds* was a huge hit on both sides of the Atlantic.

Australian actor and singer Rick Springfield's *Jessie's Girl* topped the singles chart in 1981. Several of his subsequent albums and singles have reached the top 10 in America, although a breakthrough in Britain seems as far away as ever. This is also true of the most consistent hitmakers of the first half of the 1980s in America, white soul practitioners Daryl Hall and John Oates. Regulars in the chart since 1976, the duo had reached number one in 1977 with *Rich Girl*, but 1981 saw them take three singles out of four to the top, with *Kiss On My List*, *Private Eyes* and *I Can't Go For That (No Can Do)*, while all their recent LPs have reached the US top 3. After another chart-topping single *Maneater* in 1983 Hall and Oates were dubbed by *Billboard* the most successful recording duo of all time.

241

USA CHART TOPPERS

TITLE	ARTIST	LABEL	WEEKS AT NO. 1
(Just Like) Starting Over	John Lennon	Geffen	4
The Tide Is High	Blondie	Chrysalis	2
Celebration	Kool and the Gang	De-Lite	1
9 To 5	Dolly Parton	RCA	5
Keep On Loving You	REO Speedwagon	Epic	1
Rapture	Blondie	Chrysalis	2
Kiss On My List	Daryl Hall and John Oates	RCA	1
Morning Train (9 To 5)	Sheena Easton	EMI America	3
Angel Of The Morning	Juice Newton	Capitol	1
Being With You	Smokey Robinson	Tamla	3
Bette Davis Eyes	Kim Carnes	EMI America	1
Stars On 45	Stars On 45	Radio	1
All Those Years Ago	George Harrison	Dark Horse	3
The One That You Love	Air Supply	Arista	1
Greatest American Hero	Joey Scarbury	Elektra	2
I Don't Need You	Kenny Rogers	Liberty	1
Jessie's Girl	Rick Springfield	RCA	2
Endless Love	Diana Ross and Lionel Richie	Motown	9
Arthur's Theme	Christopher Cross	Warner Bros	3
Private Eyes	Daryl Hall and John Oates	RCA	2
Physical	Olivia Newton-John	MCA	6

UK CHART TOPPERS

TITLE	ARTIST	LABEL	WEEKS AT NO. 1
There's No-One Quite Like Grandma	St Winifred's School Choir	MFP	1
Imagine	John Lennon	Parlophone	4
Woman	John Lennon	Geffen	2
Shaddup You Face	Joe Dolce	Epic	3
Jealous Guy	Roxy Music	Polydor/EG	2
This Ole House	Shakin' Stevens	Epic	3
Making Your Mind Up	Bucks Fizz	RCA	3
Stand And Deliver	Adam and the Ants	CBS	5
Being With You	Smokey Robinson	Motown	2
One Day In Your Life	Michael Jackson	Motown	2
Ghost Town	The Specials	2-Tone	2
Green Door	Shakin' Stevens	Epic	3
Japanese Boy	Aneka	Hansa/Ariola	4
Tainted Love	Soft Cell	Some Bizarre	1
Prince Charming	Adam and the Ants	CBS	2
It's My Party	Dave Stewart and Barbara Gaskin	Stiff/Broken	4
Every Little Thing She Does Is Magic	Police	A&M	1
Under Pressure	Queen and David Bowie	EMI	2
Begin The Beguine	Julio Inglesias	CBS	1
Don't You Want Me?	Human League	Virgin	3

FILMS

Arthur
Atlantic City
Chariots Of Fire
For Your Eyes Only
The French Lieutenant's Woman
The History Of The World Part I
Honky Tonk Freeway
On Golden Pond
The Postman Always Rings Twice
Ragtime
Raiders Of The Lost Ark
Reds
Rich And Famous
S.O.B.
Superman II
Time Bandits

DEATHS

Mike Bloomfield, blues guitarist
Roy Brown, R&B pioneer
Hoagy Carmichael, songwriter
Harry Chapin, singer/songwriter
Moshe Dayan, Israeli war hero
Mike Hailwood, motor cycling champion
Bill Haley, rock'n'roll pioneer
Bob Hite, Canned Heat singer
Joe Louis, boxer
Bob Marley, reggae singer
Anwar El Sadat, President of Egypt
Natalie Wood, film star

2 January: Peter Sutcliffe, a 35-year-old lorry driver from Bradford, is arrested and charged with being the Yorkshire Ripper.

18 January: A fierce fire kills 18 at an all-night West Indian party in Deptford, south London. Foul play is suspected, but an official inquest returns an open verdict.

20 January: The 52 American hostages, imprisoned in Tehran for 444 days, are released as President Reagan takes the oath of office.

27 January: Recession gloom deepens in the UK as unemployment rate breaks the 10 per cent barrier.

14 February: 49 die when fire sweeps through a Dublin disco.

24 February: Prince Charles announces his engagement to Lady Diana Spencer.

24 March: Great Train Robber Ronnie Biggs is kidnapped in Rio and taken to Barbados, where he successfully fights extradition.

30 March: Ronald Reagan survives an assassination attempt outside the Hilton Hotel in Washington.

10 April: Three days of running battle between police and blacks in Brixton, south London, leaves property destroyed, looted and burning.

12 April: The space shuttle Columbia lifts off from the Kennedy Space Center.

5 May: Hunger striker Bobby Sands dies after 66 days without food.

13 May: The Pope survives an attempt to kill him in St Peter's Square.

22 May: Peter Sutcliffe is found guilty in the Yorkshire Ripper case.

2 July: The pound slumps to $1.88, its lowest level in four years.

3 July: Race riots break out in Southall, west London. Within 24 hours the Toxteth area of Liverpool is ablaze in the worst scenes of civil disorder ever seen in Britain.

29 July: A UK national holiday celebrates the royal wedding of Prince Charles and Lady Diana.

24 August: Mark Chapman, murderer of John Lennon, is jailed for a minimum of 20 years.

6 September: Civil unrest grows in Poland as the price of bread and cereals trebles. The independent trade union Solidarity calls for free elections.

25 October: Record-breaking demonstrations are held in London, Rome, Paris and Brussels against the deployment of nuclear missiles in Europe.

13 December: General Jaruzelski imposes martial law in Poland 'to avert anarchy'. Lech Walesa, leader of Solidarity, is one of the many 'agitators' rounded up and imprisoned.

20 December: All eight crew members of the Penlee life boat die trying to rescue survivors from the shipwrecked *Union Star*.

1981

SIDE ONE
45 RPM
STEREO

Tainted Love

Made in England

ALL RIGHTS OF THE MANUFACTURER AND OF THE OWNER OF THE RECORDED WORK RESERVED. UNAUTHORISED PUBLIC PERFORMANCE, BROADCASTING AND COPYING OF THIS RECORD PROHIBITED

ABC

ASIA

IRENE CARA

RY COODER

KID CREOLE AND THE COCONUTS

CULTURE CLUB

'FAME'

A FLOCK OF SEAGULLS

GO-GOS

GOLDEN EARRING

EDDY GRANT

HAIRCUT 100

The drift away from America and towards British music which began in 1981 continued. Acts who were relatively unknown in Britain achieved fame via the influential MTV, notably A Flock of Seagulls and Asia, acts from very different ends of the spectrum.

Asia, a group who rose from the ashes of Yes, took their eponymous debut LP to the top of the US chart, while a single from it *Heat Of The Moment* was concurrently a top 5 hit. The group's follow-up LP *Alpha* was slightly less successful. So far the group's acclaim in Britain has been limited.

A Flock of Seagulls, yet another band from the Liverpool area, broke through in America with a top 10 hit *I Ran*, but were largely ignored in Britain until *Wishing* made the UK top 10 in 1983. As album sellers in Britain the group remain of minor appeal, although their second LP *Listen* reached the US top 20.

In contrast a number of British acts were very popular in their homeland but found it difficult to penetrate the American market, like ABC and Haircut 100.

ABC, from Sheffield, burst on to the British scene with three classy singles *Poison Arrow*, *The Look Of Love* and *All Of My Heart* in 1982 plus a stunning LP *The Lexicon Of Love*, which topped the British album chart for a month. In America, despite their excellent promo videos, the group scored one small hit single (with The Look of Love) and their follow-up LP was disappointing.

Haircut 100, fronted by Nick Heyward, also managed one minor US hit compared with four top tenners in the UK plus a big hit LP, but their momentum ceased when Heyward and the others fell out during the recording of a follow-up LP. Heyward enjoyed a reasonably successful solo career thereafter, but the remaining Haircuts were virtually forgotten.

Numerous bands made a minor impact in Britain in 1982, like Haysi Fantayzee, a duo who reached the top 20 with a rant title *John Wayne Is Big Leggy*; the Belle Stars, a female group; Tight Fit, a disco group who had charted with a pair of medleys of 1960s' classics then topped the UK chart with their version of *The Lion Sleeps Tonight*; the Associates, a group from Scotland who scored three hits during the year; Musical Youth, a teenage quintet from Birmingham who topped the UK chart with their debut single, the infectious and very successful *Pass The Dutchie*; and China Crisis, yet another Merseyside group who may still achieve greatness.

Not that every group enjoyed only a brief spell of fame. Yazoo, for instance (who called themselves Yaz in America), were a revelation. Formed by synthesist Vince Clarke after he left Depeche Mode, Yazoo was completed by the deep and expressive voice of Alison Moyet (familiarly known as Alf). Their first single *Only You* reached number two in the UK chart, while a follow-up *Don't Go* reached number three. Their

HEAVEN 17

IMAGINATION

RICK JAMES

JOAN JETT

GREG KIHN

LOVERBOY

ROBERT PLANT

SIMPLE MINDS

BILLY SQUIER

SURVIVOR

TEARS FOR FEARS

YAZOO

first LP *Upstairs At Eric's* also reached number two but, as their second album was being recorded the duo announced that they would go their separate ways. When the LP *You And Me Both* was released in mid-1983, it became a chart topper in Britain after they split up. Meanwhile both Alison and Vince were formulating plans for new projects.

Culture Club enjoyed far greater longevity, with lead singer George O'Dowd (better known as Boy George) a constant source of headlines due to his ready wit, his 'gender bending', and his remarkable talent as a lyricist and vocalist. When Culture Club first emerged in 1981 George was already well-known for a brief liaison with Bow Wow Wow when manager Malcolm McLaren was apparently having problems with Bow Wow Wow's singer Annabella Lwin. McLaren then suggested that George should form his own band. In fact Bow Wow Wow disintegrated in 1983 after a handful of hits and, without Annabella, renamed themselves Chiefs Of Relief, but they soon disappeared.

Rumours that McLaren was about to recruit a band around George were incorrect but led to bass player Mikey Craig approaching the Boy. The group was completed by Jon Moss (formerly with several punk bands) and Roy Hay. Their first two singles were not hits but the third, *Do You Really Want To Hurt Me*, topped the UK chart towards the end of 1982 and reached number two in America in early 1983, and their debut LP *Kissing To Be Clever* made the top 5 in the UK and the top 10 in America.

At the end of 1983 Boy George mania hit Britain with the release of *Karma Chameleon*, which topped the charts on both sides of the Atlantic, and the album from which it came, *Colour By Numbers*, made number one in the UK and number two in America. The immense expectation of the group's next LP *Waking Up With The House On Fire* was more than anyone could have been expected to fufil, and at the end of 1984 Culture Club's appeal seemed to be evaporating.

America, too, had transient stars like the Motels, a Los Angeles group fronted by Martha Davis, and Charlene, a country singer signed to a Motown subsidiary label during the 1970s whose *I've Never Been To Me* was one of the surprise hits of the year in America and even less predictably topped the British singles chart. As a result of the hit she charted again duetting with Stevie Wonder.

Heavy metal was also well represented, with Canadian quintet Loverboy achieving platinum status with each of their first two LPs, *Loverboy* and *Get Lucky*; the exceptionally talented Aldo Nova, another Canadian, scoring with his eponymous debut LP; .38 Special, whose singer Donnie Van Zant was the younger brother of the late Ronnie Van Zant of Lynyrd Skynyrd. Billy Squier, reached the top 5 of the US LP chart with *Don't Say No* in 1981 and followed it with the platinum *Emotions In Motion*, as well as taking three singles into the American top 40 in 18 months; and Survivor were fortunate enough to record the theme song of the hit movie *Rocky III*, *Eye Of The Tiger*, which topped the US singles chart for six weeks and its UK equivalent for four.

One group who must have been surprised to become rising stars of 1982 in America were Dutch hard rockers Golden Earring, who had formed back in 1964. They had reached the US top 20 in 1974 with *Radar Love*, but with major MTV exposure returned to the top 20 with the classic single *Twilight Zone*, while Donald Fagen, formerly of Steely Dan, made a convincing solo debut with his gold LP *The Nightfly*. Rumours still persisted that he might yet reform Steely Dan with Walter Becker.

Several other comparative veterans also made their mark like Robert Plant, formerly of Led Zeppelin, who released his first solo LP *Pictures At Eleven* which was a top 5 hit on both sides of the Atlantic. In 1984 Plant cut a ten-inch LP under the name of the Honeydrippers, which was also a big hit. Ry Cooder, a much praised session guitarist who had been making critically acclaimed solo LPs since 1970, took his 1982 LP *The Slide Area* into the UK top 20 although he has yet to achieve similar chart status in America.

Eddy Grant had fronted the Equals during the 1960s when they scored with *Baby Come Back*, but during the early 1970s he set up his own label Ice Records and produced other acts. He picked up his own performing career at the end of the 1970s, making the UK top 20 once a year until 1982 when he topped the UK chart with *I Don't Wanna Dance* and consolidated his position with a number two US hit *Electric Avenue*. Grant will no doubt continue making hits for some time to come.

From a similar era came the Boston-based J. Geils Band, a hard driving R&B band whose six-man line-up had not altered since 1969. They had scored occasional hits before 1982, when *Centerfold* from their eleventh LP *Freeze Frame* topped the US chart and reached the top 3 in the UK. It came as somewhat of a surprise when the group's charismatic lead singer Peter Wolf decided to leave the group for a solo career in 1983.

Major hits also came the way of others who had started during the 1960s, like the great Joe Cocker, who teamed up with Jennifer Warnes to take *Up Where We Belong*, the theme from the movie *An Officer And A Gentleman*, to the top of the US chart, and Toni Basil, a choreographer who had worked on various TV and film projects, who launched a new phase of her career as a singer and dancer for the video medium with a smash hit single *Mickey*.

The world of soul music saw a few new stars, the biggest being Rick James, who had played with Neil Young in a Toronto group the Mynah Birds during the 1960s, but only emerged as Motown's biggest funk act in the late 1970s and early 1980s. His best

known single was *Super Freak*, a US top 20 hit in 1981, the same year as his *Street Songs* LP went double platinum in America. A major feature of his live show was James' outrageous clothing and this was parodied by Imagination, a British black group who scored major hits with singles like *Body Talk* in 1981 and *Just An Illusion* and *Music & Lights* in 1982, all of which reached the UK top 5.

Rather more subtle were Kid Creole and the Coconuts who played a unique blend of

Above: Eddy Grant, who returned to the top of the British chart with I Don't Wanna Dance.

Previous page top: Boy George (right), as always the centre of attention!

Previous page bottom: Asia: Steve Howe (guitar), Geoff Downes (keyboards), John Wetton (bass) and Carl Palmer (drums) rose from the ashes of Yes and ELP.

Latin-American, West Indian and black North American music. Kid Creole was the alter ego of August Darnell, co-leader of the wonderfully bizarre, but only moderately successful, Dr Buzzard's Original Savannah Band, and his concept of a modern-day Odyssey was released under the title *Fresh Fruit In Foreign Places*. It was a huge artistic success but seemed to be going the way of the equally smooth Dr Buzzard records until a concerted publicity campaign in Britain placed three singles in the UK top 10 in six months. A follow-up LP *Tropical Gangsters* also reached the top 3.

Another face of soul music was the rap – talking rhythmically over an instrumental backing – which was popularized, unsurprisingly, by disc jockeys. The most celebrated exponent of this art was Grandmaster Flash and the Furious Five, who broke through in Britain with *The Message*, a top 10 single in 1982. Before their arrival the best known rap act was the Sugarhill Gang, whose 1979 single *Rapper's Delight* was an international hit which introduced the world to the art of rapping.

Rap was a New York phenomenon closely related to the biggest craze of the year in Britain, which was also New York

based. Back in 1980 a film about a New York school for fledgling entertainers had been a reasonable success in the cinemas under the title *Fame*, and its title song had been a hit for Irene Cara. A TV spin-off was largely ignored in America but became the cult of the year in Britain, bringing Irene Cara's record to the top of the charts and creating huge record sales from the TV show. *Hi-Fidelity* and *Starmaker* both reached the top 5 of the singles chart and two LPs, *Kids From Fame* and *Kids From Fame Again*, were enormous sellers, but by mid-1983 the show's novelty had worn off.

As ever some curious records reached the top of the charts. In America the theme music from the award-winning movie *Chariots Of Fire*, as played by Greek keyboard wizard Vangelis, reached the top, while in Britain the unlikely number ones included *Seven Tears* by the Goombay Dance Band, a German/Caribbean group, and Captain Sensible, a member of punk group the Damned, took a song from the musical *South Pacific*, *Happy Talk*, to the top.

On a less transitory note Greg Kihn, who had been making critically acclaimed albums for several years, took his sixth LP

Above: Joan Jett, who enjoyed a huge international hit and finally buried the myth that hard rock is a male preserve.

Top: Scottish hit-makers Simple Minds whose lead singer Jim Kerr (second from left) married Chrissie Hynde of the Pretenders in 1984.

Rockihnroll to the US top 40, a single *The Breakup Song* to the US top 20, and by 1983 had a top 5 single with *Jeopardy*. Laura Branigan, who had worked as a backing singer for Leonard Cohen, reached number two in America with her disco single *Gloria*.

The Go-Gos, a female quintet from Hollywood, surprised everyone when their first LP *Beauty And The Beat* was at the top of the LP chart in America, while two singles from it, *We Got The Beat* and *Our Lips Are Sealed*, reached the US top 20. A second LP

Vacation and its title track released as a single were also big hits. *Our Lips Are Sealed* was written by Terry Hall of Fun Boy Three – who teamed up with a trio of British female singers who called themselves Bananarama. The two trios combined to take two revamped oldies *It Ain't What You Do* and *Really Saying Something* into the UK top 5 within three months after which Bananarama reverted to 'solo' recording with some success.

Tears For Fears, a duo from Bath, took their first single *Mad World* into the top 3 in Britain, but astounded the world when their first LP *The Hurting* topped the UK LP chart in 1983, while Scottish group Simple Minds took their fifth LP *New Gold Dream* into the UK top 3 in 1982 and demonstrated that it was no fluke when *Sparkle In The Rain* topped the same chart in 1984.

Ex-Human Leaguers Heaven 17 impressed with their ambitious *Music Of Quality And Distinction*, which featured notables like Tina Turner, Sandie Shaw and Gary Glitter performing well-known songs with which they were not normally identified. The project was perhaps not the commercial success expected, but the group, without guest stars, went on to make hits like *Temptation*, a top 3 British hit in 1983. Blancmange, another electronic duo, began a top 10 career with *Living On The Ceiling*, which is still flourishing.

In America the single to remain longest at number one, just edging out *Eye Of The Tiger* and *Centerfold*, was *I Love Rock-'n'Roll* by ex-Runaway Joan Jett, which also made the UK top 5. Few seemed to consider it an exceptional record, but perhaps its sentiments sounded promising amid the maelstrom of five-minute wonders and short-lived crazes which seemed to typify the early years of the 1980s.

Above: Curt Smith and Roland Orzabal formed Tears For Fears, topping the UK album chart with their debut album The Hurting.

Left: Heaven 17: (left to right) Ian Craig-Marsh, Glenn Gregory and Martyn Ware scored as producers under the name of the British Electric Foundation as well as making hits on their own account.

USA CHART TOPPERS

TITLE	ARTIST	LABEL	WEEKS AT NO. 1
Physical	Olivia Newton-John	MCA	4
I Can't Go For That	Daryl Hall and John Oates	RCA	1
Centerfold	J. Geils Band	EMI America	6
I Love Rock'n'Roll	Joan Jett and the Blackhearts	Boardwalk	7
Chariots Of Fire	Vangelis	Polydor	1
Ebony And Ivory	Paul McCartney and Stevie Wonder	Columbia	7
Don't You Want Me?	Human League	A&M/Virgin	3
Eye Of The Tiger	Survivor	Scotti Bros	6
Abracadabra	Steve Miller Band	Capitol	2
Hard To Say I'm Sorry	Chicago	Full Moon/Warner Bros	2
Jack And Diane	John Cougar	Riva/Mercury	4
Who Can It Be Now?	Men At Work	Columbia	1
Up Where We Belong	Joe Cocker and Jennifer Warnes	Island	3
Truly	Lionel Richie	Motown	2
Mickey	Toni Basil	Chrysalis	1
Maneater	Daryl Hall and John Oates	RCA	2

UK CHART TOPPERS

TITLE	ARTIST	LABEL	WEEKS AT NO. 1
Don't You Want Me?	Human League	Virgin	2
The Land Of Make Believe	Bucks Fizz	RCA	2
Oh Julie	Shakin' Stevens	Epic	1
The Model/Computer Love	Kraftwerk	EMI	1
A Town Called Malice	The Jam	Polydor	3
The Lion Sleeps Tonight	Tight Fit	Jive	3
Seven Tears	Goombay Dance Band	Epic	3
My Camera Never Lies	Bucks Fizz	RCA	1
Ebony And Ivory	Paul McCartney and Stevie Wonder	Parlophone	3
A Little Peace	Nicole	CBS	2
House Of Fun	Madness	Stiff	2
Goody Two Shoes	Adam Ant	CBS	2
I've Never Been To Me	Charlene	Motown	1
Happy Talk	Captain Sensible	A&M	2
Fame	Irene Cara	RSO	3
Come On Eileen	Dexy's Midnight Runners	Mercury	4
Eye Of The Tiger	Survivor	Scotti Brothers	4
Pass The Dutchie	Musical Youth	MCA	3
Do You Really Want To Hurt Me?	Culture Club	Virgin	3
I Don't Want To Dance	Eddy Grant	Ice	3
Beat Surrender	The Jam	Polydor	2
Save Your Love	Renee and Renato	Hollywood	2

DEATHS

John Belushi, film star
David Blue, folk singer
Rainer Fassbinder, film director
Marty Feldman, comedian
Henry Fonda, film star
Princess Grace of Monaco
Alex Harvey, rock singer
Murray The K, disc jockey
Thelonius Monk, jazz musician
Marty Robbins, country singer
James Honeyman Scott, rock guitarist
Jacques Tati, film director
Joe Tex, soul singer

CURRENT EVENTS

7 January: Snow causes chaos in the worst winter in the UK for 20 years.

13 January: 81 people die when a Boeing 737 crashes into a road bridge over the Potomac River in Washington DC during a blizzard.

26 January: Unemployment in the UK exceeds three million for the first time ever.

5 February: Laker Airways collapses with debts exceeding £210 million.

19 February: The Belfast car firm DeLorean goes into receivership.

22 March: 60 Argentinian scrap merchants land in South Georgia and hoist their national flag.

2 April: In a massive sea and air operation, Argentinian forces invade and capture the Falkland Islands.

5 April: The most powerful British fighting force assembled since the Second World War sets sail to secure the recovery of the Falklands.

2 May: The Argentinian cruiser *General Belgrano* is torpedoed by a British submarine and subsequently sinks.

21 May: British troops establish a bridgehead at San Carlos on East Falkland and begin to move towards Port Darwin and Port Stanley.

15 June: Argentinian forces surrender to the British commander, Major General Jeremy Moore.

21 June: Prince William is born to the Prince and Princess of Wales.

30 June: The Palestine Liberation Organisation agrees to evacuate Beirut, now encircled by Israeli troops, who control South Lebanon.

9 July: A Buckingham Palace intruder gains access to the Queen's bedroom.

8 October: US unemployment surges to its highest level since the Great Depression.

11 October: Henry VIII's warship the *Mary Rose* is raised from the sea bed and towed into Portsmouth.

31 October: The Thames flood barrier is raised for the first time, to test its mechanism.

10 November: President Brezhnev of the Soviet Union dies of a heart attack. Former KGB chief Yuri Andropov succeeds him.

12 December: Tens of thousands of women converge on Greenham Common RAF base to protest against the siting of American cruise missiles.

30 December: Martial law is suspended in Poland.

FILMS

Annie
The Best Little Whorehouse In Texas
Blade Runner
Cat People
Conan The Barbarian
Diner
ET – The Extra Terrestrial
48 Hours
Gandhi
Missing
My Favourite Year
An Officer And A Gentleman
Rocky 3
Sophie's Choice
Startrek 2
Tootsie
Tron

Left: Dolly Parton, starring in the movie The Best Little Whorehouse In Texas *(RKO, 1982).*

Made in England

1982

SIDE ONE
45 RPM
STEREO

Pass The Dutchie

1983

SIDE ONE
45 RPM
STEREO

Billie Jean

Made in England

The world's charts were dominated by Michael Jackson in 1983. Since the success of *Off The Wall* in 1979, expectation had been growing over a follow-up. The question had been partially answered, as Michael took a duet with Paul McCartney, *The Girl Is Mine*, into both US and UK top 10s in 1982. Then came the remarkable *Thriller*, which spent eight months at the top of the US LP chart, returning to the top three times after it had been replaced and also spending eight weeks at the top in Britain. Two singles from the LP also topped the US chart, *Billie Jean* and *Beat It*, while the video for the title track of the LP attracted vast publicity as the most expensive promo clip of all time. An unplanned by-product, a compilation of Michael's work at Motown, *18 Greatest Hits,* also topped the UK album chart for three weeks. Meanwhile New Edition, a black American group apparently based on the Jacksons, topped the UK singles chart for one week with *Candy Girl.*

Among the year's other chart toppers in Britain were the Flying Pickets, whose name betrayed their political leanings, but whose acappella version of Yazoo's *Only You* was the year's big Christmas hit. Limited by both their unaccompanied format and their refusal to sing material with sexist lyrics, the group subsequently found it hard to equal that success, as did Nena, who fronted a German rock band and had a huge hit with *99 Luft Balloons* (the title used in

America) or *99 Red Balloons*, the title used when it topped the UK chart in early 1984.

Unlike the previous year several enduring talents rose to prominence, like Paul Young, previously singer with Q-Tips. Young's solo career went into orbit in 1983 with three top 5 hits in Britain, including the chart topper *Wherever I Lay My Hat* and a number one LP with *No Parlez*. Young will be releasing a new LP early in 1985.

After several quiet years Welsh singer Bonnie Tyler was teamed with producer/songwriter Jim Steinman, architect of Meat Loaf's phenomenal *Bat Out Of Hell*, and the result was a superb LP *Faster Than The Speed Of Night*, which included *Total Eclipse Of The Heart*, which topped the singles chart on both sides of the Atlantic (the USA for four weeks and the UK for two).

Tyler had been previously referred to as 'the female Rod Stewart' and her male equivalent returned to the top of the UK charts with *Baby Jane*, his first number one in five years.

The ARMS (Action for Research into Multiple Sclerosis) tour brought together on stages in Britain and America Jeff Beck, Eric Clapton and Jimmy Page, along with Steve Winwood and other 1960s' survivors. Rod Stewart was expected to take part, especially as his ex-Faces colleague Ronnie Lane was an MS sufferer, but ultimately didn't. No doubt the Police, who enjoyed their best year internationally so far with *Synchronicity*, their fifth LP, topping the charts in Britain

and America and a single from it, *Every Breath You Take*, doing likewise, would have helped out too, but the concerts were largely organized to feature Lane's contemporaries like Bill Wyman and Charlie Watts of the Rolling Stones.

The most unlikely breakthrough came from Australian group Men At Work, who had topped the US chart in 1982 with *Who Can It Be Now?*, and returned to the top on both sides of the Atlantic with a single, *Down Under*, and an album, *Business As Usual*.

However, most of the new talent came from Britain, like Nick Heyward, ex-leader of Haircut 100, whose gentle pop approach took *Whistle Down The Wind* into the British chart, and David Grant, formerly of Linx, who enjoyed three hit singles in quick succession, assisted by producer Derek Bramble, who performed a similar function in 1984 with David Bowie.

Bowie enjoyed a huge comeback in 1983 with his Nile Rodgers-produced LP *Let's Dance*, which topped both British and American LP charts, and also included a chart-topping single in the title track. Its

MEN AT WORK

NEW ORDER

PRINCE

LIONEL RICHIE

STYLE COUNCIL

THOMPSON TWINS

TOTO

TINA TURNER

BONNIE TYLER

TRACEY ULLMAN

WHAM!

PAUL YOUNG

253

success was underlined by a triumphant tour, while Bowie 1984-style produced another chart-topping LP, *Tonight*, with Derek Bramble helping.

Orange Juice, a Scottish group, later a duo, led by Edwyn Collins, reached the UK top 10 in 1984 with *Rip It Up*, but never really transcended their cult following. This seemed equally true of Aztec Camera, led by Roddy Frame, who began their recording career like Orange Juice on a Scottish independent label, Postcard Records.

Quintet KajaGooGoo's first single *Too Shy* was produced by Nick Rhodes of Duran Duran. The single reached number one in Britain and was a hit in America, but not long afterwards vocalist Limahl left the group. KajaGooGoo's fortunes have since been distinctly patchy, but Limahl himself came back strongly at the end of 1984 with *Never Ending Story*, a film theme written and produced by Giorgio Moroder which made the top 3 in Britain.

Similar progress was made by the Genesis-influenced group Marillion, who took their debut LP *Script For A Jester's Tear* into the UK top 10 and continued to grow in popularity in 1984, the Alarm, a Welsh folk/rock quartet whose calls to arms were often reminiscent of the Clash and who took *68 Guns* into the British top 20 in late 1983; Carmel, a singer from the northeast of England whose jazz-influenced style was much admired but who had few hit records to show for it; and Phil Fearon (also known as Galaxy), who took several funk singles into the British chart during 1983 and 1984.

The Thompson Twins, of whom there

were three when they came to fame, actually formed in 1977. Leader Tom Bailey added and subtracted personnel until 1982 when the group enjoyed their first minor chart success with *In The Name Of Love*. Then the final trio of Bailey, Joe Leeway and New Zealander Alannah Currie decided to opt for a synthesized approach. At first they alienated some fans, but the change paid off when *Into The Gap*, their fourth LP, topped the UK album charts, also spawning several big hit singles such as *Sister Of Mercy, Doctor! Doctor!* and *Hold Me Now*.

Equally regular in the charts were Eurythmics, a duo consisting of Annie Lennox and Dave Stewart who were refugees from the Tourists. Their first LP, released in 1981, made only minor waves, but *Sweet Dreams* topped the US singles chart, several singles became big British hits and by 1984 *Touch* had topped the UK album chart. The group were also contracted to write part of the score for the movie of *1984* and a single from it, *Sexcrime*, became a big hit.

Style Council, the group formed by ex-Jam leader Paul Weller with ex-Merton Parka Mick Talbot, managed to place a series of singles in the UK top 10 in 1983 and 1984, but never quite approached the predominance enjoyed by Weller's previous group the Jam.

Big Country, a quartet launched by ex-Skid Stuart Adamson, proved to be one of the year's big surprises, their second single *Fields Of Fire* and their first LP *The Crossing* both reaching the UK top 10. The summer of 1984 saw the group deputizing for an incapacitated Paul Young at the

Wembley Stadium concert headlined by Elton John, no doubt making many new fans who helped to take their second LP *Steel-town* to the top of the UK album chart at the end of that year.

The often-tried ploy of notables from different fields making records for once paid off, as comedienne Tracey Ullman proved by taking four consecutive singles into the UK top 10, while her first single released in America, *They Don't Know*, reached similar heights. Tracey's success in Britain continued in 1984 as her revival of John D. Loudermilk's *Sunglasses* took her back up the UK chart.

Equally unlikely was the rise to stardom of the man who had been involved with the New York Dolls, the Sex Pistols, Adam and the Ants and Bob Wow Wow: Malcolm McLaren. Having proved that even his most outrageous ideas could turn into commercial bonanzas, he hired producer Trevor Horn to help him restart a career which had been dormant since his Fagin-like rendition of *You Need Hands* in the Sex Pistols' movie *The Great Rock'n'Roll Swindle*, and no doubt wasn't a bit surprised when early singles inspired by African music, New York 'scratch' disc jockeys and street dancing all made the charts. Next he updated Puccini's *Madam Butterfly*, which was, of course, also a hit . . .

Egyptian-born meteorology student Thomas Dolby, who had worked with several promising British bands of the late 1970s, formed his own label which he called Venice In Peril. Using a Meteorological Office employee to read a weather forecast on his first LP *The Golden Age Of Wireless*,

Thomas was regarded as an amusing eccentric until it reached the UK chart. When a follow-up single *She Blinded Me With Science*, which included help from TV astronomer Magnus Pyke, reached the US top 5 and took the already mentioned LP into the US top 20, he began to be viewed more seriously.

The Fixx were another British act enthusiastically supported in America but virtually ignored at home. The quintet found it hard to be taken seriously in Britain but, when their second LP *Reach The Beach* sold around two million copies, the group became major stars in America. With Britain still showing little interest in their third LP *Phantoms*, the Fixx could hardly be blamed if they moved permanently to the United States.

One of the year's longest-lived chart singles was *Blue Monday* by New Order, the group who had been known as Joy Division before their frontman Ian Curtis committed suicide. The single refused to leave the chart for many months, although the group's determinedly low profile did little to enhance their prospects of superstardom. This relative lack of information about the group may have actually helped their 1983 LP *Power, Corruption And Lies* to feature in the top 20.

In retrospect the major new act to rise in Britain was Wham!, a duo of George Michael and Andrew Ridgeley, who are managed by industry veteran Simon Napier-Bell, at various times a successful manager of acts like the Yardbirds, Marc Bolan and Japan. Taking their debut single *Young Guns (Go For It)* into the UK top 3, Wham! followed it

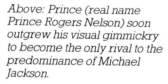

Above: Prince (real name Prince Rogers Nelson) soon outgrew his visual gimmickry to become the only rival to the predominance of Michael Jackson.

Above right: Wham! (left to right foreground Andrew Ridgeley and George Michael) built an enormous following at remarkable speed.

up with two more UK top 10 hits in *Wham! Rap* and *Bad Boys* plus a big selling LP *Fantastic!* 1984 saw even greater success with *Wake Me Up Before You GoGo* topping the singles chart in America as well as Britain, George Michael releasing a solo single *Careless Whisper*, which also reached the top, and at the end of the year another Wham! single *Freedom* at the top of the chart, with their second LP *Make It Big* in a similar position.

Amid all this British activity – even Slade returned to the top 3 with a giant Christmas hit *My Oh My* and achieved their first American gold album – America was still to some extent producing new stars such as

Alabama, a country music group who released three platinum LPs during the first years of the 1980s, supporting them with a trio of US top 20 singles, yet still remaining virtually unknown in Britain. Toto, a group composed of session musicians, had emerged in 1978 with a top 5 single *Hold The Line* and an eponymous debut LP which remained in the US chart for a year. After a hiatus of several years the group resurfaced in 1982 with two big hits, *Rosanna* and *Africa*, which helped them to win an amazing seven Grammy Awards in 1983. However, their American success was hardly reflected at all in Britain.

Huey Lewis and the News burst out of San Francisco with several US top 10 singles during 1983 and 1984, but the pinnacle of their achievements came when their 1984 LP *Sports* became one of only five LPs to top the US album chart during the first months of 1984. One of the others, which held the top slot for nearly six months, was *Purple Rain*, the soundtrack album to a film starring the year's most prodigious new American talent, Prince. The son of a band leader and a singer from Minneapolis, Prince obviously inherited his parents' musical gifts and was producing his own records by the time he was 18. His breakthrough came in 1982 when his fifth album, a double LP titled *1999*, went platinum while a single from it, *Little Red Corvette*, reached the US top 10. His outspokenly sexual lyrics seemed unlikely to gain him universal approbation but *Purple Rain* deflected the spotlight from Michael Jackson for a remarkably long time, during which two singles from the film, *When Doves Cry* and *Let's Go Crazy*, topped the US singles chart.

Lionel Richie was one of the few stars to rival Prince. After first reaching number one with his duet with Diana Ross *Endless Love* in 1981, Richie repeated the feat solo in 1982 with *Truly*, in 1983 with *All Night Long (All Night)* and in 1984 with *Hello*, as well as topping both the US and UK LP charts with his *Can't Slow Down* album at the end of 1983.

The ageless Tina Turner also made a big impression, particularly in Britain where her revival of Al Green's *Let's Stay Together* returned her to the top 10 after far too many years away. In 1984 she exceeded even this achievement when her classic *What's Love Got To Do With It* became the first US chart-topping single of her lengthy career.

Irene Cara, originally from *Fame*, involved herself in an equally phenomenal movie, *Flashdance*. The soundtrack album topped the US LP chart, the title track was a number one single for her and another song from the movie, *Maniac* by Michael Sembello, also reached the top in America.

New acts from Australia (Inxs, pronounced 'in excess') and Canada (hard rock star Bryan Adams) made a strong initial impression Stateside, and the Everly Brothers, who had split up acrimoniously ten years before, decided to stage their reunion concert at London's Royal Albert Hall, from which came a live double album, a TV documentary and practically nothing in the way of new material. For their studio album, which was released in 1984, Don and Phil were given songs from many admiring sources including Paul McCartney, whose *On The Wings Of A Nightingale* became the first Everlys' hit single in 15 years.

In a year when it seemed that everything

he touched turned to precious metal McCartney also moved into 1984 with the number one single in America *Say Say Say*, another duet with star of the year Michael Jackson. The Everlys re-formed, Paul McCartney at the top of the singles chart – why, even the Beach Boys took a compilation LP of their old hits to the top of the British LP chart in 1983.

Top: After leaving the Commodores, whom he had led to the top of the charts, Lionel Richie proved to be an even greater solo attraction.

Above: Tina Turner made a remarkable comeback with her singles Let's Stay Together *and* What's Love Got To Do With It.

257

USA CHART TOPPERS

TITLE	ARTIST	LABEL	WEEKS AT NO. 1
Maneater	Daryl Hall and John Oates	RCA	2
Down Under	Men At Work	Columbia	4
Africa	Toto	Columbia	1
Baby Come To Me	Patti Austin	Qwest	2
Billie Jean	Michael Jackson	Epic	7
Come On Eileen	Dexy's Midnight Runners	Mercury	1
Beat It	Michael Jackson	Epic	3
Let's Dance	David Bowie	EMI America	1
Flashdance (What A Feeling)	Irene Cara	Casablanca	6
Every Breath You Take	Police	A&M	8
Sweet Dreams	Eurythmics	RCA	1
Maniac	Michael Sembello	Casablanca	2
Tell Her About It	Billy Joel	Columbia	1
Total Eclipse Of The Heart	Bonnie Tyler	Columbia	4
Islands In The Stream	Kenny Rogers and Dolly Parton	RCA	2
All Night Long	Lionel Richie	Motown	4
Say Say Say	Paul McCartney and Michael Jackson	Columbia	3

UK CHART TOPPERS

TITLE	ARTIST	LABEL	WEEKS AT NO. 1
Save Your Love	Renee and Renato	Hollywood	2
You Can't Hurry Love	Phil Collins	Virgin	2
Down Under	Men At Work	Epic	3
Too Shy	KajaGooGoo	EMI	2
Billie Jean	Michael Jackson	Epic	1
Total Eclipse Of The Heart	Bonnie Tyler	CBS	2
Is There Something I Should Know	Duran Duran	EMI	2
Let's Dance	David Bowie	EMI America	3
True	Spandau Ballet	Reformation	4
Candy Girl	New Edition	London	1
Every Breath You Take	Police	A&M	4
Baby Jane	Rod Stewart	Warner Bros	3
Wherever I Lay My Hat	Paul Young	CBS	3
Give It Up	K.C. and the Sunshine Band	Epic	3
Red Red Wine	UB 40	DEP International	3
Karma Chameleon	Culture Club	Virgin	6
Uptown Girl	Billy Joel	CBS	5
Only You	The Flying Pickets	10/Virgin	3

FILMS

- Educating Rita
- Flashdance
- King Of Comedy
- Local Hero
- Monty Python's The Meaning Of Life
- Never Say Never Again
- Octopussy
- The Outsiders
- Psycho II
- The Right Stuff
- Rumblefish
- Silkwood
- Staying Alive
- Terms Of Endearment
- Trading Places
- Yellowbeard
- Zelig

DEATHS

- Eubie Blake, 100-year-old ragtime pianist
- Karen Carpenter of the Carpenters
- Jack Dempsey, boxer
- Dick Emery, comedian
- Pete Farndon, Pretender
- Billy Fury, pop star
- Ira Gershwin, songwriter
- John Le Mesurier, actor
- Felix Pappalardi, record producer
- Sir Ralph Richardson, actor
- Muddy Waters, bluesman
- Dennis Wilson, Beach Boy
- Chris Wood, Traffic saxman

CURRENT EVENTS

24 January: 63 Red Brigade terrorists are sentenced to terms of imprisonment in Rome.

16 February: Magistrates jail 36 women for breaches of the peace at Greenham Common air base.

2 March: The compact disc digital audio system is launched in Britain. A five-inch disc can contain up to an hour of music, reproduced as sound by a laser beam.

21 March: Following long-lasting drought, over a million are in need of famine relief in Ethiopia.

23 March: President Reagan claims to have evidence of 'a relentless Soviet military build-up' and urges more research on a 'Star Wars' space defence programme.

1 April: 100,000 Campaign For Nuclear Disarmament protesters join hands to form a 14-mile human chain stretching from Greenham Common to Burghfield Ordnance factory.

29 April: The Argentina Junta officially declares that the many thousands of missing persons reported since the 1970s must be considered dead.

9 June: The Conservative party are returned to office in the UK general election.

16 June: The Pope returns to his native Poland, denouncing the constrictions of the governing regime and meeting Lech Walesa for secret talks.

24 June: Sally Ride, one of the crew of the US space shuttle Challenger, is America's first spacewoman.

13 July: The House of Commons votes against the restoration of the death penalty by an unexpectedly large majority.

18 August: Radio Caroline, operating from a converted trawler in the North Sea, resumes broadcasting.

31 August: All 269 people on board a South Korean 747 are killed when Soviet fighters destroy the plane for violating Soviet airspace.

1 September: President Reagan orders an amphibious force to Lebanon following further outbreaks of fighting in Beirut.

25 September: 38 IRA prisoners escape from the Maze top security prison in Belfast.

2 October: Neil Kinnock is elected leader of the Labour Party in place of resigning Michael Foot.

25 October: On President Reagan's instructions, US troops invade Grenada 'just in time to thwart a Soviet-backed take-over of Cuba'.

3 November: South Africa extends constitutional and political rights to Indians and coloureds, but no concessions are granted to the country's 20 million blacks.

4 November: Dennis Nilson is sentenced to life imprisonment for killing and dismembering 15 young men in Muswell Hill and Cricklewood, London.

14 November: The first cruise missiles are delivered to the Greenham Common air base.

17 December: An IRA bomb kills six and injures 100 outside Harrods in Knightsbridge.

Made in England

1983

SIDE ONE
45 RPM
STEREO

Billie Jean

ALL RIGHTS OF THE MANUFACTURER AND OF THE OWNER OF THE RECORDED WORK RESERVED UNAUTHORISED PUBLIC PERFORMANCE BROADCASTING AND COPYING OF THIS RECORD PROHIBITED

BAND AID

BRONSKI BEAT

JIM DIAMOND

FRANKIE GOES TO HOLLYWOOD

HOWARD JONES

NIK KERSHAW

CYNDI LAUPER

JULIAN LENNON

MADONNA

Little progress was made in 1984 and the year turned out to be as uninspiring musically as say, 1961 or 1976. There were new stars, none bigger than Frankie Goes To Hollywood, a quintet from Liverpool who equalled the feat of Gerry and the Pacemakers in taking each of their first three singles to the top of the British chart. In truth FGTH bettered Gerry Marsden's ancient achievement, since their debut LP *Welcome To The Pleasuredome* also topped the British LP chart, something which Gerry's *How Do You Like It* failed to do. To predict long-term fame for Frankie (none of the five members of the group is called Frankie, although one of them is known as Holly) is difficult. The group appear to be little more than facets of the fertile imagination of Paul Morley, the ex-music journalist who launched the ZTT record label to which Frankie are signed, along with ace producer Trevor Horn, whom many feel contributes as much to Frankie's records as the members of the group.

Relax, their first single, spent 48 weeks in the UK top 75, five of them at number one, and four months after relinquishing the top position the group were back at the top with *Two Tribes*, which not only hogged the top position for nine weeks (in part due to a video which portrayed the Soviet and American heads of state in hand-to-hand combat) but also re-awakened interest in *Relax* which returned to number two for

several weeks. The third single *The Power Of Love* portrayed the three wise men in its accompanying video.

Bronski Beat, a group from Glasgow, took two singles, *Smalltown Boy* and *Why*, into the top 10 and their debut LP *The Age Of Consent* into the top 5. Manchester group the Smiths were fronted by Steven Morrissey, who writes the group's lyrics to the music of Johnny Marr. Apart from scoring a couple of hit singles, the group's major deeds included helping Sandie Shaw pick up her career and taking their LP titled *The Smiths* into the UK top 3.

The year's major trend was for one-man bands, using electronic backing to take their philosophies to the top of the chart. Two names in particular, Howard Jones and Nik Kershaw, had splendid years, frequently appearing in the chart. Jones, described by one writer as 'desperately normal', scored five hit singles between August 1983 and the end of 1984 – *New Song* and *What Is Love?* reaching the top 3, while his debut album *Human's Lib* topped the UK chart. At the same time Kershaw's debut LP *Human Racing* was also in the top 10. Kershaw achieved five UK top 20 singles during the year, the biggest of which was *I Won't Let The Sun Go Down On Me*, finishing the year with his second LP *The Riddle* reaching the top 10 of the album chart and its title track slipping down from its highest position at number three in the singles chart. Jones, meanwhile, took *The 12-inch Album*, a budget-priced LP containing extended and remixed versions of his hits, into the top 20 of the album charts. Its relatively average position was to some extent due to the major re-emergence of a series of compilation albums composed of current hits on which both Jones and Kershaw featured.

In previous years such compilations had been released by K-Tel and similar marketing companies, who sold not only records but anything else which might sell in quantity through TV advertising. Although various labels had attempted to release their own hits compilations, the marketing giants who had established relationships with virtually every major label found it easier to license individual hit tracks, probably because their specialist operation was not in direct competiton. Everything changed when EMI, one of the biggest companies, and Virgin, the fastest growing of the smaller labels, agreed to a joint venture at the end of 1983 whereby they would release a double album of hits under the title *Now, That's What I Call Music*. Of its 30 tracks about half were already the province of the two labels and, by offering a share of the profits (rather than simply a licensing fee) to labels from whom they wished to license other tracks, the *Now, That's What I Call Music* series, as they quickly became known,

changed the face of TV hit compilations.

The first three double albums in the series all reached number one in the UK chart, amassing sales of around two and a half million copies between them, while an accompanying series of video tapes (titled, of course, *Now, That's What I Call Music Video*) also became prodigious sellers. By the end of the year two major American companies, CBS and WEA, realized that major profits were there for the asking and produced their own version of *Now*, which they called *The Hits Album*. Like the first three volumes of *Now*, *The Hits Album* topped the British chart and in so doing actually prevented the fourth volume of *Now* from reaching its expected position at number one. The long-term effect of these comprehensive packages of hits is difficult to judge. While they may be said to stimulate interest in pop music by the convenient way in which they are packaged, at a time when new talent seems relatively thin on the ground it may also be true that sales of records by individual artists will fall since their most successful tracks can be found among the compilations.

Virtually every notable newcomer appeared on one or more of these albums, including a quartet of female singers all of whom broke through in style. Alison Moyet, known during her days with Yazoo as Alf, reverted to her real name for two top 10 hits *Love Resurrection* and *All Cried Out* to launch her solo career, but titled her debut LP, which went platinum, *Alf*. The virtually unknown Sade (pronounced Sharday), a Nigerian-born singer who had settled in England with her mother at the age of six, also achieved platinum status with her first LP *Diamond Life* assisted by three hit

singles during the year, the best known of which was *Smooth Operator*.

Both Sade and Alison owed a portion of their success to their sophisticated jazzy style which, in Britain at least, seemed to be setting a trend away from the attention-grabbing approach of the two major new American females Cyndi Lauper and Madonna. *Time After Time*, the second of Cyndi's three consecutive top 3 hits and the only one of the three to top the US chart, was, however, in sharp contrast to the brassy appeal of *Girls Just Want To Have Fun* and *She Bop*, being a more restrained offering with wider appeal. Similarly Madonna (real name Madonna Louise Ciccone) used her siren-like femininity in somewhat erotic videos which took both *Borderline* and *Lucky Star* into the top 10 of the US singles chart, and also helped her eponymous debut LP to go platinum, as did Cyndi Lauper's *She's So Unusual*.

In the heavy metal field British newcomers were scarce, although one of the ultimate heavy metal bands from the early 1970s Deep Purple finally reformed for a new LP and a world tour after several years of turning down lucrative offers to reunite. The line-up which relaunched the group with the *Perfect Strangers* LP popularly known as the 'Mark II' Purple, had originally disbanded in 1973.

From a similar era came Z.Z.Top, a Texan trio whose career since they formed in 1970 seemed to be punctuated with lengthy periods when they failed to release new material, although this could be partly explained by the remarkable length of some of their tours – in 1976, for instance, they toured for a whole year with a stage shaped like Texas complete with cactus and real

Above left: The unlikely duo of Vince Clarke and Alison 'Alf' Moyet, who relinquished their joint success as Yazoo to launch equally successful solo careers.

Above: Texan heavy metal trio Z.Z.Top, quoted as saying 'A new image is only a razor blade away'.

Left: The raucously colourful Cyndi Lauper.

buffalo. Although each of their previous eight LPs (in 14 years) had made the top 40 of the US album chart, it wasn't until *Eliminator* was released during the summer of 1983 that the group's immense following as a live act was translated into record sales. Selling over two million copies, the album remained in the chart for well over a year assisted by impressive videos for several singles taken from it.

During Slade's years of trying unsuccessfully to conquer America in the mid-1970s they frequently played as support act to Z.Z.Top, and the other major newcomer in the hard rock field, Quiet Riot, also had connections with Slade. Their cover version of Slade's 1973 British chart topper, *Cum On Feel The Noise* reached the top five in America and the group's *Mental Health* Album topped the LP chart.

Above: Ray Parker Jr, a comparative veteran, broke through with the spectacularly successful theme from the movie Ghostbusters.

In Britain a fresh outbreak of so-called 'pirate' radio occurred as a new station, Laser 558, with a very strong and clear signal, began broadcasting all over Europe and exposed a number of records which seemed to be being ignored by legal outlets, including *Big In Japan* by Alphaville, while nightclub exposure initially launched a series of dubious singles by a middle-aged transvestite known as Divine. Equally curious was the chart success of *Hole In My Shoe* by Neil (a comedian from the successful TV series *The Young Ones* in which he portrayed a hippie), and the bizarre case of *Ghostbusters*, the hit theme from the movie of the same name by Ray Parker Junior which topped the US singles chart. It became the subject of a major law suit brought by Huey Lewis who claimed that *Ghostbusters* bore a remarkable resemblance to his song *I Want A New Drug*. Since Lewis had originally been invited to write the theme for the movie, but had been forced to decline due to pressure of work, the eventual outcome of the law suit will be fascinating. Parker had become fairly well established before *Ghostbusters* with a string of hits during the previous six years like *A Woman Needs Love*, *That Old Song* and *The Other Woman*.

As usual a crop of newcomers showing varying degrees of promise emerged, like John Waite, previously a member of the Babys, who took *Missing You* to the top of the American singles chart. With another ex-Baby, Jonathan Cain, now a member of Journey, the re-issue of records by the Babys seems a certainty in the not too distant future. Hazell Dean, supposedly appealing to devotees of gay discotheques, charted with both *Searchin'* and *Whatever I Do*; Scottish pop group the Bluebells impressed with their jaunty *Young At Heart*; British

band Wang Chung (previously known as Huang Chung) made a significant dent in America without really adding to their small British following; Billy Ocean, last in the chart in 1980 but whose biggest hits came in 1976 and 1977 with *Love Really Hurts Without You* and *Red Light Spells Danger*, returned to top the US singles chart with *Caribbean Queen*. Berry Gordy's son Rockwell broke into the charts with *Somebody's Watching Me*; the gargantuan Weather Girls broke through with the catchy *It's Raining Men*; and Womack and Womack, the latest in a line of hitmakers from the same family, took *Love Wars* into the top 20.

The debut awaited with most interest was that of Julian Lennon, who had been signed by Charisma Records some time before. The delay may or may not have altered the younger Lennon's chances of starting his career with a hit, but the definite similarities between his voice and that of his late lamented father must surely have helped *Too Late For Goodbyes* into the top 10. Julian's style was not noticeably up to date and his use of producer Phil Ramone and session musicians like Barry Beckett, Roger Hawkins and David Hood, working in their hometown studio in Muscle Shoals, seemed to indicate that there had been little attempt to slot the first of the Beatle offspring to record into a particularly 1984 context.

If anything Julian seemed quite close to

the style of Elton John, who had one of the best years imaginable. He got married, had several hit singles on both sides of the Atlantic and enjoyed the great success of Watford Football Club, of which he was chairman. The team reached the FA Cup Final at Wembley and Elton returned to Wembley a few weeks later as headliner of a bill which attracted a capacity audience of over 70,000.

It was an equally good year for another comparative veteran, Scotsman Jim Diamond, who had tasted chart fame a few years before as half of PhD, who scored a major hit with the anthemic *I Won't Let You Down*. Diamond re-emerged in 1984 as a solo artist and to everyone's surprise took his first single *I Should Have Known Better* to the top of the British chart.

It was to Diamond's great credit that he publicly stated that he hoped his single would only stay at the top briefly. Unlikely as this may seem, Diamond wanted *Do They Know It's Christmas,* a single by Band Aid, to reach the top as quickly as possible. This single was recorded for the benefit of starving refugees in Ethiopia and included participation from among others Culture Club, Duran Duran, Spandau Ballet, Ultravox, U2, Wham!, Status Quo, Paul Young, Phil Collins, Sting, Bananarama, the Style Council and Heaven 17. More than 40 current stars donated their services. The idea

was conceived by Bob Geldof of the Boomtown Rats who co-wrote the song with Midge Ure of Ultravox (who also produced it). Within a few days the single had rushed to the top of the UK singles chart as the fastest seller of all time in Britain.

Such charitable thoughts from the often overfed egos of the pop fraternity were at least one good reason to remember 1984, which in many ways gave the distinct impression that after 30 years of mayhem, fun and excitement, rock'n'roll might finally be dead. Of course, to predict the demise of an institution which has been generally thriving for three decades purely on the basis of one uninspired year would be too hasty. After all, there have been several previous years among rock music's 30-year lifespan when its continuing existence seemed threatened, sometimes by ignorance and/or stupidity but more often in recent years by the pressure of big business. There is no obvious and ready solution to the problem, but neither was there in 1962, 1966, 1970, 1976, 1980 or any other period when things were looking bad. Rock'n'roll is the essence of youthful rebellion, of dreams and hope for the future, which has sustained innumerable believers for three generations, and it will certainly continue to do so for many years to come. Rock'n'roll, as the Showmen remarked during the 1960s, forever will stand. . . .

Above: The all-star group Band Aid whose single, Do They Know It's Christmas, *recorded to benefit the starving people of Ethiopia, proved that not all pop stars are uncharitable.*

TITLE	ARTIST	LABEL	WEEKS AT NO. 1
Say Say Say	Paul McCartney and Michael Jackson	Columbia	2
Owner Of A Lonely Heart	Yes	Atco	2
Karma Chameleon	Culture Club	Virgin/Epic	3
Jump	Van Halen	Warner Bros	5
Footloose	Kenny Loggins	Columbia	3
Against All Odds	Phil Collins	Atlantic	3
Hello	Lionel Richie	Motown	2
Let's Hear It For The Boy	Deniece Williams	Columbia	2
Time After Time	Cyndi Lauper	Portrait	2
The Reflex	Duran Duran	Capitol	2
When Doves Cry	Prince	Warner Bros	5
Ghostbusters	Ray Parker Jr	Arista	3
What's Love Got To Do With It?	Tina Turner	Capitol	3
Missing You	John Waite	EMI America	1
Let's Go Crazy	Prince and the Revolution	Warner Bros	2
I Just Called To Say I Love You	Stevie Wonder	Motown	3
Caribbean Queen	Billy Ocean	Jive	2
Wake Me Up Before You Go Go	Wham!	Columbia	3
Out Of Touch	Daryl Hall and John Oates	RCA	4

TITLE	ARTIST	LABEL	WEEKS AT NO. 1
Only You	The Flying Pickets	10/Virgin	1
Pipes Of Peace	Paul McCartney	Parlophone	2
Relax	Frankie Goes To Hollywood	ZTT	5
99 Red Balloons	Nena	Epic	3
Hello	Lionel Richie	Motown	6
The Reflex	Duran Duran	EMI	4
Wake Me Up Before You Go Go	Wham!	Epic	2
Two Tribes	Frankie Goes To Hollywood	ZTT	9
Careless Whisper	George Michael	Epic	3
I Just Called To Say I Love You	Stevie Wonder	Motown	6
Freedom	Wham!	Epic	3
I Feel For You	Chaka Khan	Warner Bros	3
I Should Have Known Better	Jim Diamond	A&M	3
The Power Of Love	Frankie Goes To Hollywood	ZTT	1
Do They Know It's Christmas?	Band Aid	Mercury	1

DEATHS

Count Basie, jazz bandleader
Richard Burton, film star
Truman Capote, novelist
Tommy Cooper, comedian
Diana Dors, actress and media personality
Marvin Gaye, soul star
Alberta Hunter, blues singer
Alexis Korner, R&B pioneer
Peter Lawford, actor
Eric Morecambe, comedian
Esther Phillips, R&B singer
Leonard Rossiter, actor
Jackie Wilson, pioneer soul singer

FILMS

Another Country
The Bounty
Cal
The Company Of Wolves
Electric Dreams
Footloose
Ghostbusters
Give My Regards To Broad Street
Gremlins
Greystoke – The Legend Of Tarzan
Indiana Jones & The Temple Of Doom
The Karate Kid
The Killing Fields
The Natural
1984
Once Upon A Time In America
Paris Texas
Police Academy
Purple Rain
Splash
Star Trek III
Woman In Red
Yentl

7 February: Captain Bruce McCandless emerges from the space-shuttle Challenger to walk in space 165 miles above the earth, becoming the first human to enter space without a safety line.

9 February: Soviet President Yuri Andropov dies, aged 69, after only 15 months in office. Konstantin Chernenko succeeds him.

12 March: After the National Coal Board's decision to close uneconomical pits, over half the nation's miners go on strike. Protracted confrontations between police, flying pickets and miners characterize the rest of the year. Despite various attempts to reach a negotiated settlement, the strike continues beyond the end of the year.

17 April: Shots fired at demonstrators from a window of the Libyan People's Bureau in London kill policewoman Yvonne Fletcher. All Libyan officials are subsequently ordered to leave the country as the UK breaks off diplomatic relations.

12 June: Over 1000 die during a Sikh uprising at the Golden Temple in Amritsar, India.

22 June: Virgin Atlantic, owned by Virgin Records boss Richard Branson, makes its first transatlantic flight.

13 August: During a microphone test, President Reagan jokes that he 'will begin bombing Russia in five minutes'. After tape recordings are made public, the Kremlin issues a statement deploring his sense of humour.

22 August: In South African elections, blacks, who form more than 70 per cent of the population, are still excluded from voting or participating in government. Black dissatisfaction and unrest increases over the weeks to follow.

15 September: A second son, to be known as Prince Harry, is born to the Prince and Princess of Wales.

4 October: Six million Ethiopians are reported to be in desperate straits after a prolonged drought decimated grain production. The Western world begins to ferry in aid following harrowing television coverage.

12 October: An IRA bomb explodes at the Grand Hotel, Brighton, where the Prime Minister and many colleagues are staying during the annual Conservative Party conference. Four are killed and 32 injured.

30 October: Indira Gandhi, India's Prime Minister, is shot dead by two of her personal guards, both Sikhs. Her son, Rajiv Gandhi, succeeds her as hundreds of Sikhs die in a Hindu revenge reaction.

6 November: Ronald Reagan carries 49 states to sweep to victory in the US Presidential election. His comprehensive defeat of Democrat Walter Mondale was never in doubt.

12 November: Miners begin a drift back to work after high financial inducements for the Christmas period, but the majority of strikers are resolute in their determination to win.

3 December: Over 2000 die when toxic gas leaks from an underground storage tank at a Union Carbide pesticide factory in Bhopal, India.

22 December: Following the visit of Soviet diplomat Mikhail Gorbachov Mrs Thatcher meets President Reagan to urge an early ban on space weapons.

Above: The great Marvin Gaye, the year's most notable rock casualty, who was shot dead by his father, a retired minister, after a family argument on 1 April 1984.

Made in England

1984

SIDE ONE
45 RPM
STEREO

Relax

ALL RIGHTS OF THE MANUFACTURER AND OF THE OWNER OF THE RECORDED WORK RESERVED. UNAUTHORISED PUBLIC PERFORMANCE BROADCASTING AND COPYING OF THIS RECORD PROHIBITED

Index

Photographic acknowledgments

Frank Driggs Collection, New York 8–9 top, 8–9 bottom, 12, 20, 21 top, 22, 23 top, 24, 32 left, 33 right, 38, 45 top, 47 bottom, 74, 172, 188 left, 212, 230; Duncan Paul Associates, London 264–265; Kobal Collection, London 11, 14, 34, 42, 76–77, 124–125, 132–133, 148–149, 175, 192–193, 217, 218–219, 250; London Features International Ltd 10 top, 10 bottom, 16–17, 31 bottom, 39 top, 39 bottom, 46, 48, 49 top, 53 bottom, 54, 61 bottom, 62, 63 top, 66, 71 bottom, 73 right, 79 top, 81 top right, 85, 96–97, 102 bottom, 103, 106, 108–109 bottom, 113, 118, 121 left, 122 bottom, 127 bottom, 128–129 top, 129 bottom left, 129 bottom right, 130–131, 135 bottom, 136–137, 137 bottom, 138 bottom, 139, 143 top, 145 left, 145 bottom right, 146–147, 153 right, 154 left, 155, 160, 161 top, 161 bottom, 162–163 top, 162–163 bottom, 164, 170 top left, 170 bottom right, 171 right, 180, 181, 182, 186–187, 188–189, 190 bottom, 191 bottom, 195 top, 196 left, 196–197, 197 right, 199 top, 203 top, 205 bottom, 208 top, 208 bottom, 209, 213 top, 214–215, 215 right, 216, 221 top, 221 bottom, 222, 223 top, 223 bottom, 225 top right, 225 bottom, 231 top, 231 bottom, 232, 233, 236, 237 bottom, 240 centre, 245 top, 246, 247, 248 right, 253 top, 253 bottom left, 254 left, 254–255, 256–257, 261 left, 262–263, 263 bottom, 264 left, 267; Lynda Morrison, London 257 bottom; National Film Archive, London 156 left; The Photo Source Ltd, London: Central Press Photos 123, 130 left, 159, 183; Fox Photos 82 top; Fox/Keystone 78–79 bottom, 101 top, 104–105; Keystone Press Agency 18, 57, 61 top, 68–69, 75 top, 80–81 top, 82 bottom, 90 left, 90–91, 91 top right, 100, 122 top, 136 left, 145 top right, 152 right, 153 left, 165 top, 203 bottom, 225 top left, 229, 255 right; Pictorial Press, London 9 bottom right, 13, 17 top, 21 bottom, 23 bottom, 27 top, 27 bottom, 28, 29, 31 top, 32–33, 37 top, 37 bottom left, 37 bottom right, 40 left, 40 right, 41, 45 bottom, 47 top, 49 bottom, 53 top left, 53 top right, 55 top, 55 bottom, 56, 58, 63 bottom, 64, 65, 67 top, 67 bottom, 71 top, 72 left, 75 bottom left, 75 bottom right, 81 bottom right, 89 bottom, 91 bottom left, 91 bottom right, 92 top, 92 bottom, 93, 98–99 bottom, 101 bottom, 102 top, 107, 108 top, 109 top, 110 left, 110–111, 111 top, 112, 114, 116, 117, 119 top, 119 bottom, 120, 121 right, 127 top, 131 right, 165 bottom, 168–169, 176, 178–179, 179 top, 184–185, 187 top, 190 top, 191 top, 195 bottom, 204, 205 top, 234, 262 bottom; Barry Plummer, Ascot, Berkshire 128 bottom, 135 top, 138 top, 144, 147, 151, 152 left, 154 right, 158, 169 top, 170–171 top, 177, 189 right, 198 right, 199 bottom, 206–207, 213 bottom, 214 left, 224, 228, 237 top, 239, 240 top, 241, 249 top, 256 left, 261 right; Official Elvis Presley Fan Club of Great Britain 19; Retna Ltd, London 179 bottom, 198 left, 240 bottom, 245 bottom, 248 left, 249 bottom, 253 bottom right, 257 top right, 260; Rex Features Limited, London 7, 50, 72–73, 83, 84, 86–87, 89 top, 97 top, 98 top, 99 top, 137 top, 140–141, 143 bottom, 156–157, 170 bottom left, 173, 210–211, 263 top right; Tritec Music Limited, Birmingham 238

Front cover: Back row, left to right
Elvis Presley (Rex Features Limited, London)
Diana Ross (Rex Features Limited, London)
Michael Jackson (Rex Features Limited, London)
Bill Haley (Rex Features Limited, London)
Paul McCartney (David Redfern, London)
Tina Turner (Rex Features Limited, London)
Front – Wham (London Features International)

Back cover: Left to right clockwise from top
Cliff Richard (Rex Features Limited, London)
The Beatles (Fox/Keystone)
David Bowie (Retna Ltd, London)
Little Richard (Frank Driggs Collection, New York)
Bob Marley and the Wailers (Pictorial Press, London)
Donna Summer (London Features International Ltd)
The Who (Rex Features Limited)
Abba (Pictorial Press, London)
Duran Duran (Tritec Music Limited, Birmingham)

Endpapers: Kid Creole and the Coconuts (Barry Plummer)
Titlespread: Gary Numan (London Features International)